The Shaker Way

by Charles R. Muller

Foreword by Dr. Robert Bishop

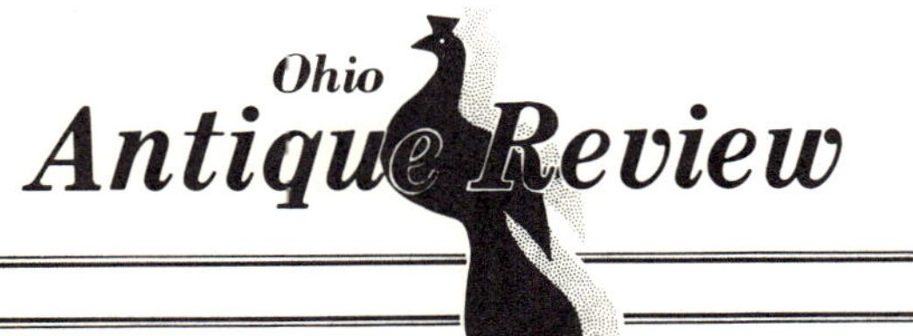

Ohio
Antique Review

The articles included in this volume are printed as they appeared in the **OHIO ANTIQUE REVIEW**, November, 1975 - August, 1979.

The cover photograph is the main hall of the Centre House, South Union, Kentucky.

First Edition

Library of Congress Catalog Card Number 79-89838

ISBN 0-9603290-0-5

Published by   Ohio Antique Review, Inc.
               72 E. North Street
               Worthington, Ohio 43085

Contents

The NOTES appearing at the end of some articles were added by the author in July, 1979.

Acknowledgements

The writing of a column over a period of almost four years requires the cooperation and assistance of many people and produces friendships that exceed the common interest in Shaker. A word of thanks goes to everyone that has shared in some way with this endeavor.

A very special expression of thanks needs to go to the following: my family, Brenda, Heather, Rusty and Jimmy, who tolerate my obsession; Pete and Ann Lowder and Jim and Lucille Loeffler who made it all possible; Faith Andrews, John Kassay, Steve Kistler, Robert Meader, Milt Sherman, Don Sprowls and Richard Steinert who have so willingly shared of their knowledge and insights; Herbert and Dee Wisbey and other members of the Shaker Seminars who have become family, especially Record and Thelma Barris, Jean Dones, Steve Metzger and Clark and Betty Rice; and all those scholars, dealers, collectors and museums who are given credit within the text.

And last, but certainly not least, graditude has to be given to Sister Mildred Barker and the late Sister Marguerite Frost who have made a people of the past a very present joy to be experienced.

Foreword

Beginning in 1976, Charles Muller, collector, student of American antiques, and writer, began a series of profusely illustrated feature articles titled "The Shaker Way" in the highly informative, popular publication *Ohio Antique Review*. In the March 1976 issue, he quoted a *New York World* article on the Shakers published on December 27, 1887: "the first and only successful attempt at Communism known in history...The Shakers have a keen appreciation of the necessity and dignity of labor, but they never hire halls to talk about it nor rush about the country exhorting each other to strike for short hours and long pay. Everyone of them has some useful work to do, according to age, sex and strength. Perhaps no class of people has done more for the country than they, when it is remembered how few they are in number."

Interest in the Shakers during the 19th century focused for the most part upon the eccentricities of the sect. Often referred to as "quaking Shakers" and described as religious fanatics, their way of life, which centered around communal precepts, brought down upon them extensive ridicule. This ridicule was based upon misunderstanding of the Shaker way of life and their search for perfection.

Many authors through the years have focused upon the Shakers and added significantly to the scholarship surrounding this field. *The Communistic Societies of the United States* written by Charles Nordhoff in 1875 and published by Harper & Brothers is an excellent source book. During the 20th century, collecting scholars, such as Edward Deming Andrews and his wife Faith Andrews, brought new understanding of the life and ways of the Shakers. Andrews' book, *The People Called Shakers, A Search for the Perfect Society,* published in 1953 by the Oxford University Press, Inc., still remains today the bible for those who wish to study the Shakers. Robert F. W. Meader, former director of the Shaker Museum at Old Chatham, New York, broke new ground in the study of Shaker artifacts in his highly informative book, *Illustrated Guide to Shaker Furniture,* written in 1972 and published by Dover Publications, Inc.

Charles Muller's series, "The Shaker Way," substantially extends the primary research of Nordhoff, the Andrewses, and Meader, for he has delved into many new areas of research and has focused especially upon the arts and crafts of the midwestern Shaker communities which had never before been as extensively researched. "The Shaker Way," in its diversity and in its rich wealth of information, is an absolute necessity for anyone interested in Shaker studies.

As might be expected, the majority of Muller's articles are devoted to the analysis of Shaker furniture for collectors of Shaker artifacts focus upon objects in this category. Additional areas of collecting, such as baskets, boxes, stoves, spirit drawings and pottery are included in "The Shaker Way" as well as several articles about the detection of fakes. Shaker life was spiritual and agrarian and these areas are also considered.

For those just now coming to awareness of the Shakers, Charles Muller has listed museum collections and restorations where major collections of Shaker furniture and other artifacts might be seen and has even recorded auction sales and prices paid for Shaker pieces when they have passed through the marketplace. It should be noted that the author has thoughtfully included the original date of publication of all articles which is of considerable import wherever prices are mentioned. In the brief period since these articles first appeared, substantive changes in values of some catagories of Shaker artifacts has already been observed.

The Shaker Way preserves for posterity the research and scholarship of Charles Muller as originally published in the antiques trade journal, *Ohio Antique Review*. This compilation in book format is a substantial contribution to the study of Shaker life and art in America.

Dr. Robert Bishop
Director
Museum of American Folk Art
New York City
July, 1979

Sites and Sights

Attempts were made to establish the Shaker faith in numerous places - the banks of the Wabash River in Indiana and near Tampa, Florida, to name just two - and among different peoples such as the blacks in Philadelphia and the Shawnee Indians in Ohio. Many of these met with limited success but eighteen communities lasted better than fifty years. Of these, twelve are in New York and the New England states and the other six in the Midwest. The majority of these now have some restoration or a museum in the area that is dedicated to the Shaker heritage. In addition, other museums possess fine collections of Shaker artifacts that should be visited by the collector and student. The first article in this section includes a map showing most of these.

But for those who desire to study the Shakers and their ways, information is not limited to these geographic sites. Numerous books have been written about the Shakers. And now, through the Library of Congress, the microfiche of original manuscripts can be obtained for reading in most any local library.

It is hoped that the articles that follow might motivate people to visit some of the places mentioned. While they share many common bonds, each is unique in its own right. The view at Enfield, N.H., is lovely; the tool collection at the Shaker Museum is superb; the collections in Lebanon bring together the styles of the East and West; and the food at Pleasant Hill is delicious. And as varied as the present day sights are, so were their predecessors and their artifacts. The round barn at Hancock and the great barn at Mt. Lebanon are individual expressions of an ingenious people. The sewing desks of Alfred and those of South Union are greatly varying forms seeking to achieve a common function. Again and again, local styles and histories gave variety to the standards of the Shakers. It is fascinating to examine how the same rules were adapted to local influences. The uniformity...and differences...should be seen in their own original settings.

Because of the way in which these articles were written, not all sites and sights are mentioned in this book. There are, though, two places that are noticeably absent...Canterbury and Sabbathday Lake. These two communities are still functioning and the last of the Shakers reside there. No visit to any other site can match the joy and enchantment that can be found in a chat in the school house with Eldress Bertha Lindsey or the sharing of cookies and tea with Sister Mildred Barker. For in them, the past is a very present reality.

The Shaker Way

On December 27, 1887, the NEW YORK WORLD spoke of the Shakers as "the first and only successful attempt at Communism known in history ... The Shakers have a keen appreciation of the necessity and dignity of labor, but they never hire halls to talk about it nor rush about the country exhorting each other to strike for short hours and long pay. Everyone of them has some useful work to do, according to age, sex and strength. Perhaps no class of people has done more for the country than they, when it is remembered how few they are in number."

It is only right that we should give, in this column, close attention to this unique group that has contributed so much to the rich history of our land and to the field of antiques. "It has been remarked, and it is worth repeating, that the Shaker vision was peculiarly and authentically American ... They had the gift to express much that is best in the American spirit. They exemplified the simplicity, the practicality, the earnestness, and the hope that have been associated with the United States." (Thomas Merton in "Religion in Wood," 1966, by Edward and Faith Andrews).

In the year that the Declaration of Independence was signed, Mother Ann Lee and her small group of followers, who had arrived in this country from England two years before, purchased land in Niskeyuna, New York, and founded the first Shaker community. From that small beginning came 27 different communities in eleven states and better than 17,000 covenant members. Two of these communities (Sabbathday Lake, Maine, and Canterbury, New Hampshire) are still functioning today. "From 1776 - the era of our national Revolution - the Shakers have been established in this country; ... The example of the Shakers has demonstrated, not merely that successful Communism is subjectively possible, but that this nation is free enough to let it grow." (John Humphrey, "History of American Socialisms," 1870).

The study of the Shakers is important in the socio-economic study of communes, religion and America. But it is also important to the antiquer because their furniture embodies a purity of design, inventiveness, craftsmanship and beauty unique to the Shakers.

Merton, in his preface to RELIGION IN WORD, says, "Shaker craftsmanship is perhaps the last great expression of work in purely human measure, a witness to the ancient, primitive, perfect totality of man before the final victory of machine technology."

But while the decline of the Shakers is decidedly related to the increased presence of machines, the Shakers were not opposed to technology. Joseph Meacham, first American convert to Shakerism, is oft quoted as saying, "We have a right to improve the inventions of man, so far as it is useful and necessary." And this they did.

In addition to improved windmills, washing machines, and lathes, the Shakers are credited with inventing machines to cut tongue and groove boards; print seed bags and labels; weave baskets; shell peas; pare, quarter and core apples; etc. Many of us have weight balanced windows in our homes ... thanks to the Shakers. Before the ball point pen, most of us used metal pens whose original design came from the Shakers. And who among us has not used a clothes pin (reputedly invented at North Union, now Shaker Heights, Ohio) or a flat broom. Of course, we antiquers always find the tell-tale marks of the circular saw to be an aid in determining the age of a piece of furniture. It was a Shaker sister who is given credit for the design of such a saw after watching a spinning wheel.

We often think of the Shakers as being prominent in the East. This is true, but we of the Midwest also have a strong tie with them. The communities in the East thrived in the early days and caused the leaders to look for other fertile ground. A great religious revival was taking place in Kentucky and attracted the attention of the Shakers. On Jan. 1, 1805, three men left New York and traveled to Kentucky and Ohio. They were welcomed into the home of Malcolm Worley who became their first convert in the area. His home (now the Otterbein Home) about five miles west of Lebanon, Ohio, became the center of what was to be the largest of all Shaker communities, Union Village.

From there, the Shakers founded communities at Pleasant Hill (Southwest of Lexington) and South Union (Southwest of Bowling Green) in Kentucky, West Union (Burso) in Indiana, and Watervliet (outside Dayton), North Union (Shaker Heights outside Cleveland), Whitewater (West of Hamilton) and Darby (West of Plain City) in Ohio. All of these communities were closed by 1912. Today, South Union is being developed and some of the other communities have some

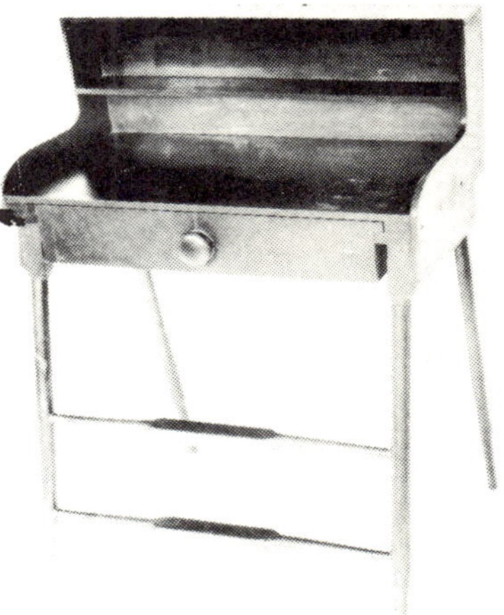

Sewing table
in cherry and poplar
from South Union, Kentucky.
(Shakertown - South Union, Ky.)

Photograph by John Kassay

restoration. Pleasant Hill is the gem of the Western Shaker communities in its restoration. It has facilities for dining and overnight lodging. The Golden Lamb and the Warren County Museum in Lebanon, Ohio, offer the best accumulation of Shaker artifacts to be found in the Midwest.

Directory of Shaker Museums, Collections and Points of Interest

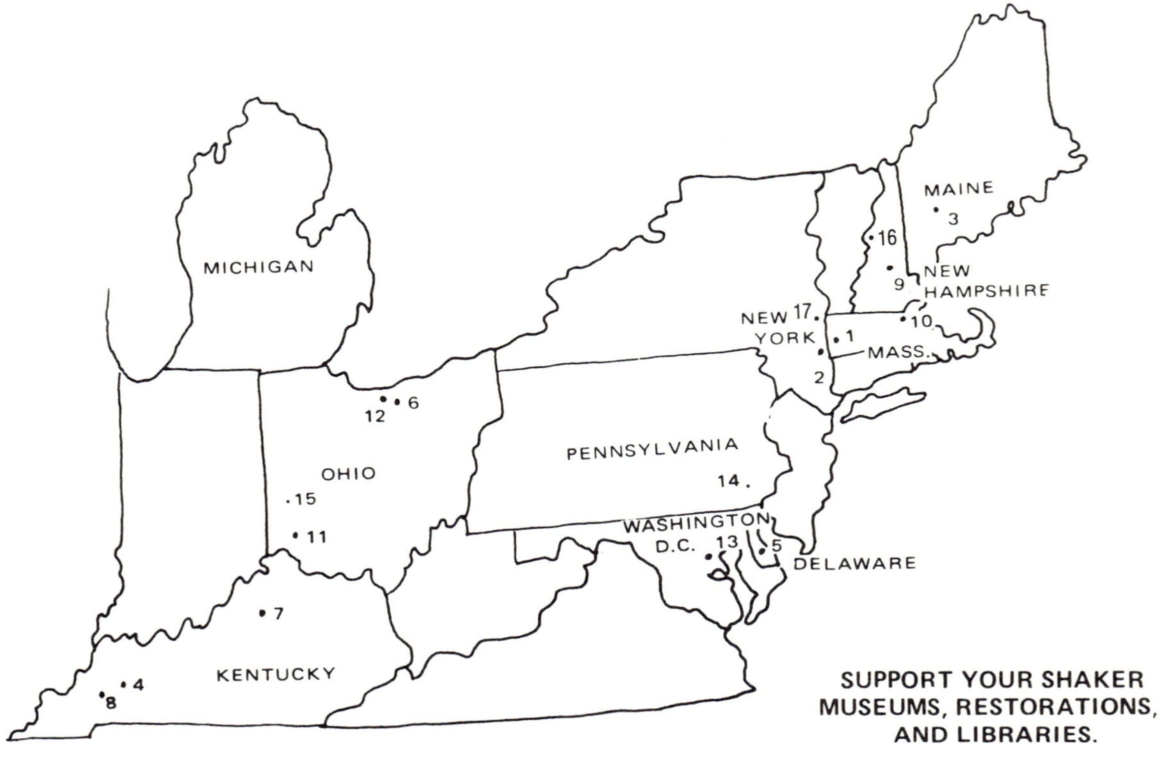

SUPPORT YOUR SHAKER MUSEUMS, RESTORATIONS, AND LIBRARIES.

1. Shaker Community, Inc.
P.O. Box 29
Pittsfield, Mass. 01201

2. Shaker Museum
Shaker Museum Road
Old Chatham, NY 12136

3. United Society of Shakers
Sabbathday Lake
Poland Spring, Maine 04274

4. Kentucky Building
Western Kentucky Univ.
Bowling Green, KY 42101

5. The Henry Francis du-Pont
Winterthur Museum
Winterthur, Del. 19735

6. Shaker Historical Society
16740 South Park Blvd.
Shaker Hts., Ohio 44120

7. Shakertown at Pleasant Hill
Kentucky, Inc.
Route 4
Harrodsburg, KY 40330

8. Shakertown
at South Union,
Kentucky 42283

9. Shaker Village, Inc.
Canterbury, NH 03224

10. Fruitlands Museum
Harvard, Mass. 04151

11. Warren County
Historical Society
Lebanon, Ohio 45036

12. The Western Reserve
Historical Society
10825 East Boulevard
Cleveland, Ohio 44106

13. New National Museum
Smithsonian Institution
Constitution Ave. at
14th St. N.W.
Washington, D.C. 20560

14. Philadelphia Museum of Art
Philadelphia, Pennsylvania 19010

For detailed information relative to museums and collections listed in our directory, please correspond directly with the museum involved.

Map & Directory courtesy of THE WORLD OF SHAKER, Guild of Shaker Crafts. Since publication of this map, the Kettering-Moraine Museum in Dayton, Ohio has opened its Shaker collection (15). — March, 1976

NOTE: *An exhibition room has been opened in the dwelling house at Enfield, N.H. (16), and restoration is under way at Watervliet, N.Y. (17).* THE WORLD OF SHAKER *has been changed to* THE SHAKER MESsenger, *a quarterly publication available from P.O. Box 45, Holland, MI 49423.*

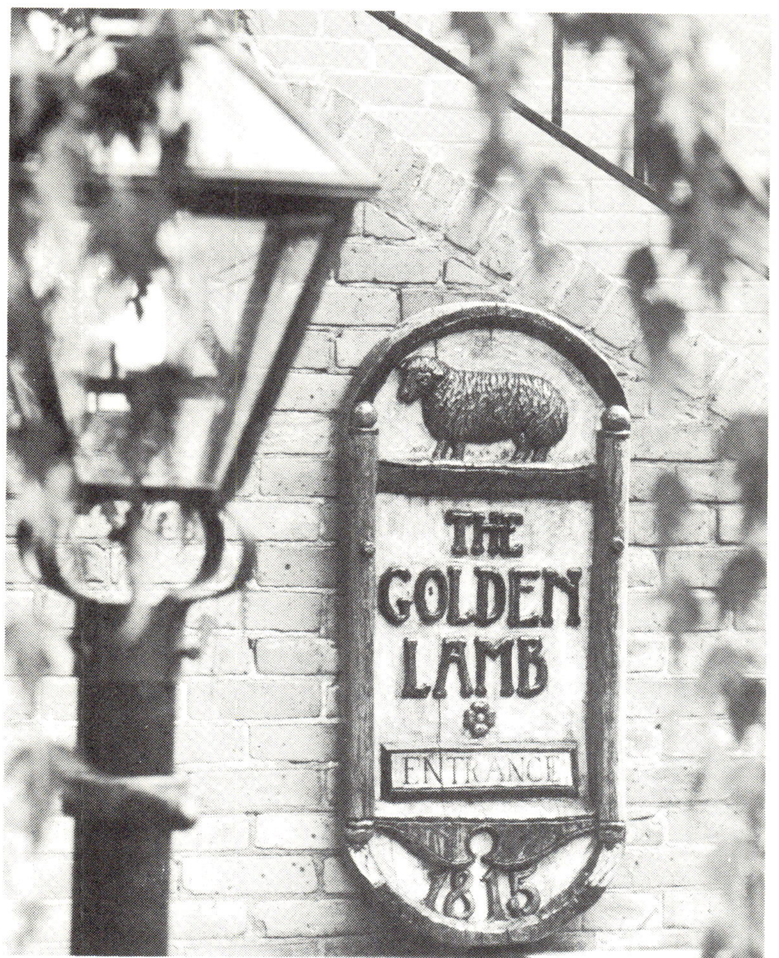

Lebanon, Ohio

in the Shaker development that existed west of town. The Museum has combined some artifacts on loan from The Otterbein Home with some from the personal collection of Mr. Robert Jones and with some of its own acquisitions to present an excellent exhibition of Shaker. Appropriately, the Warren County Museum has the finest display of Union Village furniture that can be viewed by the public.

Western Shaker (Ohio and Kentucky) furniture has long been considered by Shaker authorities, who seem to be from the East, to be the "poor cousins" in style and fineness of craftsmanship. Poorly made, clumsy, or awkward pieces are automatically described as "Western." This, I believe, to be hasty and inaccurate. An examination of the artifacts at the Warren County Museum will soon lead to an appreciation of the excellence of the work of the Western Shakers. Union Village furniture with its scalloped aprons on cupboards

There is no better mini-trip in all of Shakerdom than can be had in an excursion to the small southwestern Ohio town of Lebanon. Located midway between Cincinnati and Dayton and between I-71 and I-75, Lebanon offers the remains of the Shaker's largest community, perhaps the finest collection of Shaker furniture to be found in any small museum, and Ohio's oldest inn with its superb collection of Shaker.

What had been the Shaker's largest community with 600 members is now the United Methodist Church's largest retirement center, The Otterbein Home, with 520 members. But where there had been more than 100 buildings in Union Village a hundred years ago, only three still remain with two in active use. A visit to Lebanon might begin with a drive past these buildings, four miles west of Lebanon, about one half mile north of Route 63 on Route 741. Between the Elder's Shop

(built in 1811) and Bethany Hall (1853), stands the Trustee's Building. This building is better known as Marble Hall because of the elaborate use of imported French marble used by the Shakers in remodeling the structure in the 1890's. It stands today as the best example of the Shakers' efforts to stay in vogue during the Victorian era.

The Warren County Historical Society was formed in Lebanon in 1940 and developed Glendower which is now a state museum in a beautiful Greek Revival home on the south side of town. The present location of the Historical Society and its museum is on the main street of town, one half block south of The Golden Lamb Inn. While the Society is greatly concerned with the history of the Lebanon area from prehistoric times to the present, Mrs. Hazel Phillips, the former director, and Mrs. Elva Adams, the present one, have shown a keen interest

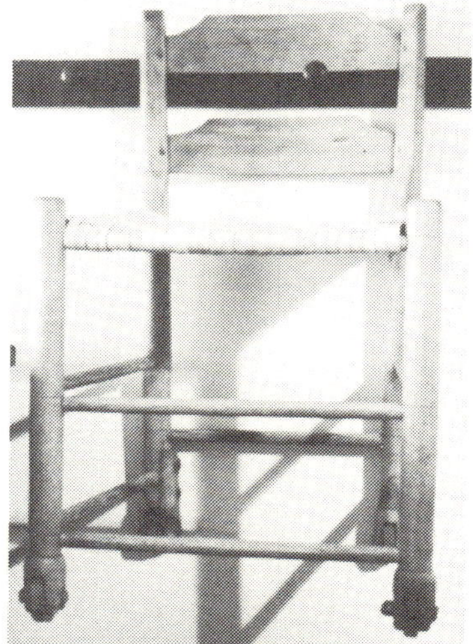

The Shakers made wheel chairs for their invalid members. But who needs a dining chair with rollers? Hanging in one of the Shaker exhibition rooms at The Golden Lamb, this chair points out the ingenuity of the Shakers. The rollers are original.

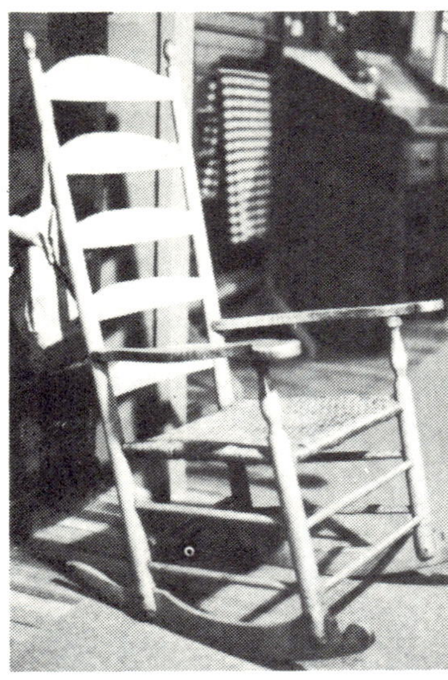

Union Village rocker in the Warren County Museum. Of special interest are the five graduated, gracefully curved, slats and the scroll work on the front of the rockers.

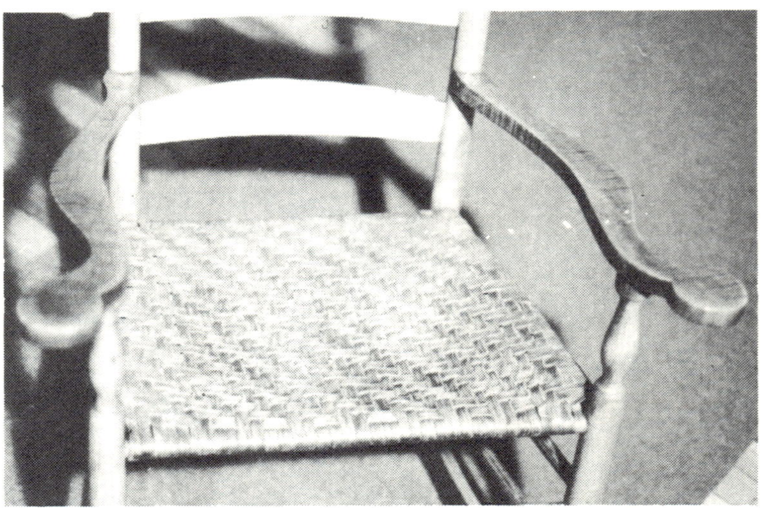

Top view showing the cyma-curved arms on the rocker. The curly maple arms blend with the maple used in the rest of the chair. Note how the arms are fitted to the back posts and pegged. This chair need not take a back seat to any Eastern chair.

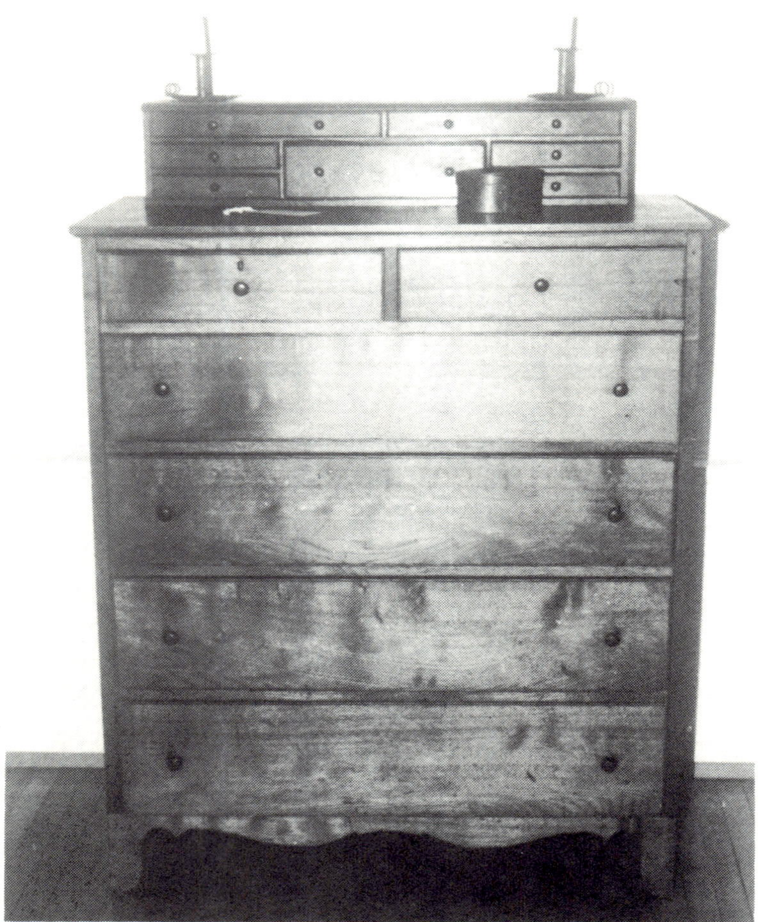

Union Village, Ohio, chest of drawers in butternut. Note the scalloped apron which is typical of Union Village. This is one of the fine pieces of Union Village furniture in the Warren County Historical Society's Museum in Lebanon, Ohio.

and chests and its cyma-curved arms on chairs does tend to be more fancy than its Eastern counterpart, but the resulting design is still very delightful and the construction superb. A tall four door cupboard with its mortised and pinned joints, inlaid escutcheon, beaded frame and quarter round molding on the doors is as well made as any Eastern piece. Five drawers centered in the bottom half add to the design of the piece. And when I stand back and look at the beautiful grain in the walnut panels, I can not recall but two or three Eastern pieces that are any better in construction or beauty.

The Shaker exhibition occupies most of the second floor of the Museum while the first floor is given to a street of shops of yesteryear and the basement features a variety of displays from archeology to weaving. There are few small town or county museums that surpass the Warren County Historical Society. It is open from 1:00 to 4:00 Tuesday through Sunday.

After a pleasant drive through the country to visit the former Union Village community at The Otterbein Home and a stroll through the Museum, you will want to relax and savor the excellent cuisine of The Golden Lamb Inn. Started in 1803, the present building dates from 1815. Over the years, ten Presidents have

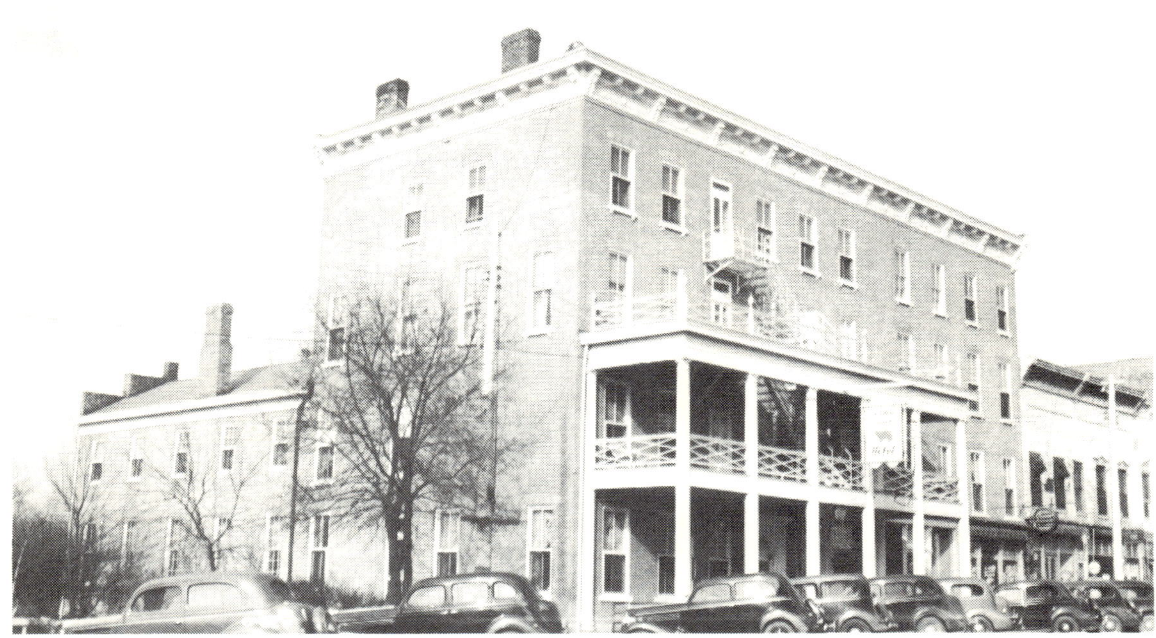

The Golden Lamb Inn as it appeared in the 1930's. From 1815 to the present, it has changed little in appearance.

stayed at the Inn as well as other notables such as Henry Clay and Charles Dickens. Even today, overnight accomodations are provided in the antique furnished rooms that bear the names of famous lodgers of the past.

Since 1969 when the long time owner and operator of the Inn, Mr. Robert Jones, retired, The Golden Lamb has been under the guidance of the Comisar brothers of Cincinnati who also operate the famous Maisonette Restaurant in that city. Mr. Jack Reynolds is the present manager and a very gracious host as well as an enthusiastic supporter of Shaker preservation. Under his leadership, the Inn has kept its ties with the past through its menu and furnishings. Warren County turkey is a regular on the menu. Sister Lizzie's Sugar Pie, Shaker Lemon Pie, or some other Shaker dessert is always available.

Either before or after the meal, allow time to walk through the Inn. If rooms are not occupied by overnight guests, they are left open to visitors. On the top floor, two rooms have been arranged exhibiting Shaker furnishings from the Jones collection. Mr. Jones was an early collector of Shaker and acquired many excel-

lent pieces long before Shaker became a part of the antique vocabulary in Ohio. While some of the items were acquired locally, Mr. Jones purchased most of his collection in the East and from those communities. Therefore, a visit through the

Warren County Museum and The Golden Lamb offers the best cross section of Eastern and Western Shaker to be found anywhere.

In addition to the two rooms on exhibit, Shaker furnishings are used throughout the Inn. A cupboard holds silverware in one

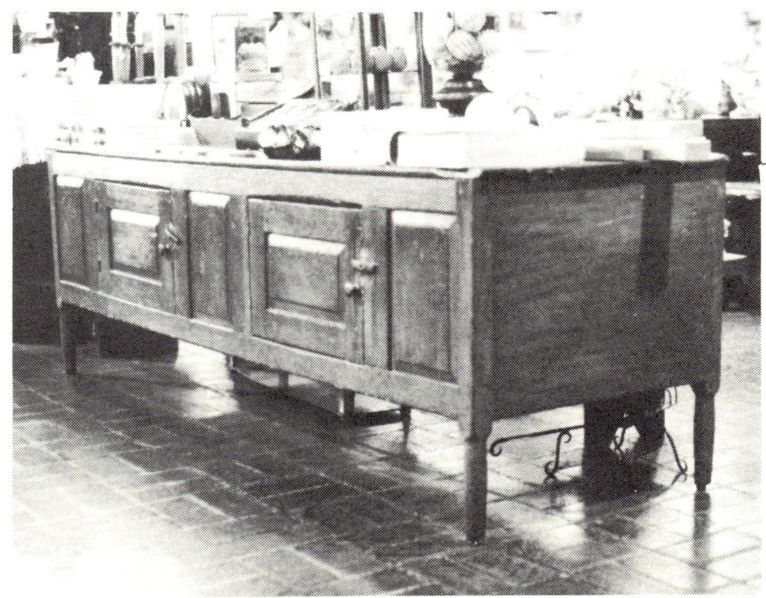

If a visitor to The Golden Lamb does not look carefully, he might miss some excellent Shaker furniture such as this serving table being used in the gift shop. In original red, this table is 7 feet long. It is from the Washhouse at Enfield, New Hampshire.

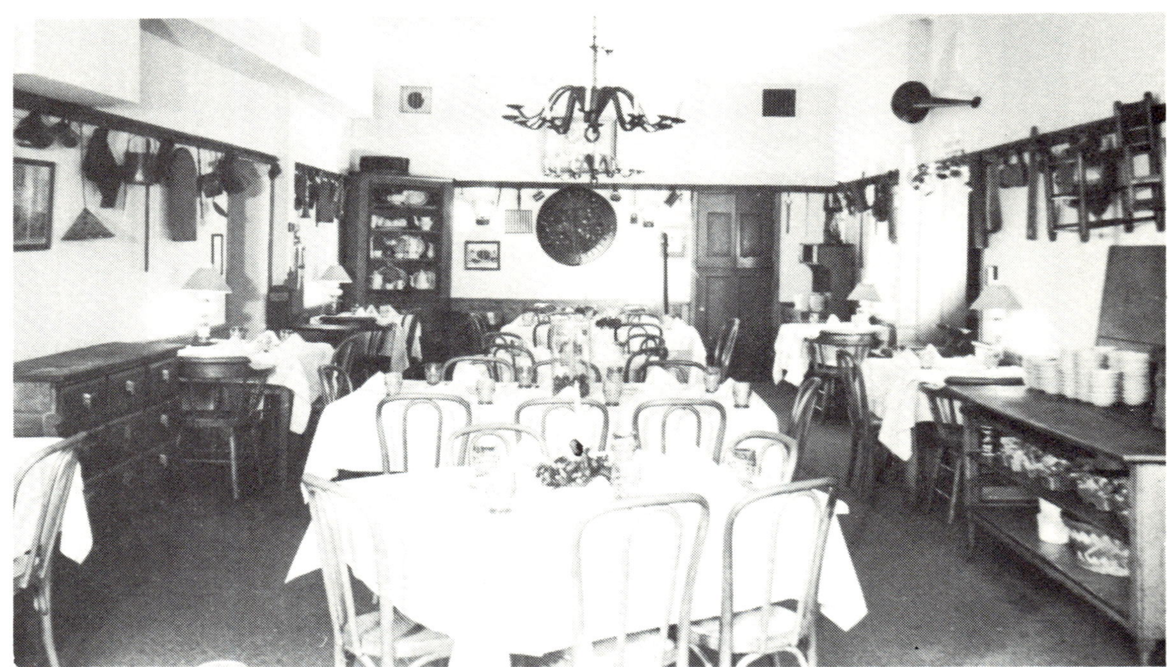

My favorite dining room at The Golden Lamb is The Shaker Room. In between the good food and conversation, it is always fun to walk around the room and examine the Shaker artifacts adorning the pegboard along the walls.

dining room. A large sewing counter serves as a buffet in another dining room. One drawer cherry stands hold candy in the lobby while a sorting table in original green paint is used for displaying rag dolls in the gift shop. A curious and perceptive eye can learn a great deal about the Shaker furniture by simply wandering through the halls of The Golden Lamb Inn. And if you have visited the Museum down the street, you will have seen more original Shaker furnishings than anywhere West of the Hudson River. For the follower of Shaker, Lebanon, Ohio, offers insight as well as delight.

— May, 1977

NOTE: *Since the opening of the Kettering-Moraine Museum in nearby Dayton, additional furniture from Watervliet, Ohio, has come to light. See pages 70, 71 for examples of chairs.*

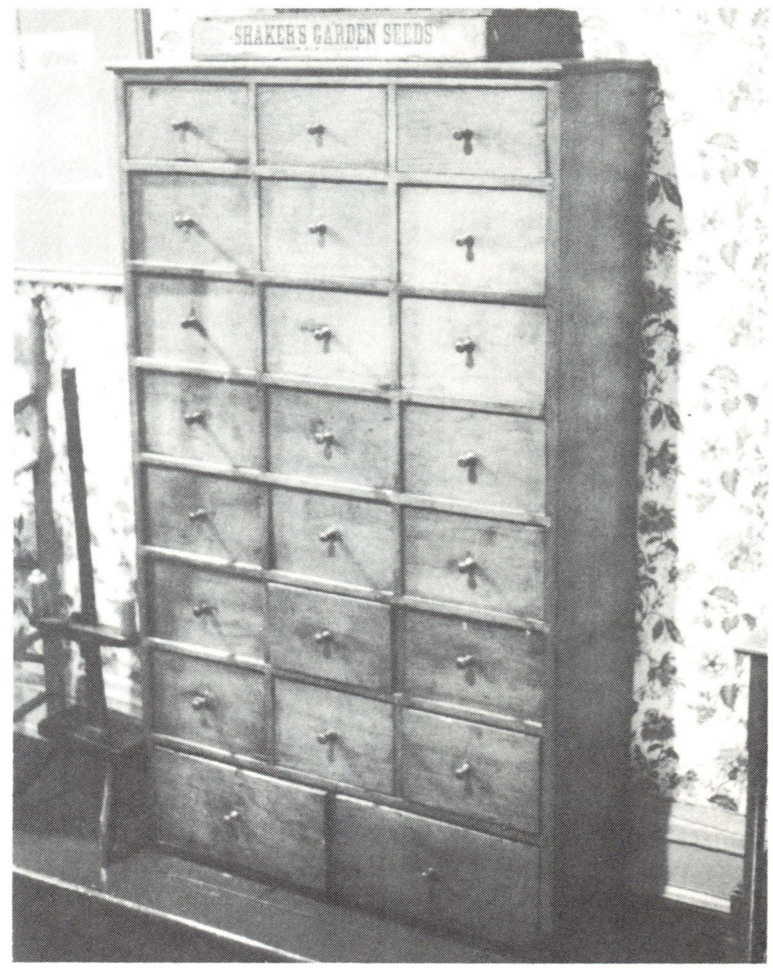

This case of drawers stands at the top of the stairs leading to the second floor in The Golden Lamb. It is 60" tall and 36" wide and has a molded base at the floor. The peg knobs are extra long. This piece is one of two that can be attributed to Watervliet (Dayton), Ohio, Shakers.

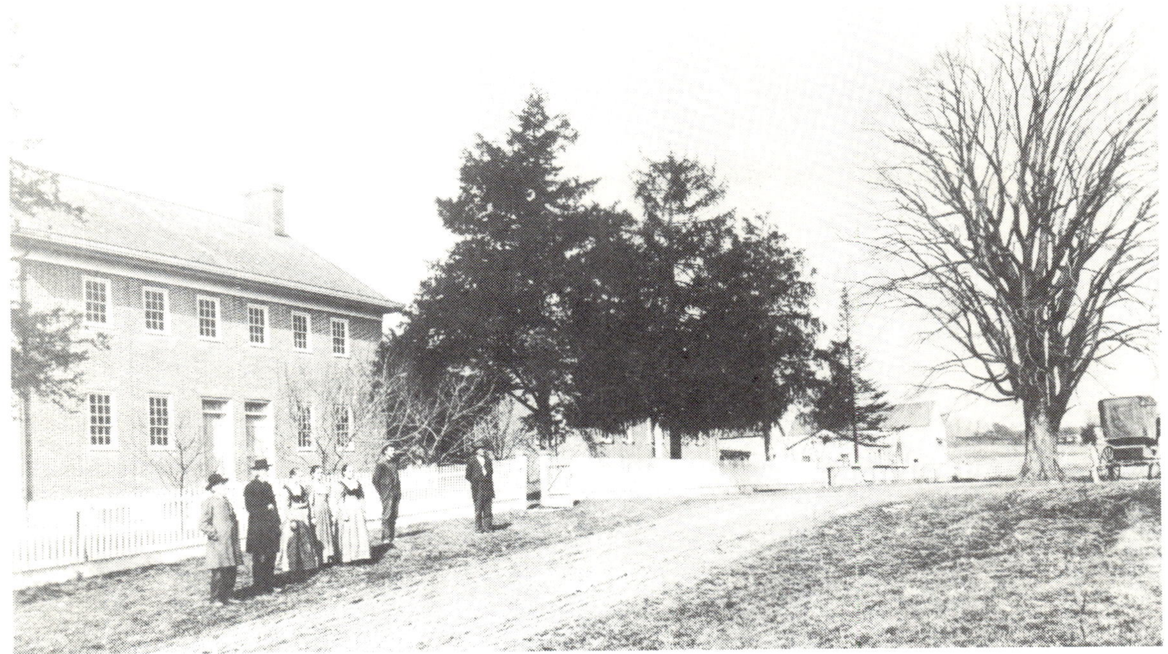

Early photograph of North Family Meeting House (foreground) and Dwelling House. The latter is obscured by some of the pine trees of the 2500 purchased from North Union (Shaker Heights, Ohio) in 1856.

(Original photograph is from the collection of Steve Kistler.)

Whitewater, Ohio

Two years ago, there were only five or six serious Shaker collectors and some knowledgeable antique dealers who joined the crowd at a farm auction outside Cincinnati, Ohio. They came because that farm had been the Whitewater Shaker Village, and the auction promised to reveal some of the contents of the dwel-

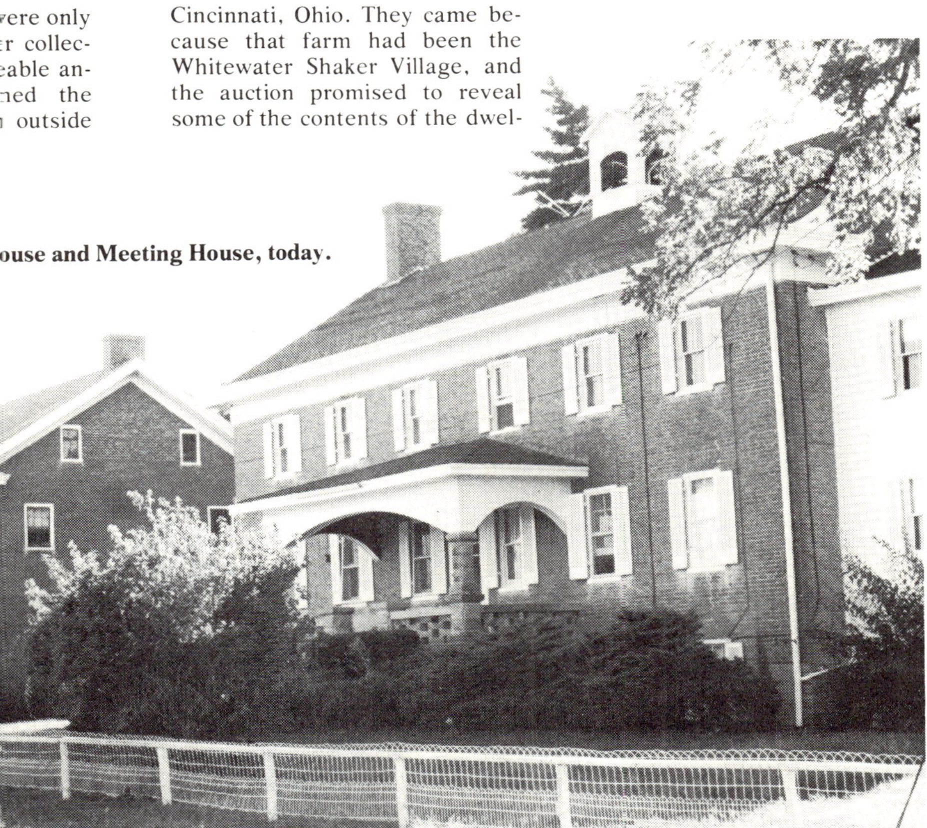

North Family Dwelling House and Meeting House, today.

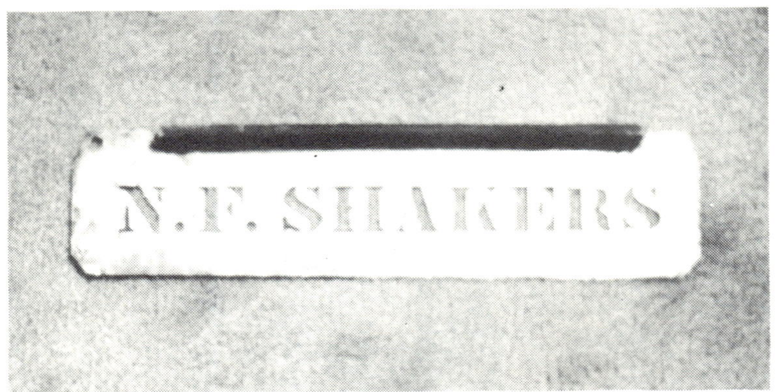

Brass stencil from Whitewater Ohio, North Family, Shakers. This was one of the choice items that came out of the November, 1974 auction. (Private collection)

lings that had been in one family's possession since being purchased from the Shakers in 1909. The Meeting House, dwelling house, six out-buildings, and better than three hundred acres had been sold to a group for development purposes. Today, the Meeting House has been sold and great attention is being focused on the preservation of the dwelling house.

By the year 1823, Union Village, outside Lebanon, Ohio, had reached its peak in membership, had stabilized itself as the Bishopric of the West, and was seeking new growth. In that year, the Shakers enlarged their membership by, among others, a convert from northwest of Cincinnati and a group known as The New Light Church from Darby Plains. It was decided to begin a new community with the New Light Church people as the core, and a Meeting House was built on the land west of Plain City, Ohio. But it was soon recognized that a community could not be sustained on that land, and the people were moved to join with the convert Northwest of Cincinnati.

There, in an 18 foot square cabin on a forty acre lot, began the Whitewater Shaker community. Illness, poor land, and unfaithfulness took their toll on the new community, but with the financial and leadership assistance of Union Village, Whitewater was able to grow and mature. In 1825, 215 acres of better land was purchased and the community moved. In 1827, another 345 acres was added towards the eventual total of 1500 acres. That same year, West Union, in Indiana, was broken up and many of the members from there joined Whitewater. Later that year, the Meeting House, which still stands, was built.

Among the buildings and industries that occupied the Shakers at Whitewater were broom making and the raising and selling of garden seeds. The frame building that housed the broom making was set up in 1876 and still stands although empty and in great need of attention. In 1829, Shaker brooms and mats sold for $2.25 per dozen. By 1865, the price had risen to $7.00 per dozen. In 1839, 17 acres of broom corn was raised and used to provide revenue for the community which four years earlier had become debt free.

The garden seed industry reached its peak in 1857 with a better than $5,000 profit. It is interesting to note that although seeds were sold throughout the Midwest, none of the packages had evidently made it to our time. In fact, I have not seen any labels or boxes from any of the Western Shaker communities except South Union. Whitewater gave up the seed business in 1873 when colored packages became prominent.

"That our seeds did not take, as they were put up in a brown colored paper and a plain stained box. It was conclusive we must keep up with the times or step down and out, which we did."*

* Page 431 in "Ohio State Archaeological and Historical Society Publications. Volume 13"

Another Whitewater industry of which we have no lasting evidence and little reference is the brewery that was constructed in 1832. Fourteen years later, the use of intoxicating beverages as well as tea, coffee, and tobacco were prohibited.

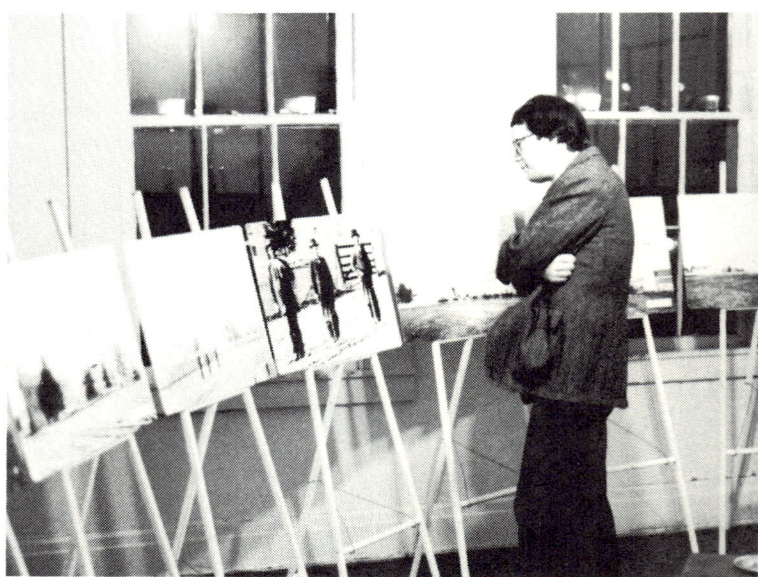

Exhibit of early photographs of the Whitewater Village, recently found in New York. These will be on display at the Kettering Moraine Museum in Dayton until mid-December and the Warren County Musuem, Lebanon, Ohio, in January.

The history of Whitewater is a fascinating account of one Shaker community and reflects the Shaker's openness to work and progress. There is often a tendency to think of the Shakers as "old fashioned" and unwilling to change. Such is not the case. They built dams and mills, produced their own brick, and purchased the latest machinery. In 1853, they converted the mill from water to steam. They put in steam laundries and installed hot air furnaces (1886); purchased one of the first tractors in the area (1893); made use of steam heat and hot water (1897); and introduced the telephone into their office (1901). Whitewater was an example of the Shaker spirit of peace, perservance, productivity and progress. And it still stands within our grasp today!

Like the other Shaker communities, Whitewater felt the pains of the Civil War and the industrial revolution as can be seen in the decline of the seed industry. By the 1890's, lands were being rented out because of insufficient members to care for them. The end came in 1907 and the lands sold to families in whose hands the property had remained until two years ago. During these past two years many prospective buyers have examined the property but only the Meeting House has been sold. And in this the original hardware, pegs and paint seem destined for history as the new owners begin to dismantle the old and remodel for modern living.

Recently, there has been an attempt to purchase and restore the North Family Dwelling House to its proper historical significance. On November 13th, Mr. Steve S. Kistler hosted a party of interested persons in Cincinnati and displayed an exhibition of old photographs of the Shaker Whitewater Village. These photographs had been found by Mr. Ron Emery, New Lebanon, New York, in that distant area. Steve hoped to form a non-profit organization and raise the necessary $60,000 to buy the building. He has experienced the same frustrations that I had some years ago in an attempt to restore Rose Cottage at Union Village. Unfortunately, the Shakers of Ohio do not arouse the interest and/or finances necessary. In my efforts with Rose Cottage, the response was to wait for Whitewater; however, the opportunity is passing there, also!

— December, 1976

NOTE: *The Warren County Historical Society has a seed box from Union Village. The Meeting House and the dwelling house have changed hands and are being restored.*

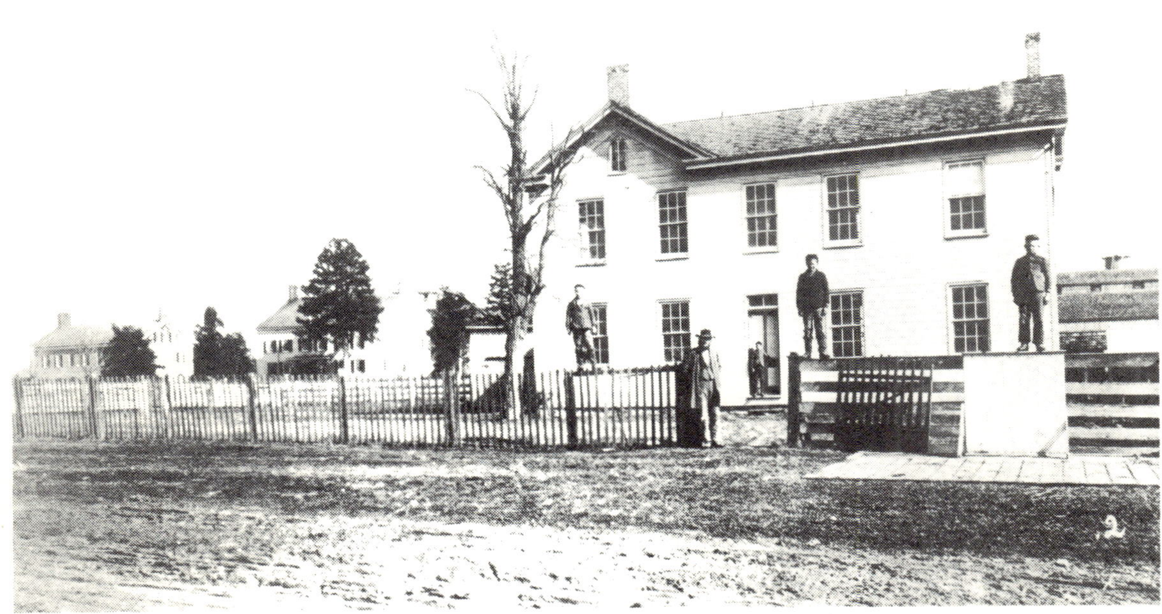

This frame structure was built in 1876 for broom making. It stands today but the buildings in the background burned in 1885. The wagon scales are seen in the foreground (1884). These structures were part of the South Family complex, still privately owned.

(Original photograph is from the collection of Steve Kistler.)

The Collection of the Ohio Historical Society

For the state that had the largest Shaker community in the world within its bounds, Ohio has a surprisingly small Shaker Collection at the Ohio Historical Society Museum in Columbus. The only pieces of furniture in the collection are two chairs...and those are from Eastern communities. In fact, the entire contents are from the Eastern communities. None of the rich heritage of the Shakers in Ohio is preserved in the Society's Shaker Collection.

Most of the collection is not on public view and came to the Society from John P. MacLean, who wrote extensively on the Ohio Shakers shortly after the turn of the century. His articles on all of the Ohio communities were published in the quarterly of the Ohio State Archaeological and Historical Society. In 1907, these articles were compiled, along with others, in his book *Shakers of Ohio* which remains the most extensive publication on the subject. The preface of that book states that "Elder Daniel Offord, of the North Family, Mt. Lebanon, New York, stated, that of all who had written about the Shakers, the author had been the fairest, and the only one who had a thorough knowledge of the subject." Because of this mutual friendship and respect, MacLean was the recipient of many gifts

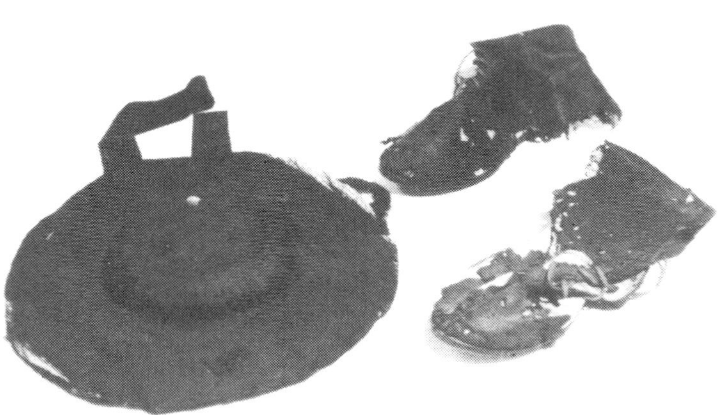

Hat and Shoes reputedly worn by Mother Ann Lee.

from the Shakers, primarily in Mt. Lebanon, N.Y. These gifts now make up the greater part of the Shaker collection.

Perhaps the most fascinating of all the artifacts...and the most significant...are items reputed to have belonged to Mother Ann Lee. Ann Lee lead a group of eight followers of the Shaking Quakers from England to America in 1774. Two years later, the Shakers bought land in Niskeyuna (Watervliet), New York. From there, Mother Ann traveled, preached and gained new followers in Connecticut, Massachusetts and New York. She died in 1783. It was not until four years later that the Shakers became established as a formal community and separated from the world. It is difficult to imagine that the belongings of the founder of a sect would be so well preserved, especially since the institution had not yet been created at the time of her death. But while it is difficult to imagine, it is fascinating and delightful and, for lack of contrary evidence, apparently accepted as true.

Included in the Shaker collection at the Ohio Historical Society are the hat and shoes worn by Mother Ann as well as a number

of pieces of cloth that were supposed to have come from her petitcoat, short gown and dresses. Similar pieces of cloth can also be found in the Shaker Museum in New York and at the Canterbury, New Hampshire, community. The Shaker Museum also has a cup and saucer that were reputedly brought from England to this

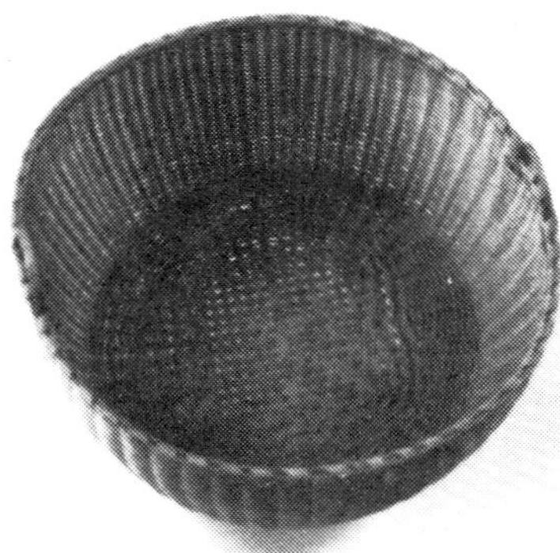

Basket w/ floral design woven in bottom.

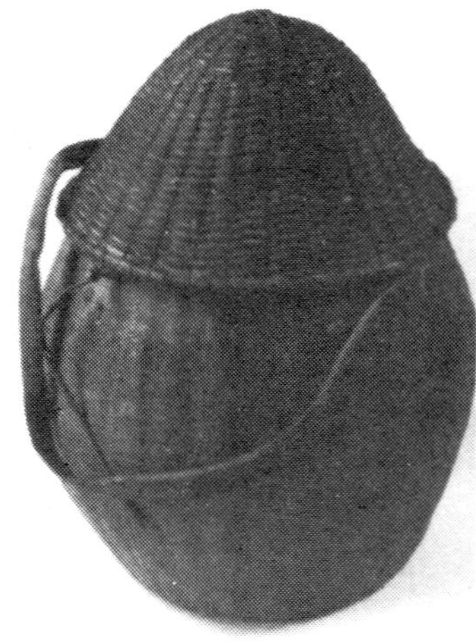

Leather covered basket w/ hinged top, intended purpose not known.

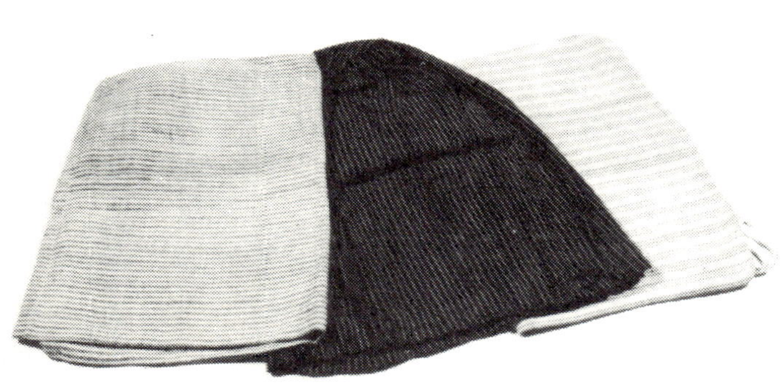

Pieces of material reputedly from Mother Ann Lee's petticoat, short gown, and dress.

country by Mother Ann although her journey predates the period of these pieces. Such is not the case, though, with the hat and shoes. They are of the style, material and workmanship that would be contemporary with the life of Mother Ann. The fact that these were given as a gift to MacLean long before there was much historical interest in the Shakers would add to the credibility of the origins of these unique artifacts. And these artifacts, in turn, give a uniqueness to the Society's collection.

Many of the other items also have a written history with them. With one of the brethren's hats is the note: "Hat belonged to Elder Daniel Boler, who at the age of 10, walked all the way from Kentucky to Mount Lebanon, N.Y. in company with his father to join the Shakers in this place. Church Family, Mount Lebanon, Columbia Co., N.Y., E.J. Neale, Trustee." Two striped linen hand bags carry the tag: "Bag owned by Patty Bumnell, sister of Elder Richard Bumnell, oldest sister. Her father opposed to her belief. Died in 1850. Donated by Eldress Sarah Collins." These little notes add much interest to the small collection.

While neither of the two baskets pictured have such a well described history, their association with the collection for so many years adds validity to their being Shaker. The one basket has a hinged top and is covered with leather. Its intended purpose is not known. The other is a finely executed square basket with the bottom plaited in a beautiful floral pattern. But while these baskets are as fine as any to be seen, their authenticity as Shaker rests upon their history since the Shakers made baskets by the same methods as did their neighbors.

Mold, tools for cutting uniform strips, notched and shaped handles, conical or domed bases, and styles of weaves were all familiar to the Indians and other basketmakers. In fact, many of the techniques of basketmaking employed by the Shakers were introduced to them by neighboring Indians. With the exception of poplar ware and some styles of sewing baskets, there seems to be no method or characteristic that is not found among the basketmakers of the world as well as among the Shakers. The Shaker sisters themselves have said that, although they made baskets in their younger days, they can not tell whether or not a basket is Shaker made. Perhaps the best reading on this subject is in Gloria Roth Teleki's *The Baskets Of Rural America.*

In addition to these noteworthy items, the collection includes other small items that are representative of the Shakers and their lives. There is a doll of the kind that the Shakers dressed and sold to the world through their gift shops; brethren's hats of felt and palm with the names of the owners; numerous brushes and sewing implements; boxes for spices; eye glasses and cases; and a sampling of Shaker clothes. My favorite item in the lot is the finely turned spool dated 1836. It seems to capture in its simplicity the grace and beauty of the Shaker spirit. It reflects the Shaker concept of beauty: "That which has in itself the highest use, possesses the greatest beauty."

. . . .

Again this year Elmira College is offering a summer seminar entitled "The Shaker Experience." The course is held at Darrow School, the former Mt. Lebanon Shaker community, July 5 - 10. Three college or graduate credits

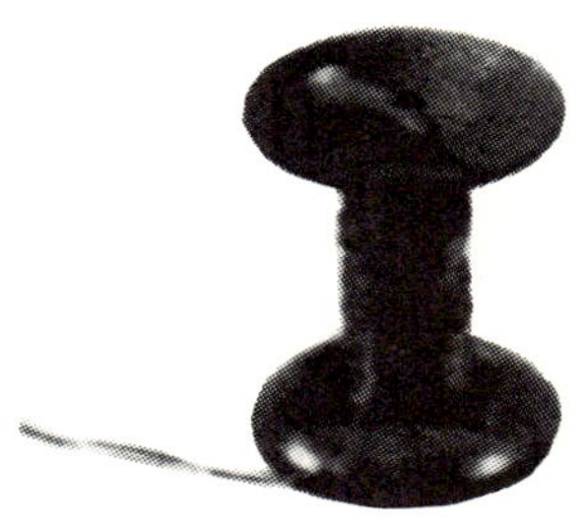

Turned spool dated 1836.

can be earned. The course includes lectures, visits to nearby museums and former Shaker communities and discussions with friends and scholars of the Shakers. It is a delightful way to have a vacation, earn some college credits, or simply relax in the old Shaker dwellings. For further information, contact Dr. Herbert Wisby, Continuing Education, Elmira College, Elmira, New York, 14901.

— June, 1976

Pleasant Hill, Kentucky

Thirteen years ago I pulled off of the state highway to spend thirty minutes looking at a small exhibition of what had been a Shaker settlement. Now, the highway by-passes the community and that exhibition has been expanded into one of the finest memorials to the Shakers to be found. While Sabbathday Lake and Canterbury still are being used by the Shakers and Hancock and the Shaker Museum hold the best collections of Shaker artifacts, Pleasant Hill, Kentucky, lives up to its name and reflects the quiet spirit of the people who occupied the bluegrass fields 65 years ago.

Pleasant Hill began its history as a Shaker community in 1805 and had its earliest remaining building erected in 1809. This stone structure is the oldest Shaker building west of New York still standing. Rose Cottage in Union Village, Ohio, was erected in 1810. From the first conversions and donations of rolling hills, the community grew to better than 2,500 acres and 500 members before beginning the decline that was hastened by the Civil War.

John Batstone, an Englishman, recently visited Pleasant Hill and wrote his impressions for THE WORLD OF SHAKER. Among other comments, he offers the following:

"Freedom and absence of 'hassle' is the keynote of Pleasant Hill. Within the buildings themselves the visitor's essential privacy is not intruded upon. In the Centre Family Dwelling House, for instance, the visitor is free to wander from room to room as he pleases, and the arrangement of the features of Shaker life is such that there is no sense of 'deadness' as in some museums. Museum is what Pleasant Hill most definitely is not. There is a real sense of 'life' as the Shakers lived it and what comes over is both the practical zeal and the common sense of these remarkable people. Their efficiency at a domestic level, their inventive ingenuity, coupled with their ability to promote a thriving economy show them to be no cranks or 'nuts.' That the movement declined during the latter part of the nineteenth century and finally died is perhaps as much a comment on our world and its values as on their own."

What Mr. Batstone found were twenty-one buildings, primarily of limestone, housing exhibitions of broom making, coopering, weaving, spinning, and cabinet making as well as educational materials and overnight lodging and dining facilities. The lodging is in the restored dwellings and shops and are furnished as authentic retiring rooms, using reproduction Shaker furniture and hand woven curtains, rugs and bed spreads. But the air conditioning and pri-

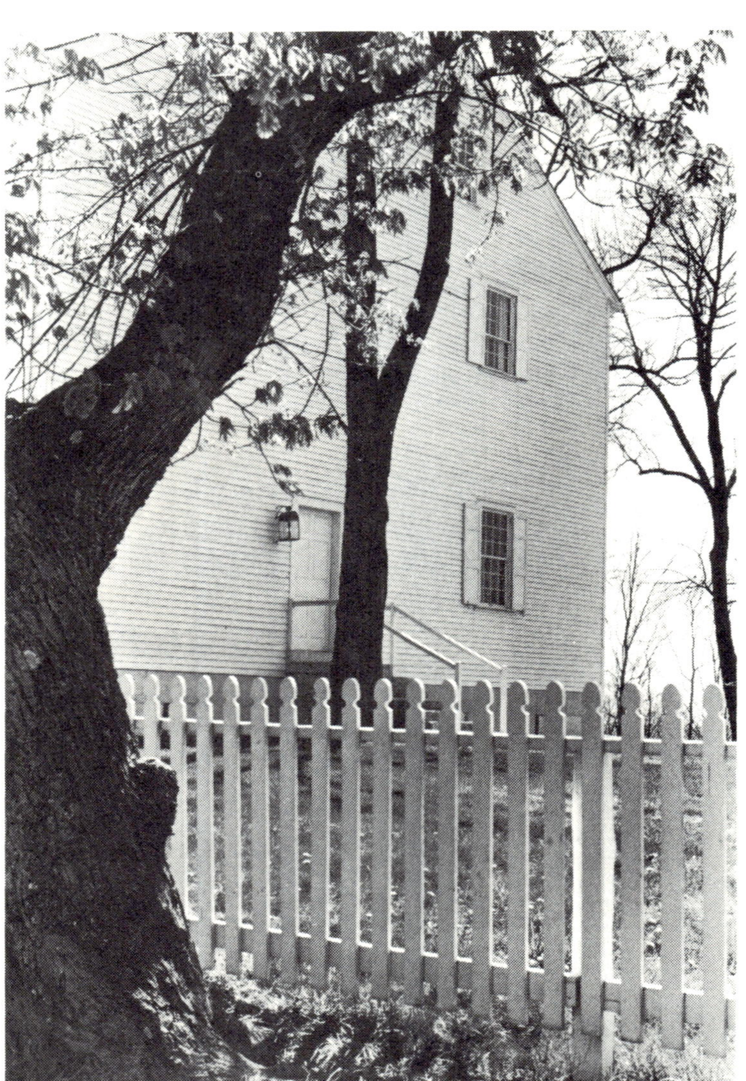

The vast meeting House stands as an invitation for visitors to ponder those frenzied, whirling dances which were the Shakers' worship service, and which actually gave rise to their name. A white clapboard building of 1820, it is still an engineering achievement with an unsupported room span of 60' x 40'. It is hard to find words for a feeling of serenity that is expressed by this simple room with its small pane windows, white-washed walls with dark blue trim, and highly polished black ash floors. (Photograph courtesy Pleasant Hill, Inc.)

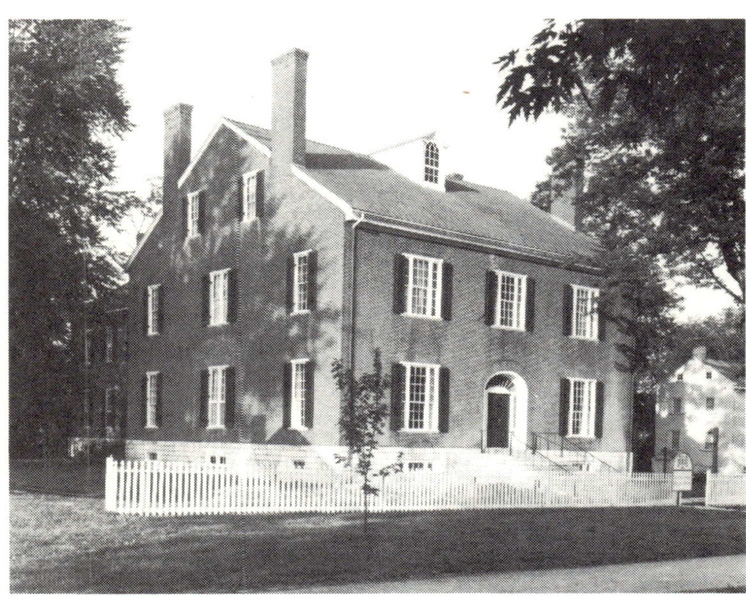

Pleasant Hill's Trustees' House was used in Shaker days to welcome "the world's people." Shaker hospitality still abounds there; today the Trustees House offers fine dining and lodging. Overnight accommodations are available in eight original buildings throughout the village, and all guest rooms are furnished with authentic Shaker reproduction furniture. (Photograph courtesy Pleasant Hill, Inc.)

the buildings have been restored to their original paints, while others have exposed lath boards so that the construction beneath can be seen.

The furnishings at Pleasant Hill are also worth noting. It is easy to be impressed with the tremendous variety of styles and construction of Shaker items. This becomes very apparent at Pleasant Hill. Chests of drawers and chairs are very much like many Ohio and Kentucky pieces and are indistinguishable as being Shaker if they were to be seen outside the community. A side trip to the nearby town of Harrodsburg and the museum there points this out. Chairs in that museum are documented as having been in the same family from times prior to the formation of the Shaker community. But without such documentation, those chairs might easily be passed off as "Kentucky Shaker."

vate baths add a luxury that the Shakers did not know.

The dining takes place in the Trustees' House which was originally used to greet visitors from the outside world. Included in this dwelling are the twin seemingly free-standing spiral staircases that fascinate the innocent child and educated architect alike. I have yet to meet anyone who was displeased with the eating at Shakertown. To walk beneath the trees that line the stone walk during the day or to stroll between the gaslights at night, Pleasant Hill is a delightful place to "get away from it all." (Reservations are necessary for lodging and/or dining. For information, write Shakertown at Pleasant Hill, Rt. 4, Harrodsburg, Ky. 40330.)

Pleasant Hill uses a combination of limestone, brick and frame in their structures. Many of the buildings, like the Trustees', reflect what Edward Andrews called "Shaker Georgian." The restored condition of the buildings sets Pleasant Hill apart from its Eastern counterparts. Many of

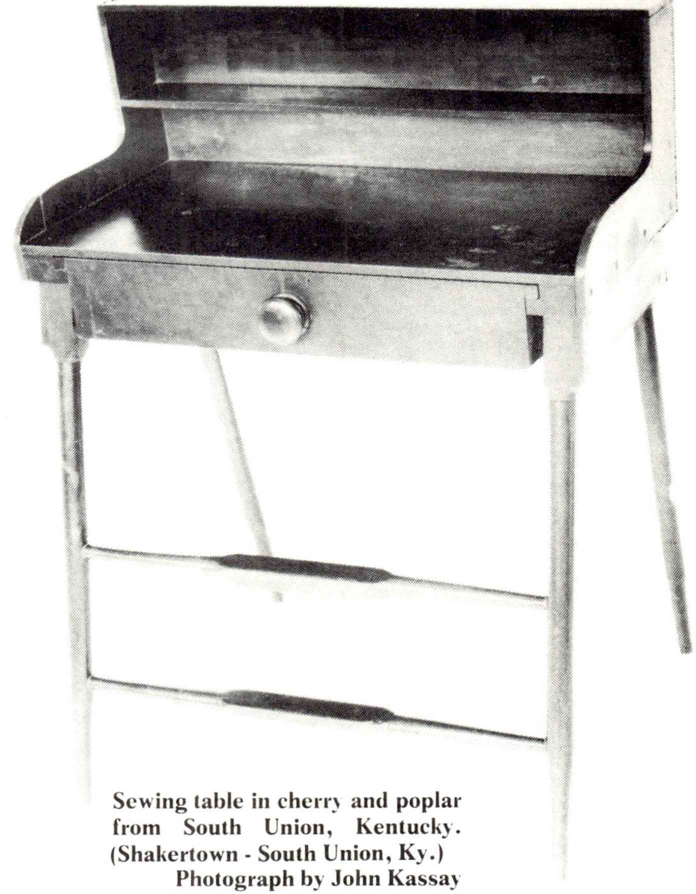

Sewing table in cherry and poplar from South Union, Kentucky. (Shakertown - South Union, Ky.) Photograph by John Kassay

The other impressive feature of the furnishings at Pleasant Hill is the fineness of the quality. Pictured herein is a sewing desk like one at Pleasant Hill. It is as dainty and delightful as any from the Eastern communities. Numerous chairs could be placed side by side with their Eastern counterparts and come away as the winner in a show of craftsmanship, lightness, and aesthetics.

— July, 1976

NOTE: *There are now twenty-four restored buildings open at Pleasant Hill which include sixty-two rooms for overnight accommodations. There are very few tourist spots in the midwest that provide the serene solitude that can be found in the gas-lit village. For the person who spends a night at Pleasant Hill, jogging up the main road in the morning dew or strolling along the stone walks at dusk instills the sense of peace that Shakers must have found a century ago. And the community should not be ignored in winter. It is open every day of the year except Christmas and offers the off-season visitor an added measure of quietude.*

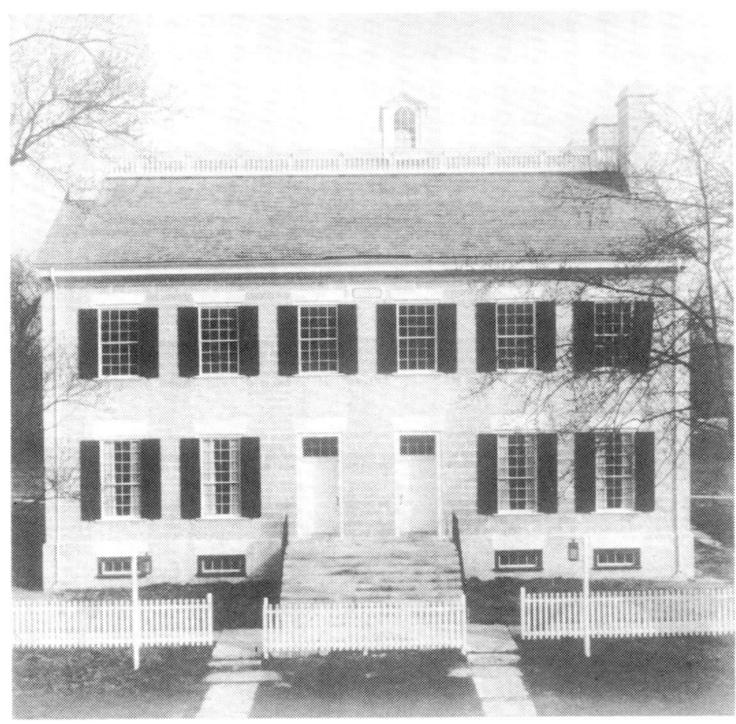

In its restored state, the village is a simple and graceful statement of the Shaker way of life and provides an open window into its history. Hostesses in Shaker dress who greet travelers in the massive Centre Family House call attention to the twin, deep, paneled doorways, one for each sex, that were necessary for communal but celibate living. Both sexes, though separate, were equal since the group believed its Messiah, Mother Ann Lee, was actually the female incarnation of Christ. Men and women occupied the same buildings, but their paths never crossed. Separate entrances, separate living quarters, and separate community duties in separate shops were included in the living arrangement for all members of the community.

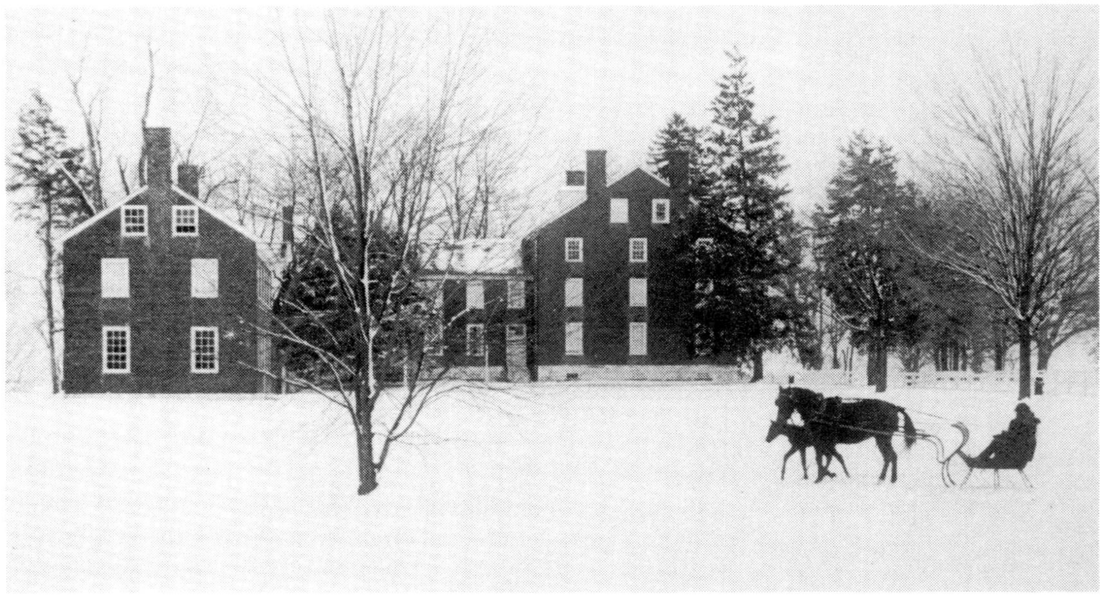

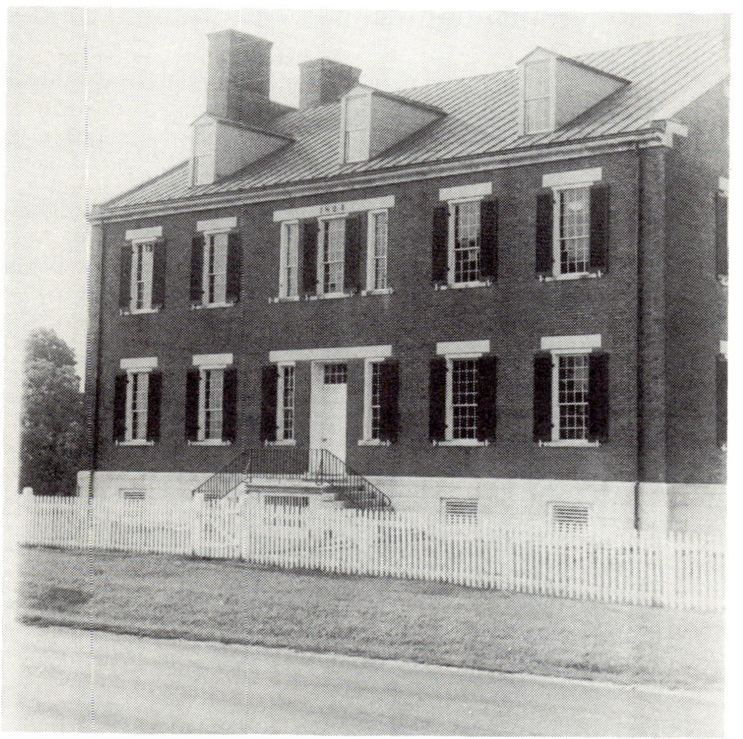

Although the date on the Centre House says 1824, it was actually started two years earlier and not finished until nine years later. The gutters on the building are limestone.

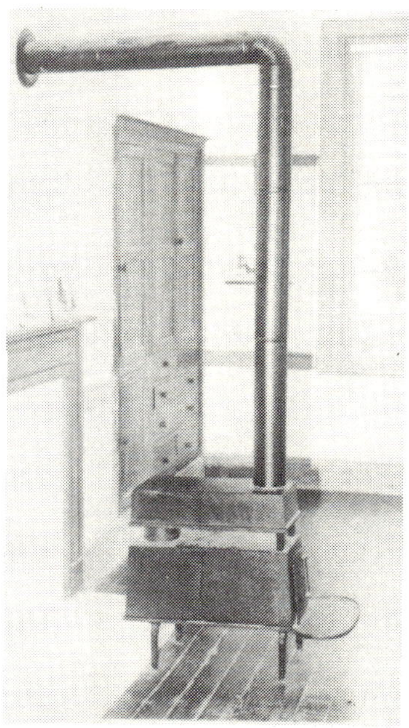

The South Union stoves were designed by the Shakers but manufactured in Cincinnati from where they were shipped in August of 1833. Notice the built-in cupboard to the rear.

South Union, Kentucky

"Delightful, refreshing, admirable" were only a few words heard recently describing the restoration and museum at the most Southwestern point of the Shaker network of societies. Shakertown at South Union, Kentucky, was started by missionaries from Union Village, Ohio, in 1807; closed in 1922 as the last of the seven western Shaker groups to be disbanded; and reopened as a museum on its present site in 1971. Today, six major buildings stand as a remembrance of a thriving community of more than 200 structures and 6,000 acres and as a symbol of the fulfillment of dreams through hard work of local citizens.

The Southwestern Kentucky society was established and organized under the leadership of Benjamin Seth Youngs who stayed until 1836. While Youngs came from the Mother Mt. Lebanon, New York, community and brought with him the established standards and regulations, South Union was the furthest from the mainstream of Shakerism and often made adaptations in keeping with its geographical and stylistic heritage. Early converts brought with them all of their possessions, including slaves which lived in cabins behind the main buildings. When the Shakers freed their slaves in 1819, this separate black family was abolished and the members of it integrated into the other families (the Shaker communal groups) as had been done in the Northern communities.

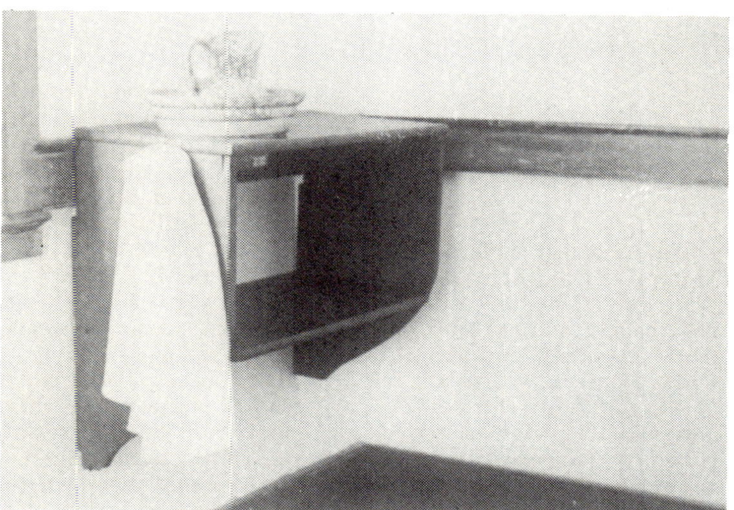

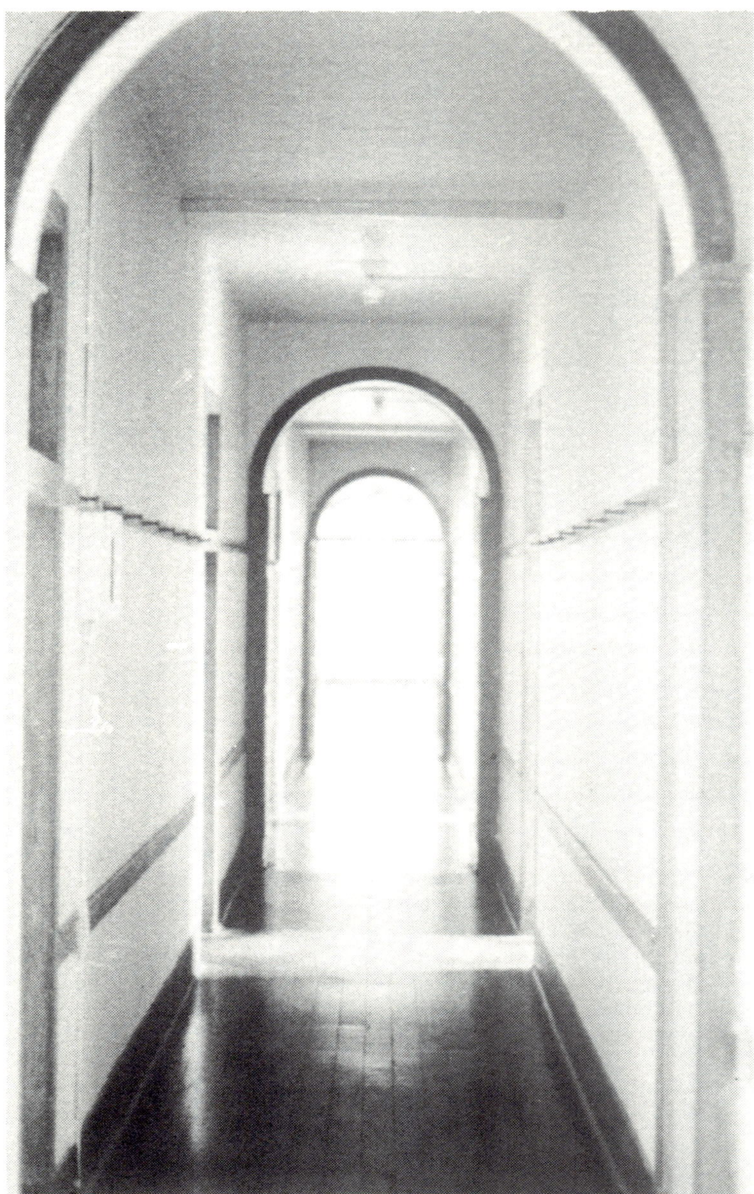

The hall on the second floor of the Centre House show the visually effective use of arches in its construction.

The Georgian influences of Virginia and the Carolinas from which most of the early settlers in the area had come can be seen in the construction of the 1824 Centre House as well as in much of the furniture. The peg rails have a beaded edge on top and bottom, a characteristic not seen elsewhere. The colors are vibrant - ochre woodwork except the baseboards which are red. The built-ins are not as large as those of the East, more abundant than at Pleasant Hill, uniform in size and placement, and include a small door at the base that might have been put in especially for a chamber pot. The many arches and mantels (although the building was heated by stoves) give the structure an element of added beauty beyond its utilitarianism that have led many to call it "probably the finest dwelling house in all of Shakerdom."

Heavier than its Eastern counterparts but not as heavy as Ohio Shaker, the furniture of South Union reflects the time of its greatest production, the Sheraton Period, as well as its Southern ties and a few characteristics uniquely its own. Chest and beds have turned legs and posts. Candlestands have bulbous turned pedestals. Built-in corner cupboards appear to be features of the Kentucky communities (Pleasant Hill has one in its kitchen) and the punched tin pie safes are strictly South Union. The cherry trestle tables have heavy but graceful cut out feet with tops having boards running across the width rather than lengthwise. The banister rail for the Sisters Shop exhibits two design elements as an inversion of the posts are duplicates of some table legs and the spindles with turned ends and squared centers are mates to the stretchers of sewing tables.

The South Union Shakers were primarily agriculturists...marketing seeds, fruit, cattle, etc. throughout the region and by river and railroad to New Orleans and Texas. They raised silk worms, spinning the silk and shipping it East for further processing and manufacturing by sister communities. In 1869, a hotel was built on the nearby railroad and leased to others for the operation of it. The Shakers had the first automobile in the county and had telephones installed as soon as possible.

The endeavor at South Union reached its peak 349 members only twenty years after its founding. For the next hundred years, it experienced a steady decline of membership and religious fervor

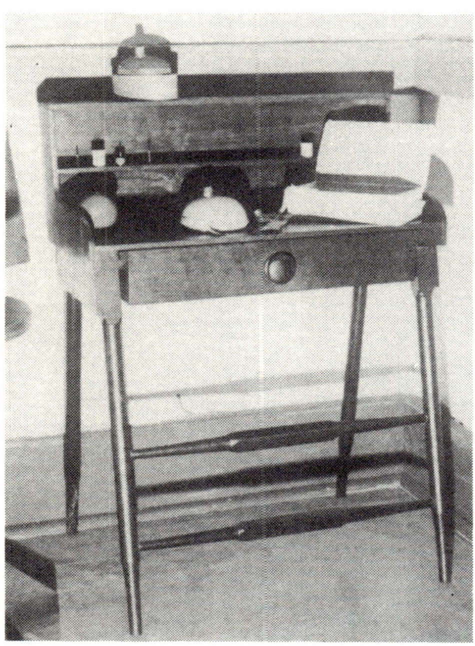

The stretchers on the South Union sewing desk are almost identical to the spindles in the stair railing of the Sisters Shop. The corner posts, inverted, are like the legs on some tables.

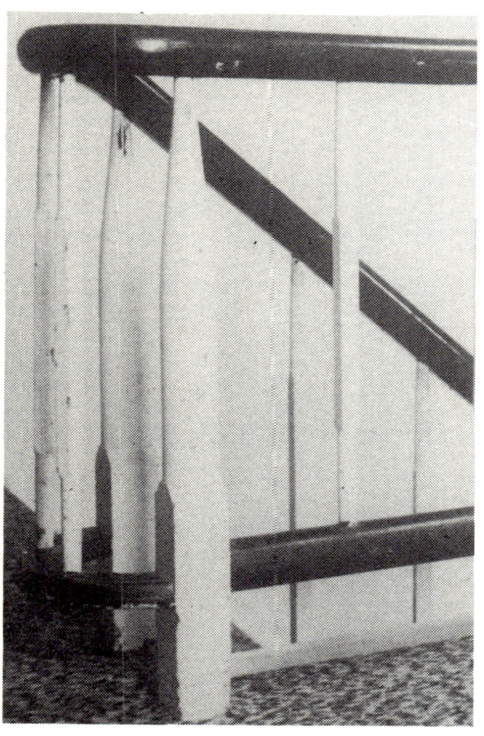

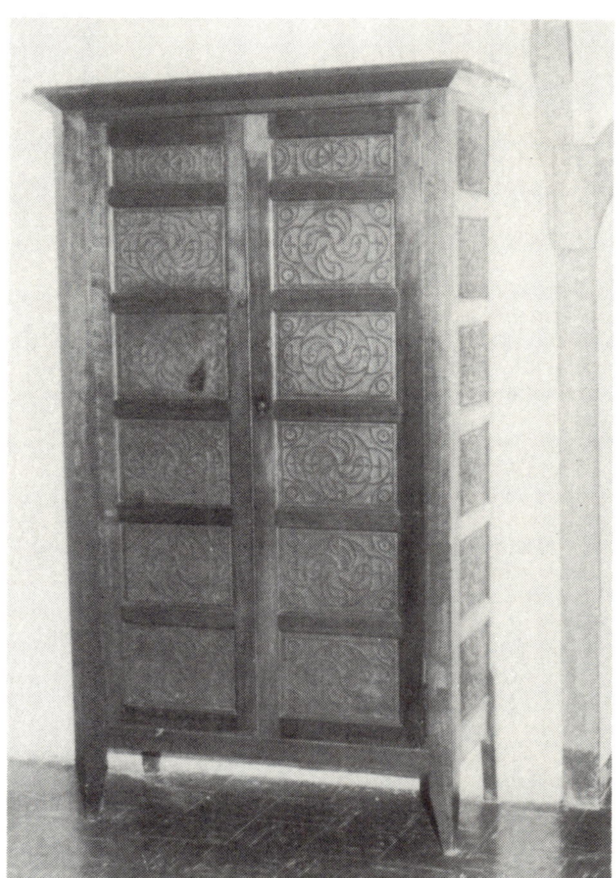

While the design in the tins is not a Shaker exclusive, the punched tin pie safe was in the kitchen of the Centre House when it was sold at auction in 1922. The wooden tube to the upper right of the safe is the channel where the rope ran from the bell on top of the building.

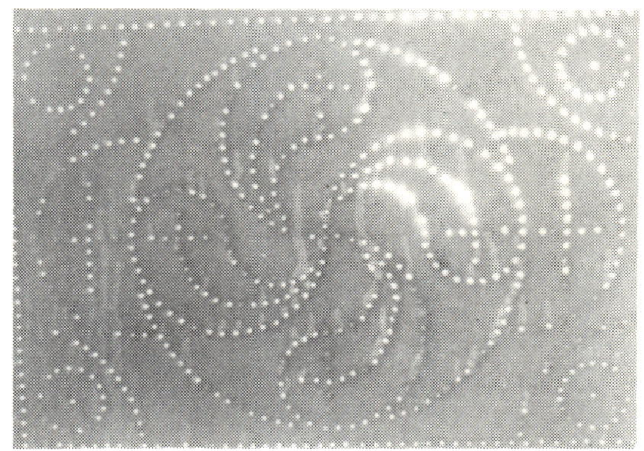

—helped along by the Civil War—until two of its last nine members moved to Mt. Lebanon. The other seven were given $10,000 and chose to stay and live out their days in the surrounding Kentucky countryside. Much of the property was sold to a company that harvested the forests for making railroad ties. In 1949, the Order of Benedictine purchased part of the land and three major buildings for a seminary. The Sisters Shop is still maintained by the Benedictines as a retreat house while the Centre House and Preservatory were sold to a non-profit organization for development as a museum.

Shakertown Revisited, Inc. was started in 1962, largely through the efforts of the current co-directors, Mrs. Curry Hall and Miss Julia Neal. To this day, these two ladies continue to give freely of themselves...greeting visitors at the door, studying manuscripts, securing grants, conducting tours, writing books and removing paint. Along with many other volunteers and the addition of the 1917 store a mile and an half away, Shakertown at South Union has achieved great

NOTE: *Richard Steinert, offical of the Connecticut State Prison on the former Shaker grounds, points out that posts protruding from the ceiling for clothes lines were not unique to South Union. They were also on the second floor of the laundry building and in the basement and attic of the seed house at the Center Family of Enfield, CT.*

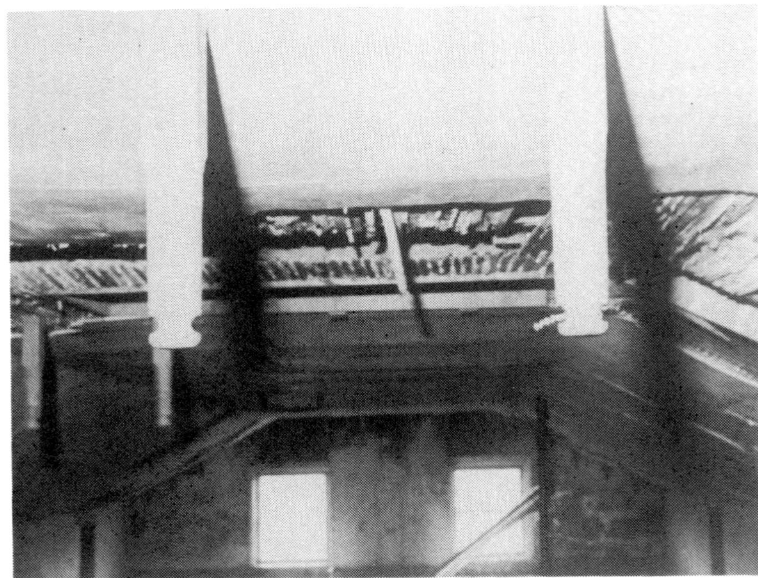

Probably unique in Shaker buildings, these posts protruding from the ceiling of the attic in the Sisters Shop were used for the clothes line.

accomplishments in the past few years. The exterior restoration of the Centre House has involved a new roof, rebuilding chimneys, replacing windows with small panes, addition of shutters and tuckpointing of the brick. The interior is yet to be carefully restored. Until that time, the visitor to South Union has the opportunity to see a true diamond in the rough and meet some who have discovered the depth of its beauty.

— August, 1979

A full moon over the famous round stone dairy barn in Hancock Shaker Village, Pittsfield, Massachusetts.

The Berkshires

While a trip to Pleasant Hill, Kentucky, can be an enjoyable weekend excursion, the world of Shaker in its fullest is to be seen in the Berkshire Mountains. There, where New York and Massachusetts meet outside Pittsfield, Massachusetts, is to be found the largest concentration of Shaker buildings, artifacts and knowledge in any one section of the country.

Mt. Lebanon, New York, was the first and largest Shaker community to be organized into Gospel Order (1792). It is now divided between a private school, Darrow, an international communal group called the Sufi, and private residences.

The Darrow School purchased the Church Family and its buildings from the Shakers in 1932. At the time, it was full of furniture and even after a number of sales (the last one in 1973), there is still an ample supply of unique examples of Shaker craftsmanship. In addition to the round pedestle tables, measuring 42 inches across, the 1806 tall clock and numerous free standing cupboards, the Darrow buildings reflect the Shaker tradition of constructing furniture into the buildings themselves. Vast expanses of drawers, drying racks that pull out of the walls next to the fireplaces, built-in cupboards measuring up to fifteen feet in length, and walk-in wardrobes remain as examples of Shaker ingenuity and practicability.

The buildings themselves are noteworthy. In addition to the many structures that were exceedingly large by early 19th century standards, there are two that are especially important. The great stone barn, completed in 1858, was 196 feet long and 50 feet wide. It had five floors, four of which could be entered at ground level off of the surrounding hillside. With this construction, the law of gravity could be used to lighten the work load. Systematically, hay could be taken in on one level, dropped to the level below for animals. The dung of the animals could then be shoveled through trapdoors to a lower level where it was gathered and dumped into wagons that were waiting below at yet another level. Burned by an arsonist in 1971, the thick stone walls stand as an eerie reminder of another time and people.

The second important structure at Mt. Lebanon is the Meeting House. Being the center of the faith, Mt. Lebanon possessed the finest of the houses of worship. Erected in 1824, the main section of the interior is one room 80 feet long and 65 feet wide. The ceiling in this room arches 25 feet above the floor in one clean span without support. It was in this room that the Shakers performed their worship in dance. To support this synchronized stomping and shuffling of feet, the floor rests upon massive piers of stone that have been placed every ten feet. It has been said that almost half the work in the construction of this building rests beneath the floor.

The last Shakers left Mt. Lebanon in 1948 and moved to Hancock, Massachusetts, less than ten miles down the road. Twelve years later, the Shakers left there and moved on to Canterbury, New Hampshire, where they continue to live out their years. At that time, a group of interested persons organized the Shaker Community, Inc. and purchased the land and buildings. Today, the 1,000 acres and twenty buildings are open as a public museum illustrating the Shakers' culture and contributions.

Perhaps the most noteable attraction at Hancock is the round stone dairy barn, originally built in 1826. It is an example of the Shakers' efficiency since one man could work in the center of the structure and feed and water all the cattle which had been placed with their heads facing inward. In the process of restoration in 1968, all of the three foot wide stone wall was dismantled and rebuilt. Today, as in the day when it was

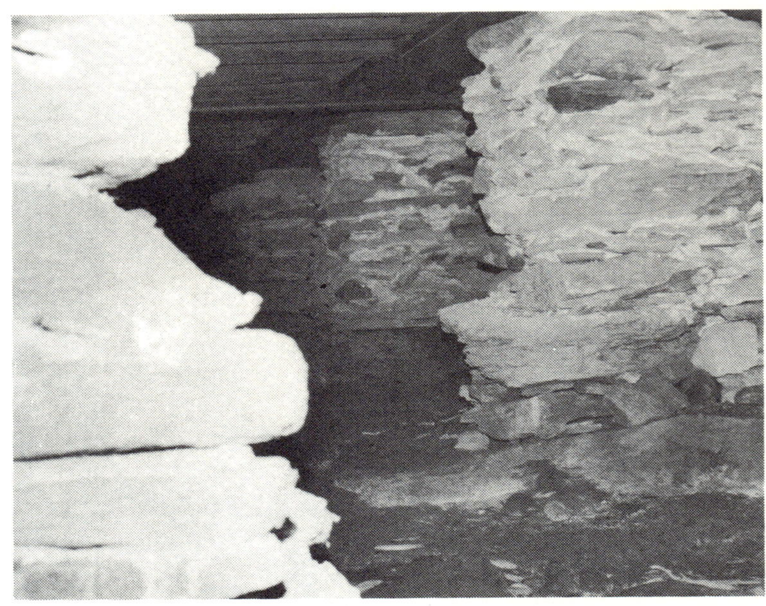

The massive stone supports beneath the floor of the Meeting House at Mt. Lebanon, New York. These were centered every ten feet in each direction.

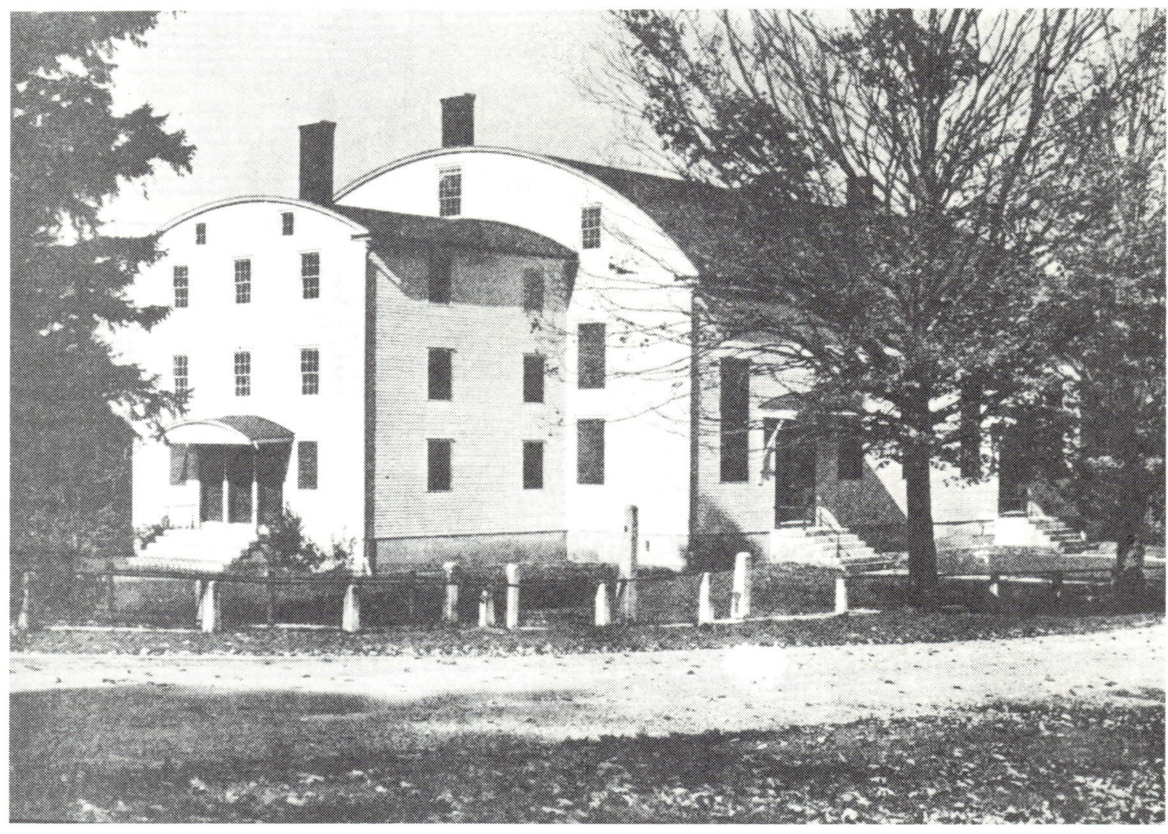

Meeting House, Mt. Lebanon, New York.

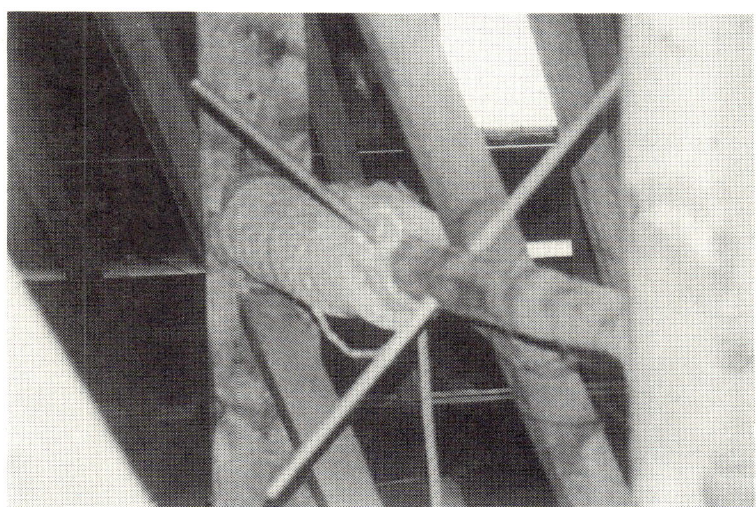

A large winch used to lower the lights in the Meeting House so that they could be lit. They were then cranked back up out of the way of the Shaker marches and dances.

built, it stands as a concept in functionalism.

Hancock village is a working village with guides and volunteers involved in the Shaker crafts and operating a kitchen wherein Shaker herbs and foods are prepared and used. Supplement this with a superb exhibit of Shaker furniture and it all adds up to the primary site for an education in Shaker and its heritage.

If a visit to Hancock does not fulfill a desire for learning about the Shakers, then a twenty minute trip to Old Chatham, New York, and the Shaker Museum should add the finishing touch. Therein is contained an excellent collection of Shaker furniture and other artifacts with emphasis upon tools. Its library of manuscripts affords the scholar a wealth of material and insights that are not contained in books.

And for the antique hunter, no other section of the country offers as many quality dealers in Shaker. In addition to Mt. Lebanon and Hancock, Watervliet, New York, and Tyringham, Massachusetts, are within forty miles. Because of the great amount of items that did exist, and still do, in the area, the dealers in this section have more "coming out of homes" than in any other area. If you want to see, learn and hunt Shaker, a visit to the Berkshires is an excellent way to begin.

— August, 1976

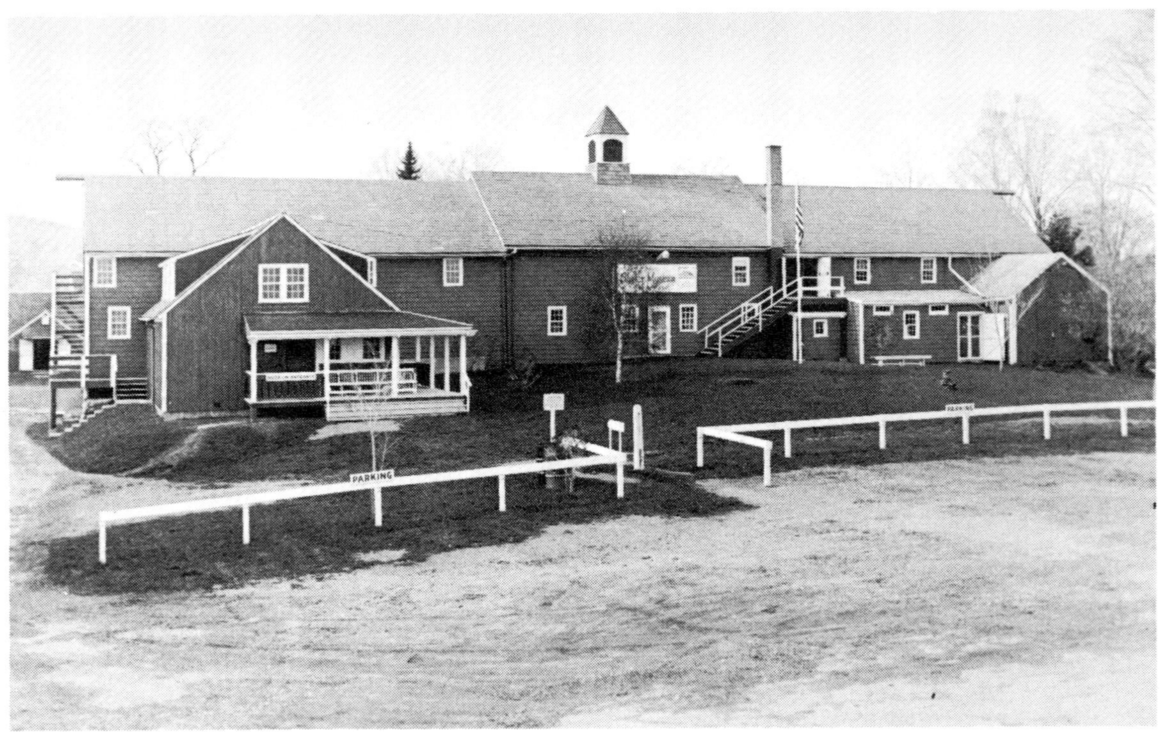

The Shaker Museum, Old Chatham, New York (Photo by Lees Studio, Chatham, N.Y.)

The Shaker Museum

Snuggled away in the Berkshire Hills of New York is the Shaker Museum. Therein is contained the largest collection of Shaker artifacts in the world. No where else does a person find a better accumulation of fine Shaker furniture and examples of the Shaker industries.

The museum is the result of the collecting of one man, Mr. John Williams. Williams was a collector of many things, including tools. As he searched the countryside about him, he constantly came upon Shaker tools as well as farm implements and furniture. It was not long until he started picking up the artifacts for himself and sought out their creators who were still living in nearby Mt. Lebanon, New York, and Hancock, Massachusetts. It was one of the Shaker sisters who suggested to Williams that he ought to open up his collection to the public as a museum. Thus, in 1950 the Shaker Museum was opened in some barns on the Williams property outside Old Chatham, New York.

Another director, Robert F.W. Meader, came to the museum in 1959. He retired from the position this past year, having brought guidance and stature to the museum for 17 years. During his tenure, the herb house was added, having previously been used as the dairy house in Enfield, Connecticut; the library was doubled in size, catalogued, and made readily available to scholars; the galleries were rearranged; carpenter shop and mill shop built; and a small barn converted into an orientation center.

Perhaps Meader's best known contribution to the museum and to the world of Shaker has been the publication of his book, *THE ILLUSTRATED GUIDE TO SHAKER FURNITURE.* It grew out of his work at the museum and brought added stature to the museum. But while this is the most popular guide book to Shaker furniture, it needs to be remembered that it, like any book on Shaker furniture, can not tell everything. There are always exceptions to the often repeated rules and insights. Meader's own advice is "Avoid certainties when talking of Shaker furniture."

From his perspective as the director of the Shaker museum for almost two decades, he suggests three items as being Shaker inventions. The first of these is the circular saw. Although this had been invented in Europe centuries before, says Meader, it was invented anew in the Western Hemisphere by the Shakers. The second distinctly Shaker contribution to the world was the oval fingered box. While there are oval boxes made by other people, the construction of these pantry boxes with Gothic style fingers to avoid splitting the lap is uniquely Shaker. The third invention of the Shakers was the tilter chair, a ball and socket arrangement that permits the chair to remain firm upon the floor even if the user should lean backwards.

Meader has retired from the museum but remains active, currently working on a book of Shaker small crafts and writing a history of his Church's parish in Kinderhook, New York. He is also in the antique business in Kinderhook. It would be one of his strong hopes for the future of the museum that it might be tied in more closely with the educational

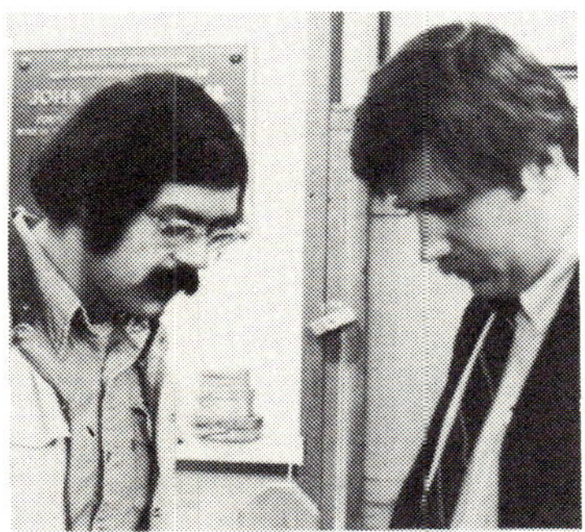

R. Peter Laskovski (right) new director of the Shaker Museum, discussing the construction of oval boxes with Jerry Grant, maker of oval boxes for the Guild of Shaker Crafts. (Photo by Cheri Dorschner)

system of the surrounding area. This hope is becoming a reality through the leadership of the new director, R. Peter Laskovski.

Mr. Laskovski is a graduate of State University of New York at Cortland with a B.A. in anthropology. He spent a year at the University of Jaime Bames in Mexico and studied at the University of Wisconsin before joining the Cooperstown Graduate Program. He has recently completed his degree requirements in ''American Folk Culture'' as has his wife Pati. For three years, he served as the archivist at the Archives of the New York State Folk Life. Mrs. Laskovski was the staff photographer for the New York State Historical Association.

One of the Laskovskis' earlier projects was a study in Costa Rica where they worked with the government in establishing an outdoor living history museum. After doing a folk culture survey of the country, they helped in the use of modern methods of study and in implementing the preservation of the materials of the folk culture. Mr. Laskovski's love for identifying and studying culture through the material objects of a culture combined with his strong interest in communistic groups make him a desirable director for the Shaker museum. He sees the museum as a laboratory for studying culture and making people aware of cultural variations. The Shaker musuem is to be his laboratory. He sees it as a tremendous resource for the study of Shaker culture because it is the best collection of Shaker aritfacts. In the past, the museum has collected. Now it is time to interpret.

It is the new director's desire to turn the ''visual storage'' into working models. He intends to redesign display areas so they will be more interpretive. An introductory exhibition will be constructed for people who are new to Shaker. Some of the galleries will be rearranged so that work can be done in them by people skilled in the crafts. Through actual doing, or by art

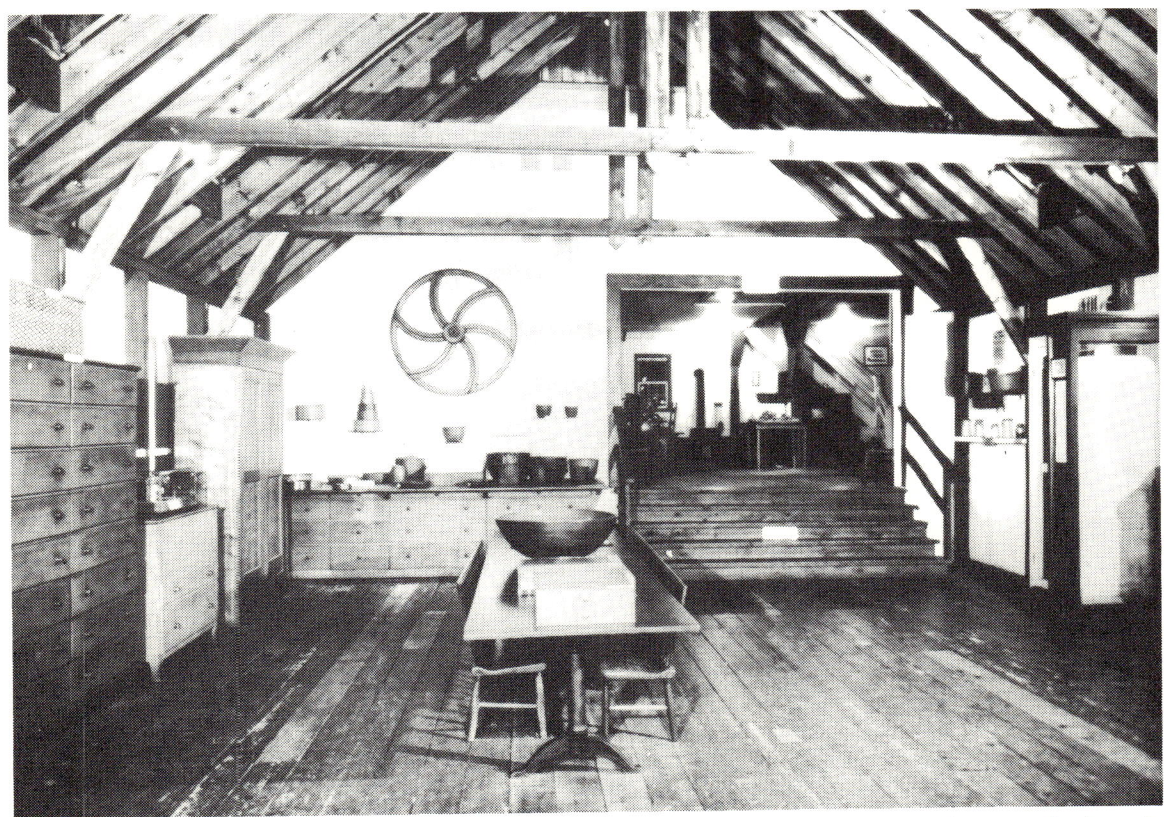

Entrance room at the Shaker Museum showing a trestle table from Hancock, Mass. In this room is the only known complete Fountain Stone from the Holy Hills used by the Shakers as special places of worship in the first half of the 19th century. (Photo by Lees Studio)

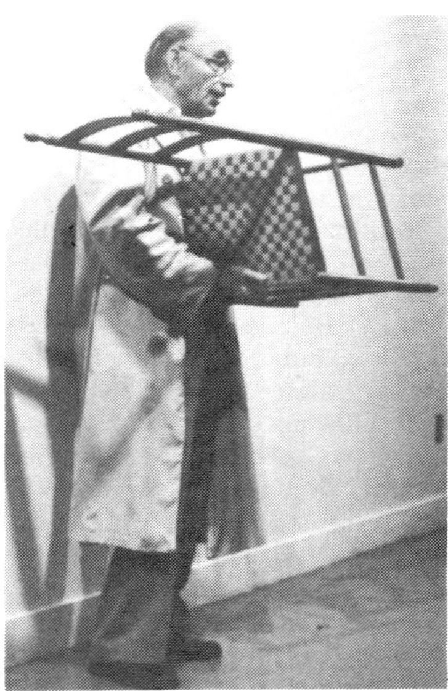

Robert F.W. Meader, Director Emeritus of the Shaker Museum, pointing out in a seminar the unique tilting devise invented by the Shakers and patented in 1852.

(Photograph by Cheri Dorschner)

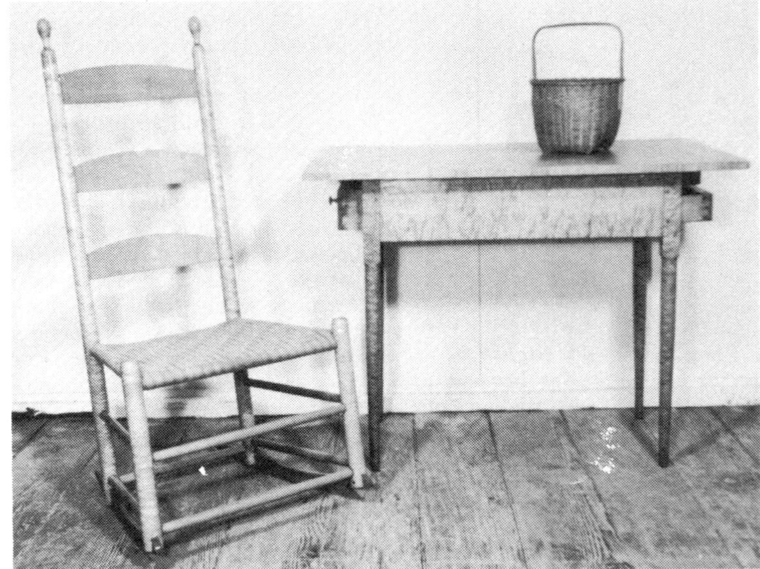

One of the display rooms at the Shaker Museum showing a Canterbury, New Hampshire, rocker and table. Both are of curly maple wood and the table has two drawers at one end and only one at the other.
(Photo by Lees Studio)

work, more interpretation of the artifacts will be given.

In addition to the work on the galleries. Laskovski is going to try to make joining as a friend of the museum more worthwhile. He has already started a newsletter. Within this newsletter will be news of upcoming events in the world of Shaker, technical advice will be offered, and some reproduction items will be offered. It is also hoped that the library might continue to be developed for research. As the future unfolds and Laskovski becomes settled in his new position, he has started to fulfill one hope of his predecessor. He has obtained a government grant for the securing of an educational coordinator to work with schools in the area.

The collection of the Shaker Museum at Old Chatham is excellent. It has established itself as a depository of Shaker artifacts. It will be most interesting to watch a new, young director seek to interpret these artifacts for himself and the world. Those of us in the world of Shaker are anxious to join with him in the interpretation of the Shakers in their relations with others of their time and like mindedness as well as their uniqueness of thought and industry as a religious sect.

To the past director, Robert Meader, goes a tip of the hat and a thanks for his contributions. To the new director, Peter Laskovski goes an extended hand and words of enthusiasm. If you have the opportunity, visit the Shaker Museum and meet its new leader.

— August, 1977

The Enfields

Two of the four towns in the United States that carry the name Enfield are bound together by their foundings and the presence of formerly thriving Shaker communities. While there is no connection in the establishment of the Shaker faith at Enfield, Connecticut, and Enfield, New Hampshire, I find there to be more in common between these two Shaker settlements than their names.

Both Enfields are among the earliest organized (Connecticut in 1790; New Hampshire in 1793). Of the communties begun before the start of the 19th century, only the much smaller ones of Tyringham and Shirley, Massachusetts, closed earlier than the Enfields. It might be suggested that one met its demise because of its closeness to the world while the other was too far from the main stream of commerce. In either case, they both are among the most overlooked and least known of the Shaker settlements.

The town of Enfield, Ct., was started in the 1680's by John Pease and his son. A century later this early family was also an integral part in the beginning of the Shakers in that area. Eight of the sixty-five signers of the 1812 Covenant were Peases. In all, there are eighteen by that name buried in the Shaker cemetary at Enfield, Ct. Today, the South Family property is privately owned while most of the remaining former Shaker ground is owned by the State of Connecticut and used as a prison. All that still stands on that land is the hired man's house, the meeting house (now the paint shop) and the oxen barn. The only other great barns still standing in any of the other Shaker settlements are the round stone one at the restored village of Hancock, Mass., and the 1854 one at Enfield, N.H.

Under the landgrants of the King of England, the town of Enfield, N.H., was founded twice: once under a grant from the governor of New Hampshire and again under a grant from the governor of Connecticut. Although some of the facilities in the town still carry the New Hampshire name of Relham, it was the settlers from Enfield, Ct., who came to the area and endured, endowing their new home with the same title as their former. Shakerism came to the area in 1782 through the conversions of James Jewett and Asa Pattee. It is interesting to note that while the town of Enfield, N.H., finds its roots in that of Enfield, Ct., the names appearing in the Shaker history of either community have no counterpart in that of the other. For example, there were no Shakers by the name of Pease in New Hampshire, nor any named Jewett in Connecticut.

Enfield, New Hampshire, is best known for its bridge that spanned Mascoma Lake to gain access to the railroad and its great stone dwelling house. The granite structure was erected in 1837 and had more than 800 drawers built into it. A team from the U.S. Department of Interior recently did a study on the building and was fascinated to discover that the width of the massive six story building varied by less than an inch from end to end of its one hundred feet length. Today, the dwelling house and the surrounding grounds are the focal point of

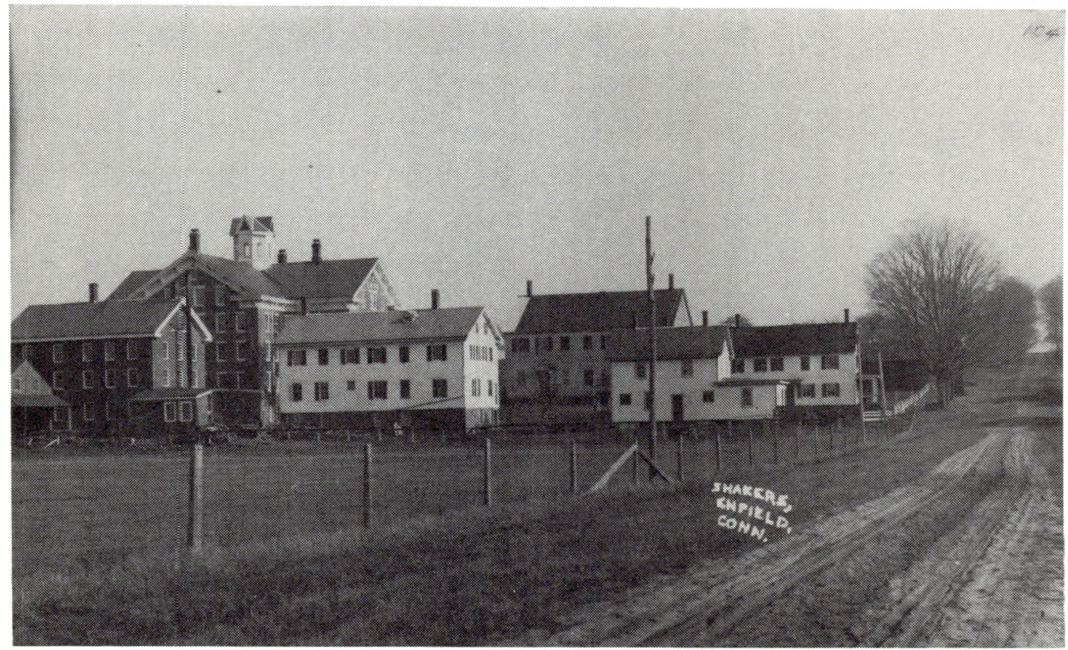

This postcard view of the Enfield, Ct., Shaker community was taken in 1914. Only the meeting house at the extreme left is still standing.

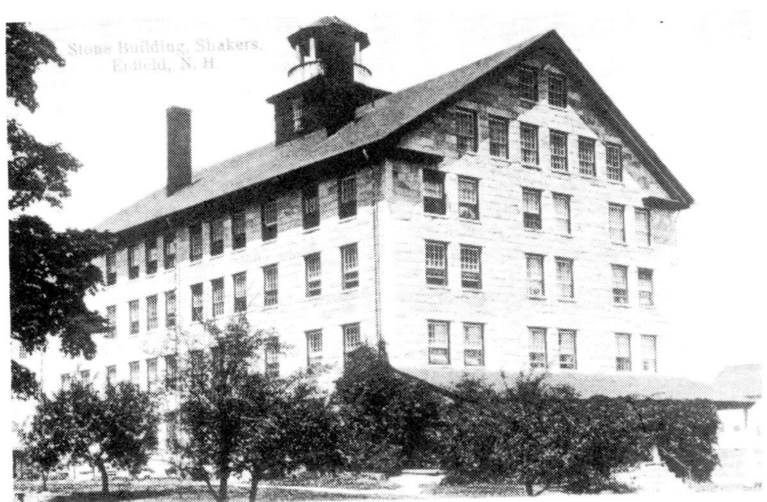

The granite dwelling house at Enfield, N.H., is one hundred feet in length, fifty-eight feet wide and has more than two hundred windows of twenty panes each.

a retreat center owned by the LaSalette order of the Roman Catholic Church.

The two Enfields shared an interest in at least two dominant industries. Both raised and widely distributed seeds. The Connecticut business had depended largely upon its routes in the South and met a great decline in business with the Civil War. As late as 1874, the New Hampshire community was doing a yearly business of $30,000 in seeds. The seed boxes from that community are unique because of the metal spring latches that keep them closed. Coopering was the other industry that was prominent in each of the Enfields. Of all the reputedly Shaker buckets that I have seen, any marked ones have had the name "Enfield." In both communities, the industry was centered in the North Family and, thus, many inscriptions read "N.F." Those from Connecticut will often also carry the mark "CT." By far the most buckets come from New Hampshire where it has been said that 95% of the sap buckets found in that state were made by the Enfield Shakers under the guidance of Caleb Dyer.

Another common bond between the two Enfields seems to be their variance from the norm in furniture styles. The New Hampshire community strayed towards a more fine, light style. Table legs tended to be more delicate, some even terminating in a turned foot no larger than the end of a person's little finger. A small collar often separates the square stile and the beginning of the turning. The flame finials on the top of chair posts are always more slender and fine than that on chairs from any other community. The chairs are also the lightest in weight, usually weighing only five pounds.

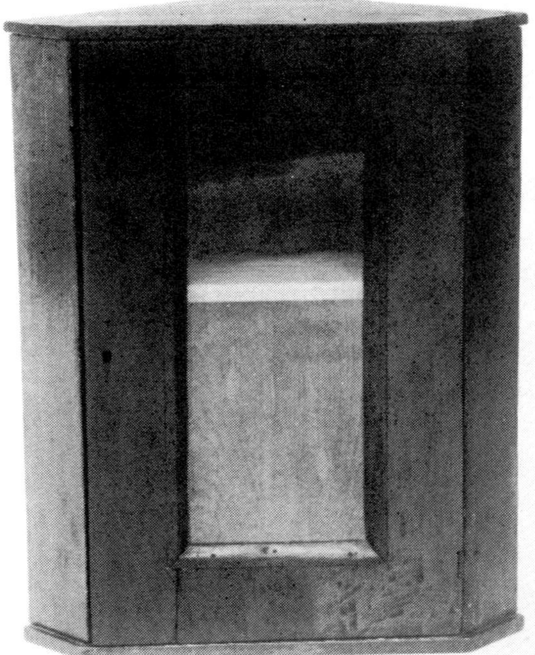

Probably unique among Shaker furniture, this small hanging cupboard is from Enfield, Ct. Photograph courtesy of Ed Clerk.

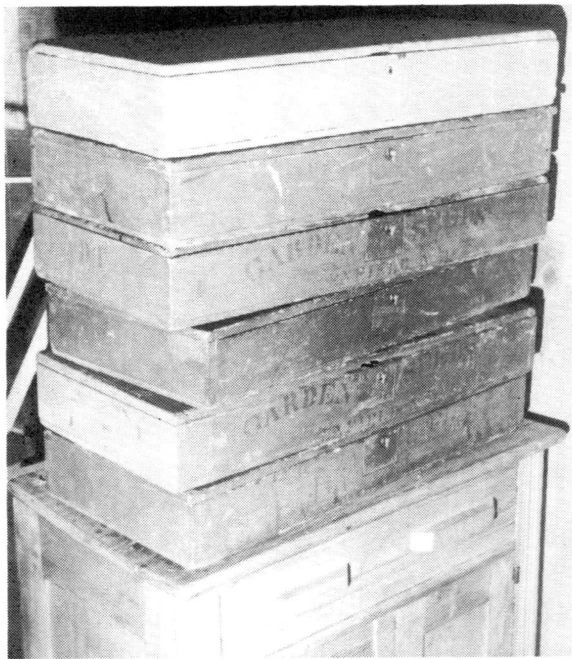

Stenciled with the Enfield, N.H., name, these seed boxes have wider hand-dovetailed corners than their Mt. Lebanon, N.Y., counterparts and make use of a metal catch.

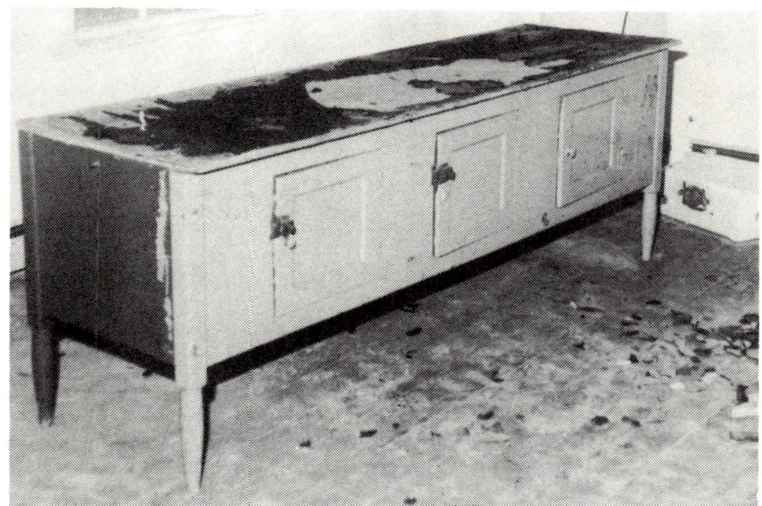

Discovered in the attic of one of the Enfield, N.H., buildings, this wash stand is very much like one now at The Golden Lamb Inn in Lebanon, Ohio. It is from the same community. Both pieces have the small ring collar that separates the square stile of the leg from its turning.

Furniture from Enfield, Ct., strays from the usual Shaker form with more elaborate turnings and added touches of fanciness. The hanging corner cupboard apparently is a phenomenon among the Shakers only at this community. Many chests, sewing desks, and boxes were decorated with ivory escutcheons, often in the shape of a heart. Thomas Fisher, the creator of octagon oak tables, carved oak chairs and other un-Shakerlike pieces of furniture, was a member and trustee of the Connecticut Enfield. Probably no other Shaker community, except perhaps Alfred, Maine, produced more out-of-the-ordinary styles.

While the two Enfields are often overlooked in studies and in travels, they are an early and important part of the Shaker heritage. This is especially true of their artifacts, which represent much of the unique, decorative, and collectible of Shaker. In both cases, the furnishings passed into private hands as the Shakers were preparing to close the communities and move to others. One gentleman relates how his father purchased beds from the Shakers to be used in their summer cottage on Mascoma Lake. That was more than 50 years ago and the beds have long since been disposed of in favor of army surplus metal cots. In the sixty years since the closing of the Enfields, many Shaker items have been destroyed; those remaining are cherished by old neighbors who harbor fond memories of their former friends.

— October, 1978

NOTE: The photograph of the small hanging corner cupboard is used by permission of United Cerebral Palsy Association of Greater Hartford, CT. It first appeared in the catalog for a 1975 exhibit. The catalog, a necessity to any Shaker library, is still available from that sponsoring organization.

Compare the wash stand on this page with the one on page 11.

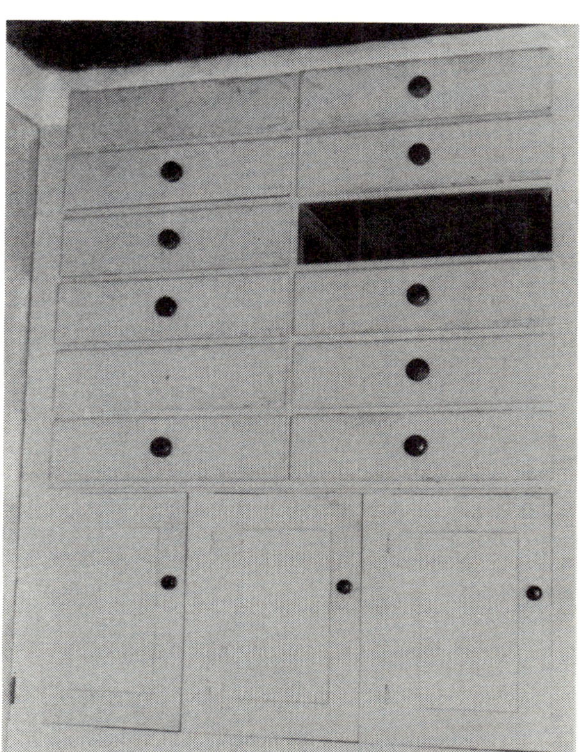

The interior of the New Hampshire dwelling house contains more than 800 drawers. Between every pair of sleeping quarters is a small room that contains a wall furnished such as this.

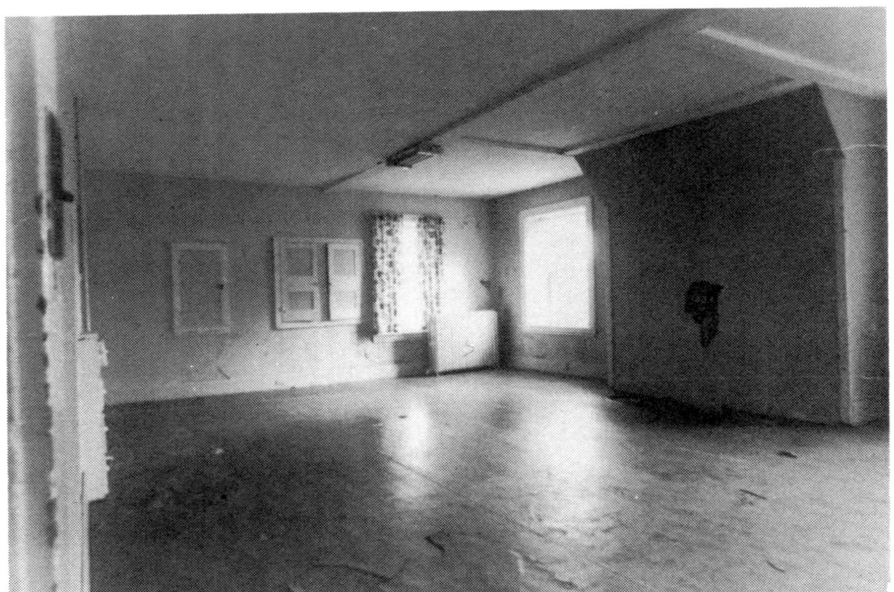

The printing press of Union Village leader Richard McNemar was probably set up in this large room.

A Thing of the Past

Two events in the last couple of months point out how values increase because of diminishing supply. In the town of Enfield, Connecticut, the state found it necessary to condemn and raze a Shaker structure for the benefit of a wider highway. In Lebanon, Ohio, a recent article in the local newspaper told of the intended tearing down of Rose Cottage, the oldest brick Shaker building West of New York.

The house in Connecticut had been moved from the Shaker land many years ago and had gained a number of additions during the course of its history. But beneath all its alterations was the original four room structure, complete with original hardware and a matching pair of built-in cupboards. In spite of the efforts of the owner to sell the building separate from the land, time and other complications did not co-operate and another Shaker house was demolished. (It is my understanding that the cupboards, at least, were salvaged.) On the former Shaker grounds in that state, nine buildings have met their demise over the last eighteen years. Of these, only an ell from the North Family Sisters House was saved by giving it to the Shaker Museum at Old Chatham, New York, where it now serves as the Herb House. The authorities of the Connecticut Correctional Institution, current owners of the land, tried to give the buildings to historical societies and/or museums. Occasionally, some of the fixtures and hardware were claimed but no one was found who wanted an entire building.

Rose Cottage and its predecessors of Union Village follow a similar pattern. At one time, more than one hundred buildings occupied their places on the 4,400 acres of Shaker ground. Today, there are only four. Many attempts were made to preserve the former Meeting House and Bethany Hall but with little success. Rose Cottage itself was slated for demolition in 1968 but was spared when the Ohio State Historical Society paid for the cost of outside painting. A committee was formed in 1972 which met with little success. Owned by the Otterbein Home, a United Methodist Church home for the elderly, the old Elders Shop and post office has been unusable for any meaningful purpose to the home except storage since 1966 when the local pastor moved from it. What does a retirement home do

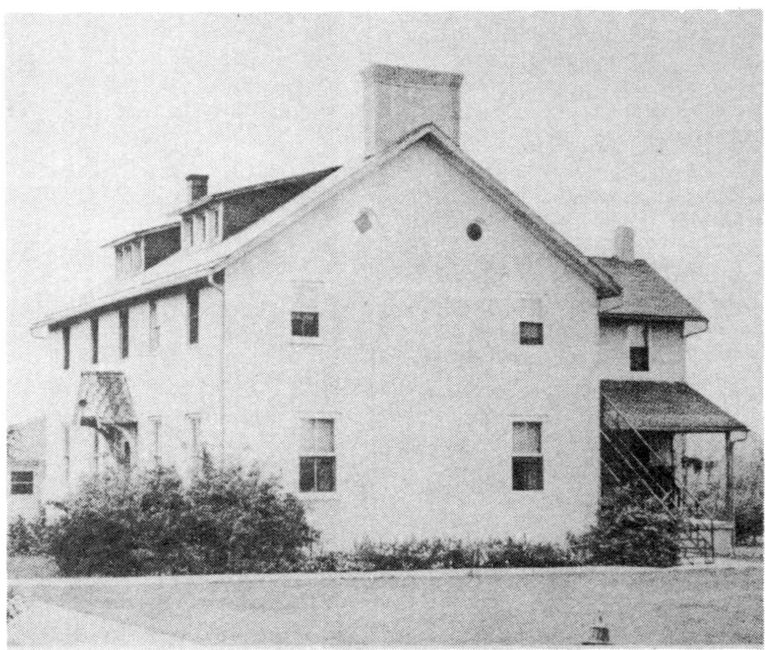

Rose Cottage, Union Village, Ohio. The back section is the half of another house that was moved from the farm and added by the Shakers.

with a deteriorating 1811 brick dwelling? The administration, and others, have vigorously sought some way to make the preservation of this historical structure a justifiable expenditure of monies that are given for the care of the elderly residents. It was even rented to me for a nominal fee and a coat of paint in an attempt to prolong its longevity.

For a brief six months period in 1977, I was able to closely examine, and appreciate anew, the craftsmanship of the United States' most successful communal group. Knowing the probable doom of the Elders Shop, I limited my efforts to cleaning and painting. With a fresh coat of proper colors, some pegboard replaced, and furnished with a few authentic pieces of Shaker furniture, the old structure reflected the style of life and work of a more glorious time. Whether it was its location on the edge of a retirement community, its large spacious twelve rooms, its simple architecture, or the spirits of a bygone people, Rose Cottage was the most serene dwelling in which I have ever lived. It is a part of my personal life and history as well as that of the Shakers in Ohio.

Unfortunately, Rose Cottage will be torn down this summer. The Otterbein Home does intend to salvage all materials worth preserving...window frames, stair rails, doors, etc. Their efforts to preserve the structure intact have proven fruitless. It was even offered as a gift to the Ohio Historical Society but this offer was rejected. Part of the rationale given for rejection was "that first consideration for state preservation of Shaker structures in Ohio shall be given to those of the Whitewater settlement...which are the least altered and the most spectacular in quantity and quality in private hands in the nation." Ironically, Whitewater property, including the Meeting House, was available to the Society two years later but saw no action. (see "The Shaker Way," December, 1976). The property was on the real estate market for three years before being purchased by people who had little

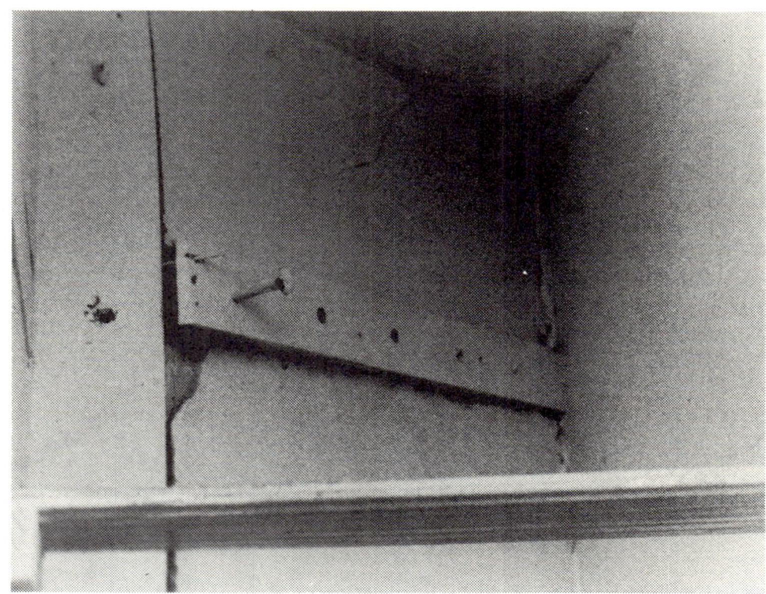

All of the original pegboard remains on the second floor although there are only three pegs in it.

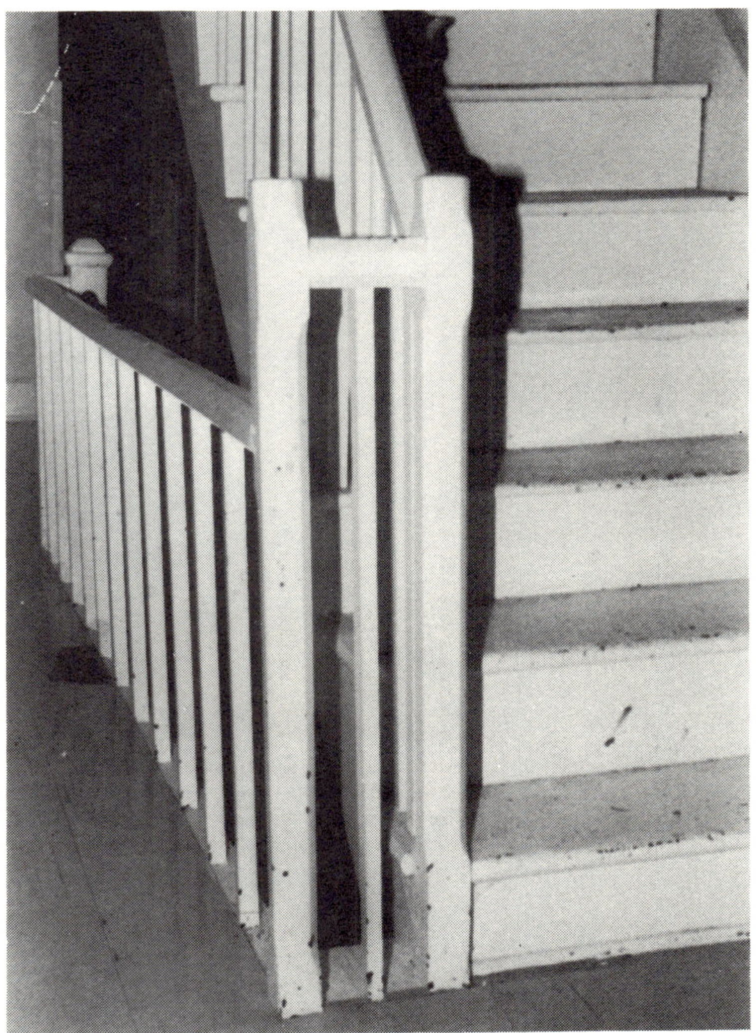

Probably the finest remains of Shaker craftsmanship in the structure are champhered stairposts and rails.

interest in Shaker. In the foreseeable future, ''I think Marble Hall will possibly face the same thing, (demolition).'' states Dr. Charles Peckham of the Otterbein Home. The end of this unique expression of Shaker architectural tastes seen in the remodeled 1810 Trustee's Office would mean that the only remnants of one of the two largest Shaker settlements are brick shells of a milk shed and a dwelling house. Union Village, like North Union and Watervliet, will only be names in the history of the Shakers in Ohio.

It has been sixty-seven years since the Shakers closed their communities in Ohio. While there are two communities still in existence in Maine and New Hampshire, the announced destruction of Rose Cottage reminds Shaker enthusiasts of the growning scarcity and increased value of the artifacts of the once thriving sect. The passing of another Shaker landmark enhances the value of what remains, for Shaker becomes more and more ''a thing of the past.''

— February, 1979

NOTE: *The Whitewater property was recently sold and now appears to be in the hands of people who intend to preserve and restore it. Rose Cottage is being given (Fall, 1979) to the Warren County Historical Society who will remove all useable pieces for inclusion in a new addition to its musuem in Lebanon.*

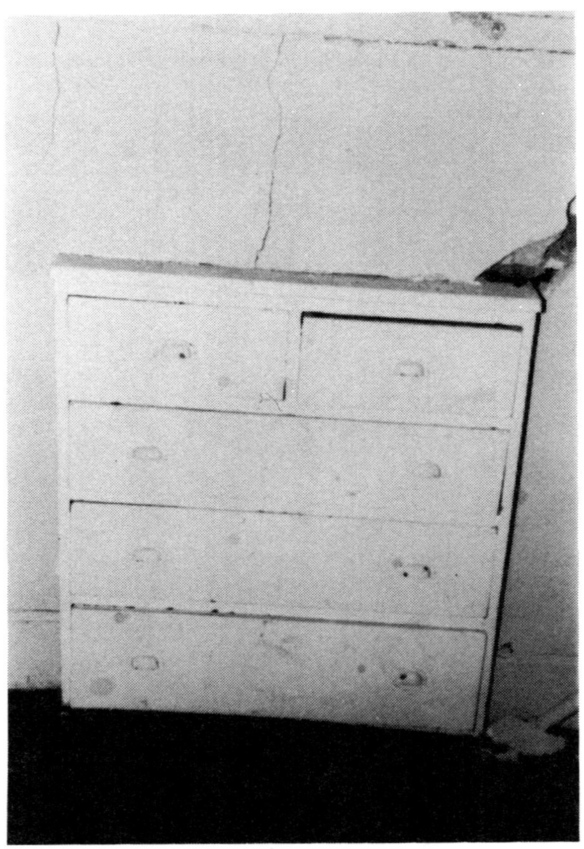

Although not originally a built-in, this chest of drawers is Shaker and was recessed into the wall. The crack on the upper right illustrates the problems that have come with 168 years of settling foundations.

The Products of Shaker Hands

Largely because of the nature of the publication in which these articles first appeared, the majority of them are concerned with the furniture and crafts of the Shakers. Sometimes attention was given to the influence of the Shaker faith upon their products for an understanding of some of the beliefs can be a great help in determining whether or not an item is Shaker made. At other times, the subject was the design characteristics of one community and/or a particular furniture form. Many of the subjects such as pottery, corner cupboards, and Ohio furniture have not previously been explored in writings about the Shakers.

As *The Shaker Way* grew, and continues to grow, the author has arrived at four generalizations relative to the study of the products of Shaker hands. The first comes from a familiarity and comparison with other forms of early American furniture: while there are distinguishing styles, there is no method of furniture construction that is unique to the Shakers. Mortised and pinned door frames, spline joints, H-hinges, etc., were all used by craftsmen contemporary with the Shakers. The second generalization is that there were excellent Shaker craftsmen...and some bad ones...as there were with ''the world's'' craftsmen. The simple fact that a piece is well made does not make it Shaker. Nor does poor workmanship exclude it from having been made by a Shaker. The third generalization is that little has been done in the systematic study of Shaker made products. With the exception of the book by Edward Andrews on the industries of the New York communities, little research and reading of the old manuscripts has been pursued in the determination of the styles and production of Shaker furniture. Finally, there is the generalization that exceptions can usually be found to any conclusion. Because of the long history of the faith, the many artisans, and the concept of items being made for a particular place and purpose, many pieces produced were individual creations and do not always fit any specific patterns or rules.

Philosophy of Work

Time and again, people are impressed with the simple beauty that came from the hands of the Shaker craftsmen. Behind the combination of skill and knowledge that produced these much sought after reflections of a former time and people, there is a philosophy of work that served as the inspiration. Edward Deming Andrews' book title *Religion In Wood* is a fitting title as well as commentary about the Shaker craftsman. The Shaker was motivated by a philosophy of his industriousness that is non-existant today (except perhaps in some communal groups). Thomas Merton in his introduction to that book raises the question of whether the excellance of the Shaker craftsman is forever lost in our technological age since we can not recapture the spiritual motivation.

While the foundation for this philosophy of work has deeper roots in the religious principals of the Society, there are four concepts that are important in understanding the Shaker craftsmen. The first of these is perfection - in effort as well as in design. The Shakers were believers first and craftsmen second. This meant that their work was an outgrowth of their dedication to a higher calling. Mother Ann Lee admonished her followers to "Put your hands to work, and your hearts to God." This moved the Shaker craftsman to do his work well since it was not just for himself. He was called to give of his best for God and the Shaker Community. Long after he was gone, his work would be needed. "Do your work as though you had a thousand years to live, and as if you were to die tomorrow," said Mother Ann.

The other aspects of perfection was one of "form follows function." Unless something had a purpose, it was undesirable. Decorations and superfluities were forbidden unless they were functional. Some of their sayings were as follows: "Beauty rests on utility;" "There is great beauty in harmony;" "All beauty that has not a foundation in use, soon grows distasteful, and needs continual replacement with something new;" "That which has in itself the highest use, possesses the greatest beauty." Any piece of furniture and craft must first be useful. It needed to be perfect in the sense of being suited for the

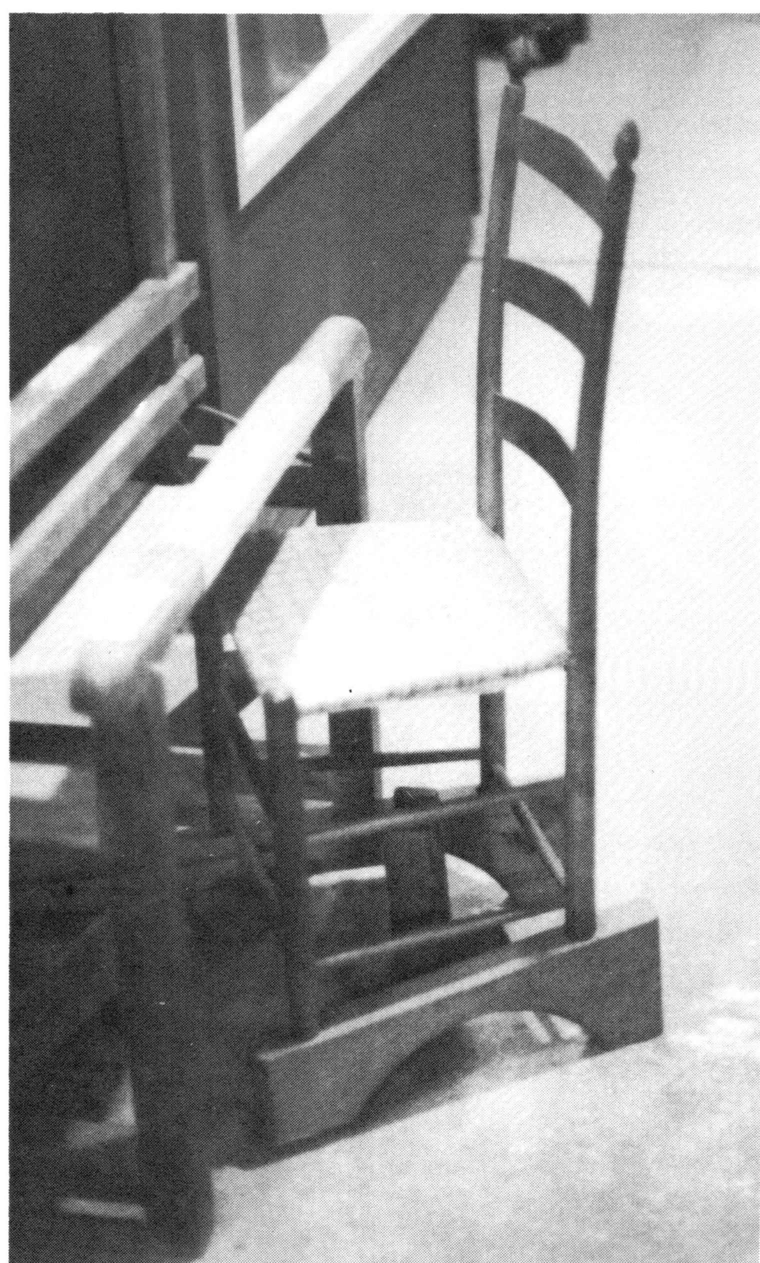

Weaver's Chair - This chair reflects two of the Shaker concepts of work. The straight leg and bent back identifies this chair as being after 1860 when a more comfortable style had evolved. The added base to give an ordinary chair necessary height to be used with a loom is an example of the Shaker inventiveness.
- Shaker Museum, Old Chatham, New York

purpose to which it was designed. Such an idea of perfection in form was not rigid though. There was the recognition that a more perfect way might yet be obtainable.

This evolving perfection leads to the second concept of work - inventiveness. There was constant striving to make an object or item "more perfect." Forms were evolving so as to better meet their intended purposes. An example of this can be seen in the design of chairs where the early ones had back posts and legs that were vertically straight. The next step had the back and legs canted backwards for greater comfort. Finally, the chairs were made with straight legs and the back posts bent backwards. This idea of evolving perfection accounts for part of the great diversity in Shaker furniture with tables, sewing desks, cupboards, etc. varying from piece to piece. Among major pieces of Shaker furniture, virtually no two pieces will be exactly alike. Theoretically, a better form or some improvement could be found since the last similar piece had been made. Joseph Meacham, the Shaker organizer, said: "We have a right to improve the inventions of man, so far as is useful and necessary, but not to vain glory, or anything superfluous." This concept led to many inventions as well as to improvements in design. Some of these inventions were a splint-cutting machine, lathe with screw spindle for wood turning, turbine water wheel, basket-weaving machine, revolving oven, and the common clothes pin.

A third concept contributing to the Shaker philosophy of work is diversity. By this is not meant the diversity in styles attributable to evolving designs but the diversity of labor. It is one of the geniuses of the Shaker structure that they provided variety in doing everyday chores and, thus, avoided boredom. Tasks in the kitchens and fields were rotated. Different seasons and events brought different jobs. When Mt. Lebanon

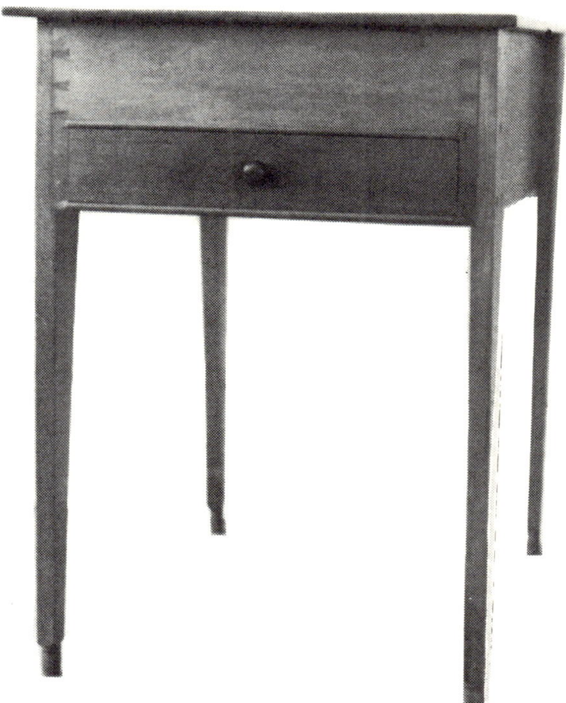

Table - A very interesting table that shows the best of Shaker craftsmanship along with some inventiveness. Note the beautiful construction of the case and the fine lip above and below the drawer.

Darrow School, Mt. Lebanon, N.Y.

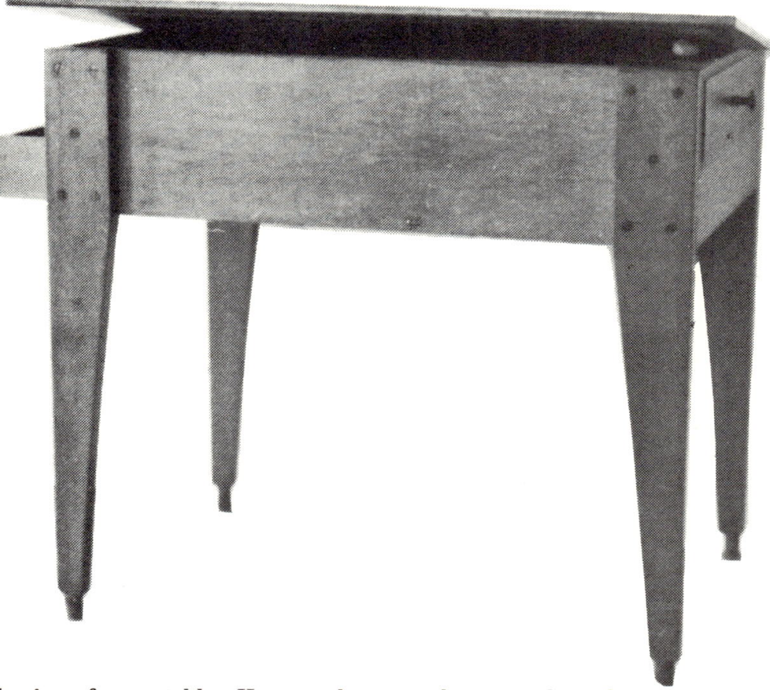

Side view of same table - Here can be seen where, at a later date and for no explainable reason, someone altered the top so it could be lifted. Note the "pencil post" end on the legs. These very plain legs are rather simply screwed onto the outside of the beautiful case! Why? Perhaps this can only be explained by the diversity and/or inventiveness of the Shaker craftsman.

experienced its great fire of 1875, everyone worked together in construction on new buildings. When apples ripened, the labor of the day was picking and canning apples. It is interesting to read the tremendous variety of labors. Among the minor chores, Richard McNemar was also a preacher, bookbinder, chairmaker, weaver and printer. Henry Blinn of Canterbury. New Hampshire, had more than a dozen different occupations from beekeeping to dentistry. And no matter what the position in the Society, a person was expected to work. "No one who is able to labor can be permitted to live idly upon the labors of others. All, including ministers, elders and deacons, are required to be employed in some manual occupation, according to their several abilities, when not engaged in other necessary duties."

It can be easily seen that such rotation or diversity in work would lead to diversity in craftsmanship and its quality. Two men making chairs in successive weeks might make them slightly different. Or, the same man might give two chairs different characteristics and quality if he had allowed an extensive period of time to lapse while he was doing other jobs such as filling teeth.

The last concept of work important to understanding Shaker craftsmanship is the common bond and good of the community. The Society took precedence over the individual. This ideal ties in with the previous comments on perfection, working for a greater good than the individual self. Extra care was called for in the manufacture of items since they would be used by many persons in the community and would serve as a spiritual witness to those outside. Meacham stated that "We are not called to labor to expell, or be like the world: but to excell them in order, union and peace, and in good works."

This concept of "for the common good" also adds to the fascination of collecting Shaker. The individual works for the community and not for himself. Therefore, he does not take personal credit for his labors. In fact, putting names on furniture was forbidden by the Millenial Law. Pieces of Shaker furniture that bear the maker's name are very rare.

The Shaker craftsman achieved such a high degree of excellence because of his philosophy of work which involves perfection, inventiveness, diversity and a sense of community.

— October, 1976

Progressive

People often make the mistake of confusing the Shakers with groups such as the Pennsylvania Dutch, Amish or Mennonites. There are, though, many differences between the Shakers and such groups in their theology, family relations, life styles, and methods of industry. Generally speaking, the major difference can be expressed in the idea that the "plain people" are conservative while the Shakers are progressive. In philsosphical views, methods of living, and use of better manufacturing techniques, the Shakers are to be counted among the most progressive of peoples. Their concepts of equality of the sexes preceeded the modern women's movement by two centuries. Some of their leaders were very vocal spokesmen for the abolition of slavery. And time and again, they developed new machines to take over what had previously been done by human hands.

Many of our common everyday articles are attributed to the Shaker spirit of inventiveness. The common clothes pin is thought to have originated at North Union, the Shaker community located in the city now called Shaker Heights, Ohio. The metal ink pen is another formerly common article credited to the Shakers. The flat broom of today is also a product of Shaker ingenuity attributed to Brother Theodore Bates of Watervliet, N.Y. Before 1800 the Shakers raised broom corn, and they were engaged in the manufacturing of brooms and brushes at that early date. To aid in this enterprise, the Shaker brothers invented a machine for sizing and cutting the broom corn and a lathe with an

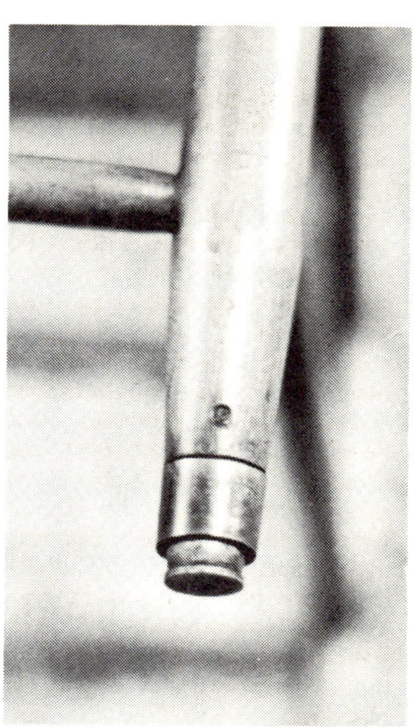

This end of a chair's back leg shows the unique Shaker "tilter." This one is made of brass and bears the stamp "patented 1852." Others were made with pewter but most were wood held in by leather thongs.

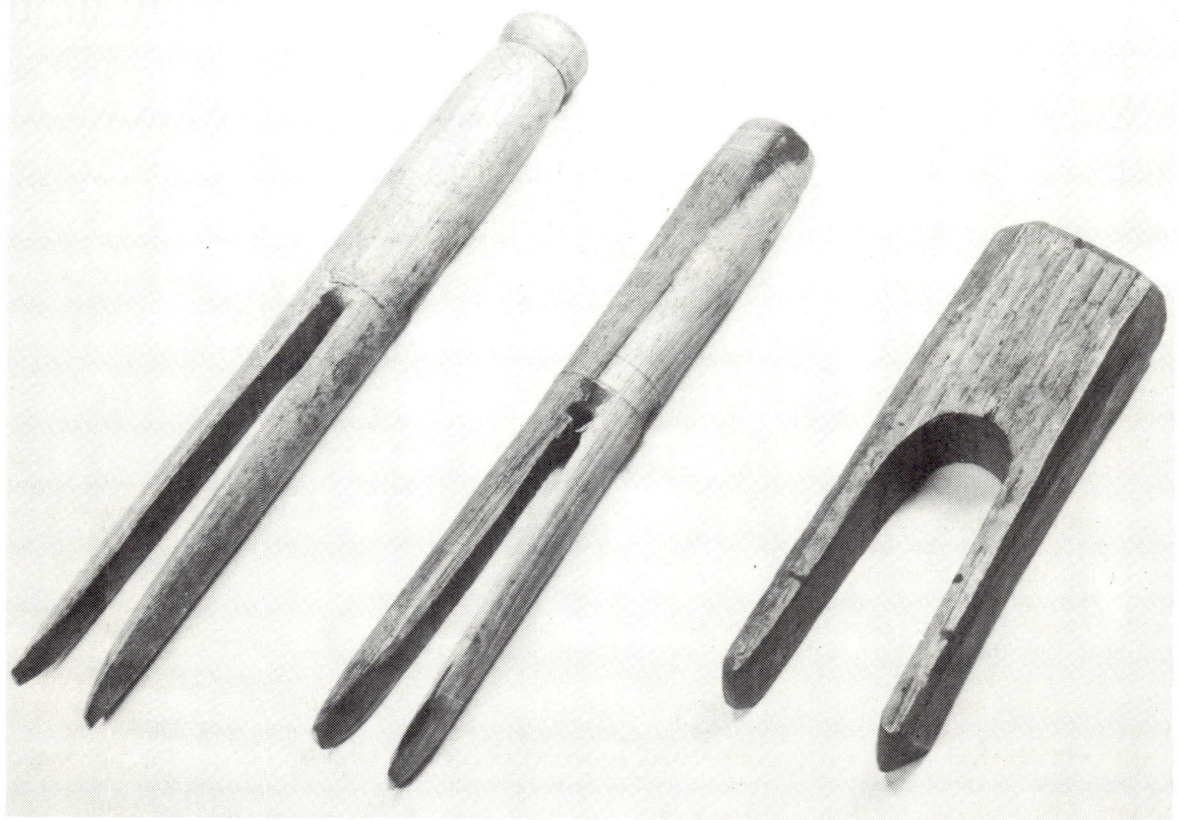

The Shakers of North Union (Shaker Heights), Ohio, are given credit for the invention of the common clothes pin. Photograph by the Lees Studio, Courtesy of The Shaker Museum, Old Chatham, N.Y.

automatic feeder for turning the handles. Such improvement and efficiency were natural outgrowths of the Shaker philosophy of progress expressed by Father Joseph Meacham in 1795: ''We have a right to improve the inventions of man, so far as is useful and necessary.''

Perhaps the most useful of those inventions attributed to the Shakers is the circular saw. Robert Meader, author of *The Illustrated Guide of Shaker Furniture,* contends that the circular saw was in use among carpenters in England prior to the Shaker's discovery but had passed from useage. He credits the Shakers with rediscovering it. It is said that Sister Sarah Babbit of Harvard, Massachusetts, gave attention to the lost motion of some of the brothers in sawing as well as to the constant movement of her spinning wheel. By experimenting with a notched disk of tin fastened to her wheel, she was able to give to the world a better way of cutting wood.

The list of Shaker improvements in the mechanical world includes a threshing machine (1815), a revolving harrows developed at North Union, a screw propeller, fertilizing machines, a machine for making planks, and another for cutting tongue and grove boards. Today, Shaker baskets are very desirable among antique collectors. Would it harm their value if people were more aware of the inventions of Brothers Daniel Boler and Daniel B. Crossman of Mt. Lebanon, New York, — a machine for splint making and basket weaving?

In the area of architecture, the Shakers again expressed their efficiency and spirit of progress. They constructed their buildings with the interior walls having windows so that the outside light could illuminate the halls and center rooms. They developed and hand cast the sash balance that was the prototype for those still being used in windows. Their barns were the epitome of efficiency with different levels for hay, the cattle, and the removal of manure. The feeding (even hot meals prepared for the animals at North Union) and the hauling of

---

SHAKER'S
WINDOW SASH LOCK.

A new device for securing ventilation.

SIMPLE AND EASILY MANIPULATED, ADJUSTABLE TO ALL WINDOW SASH, SAFELY HOLDING EITHER AT ANY POINT, WITHOUT MARRING PAINT OR VARNISH.

It consists of a clamp bar let loosely into the left side of the window frame, having two small lever eccentrics attached thereto by a screw or rivet, at the center where the sash comes together. The strip which holds the sash in place is let on the eccentrics, the lever or points only being visible. If a parting strip is used it should be cut off at the bar, so that the top may be used at pleasure. 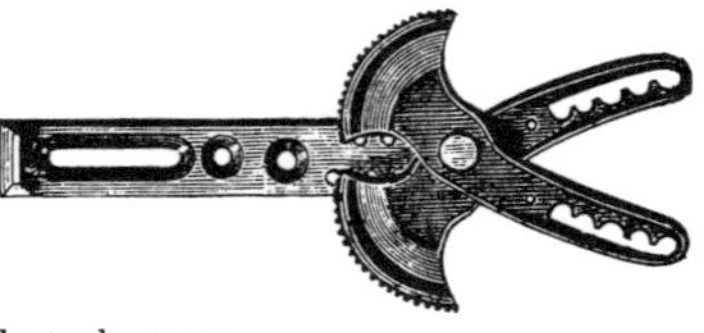

By pressing on the points the position of the eccentrics are changed so as to press against the lower sash, causing the catch on the end of the bar to pull against the top sash, thus locking them so tight that it is impossible to move either without opening the points.

Also, the eccentrics, if desired, may be put on the left face of each sash frame, in which case they will perfectly lock and tighten the sash and destroy all shaking and rattling by winds or otherwise. In this case the eccentrics are visible. The strip must be sawed off from the lower eccentric upwards, the thickness of the eccentrics, so that it will work against the under frame. When the sash is too loose to be tightened by the eccentric, tack two bits or a strip on the right-hand edge.

In short, it is the simplest, safest and best sash lock in existence, and needs only to be seen to be appreciated. Sample sent by mail for twenty-five cents.

South Union, Logan Co., Ky.   S. J. RUSSELL.

---

manure involved using a cart and rail system. The barn at Shirley, Massachusetts, had a stream running through it for the watering of the cattle. Perhaps one of the most influential areas of Shaker creativity is horticulture. The Shakers were in the business of selling seeds as early as 1794 and are credited for being the first people to raise crops strictly for seed purposes and to package seeds for sale. From this industry came further inventions for the printing and filling of seed and herb packets. The herb industry itself was the first to mass produce herbs in this country.

The Shakers recycled paper into jewelry boxes and made

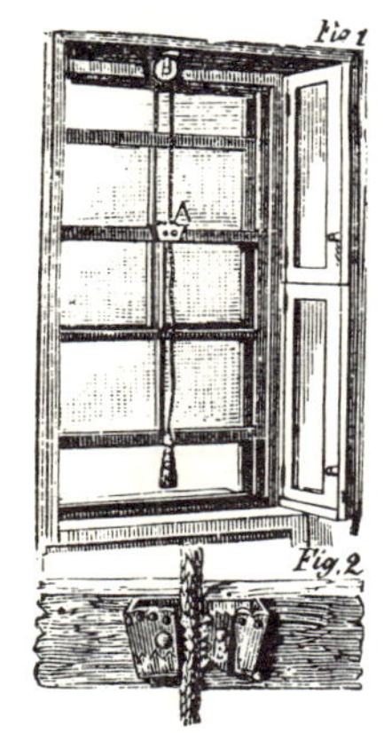

From the Scientific American

Our illustration represents a very simple and ingenious device, which does away with the usual cords and pulleys on windows, making one sash balance the other.

It is cheap and readily applied and will afford all the means of ventilation that side-weights do.

Samples by mail for $1.25—Agents wanted *Address.* S. J. Russell, Patentee.

South Union, Ky.

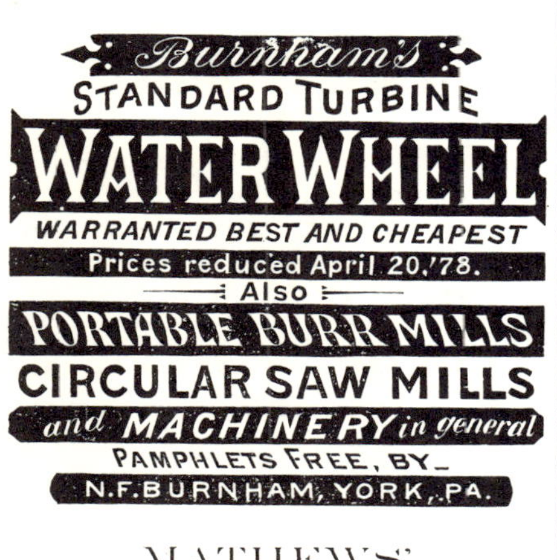

MATHEWS'
CARRIAGE MART
CONCORD, N. H.

Manufacturer of and Dealer in fine Carriages and Sleighs, second hand Carriages and Sleighs constantly on hand. "Best Bargains in the City.

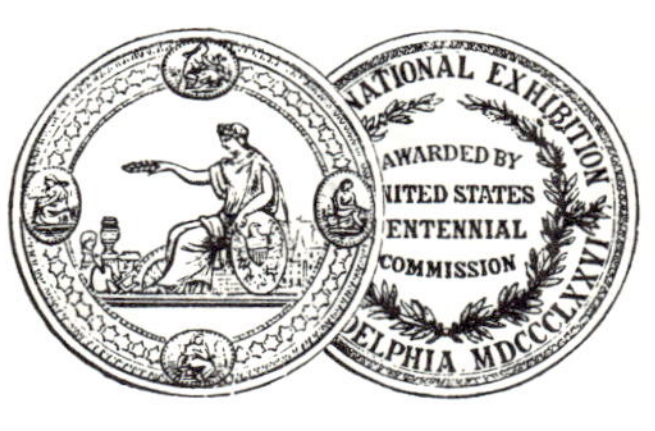

IMPROVED SHAKER WASHING MACHINE, BUILT AT SHAKER VILLAGE, N. H.

For Laundries, Hotels, Asylums and other large Institutions. Preference given in Report of Judges at the Centennial Exhibition. Medal and Diploma Awarded. N. A. Briggs Shaker Village, N. H.

Patented July 23, 1877.

Washburn & Moen Man'f'g Co.
WORCESTER, MASS.
Sole Manufacturers East of Chicago, of

PATENT STEEL BARB FENCING,

A STEEL Thorn Hedge. No other Fencing so cheap or put up so quickly. Never rusts, stains, decays, shrinks, nor warps. Unaffected by fire, wind, or flood. A complete barrier to the most unruly stock. Impassable by man or beast. TWO THOUSAND TONS SOLD AND PUT UP DURING THE LAST YEAR. For sale at the leading hardware stores, with Stretchers and Staples. Send for illustrated Pamphlet

Also

Manufacturers of all kinds of IRON AND STEEL WIRE.

A Speciality made of TINNED BROOM WIRE.

some of the first wrinkle-proof material with the use of a heated press at Sabbathday Lake, Maine. They also gave to Gail Borden the idea of utilizing the vacuum pan in the extraction of herbal products. This led to Borden's invention of evaporated milk.

The list of their expressions of progress goes on and on and they were happy to share their genius with the world. While they were generous in allowing anyone else to use the products of their inventiveness, they were also practical enough to realize the necessity of patenting some devices for the protection of their own interests. Three particular items that were patented are noteworthy. The **first was the tilter on the rear legs** of chairs, patented in 1852. This idea appears today on almost all tubular steel furniture. A second patented invention of the Shakers was a washing machine patented **by Brother David Parker in 1858.** This was sold to many hotels from Boston to Chicago. It is said that 14 women lost their jobs when one was put into use at the Girard House in Philadelphia in 1857. The third noteworthy patented Shaker product was a revolving oven designed in 1876 by Eldress Emeline Hart of Enfield, Connecticut, to bake 60 pies at a time.

The improved Shaker Washing Machine that won a medal at the 1876 Philadelphia Centennial Exhibition is advertised in the back of the July 1878, *Manifesto,* a monthly publication of the Shakers.

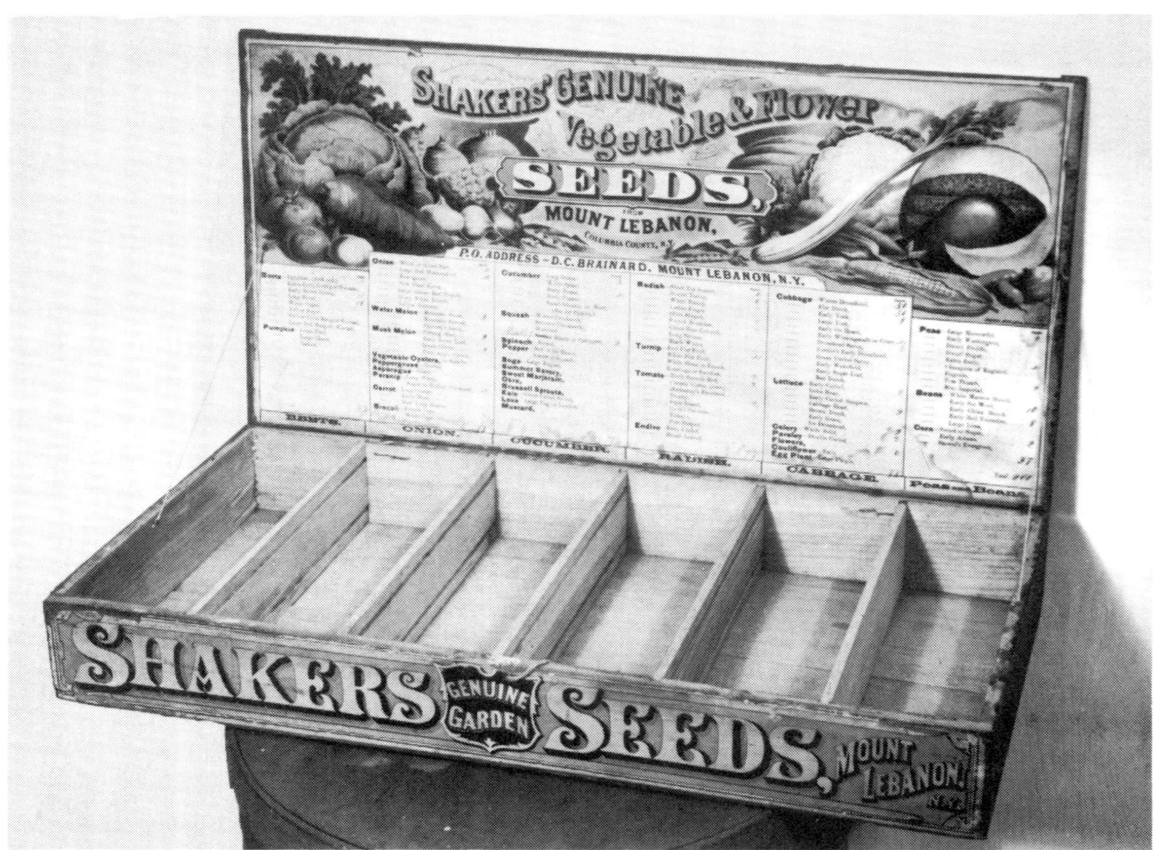

The Shakers are considered the first people to offer seeds for sale in paper packets. Prior to that method seeds were sold in bulk with the storekeeper weighing out the amount desired. Boxes such as this were left in stores in the Spring. When they were picked up in the Fall, the money was collected less a commission. It has been suggested that selling on consignment was another Shaker innovation. In 1819, the Shakers leaders agreed to "not, hereafter, put up, or sell, any seeds to the world which are not raised among believers (excepting melon seeds)." Photograph by The Lees Studio, Courtesy of The Shaker Museum, Old Chatham, N.Y.

It can be seen from these few examples that the Shakers were not, and are not, backwards or conservative. They believed that if there was a better way of doing something, the Lord would want it to be done that way. From their earliest day, they were progressive in their ideas and work methods.

— June, 1978

While the Shakers in Kentucky were raising silk worms and making silk material, the Brothers and Sisters of Sabbathday Lake, Maine, produced the first no-iron cloth in the 1840's. Layers of linen were pressed between chemically treated papers in this press which was heated from below.

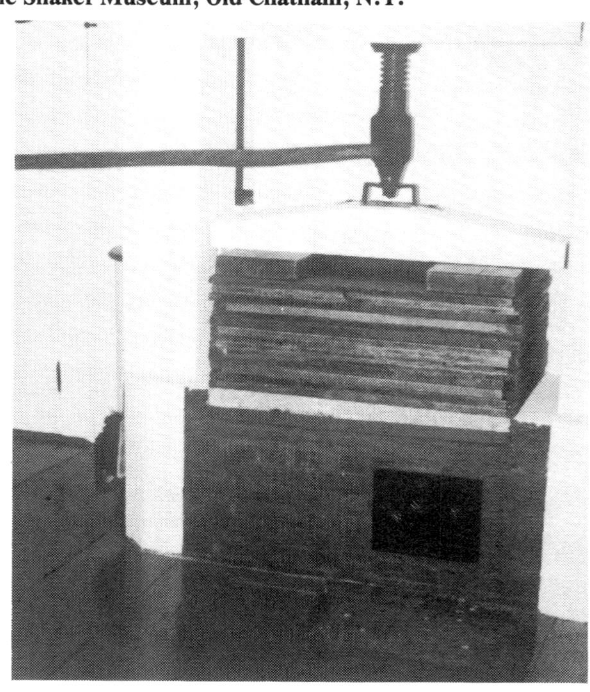

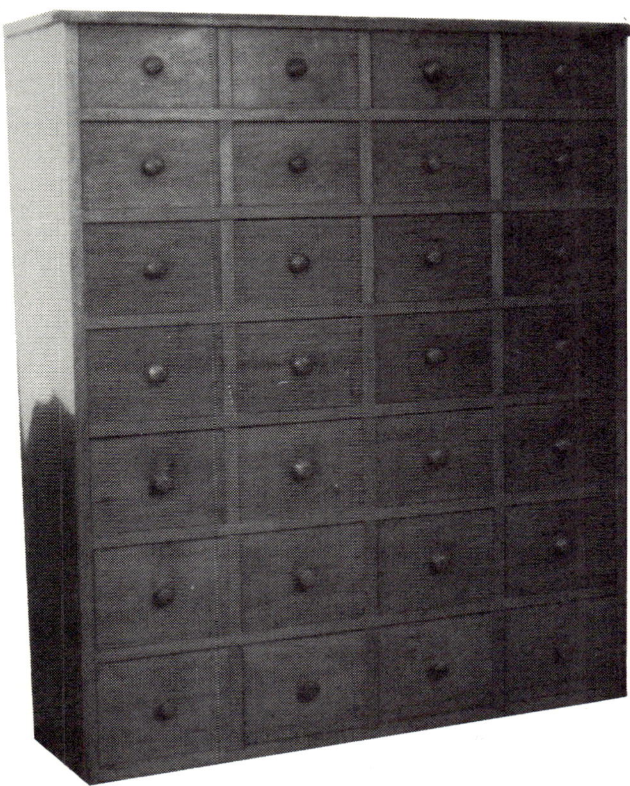

Case of drawers from Enfield, Connecticut. Made of butternut, this piece was used for the keeping of herbs. The herb labels are still on the drawers. Salvaged from a "burning of trash," this chest was originally built-in and the top has since been added.

(Private Collection)

Orderliness

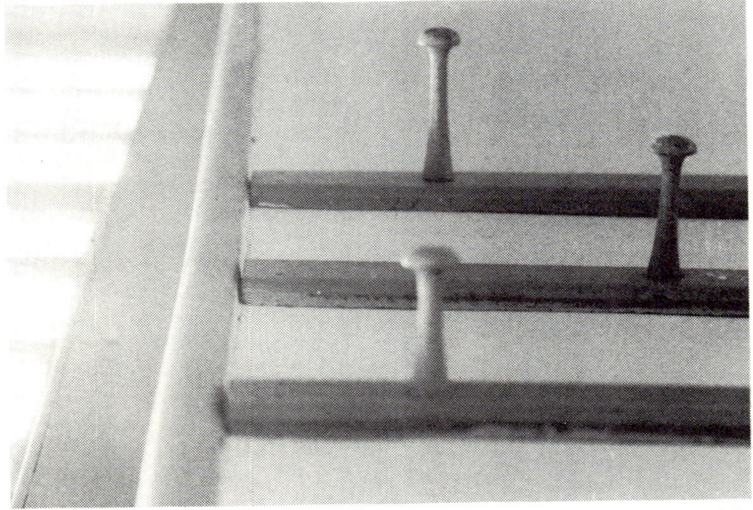

Three rows of pegs that line the walls of the Meeting House at Mt. Lebanon, New York. Cloaks and hats of the Believers and their visitors could be hung from these. (Library, Darrow School, New Lebanon, N.Y.)

People were, and still are, impressed with the cleanness and order of the Shaker way of life. From the well swept floors to the clean lines of the furniture, the word Shaker means neatness. This is in sharp contrast to some of the communal settings of our day. But for the Shakers, order was a necessity. First of all, it was practical. When hundreds of people are living together, there needs to be order for everyone to have the best of life. It promotes equality, cleanliness and safety. Secondly, there was a sense of imitating the heavenly kingdom. The Shakers believed that the Kingdom of God was present here, and their communities ought to be "heaven on earth." Therefore, order was a practical and religious necessity in the lives of the Shakers. A common saying and reflection upon this attitude is "a place for everything and everything in its place."

Shaker shops and dwellings reflected this philisophy in their construction and furnishings. Kases and chests of drawers are popular today with many owners of old homes because of the lack of storage space in these homes. Such is not the case with Shaker buildings. The most common example of the proper placement in Shaker buildings is the great use of pegs on the walls. All rooms were lined with pegboard. From these, garments could be hung. From these also, sconces, mirrors, shelves, clocks, cupboards, and other items could be hung as well as chairs. In this way, the floors were kept uncluttered and could be easily swept. The chairs were hung upside down when not in use so that dust would not accumulate on the seating surface.

Most of the pegboard has pegs that were made to be hammered into their holes and held by their tight fit. The pegs often protrude out the back side of the board. Some pegs were threaded so as to screw into the board. Robert Meader in his book **The Illustrated Guide to Shaker Furniture** suggests that threaded pegs were a characteristic of Hancock. I would add neighboring Mt. Lebanon as another community that used threaded pegs. In my

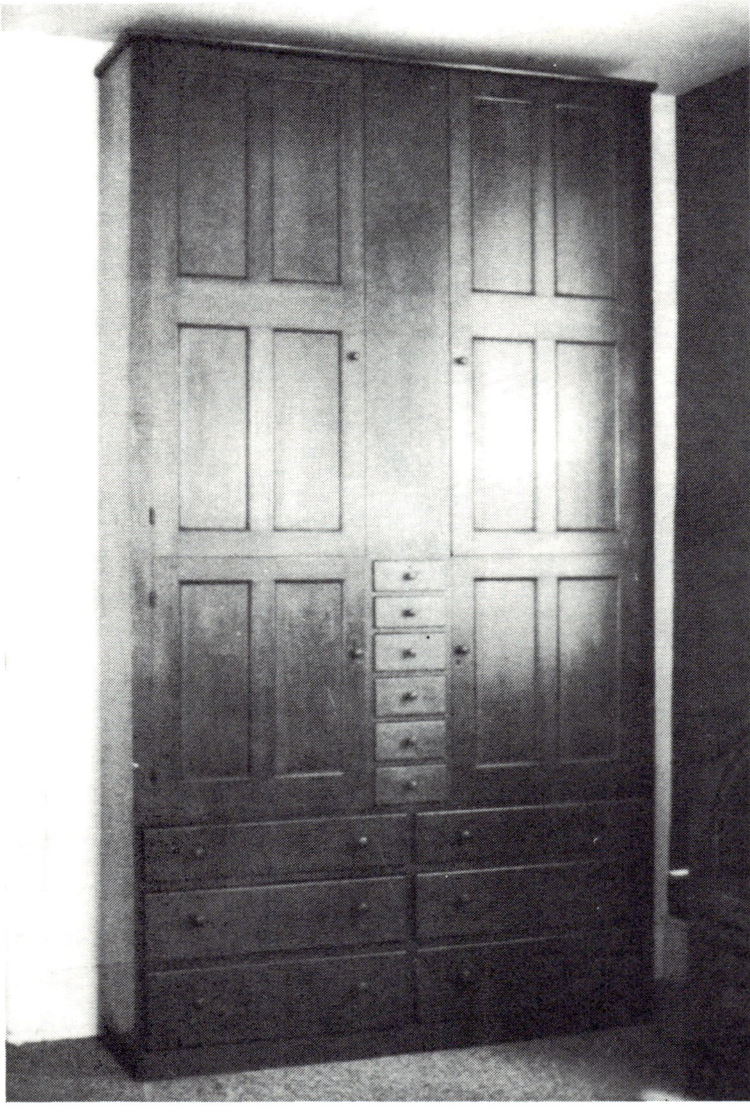

Perhaps the finest Shaker cupboard-case of drawers. With quarter round edging on door panels. And free standing, this piece is unique for its stack of center drawers.   (Darrow School, New Lebanon, N.Y.)

observations, not every peg in a board having threaded pegs would be threaded. One theory for this and the use of threaded pegs is that these could be removed in order to hang some of the shelves, etc. since the holes in hanging items are often smaller than the heads of the pegs. Pegs range in size from one half inch under window sills to hold brushes to six inches for the holding of the Brethren's hats.

Today, sections of pegboard can be found with the remnants of white plaster on half of the top and bottom edges. This is because the boards were put in place and then the walls were plastered up to the boards. When purchasing pegboard, look for the remnants of this white line on the edges. Look carefully, too, at the pegs. While even the Shaker replaced broken pegs with others that did not exactly match, many pieces of pegboard have been restored by adding new pegs. Thousands of feet of pegboard with the pegs long gone have been purchased when Shaker buildings have been destroyed with the idea of adding pegs and then selling.

The attics of the dwelling houses contained hundreds of pegs for the hanging of out of season clothing. Built-in drawers also served this purpose. Meader suggests that more clothes were stored folded in drawers than were hung from pegs. The space under the eaves was filled with great cases of drawers. Sometimes these would run the length of the attic. Visitors to Pleasant Hill, Kentucky, can see the enbankment of drawers in the Center Family Dwelling. The dwelling house at Canterbury has 88 drawers as well as many cupboards built into the attic. Today, these are difficult to use because of their size and the fact that they usually have no top or sides since they were built in. The drawers in the attic at the headmaster's house of the Darrow School (formerly Mt. Lebanon), have handles cut into the sides so that they could be easily carried to the room where they were to be filled for storage.

Drawers are to be found everywhere in Shaker communities.

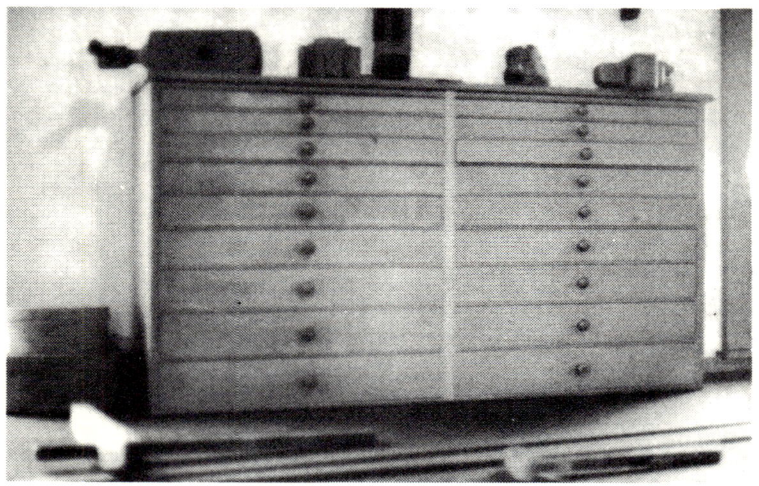

Small case of drawers (39'' x 22½'' x 15½'') used in a shop. It is very interesting because of the writing on the bottom of two drawers. On one is inscribed the following:

- H. C. -
Amusing himself 'sortin'
- tacks -
April 15, 1916

"An idle mind is the devil's workshop" Yea! On the second drawer is written: "Our lips mumble the phrases of a bygone Shakerism but our hearts dwell in the camp of the hypocrit."

(Shaker Museum, Old Chatham, N.Y.)

Built-ins and free standing cupboard-case of drawer units were made for dining and residence rooms. Some of the built-ins were made so that the drawers could also slide through the wall and be accessible from two different rooms. This proved to be a convenience at Union Village as dishes could be put away in the kitchen, then later taken out on the other side of the wall and used to set the dining tables.

Shops also used drawers extensively. Some of the drawers had covers in order to keep out the dust. Others used in the herb industry had holes in the bottom or shelves inside to permit the circulation of air. Shaker cases of drawers come in all sizes to meet the various needs of the people and the items they needed to store. Whatever the item or its purpose, there was a proper place for it.

— November, 1976

NOTE: *See photograph and caption on page 33. Threaded pegs appear to be more common than previously believed as examples are readily available from Union Village and Enfield, Ct., as well as Hancock and Mt. Lebanon.*

Made to Hang

Perhaps the most familiar of Shaker furnishings is the pegboard. In almost every room, hallway or shop, the pegboard and its many variations of pegs served the Shaker community's need for order and cleanliness. In attics, pegs were placed from opposite sides into a board suspended between rafters so that herbs or out of season clothing could be stored. In Meeting Houses, three rows of pegs were staggered one above the other to accommodate the hats and coats of the brethren and sisters during their celebrations of Life in the dance. But the pegboard was functional for more than just holding clothes. Numerous small articles of furniture were made to hang from the pegs and/or the rail.

One of the tenets of the Shaker way of life was "a place for everything and everything in its place." With the use of the pegboard, many items could be hung from the wall and, therefore, kept off of table tops or the floor. Chairs were, and still are, hung from the pegs. When not in use, these are suspended upside down so that dust will not accumulate on the sitting surface. There is an interesting photograph of some Mt. Lebanon sisters weaving palm leaf in which a small two step stool is hanging from the rail. In later years, pictures found a natural point of suspension from the pegs. Brushes, brooms, dustpans, coat hangers and kitchen utensils were commonly made and hung. But the Shakers also made the following specifically to be hung from the pegboard: pipe racks, cupboards, mirrors, candle sconces, plate racks, shelves and clocks.

Small one door cupboards were constructed with a one board back that came up to a rounded peak protruding above the case. A small hole was made near the peak for suspension. Larger cupboards had two stiles up the back

This mirror has the unique feature of having two holes for the adjustment of height. Two screws above the peg hold the mirror and its rack securely to the pegboard. Shaker Community, Inc. Hancock, MA.

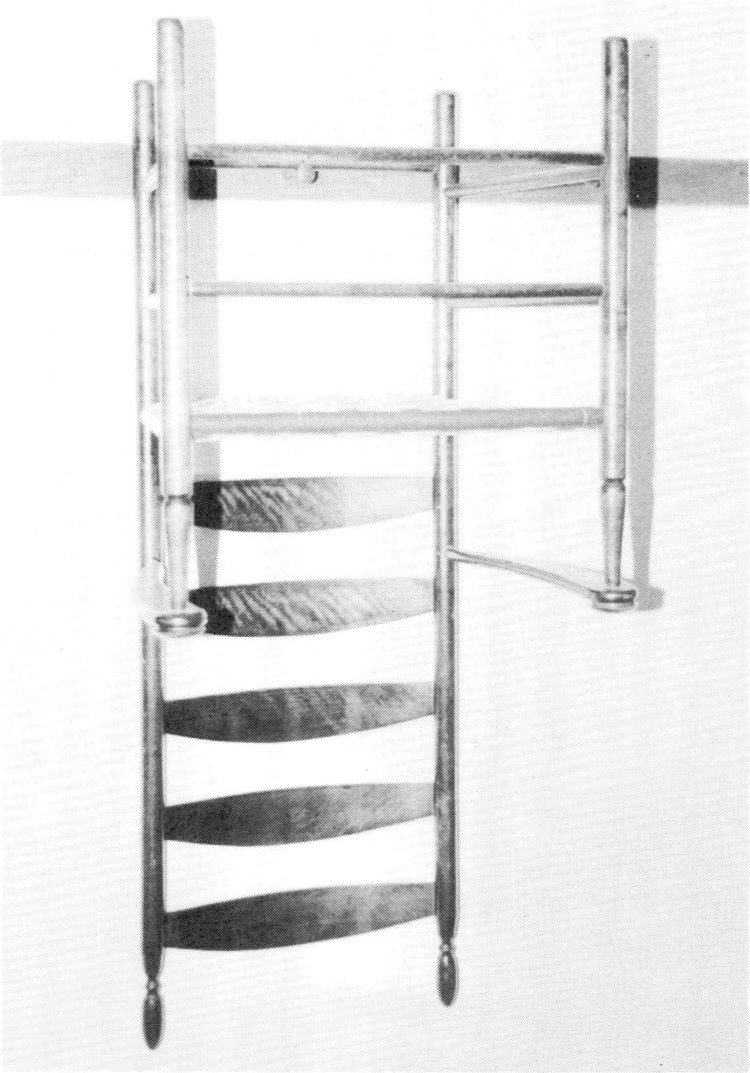

An easy way to clean the floor is to pick up everything including the chairs. When not used often, chairs were hung upside down in order to prevent dust from accumulating on the seats.

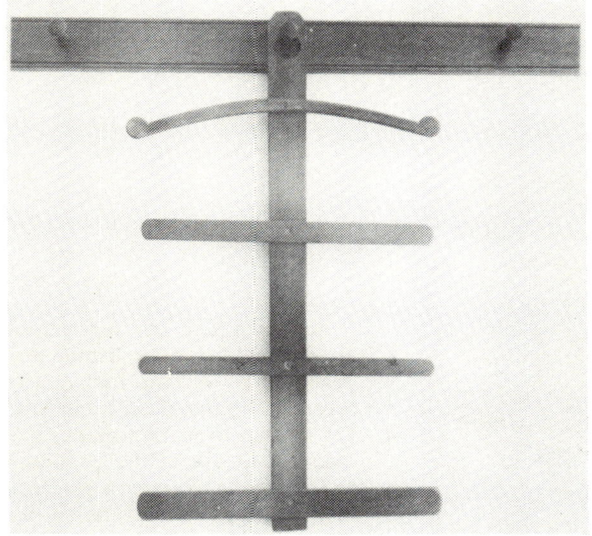

Multiple garment hanger, stained brown, Canterbury, NH., circa 1840. A plausible explanation for the different size and shape of the cross bars is that each was designed to hold a specific type of garment. Private collection. (Photograph and description by John Kassay)

Tilting sconces, cupboards and clocks must have been a constant problem and were secured in place by one of two means. The first was to simply run screws through the stiles and into the pegboard. The second method was through a three point suspension system using rings and wire. John Kassay of San Bruno, California, has discovered this arrangement on the candle sconce (plate 12), the wall cupboard with holes in them usually large enough to go over the head of the peg. While many sets of shelves used a similar means of suspension, some were also made to be suspended by a rope or to be directly screwed into the rail. In the latter case, the stiles were notched to be fitted over the peg rail.

Mirrors were constructed in two pieces: the mirror itself and the rack to hold it. The mirror rested in a grooved rail on the front of the rack. At the top of the mirror, a ring held a cord which was fastened to the rack. This would permit the mirror to be held at the right angle for the person using it. It is interesting to note that while the mirror and rack were made to be hung from a pegboard, they, in turn, have their own rail from which brushes and combs could be suspended.

Candle sconces of the West vary from those of the Eastern Shakers in their ability to be adjusted. Constructed of a platform fastened to an upright stile, sconces from Ohio and Kentucky could have their height varied because of four or five holes in the stiles. The platform on these sconces is often round with a bentwood rim that would keep a sliding candlestick on a tilted sconce.

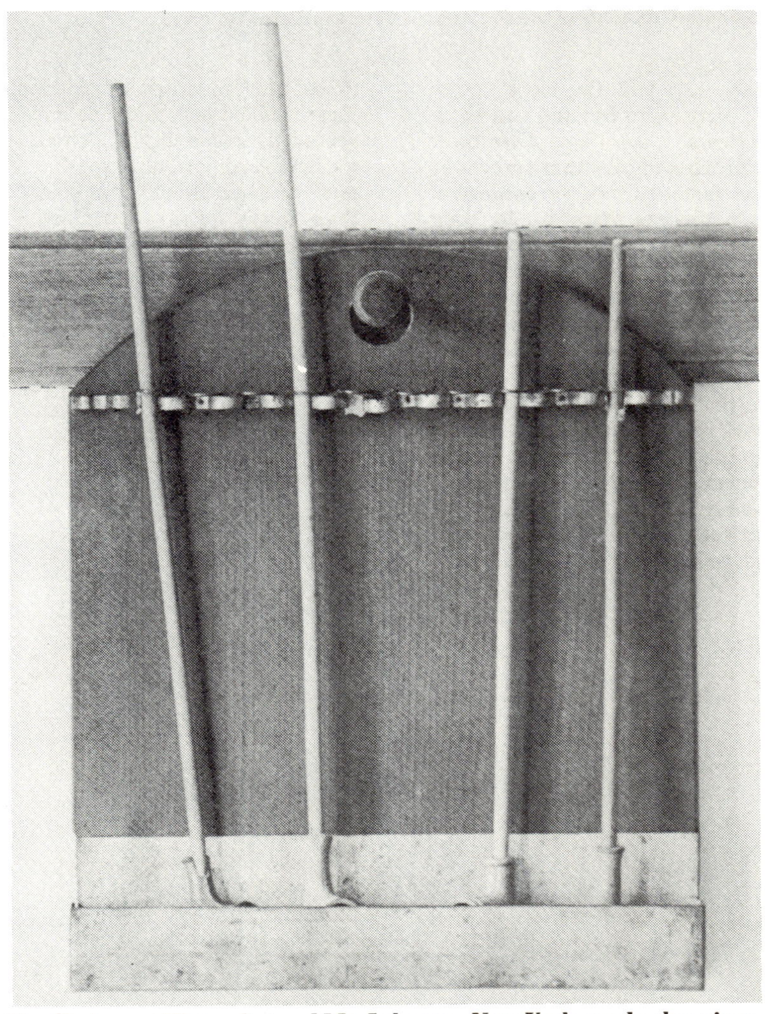

The Shakers at Watervliet and Mt. Lebanon, New York, made clay pipes in the early 1800's as well as the pipe rack. The tray and pipe holders are made of tin. Shaker Community, Inc.

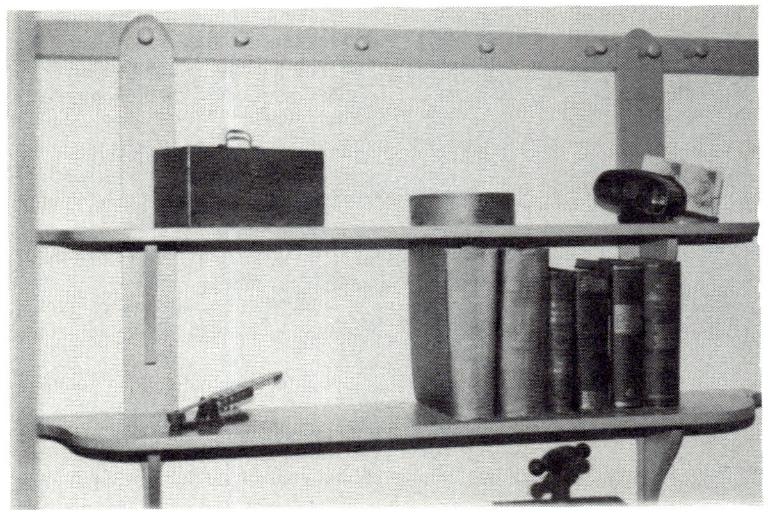

It can easily be seen that the holes in the stiles of this hanging shelf are not large enough to fit over the heads of the pegs. The pegs are threaded and can be removed and re-inserted. Also, note the irregularity of the pegs to accommodate the shelves. Shaker Community, Inc.

(plate 13), and the clock (plate 42), pictured in Deming and Faith Andrews' *Shaker Furniture.* There is evidence that screws or rings fastened into the corners of these pieces. Wire would then secure these to pegs on either side of the piece.

It will be noted that the holes for suspension are often not large enough to fit over the heads of pegs. This is true on the set of shelves pictured, the small one-door cupboards previously mentioned, and many clocks and sconces. Pegs were either made to be driven into the rail or to be screwed into it. Threaded pegs and rail appear in the midst of those held together by friction. The threaded pegs could be easily removed, placed through a hole in a clock backboard or a shelf stile and screwed back into place, thus firmly holding the clock or shelf in place.

Pegboard and its accessories are among the most useful and desirable of Shaker items. The recent exhibition illustrating Shaker influence on Danish designs made great use of the pegboard as the means to support placards that provided interpretation for the exhibit. Shakertown at Pleasant Hill, Kentucky, has for many years produced a calendar made to be hung from pegs. And when the *Ohio Antique Review* recently enlarged its office space, it put up some pegboard as an efficient means for hanging calendars and coats.

— February, 1978

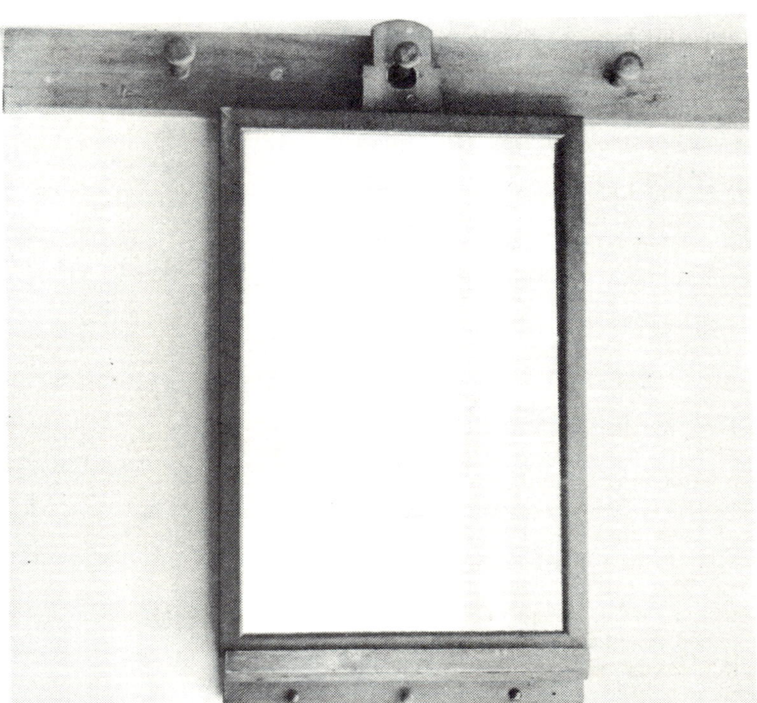

Early 19th century looking glass and hanging shelf; Community origin unknown. Collection of the Golden Lamb Inn, Lebanon, OH. (Photograph and description by John Kassay)

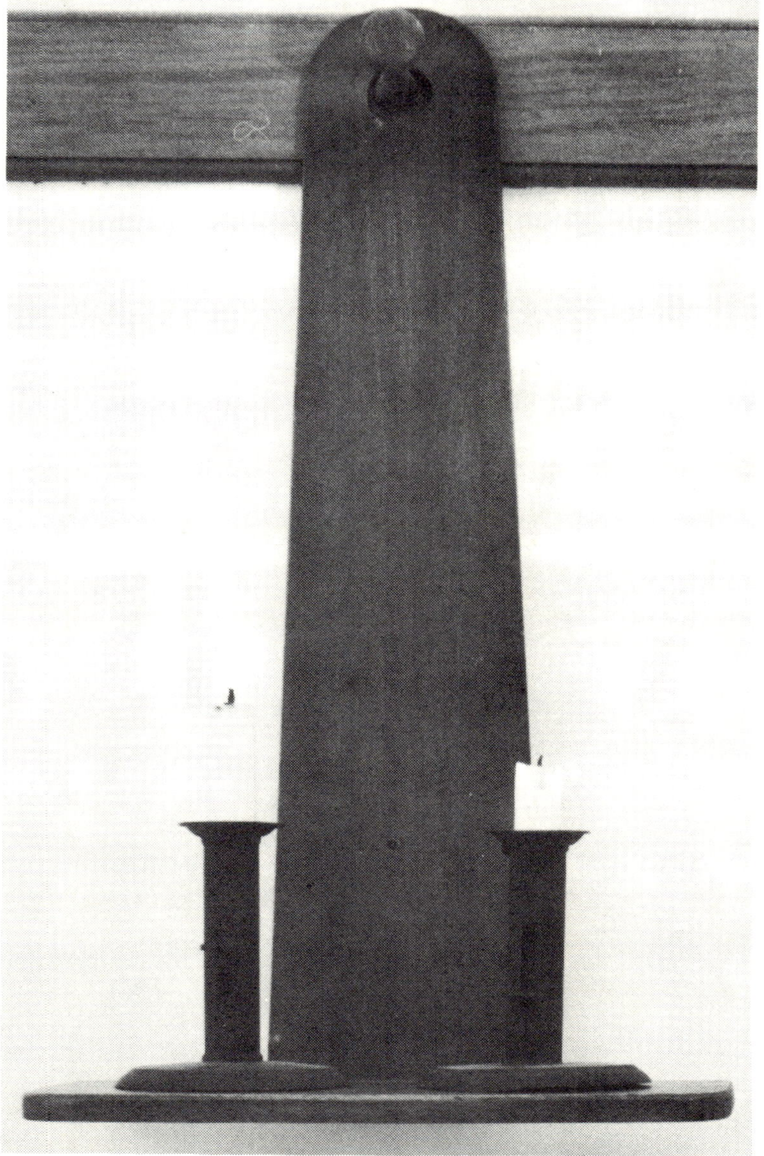

Of unknown origin, this early 19th century candle sconce holds two candles and was probably used in a large room where more light was needed; i.e., meeting, dining, gathering or work room. Collection of the Shaker Community, Inc., Hancock, MA. (Photograph and description by John Kassay)

Add - Ons

Certain styles such as Gothic fingered oval boxes, tilters on chair legs and pencil post legs on tables appear to be unique to Shaker furniture. Certain other styles and characteristics such as nipple finials on chairs, oval boxes with one pointed finger on the bottom and another on the lid, and built-in cases of drawers are most often Shaker but were also known to have been made by people outside the Shaker communities. Add-ons are in this latter category. One characteristic of furniture found only occasionally in the world but with great frequency in the Shaker communities is the addition of drawers, surface areas, or longer legs to pieces that were constructed years before and were already in use.

With the exception of chairs, Shaker furniture was made for use in the community and, usually, for a particular place. The sewing desks with many drawers were constructed with finished backs because the craftsman knew when he built it that it would be sitting in the middle of a room. Cupboards often have

A unique chair is this Union Village, Ohio, dining chair with rollers added. - Golden Lamb Inn, Lebanon, Ohio.

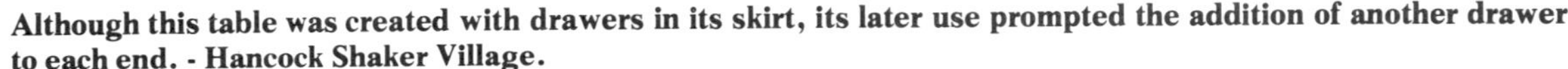

Although this table was created with drawers in its skirt, its later use prompted the addition of another drawer to each end. - Hancock Shaker Village.

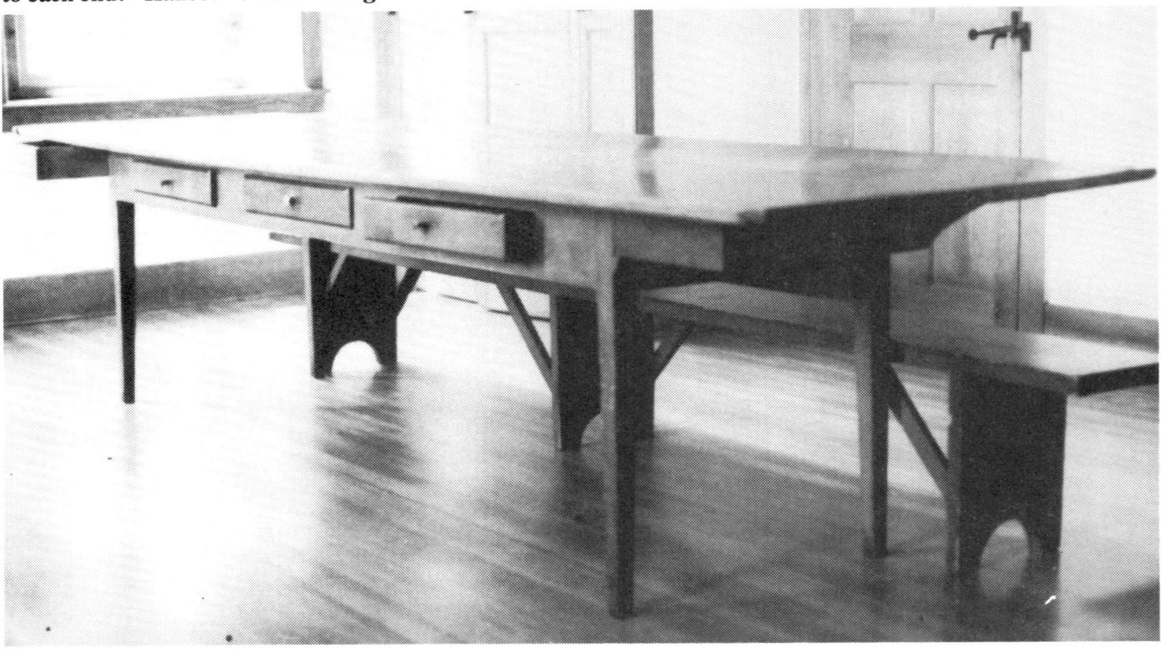

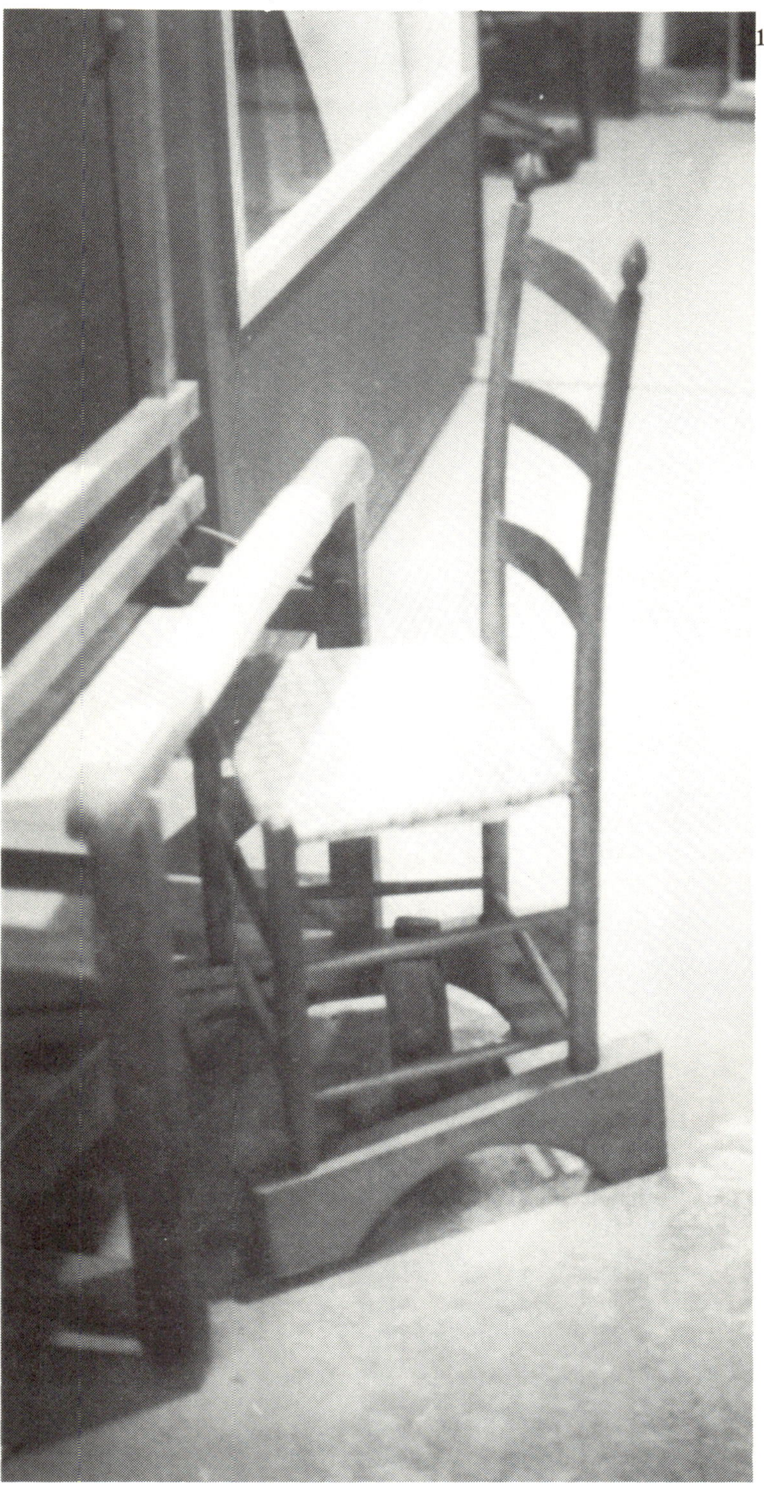

While many chairs simply had boots added to their legs, this one has had a platform added to give it added heighth and make it suitable for use at a loom. - Shaker Museum, Old Chatham, New York.

knotty wood on one side and a better grade on the other. This was because the carpenter was making that cupboard for a specific spot where the one side would be in the corner and not show. There is a cupboard between the doors in the dining room at Pleasant Hill, Kentucky, where the back is wider than the front, thus permitting the doors on either side to swing completely open. That cupboard was made for that special place.

With furniture being made for a particular place and purpose, it can be easily seen that as the desired use changed, so might the design and construction. A table might have been used against the wall. At a later date, it might have been desirable to pull the table out from the wall so that two Shaker sisters could work from opposite sides. Thus, rollers would be added to pull the table out from the wall in the morning and push it back out of the way at night. Rollers were often added to tables and beds and, once in a while, to chairs.

These rollers on tables would have the added benefit of giving them more height. Many Shaker tables and chairs gained "boots" in order to give them added height (Photo #1). In this way, a chair intended for the sitting room could be adapted for use at the weaving loom.

Besides the addition of rollers and boots. Shaker furniture frequently gained a drawer or two. Tables had drawers added on the ends or beneath while blanket chests would frequently have another drawer added. Between the feet and fashioned onto the bottom, another drawer often provided additional space (Photos #2 & 3) I have heard of one Shaker dealer who passed up a piece because of this feature. He thought of it as having been "altered." If this addition were offensive, as it frequently is to the esthetics of a piece, the drawer could have been removed and put in storage. The runners for the drawer are on the underside of the base and not readily visible to the eye. The piece could have been returned to its first state without destroying the add-on

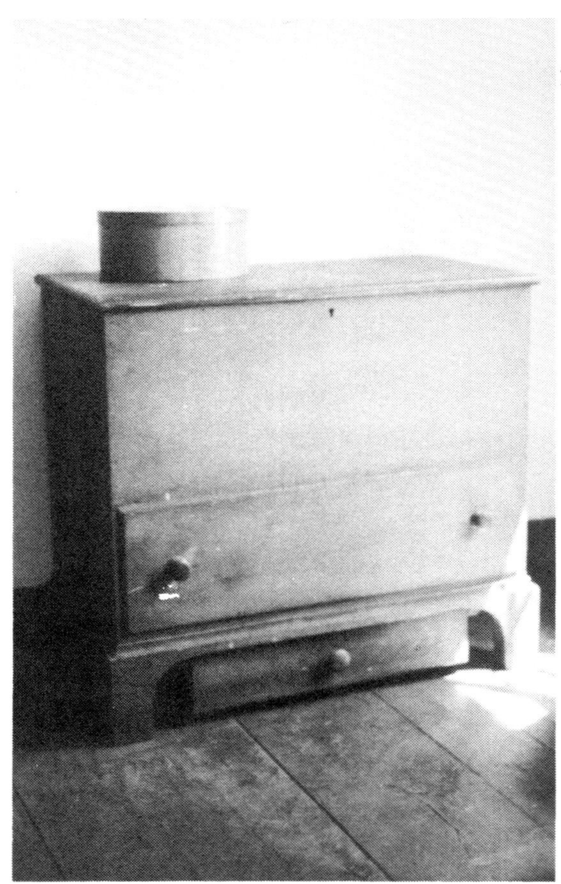

2.

This blanket chest from Harvard, Massachusetts, was made in 1821 and obtained an additional drawer at a later date. - Hancock Shaker Village.

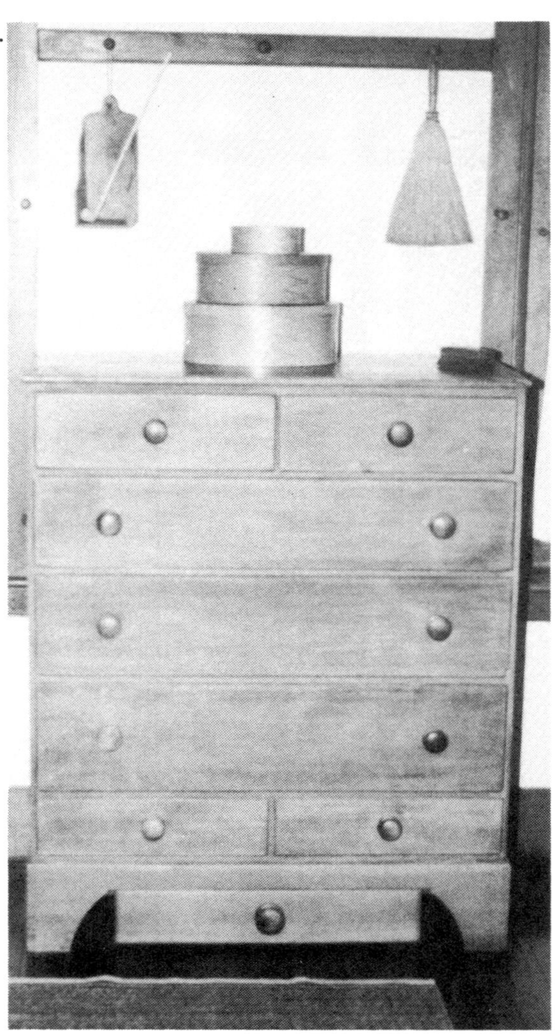

3.

The drawer below was added some years after this chest of drawers was originally constructed. This is apparent from the lack of beading on the added drawer while the others have it. On the added drawer is the inscription: "Thomas Hammond - this belongs to his case of drawers." Hancock Shaker Village, Pittsfield, Massachusetts.

feature. More importantly though, the piece was made more desirable by the add-on. Add-ons are characteristic of Shaker furniture and reflect the importance of changing functionalism in the Shaker philosophy and life style.

In addition to height to chairs, rollers to tables and drawers to chests, the Shakers added leaves to tables, pegs to the sides of pieces and lift top compartments where there had previously been only a drawer. In fact, the add-on feature became standardized in many of their common products.

Chairs had tilters added and then were manufactured with the tilters in mind. Cushion rails, or shawl rails, were added and became standard as there became a desire to soften the hard slat backs of the chairs. Even the stoves reflect this changing functionalism and add-on feature. Another heat chamber was added to the top of their stoves to permit more heat to radiate into the room. (Photo #4).

Small candle stands were made in the early days of Shakerism without drawers. A little later, one drawer separated the pedestal from the top. Then, two drawers were hung from the underside of the top to permit two sisters to use the same stand while doing sewing. Today, this style stand is among the most desirable of Shaker artifacts. If you find a stand like this or another piece of Shaker furniture with an "add-on" feature, do not reject it for this is a Shaker characteristic. Add-ons reflect the Shaker concept of functionalism and willingness to change.

— October, 1977

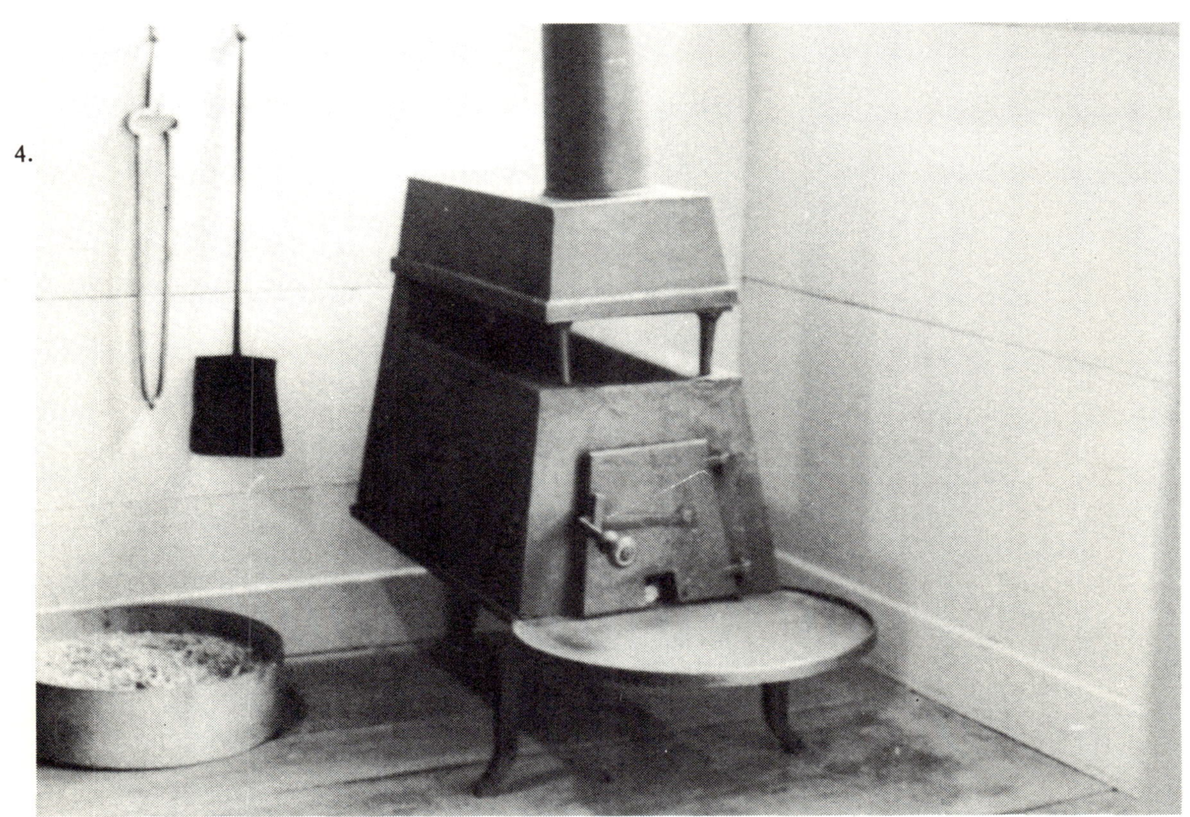

4.

The ''Super-heater'' stove is an example of a Shaker ''add-on'' that
became standard in later years. - Shaker Museum, Old Chatham, N.Y.

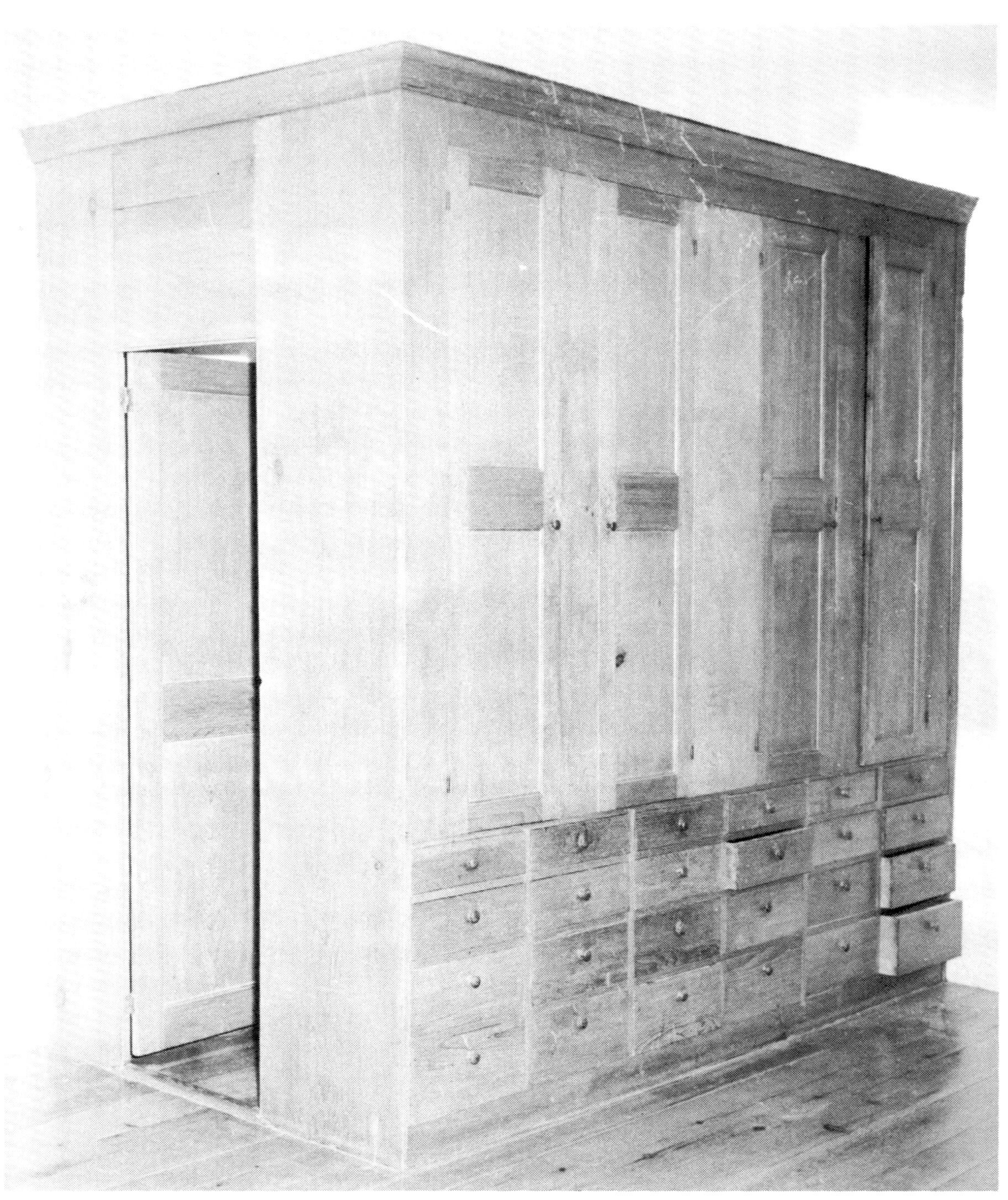

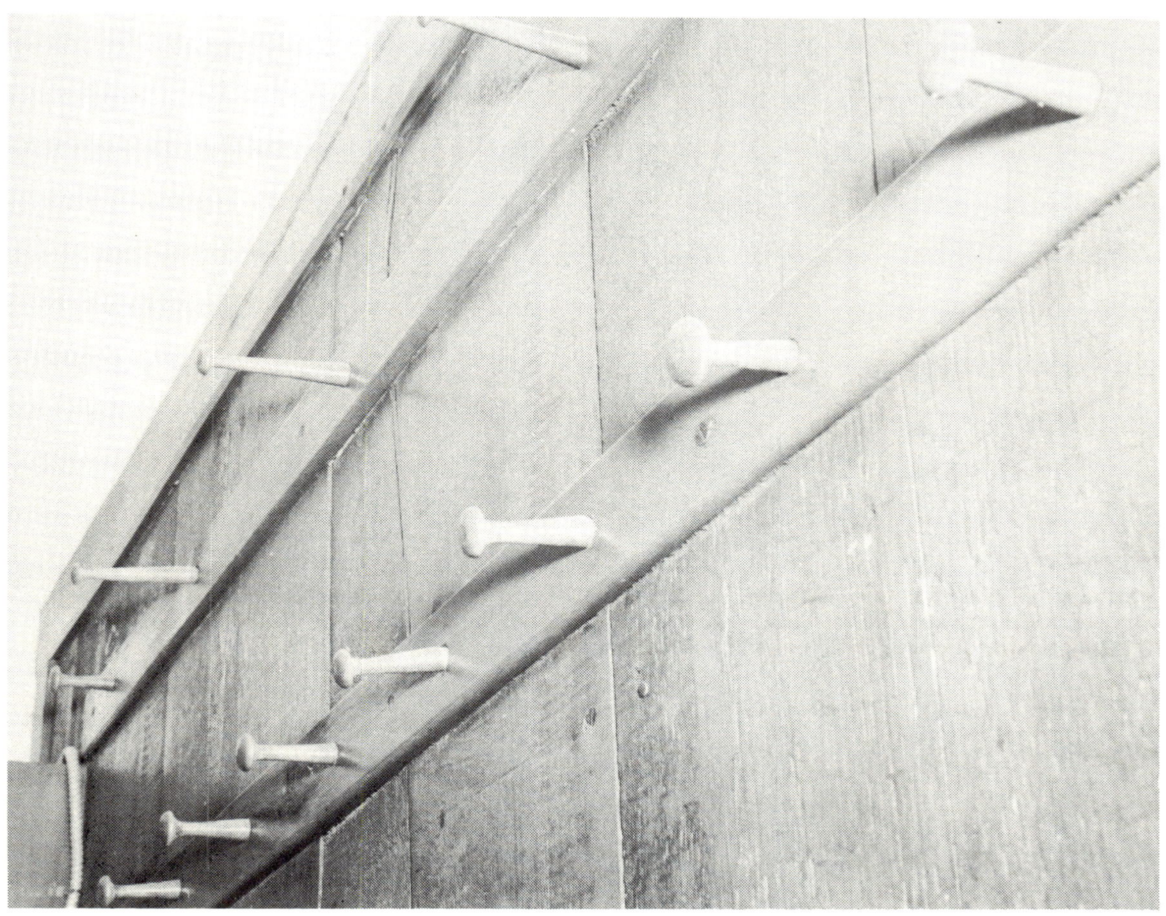

The ultimate in "add-ons" is this piece. Originally free-standing against the wall, this cupboard over drawers was moved out and a walk in closet added behind, complete with peg rails. One door on this cupboard holds the markings for the sizes of the Shaker brothers and sisters to be used in the making of their garments. - Darrow School, New Lebanon, New York. (Photograph by Clark Rice.)

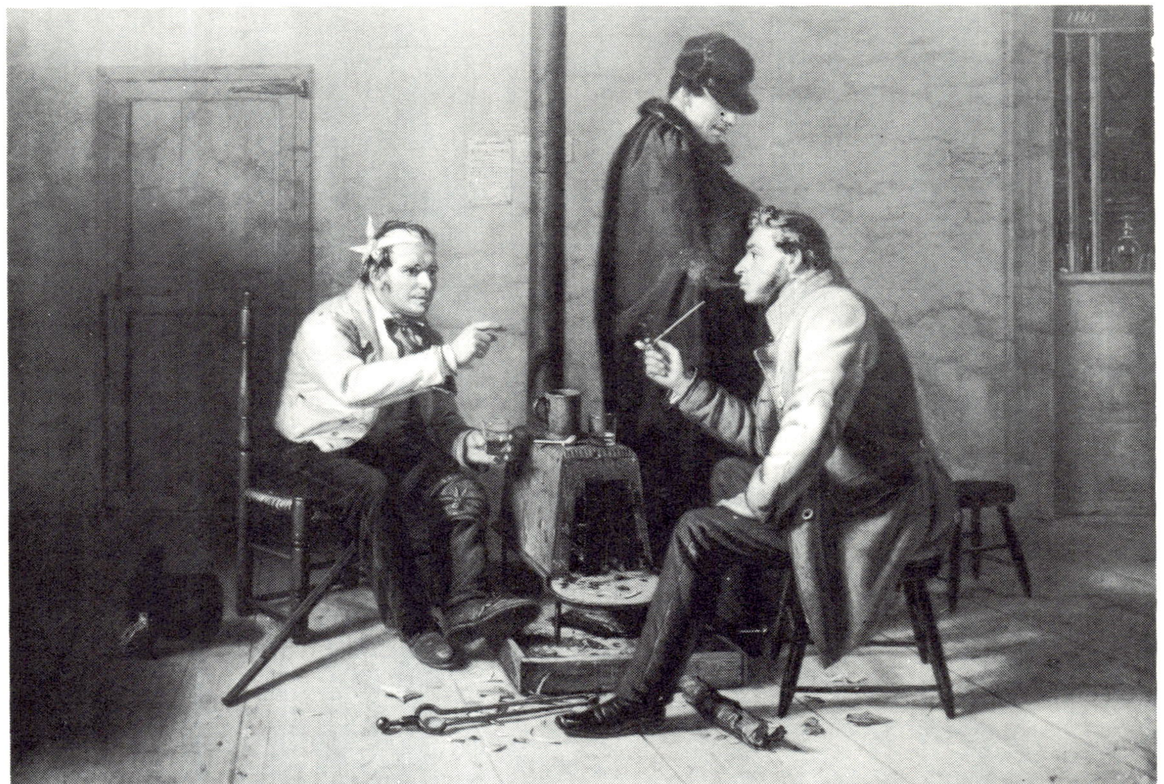

"The Long Story," an oil painting by William Sidney Mount was painted in 1837 at Setauket, Long Island. The stove depicted here would indicate that the Shakers were selling stoves to the world, and at a relatively early date. (In the collection of the Corcoran Gallery of Art, Washington, D.C.)

Stoves

In this day of energy problems, the Shaker stove is as right today as it was almost 200 years ago. A gentleman in downtown Cincinnati recently purchased one to use in heating his home, while in New Hampshire another family had one warming their living room during the recent blizzard. The style, use, and efficiency of the Shaker wood burning stoves have changed very little in their two century history.

Stoves were used very early in the Eastern Shaker communities. Although the Meeting Houses built by Moses Johnson at Mt. Lebanon, New York (1786), and Enfield, Connecticut (1791), had large chimneys to accommodate fireplaces, those of Canterbury, New Hampshire (1792), Shirley, Massachusetts (1793), and Sabbathday Lake, Maine (1794), were constructed to use the small stoves for heating. In the West, Pleasant Hill, Kentucky, replaced many fireplaces in the community with stoves in the 1820's while the Meeting House built at the beginning of that decade incorporated

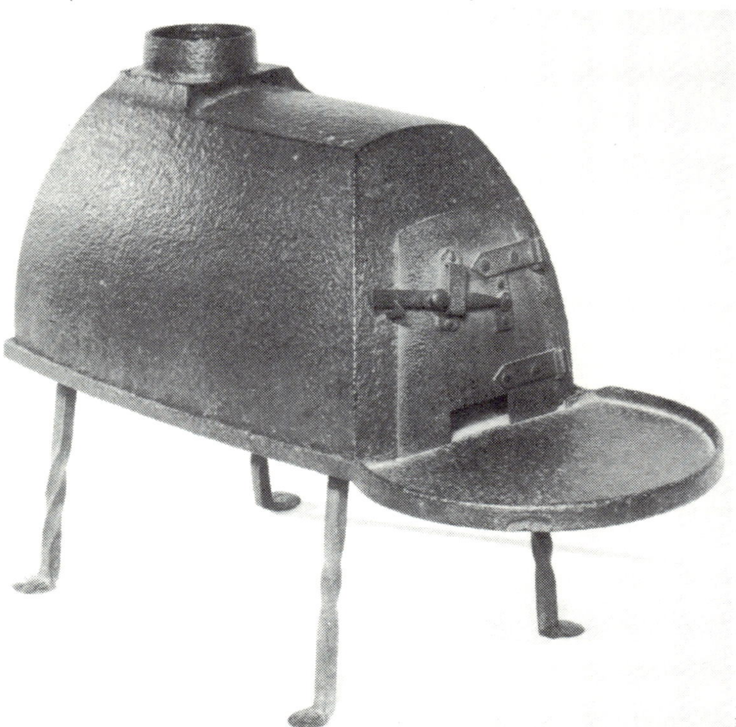

Although similar, this stove was not designed by the Shakers but by Dr. Eliphalet Nott. Dr. Nott made stoves like this for use in the students rooms at Union College, Schenectady, New York, where he was headmaster. (Photograph courtesy of The Henry Ford Museum, Dearborn, Michigan)

stoves from its beginning. The Meeting House at Union Village, Ohio, had fireplaces in use throughout its life. The consistent use of fireplaces and their wood fireplace doors are apparently unique to the Southwestern Ohio Shaker communities although many communities had fireplaces in shops and out buildings.

Eugene Dodd in "Functionalism in Shaker Crafts" (*Antiques,* October, 1970) refers to an inventory of better than 200 variations in Shaker stoves. Some were made of sheet metal with cast iron legs. Others had sheet metal bodies and cast iron legs and doors. But most were entirely of cast iron. Of these cast iron stoves, there are basically two styles: the box stove and the panelled.

The box or coffin stove was the most common form, having been produced at Mt. Lebanon and Hancock, Mass., and for the Kentucky settlements. It consisted of five parts: the body, cast in one piece; a plate upon which the body set; the legs to keep it off of the wood floors; the door; and the small draft door to regulate the air supply. Many variations of this stove have been found. The shape of the legs varies from cast pegs to cabriole to wrought iron with penny feet. The intended purpose also dictated variations in design. Some had angled sides with a ridge to hold irons for the laundry room. Others were cast with a pan on top to act as a humidifier. Still others had a small unit on top which would provide more heating surface and, thus, more heat. This variation has been called a "super heater," "double decker," "double fire box," and a stove "with radiator."

The second basic style, the panelled stove, has the body consisting of five plates that are held together with long bolts. This style appears to have been designed, manufactured, and used primarily at Canterbury and is often referred to by the name of that community. While this stove is more ornate (some have cabriole legs with claw feet), it is also considered by modern day users to be more efficient.

Canterbury, like many of the communities including Mt. Lebanon, Hancock, and Enfield, Ct., had its own foundry and could have produced its own stoves. Canterbury did this until its later years when the stoves were cast by the Ford Foundry in nearby Concord from Shaker made patterns. Pleasant Hill and South Union, Ky., had their stoves made outside the commun-

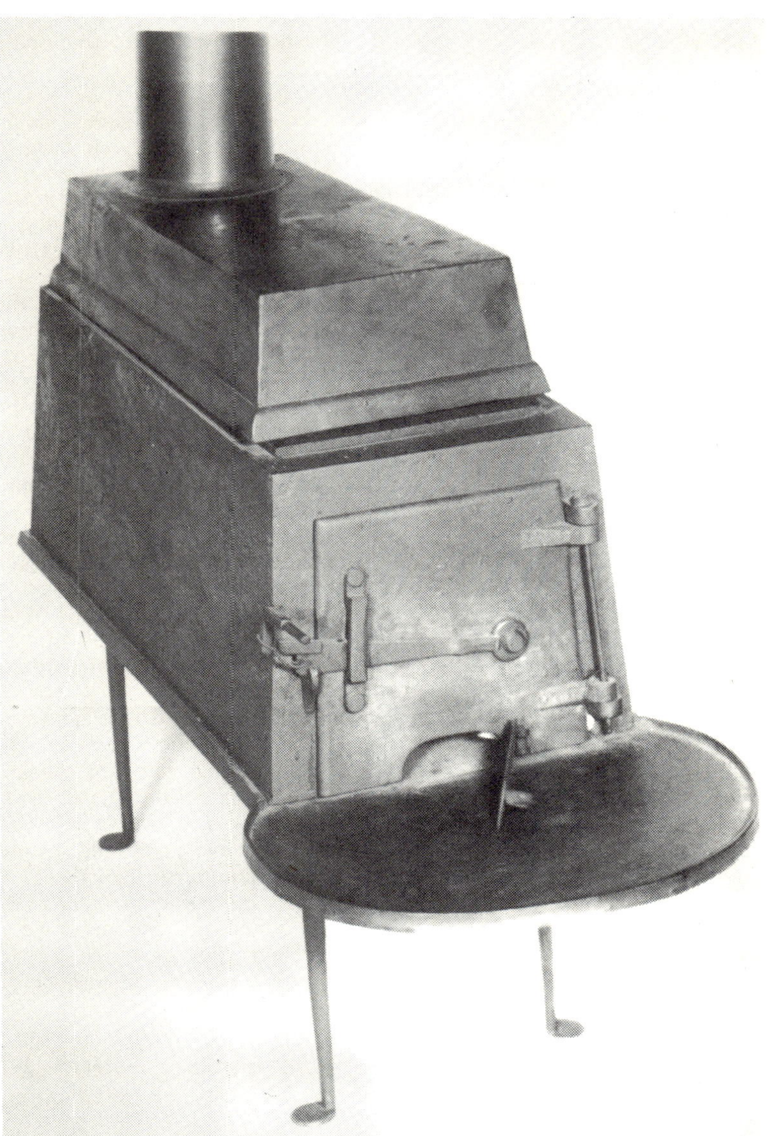

C. 1780. Coffin shaped cast iron Shaker stove. On top is a raised section (evaporating tank to control room temperature) at the rear of which is the flue opening. In front is a plain hinged door with a latch handle. At the bottom of the door is a small single hinged door used for a draft. In front is a plain round tray (cast in one piece with the bottom of the stove) with a raised edge. The stove stands on four plain wrought iron legs with flat round feet. (Photograph courtesy of The Henry Ford Museum, Dearborn, Michigan)

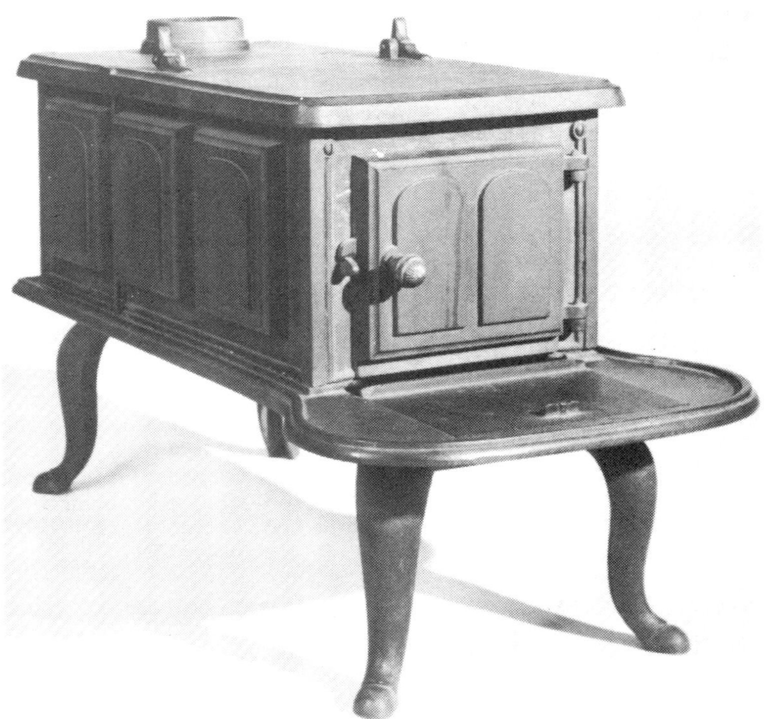

Designed and originally made at Canterbury, similar stoves were cast for the Shakers by the Ford Foundry in Concord, New Hampshire, which operated from 1834 to 1944. A stove like this is still in use in the school at Canterbury and bears the "W.P. Ford & Co." name. It is likely that similar stoves were cast elsewhere since Enfield's order to the Royal Blake foundry calls for one with "a hinge in the top of the stove so that a portion of the cover will swing up." (Height 35¼"; Width 19"; Depth 14¾"). (The photograph is from the New Hampshire Historical Society)

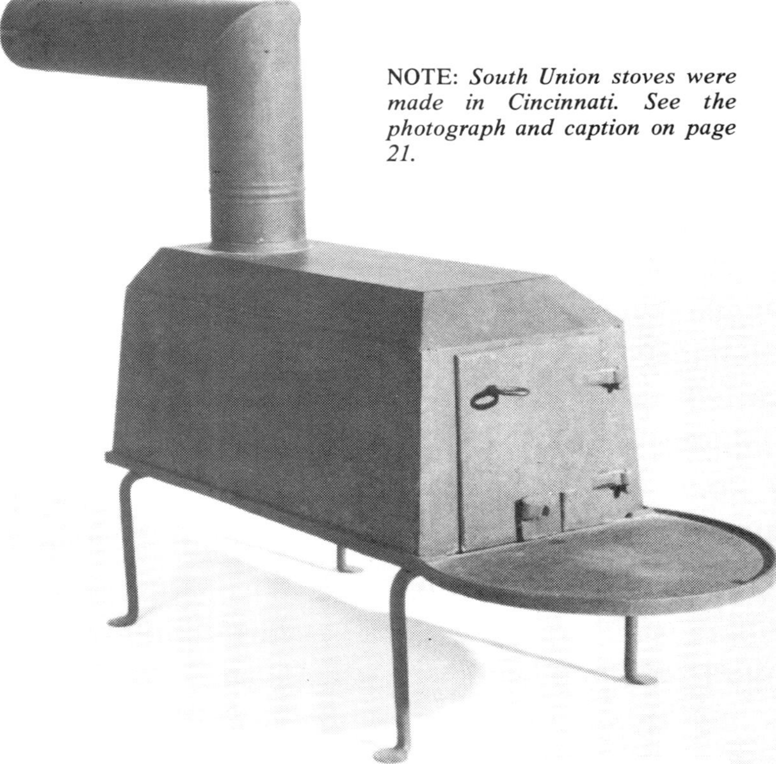

NOTE: *South Union stoves were made in Cincinnati. See the photograph and caption on page 21.*

ity at commercial foundries in Western Kentucky. Enfield, New Hampshire, also had its stove made outside the community. The following is quoted from the New Hampshire Historical Society's *"True Gospel Simplicity; Shaker Furniture in New Hampshire."* It is a manuscript from Enfield to the Royal Blake ironworks in Brandon, Vermont, and dated 1855.

"About 10 days since I wrote you and ordered some cooking stoves but had not heard from you since. We have promised a number of the stoves and should like them sent forward so that we can supply our customers. We would also like a large box stove for warming our Mill. I think they are about 3 feet long with a hinge in the top of the stove so that a portion of the cover will swing up. Also we would like 3 small box stoves for warming chambers for sleeping rooms. Write by return of mail if you can not send them."

The letter is interesting not just from its insights into outside manufacturing but also because of the expression of the need to "supply our customers." When this letter is coupled with the William Sidney Mount painting, "The Long Story," it can be readily concluded that stoves are to be included among the quality items that the Shakers produced for sale to the world. Mount was a native of Long Island, New York, and painted scenes familiar to him there. No doubt, the corner grocery of his day found the Shaker stove as efficient and desirable as the energy saving collectors of our day do.

— March, 1978

Circa 1825-1850, this stove is from Enfield, N.H., and is probably like those made by the Royal Blake Foundry in Brandon, Vermont. Height 16", Width 12", Length 29½". (Photograph is from the New Hampshire Historical Society)

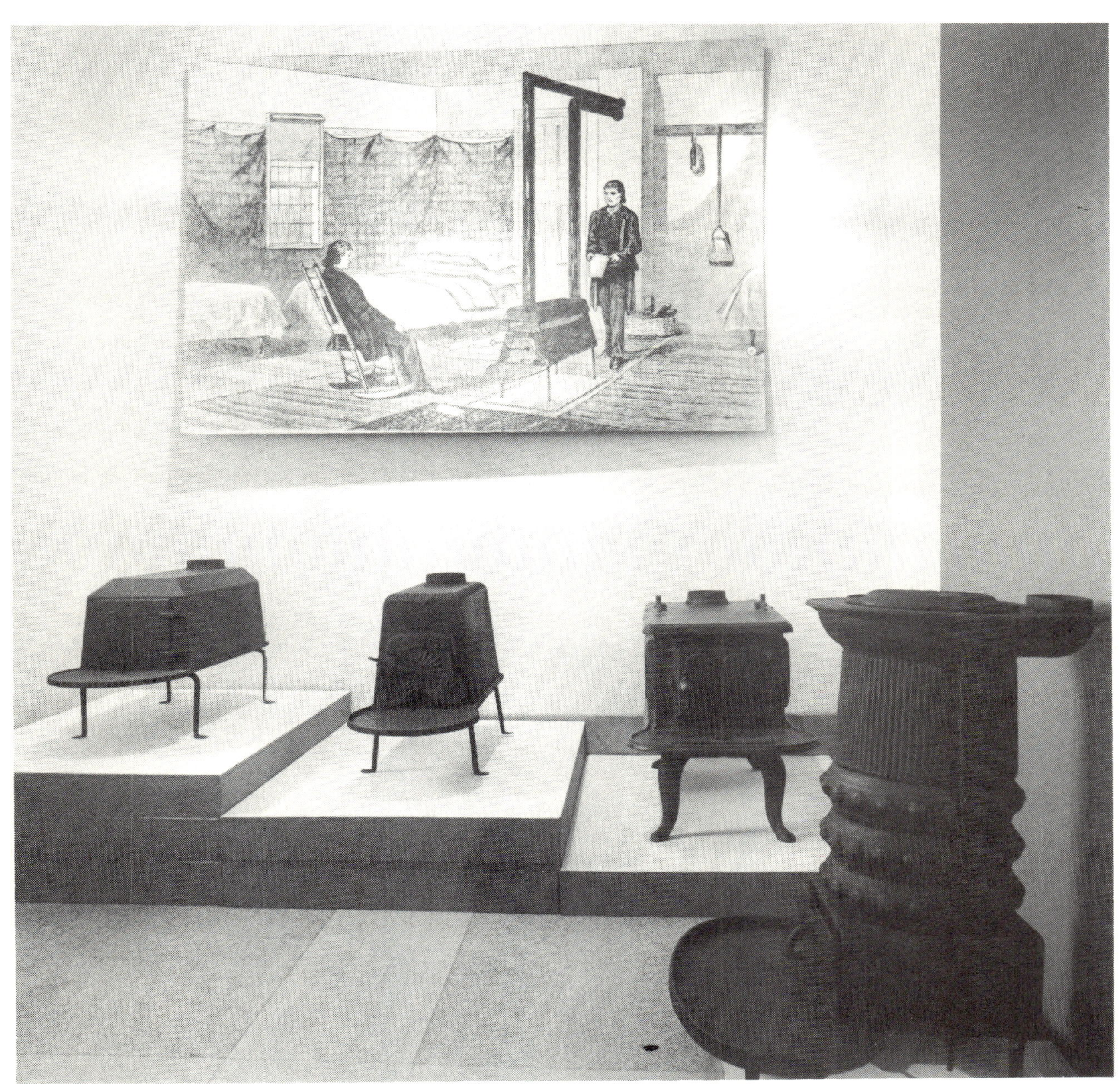

This stove exhibit was on display at the New Hampshire Historical Society in the Spring and Summer of 1977. Note the ''super heater'' in the copy of the early illustration that hangs as a backdrop. (Photograph is from the New Hampshire Historical Society)

Boxes and Baskets

Oval covered boxes and finely made baskets are two articles that are almost synoynmous with Shaker in the world of antiques. The boxes are readily distinguishable as Shaker while baskets are not.

From the earliest days the Shaker made for their own use and for sale to the world oval boxes to be used to hold sewing articles, spices, and a myriad of other small items that would need to be stored in a handy container. In 1805, they were sold for about $1.25 a nest. At that early date, a nest usually consisted of twelve boxes while in later years, it was nine or seven boxes. A nest of eleven boxes could still be purchased at the beginning of the 20th century for $5. Today, such a nest would cost well over $1,000.

The Indians are given credit for teaching the Shakers how to make baskets. They probably also deserve the credit for oval boxes. Oval boxes made of birch bark and having the lapped joint sewn with leather were a product of the Indians. An oval pine box of Shaker origin, signed and dated 1808, was sold at Clark Garrett's auction in Montgomery, Ohio, last September. It had its lapped joint cross-stitched with leather and illustrated a transition from the Indian birch bark oval box to the typical Shaker style. At the same time, though, oval lapped boxes were being made throughout early America. Most of the styles and techniques of the world's box makers were employed by the Shakers: buttonhole laps; straight seamed and tacked laps; lapped and tucked; single finger lap.

Only two styles appear to be distinguishable as uniquely Shaker. The first is made with a lap where the edge is cut like a sawtooth with the length of the teeth varying from about one fourth of an inch to an inch and a half. This sawtooth lap is uncommon and found almost exclusively on boxes that were made at Alfred, Maine. The second peculiarly Shaker design is the Gothic lap wherein the edge of the lap is cut in a series of Gothic arches making from two to six fingers. The Shakers discovered that a straight seam held with a series of nails did not allow for shrinkage. Therefore, the edge of the lap had a tendency to buckle between the nails or split at the nails. The use of fingers prevented splits and became the standard of production among Shaker oval box makers so that boxes made in 1830 have the same form and durability as those made more than a hundred years later.

Some knowledgeable Shaker collectors and dealers commented on some of the boxes in the recent Michigan auction(See August's O.A.R.) as being non-Shaker. They were referring to those with only a single finger. These are called "Harvard" boxes because

This oval box shows the multi-fingers with Gothic arch that was employed by the Shakers to keep the edge of the lap from splitting. The carving on the top is unusual. Photograph courtesy of The Shaker Museum, Old Chatham, N.Y.

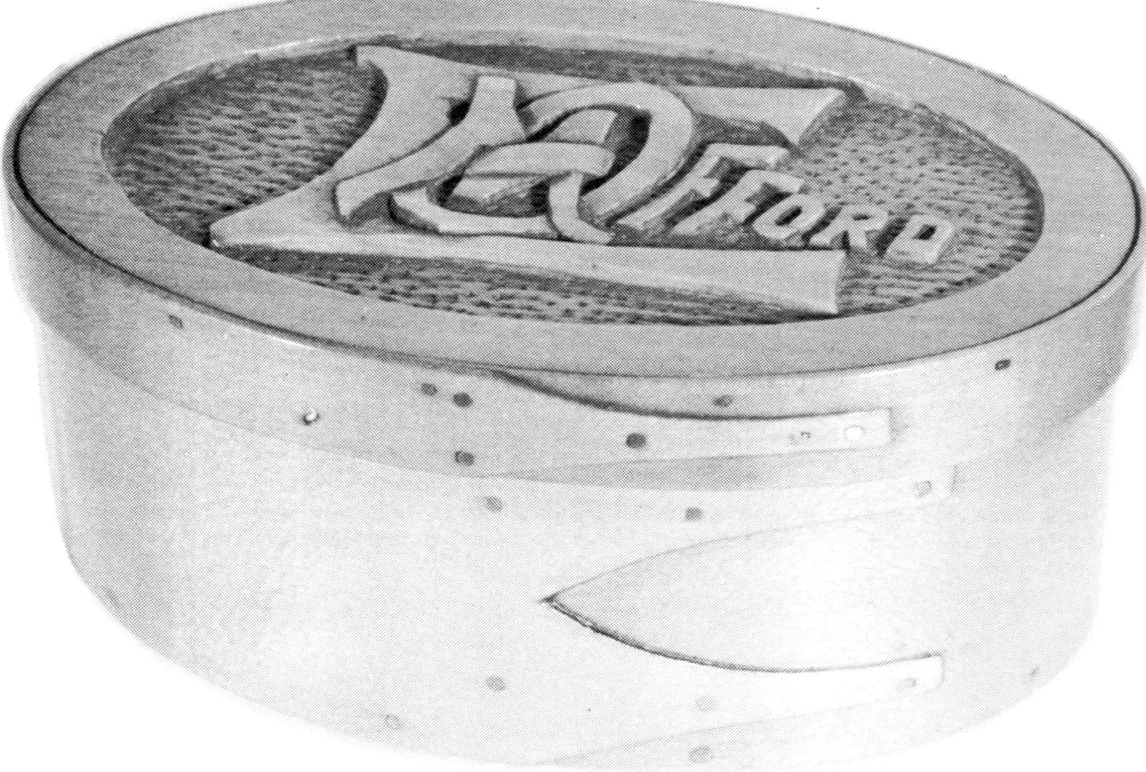

they were manufactured by the Harvard Shaker community. But that style was also made by non-Shaker box producers. Again, with the exception of some saw-tooth boxes, it is generally agreed that boxes having two or more fingers and the Gothic arch are the only ones that can be readily identified as Shaker. Robert Meader, former Director of The Shaker Museum in Old Chatham, New York, offered the following summary:

"The so-called 'Harvard' type, which had but one body-finger, triangular in shape, not Gothic, generally pointed to the left, while the cover-finger went to the right. That, I have always felt, was less attractive. We consider that, generally speaking, if the fingers of such a type oppose, the box is **probably** Shaker; if they do go in the same direction, it **probably** isn't. However, I've seen undoubted Shaker boxes with parallel fingers, so it is an iffy business at best. Lots of non-Shaker boxes were single-fingered, but multiple-fingered ones were always Shaker — one of the very few apparent certainties in Shaker design!''

Shaker oval boxes were made with pine bottoms and tops and predominantly maple sides, although some were made with cherry or oak sides. Once in a while a box is found that has a plywood top or bottom. These were made by a hired hand who worked for many years for the Shakers at Mt. Lebanon, learned the Shaker methods, and used their molds. The sides of the boxes were cut and then bent by steam or soaking in water around molds before having the top/bottom recessed into it and held in place by tacks or wood pegs. The finger laps are held by tacks made of copper or iron. Again, quoting from Robert Meader: "Some people still insist that if the box be truly Shaker, only copper tacks were used, never, **never** iron. Balderdash! The iron predomi-

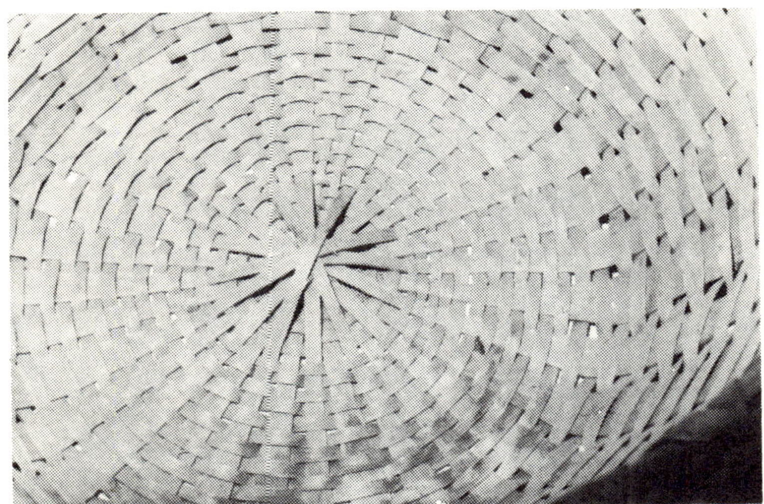

Round Shaker baskets usually have a cone shaped bottom.

Shaker baskets, like most early quality baskets, are known for their finely shaped notched handles.

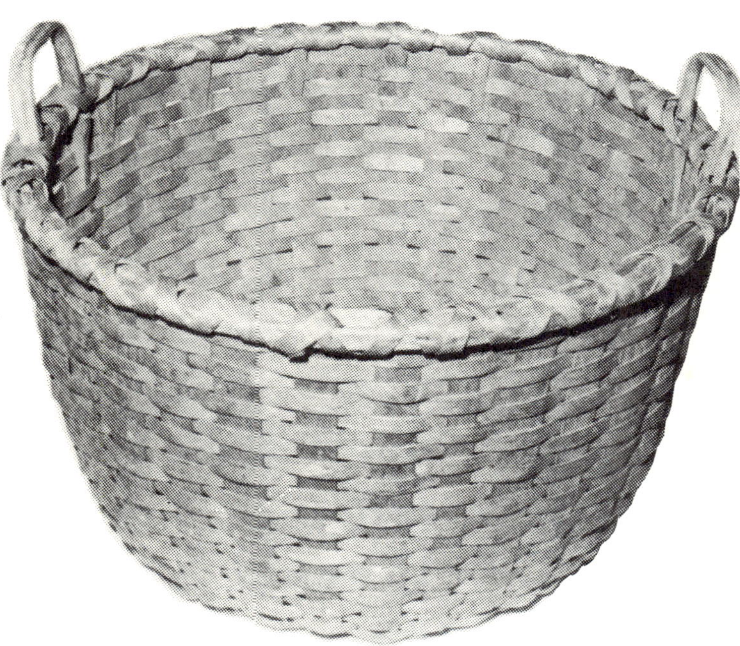

Notice the uniformity of the splint and the wrapped rim used in this Shaker laundry basket from Sabbathday Lake.

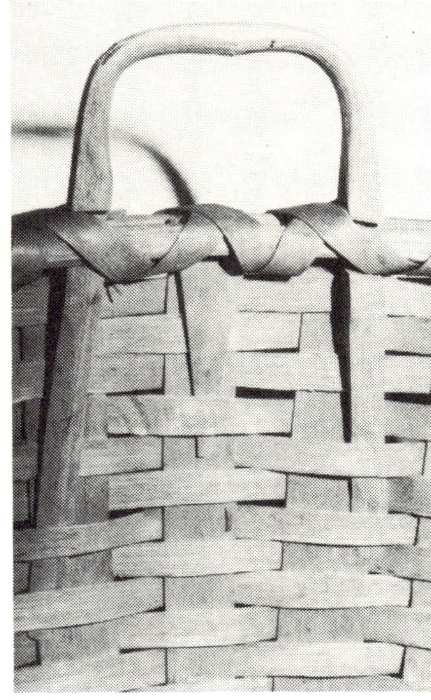

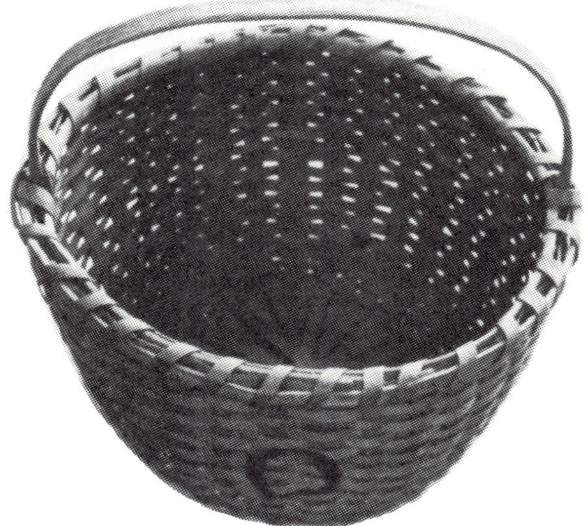

The "O" painted on the side of the basket stands for "Office" which is written on the handle. It was purchased from the Canterbury, N.H., community.

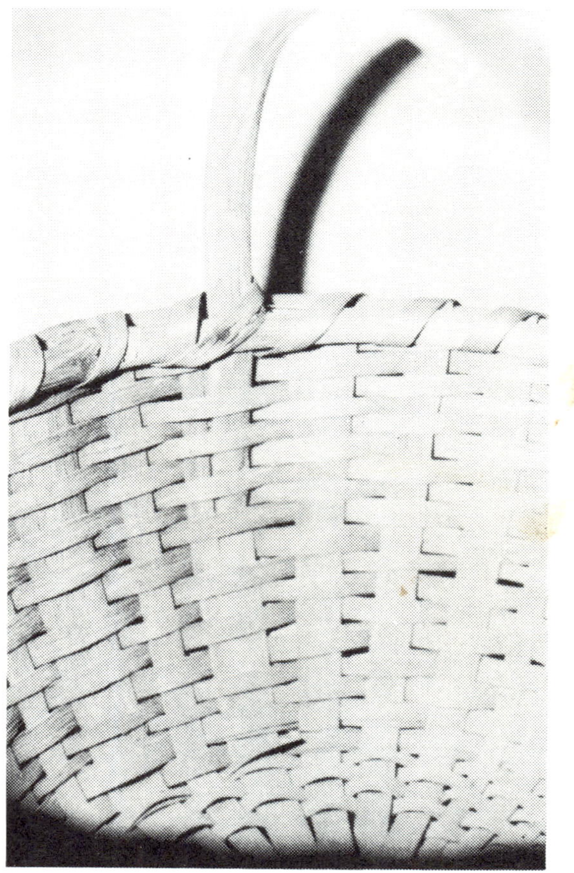

Even though the handle is notched, it has been fastened to the basket by a nail.

nated by 80%, I'd guess. Surely all the oldest were iron. It is also stronger than copper. Sometimes square shoe-pegs were used to attach the bottoms and the tops to their respective strips; fully as many were, I'd guess, tacked — certainly so in later days." There are a few examples where the ends of the fingers are pushed through a slit in the side of the box and doubled back on the inside. The "tacks" holding the fingers are wood.

Prices on the Shaker multi-fingered oval boxes run from $50 to more than $700. The prices vary with size, number of fingers, and color. Last year a yellow five finger box sold for $625 at auction and was quickly resold. Good original paint tends to almost double the value of a box. The last Shaker box was made in 1961 by Delmar Wilson at age 88 in Sabbathday Lake, Maine. The boxes made by him in those last years vary little in style and hand craftsmanship from those made by the Shakers in the earlier days. Today, there are many reproductions. Some of these are excellent such as ones made by a fellow in Maine and another in Michigan who use hand craftsmanship, old forms, and even hand made copper tacks. Fortunately, most of the reproductions bear a stamp or burned mark that indicate their recent vintage.

Unlike the oval box, the basket lacks a Shaker mark of manufacturing. With the possible exception of some small open weave sewing baskets, Shaker baskets are indistinguishable from those made in the world. One dealer has told me that he knows of a couple families who have been making baskets for decades and whose work has all the marks of being Shaker made.

All of the characteristics of Shaker made baskets can be

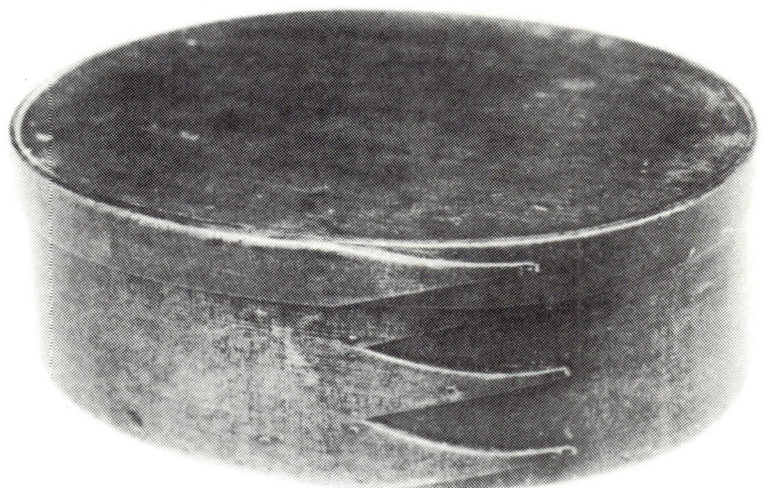

A very early oval box, it has the tips of the fingers inserted through slits on the side and bent back to insure a tight fit. All "tacks" holding the fingers as well as those holding in the top and bottom are wood pegs. Of four examples of this type, three are finished with a red stain.

found in non-Shaker made baskets. These include hand whittled notched handles; cone shaped bottoms; having been made on a mold and, therefore, uniform in size and shape; and an even width to the plaits. Gloria Roth Teleki in her book, *The Baskets of Rural America,* uses the phrase "could be Shaker" and states "without proof of provenance, positive identification is all but impossible." A New England dealer who is a close friend of the Canterbury Shakers related his conversation with Sister Bertha Lindsey in which she expresses her uncertainty in identifying Shaker made baskets although she had made many of them in her younger years. Unlike oval boxes, baskets can not be identified as having been a product of Shaker hands.

— September, 1978

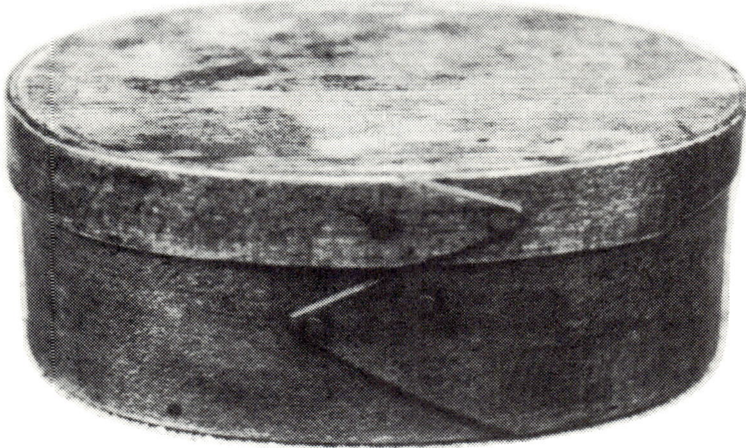

Although this particular box is signed by a Shaker sister, it represents the "Harvard" style that was also made by many box manufacturers besides the Shakers.

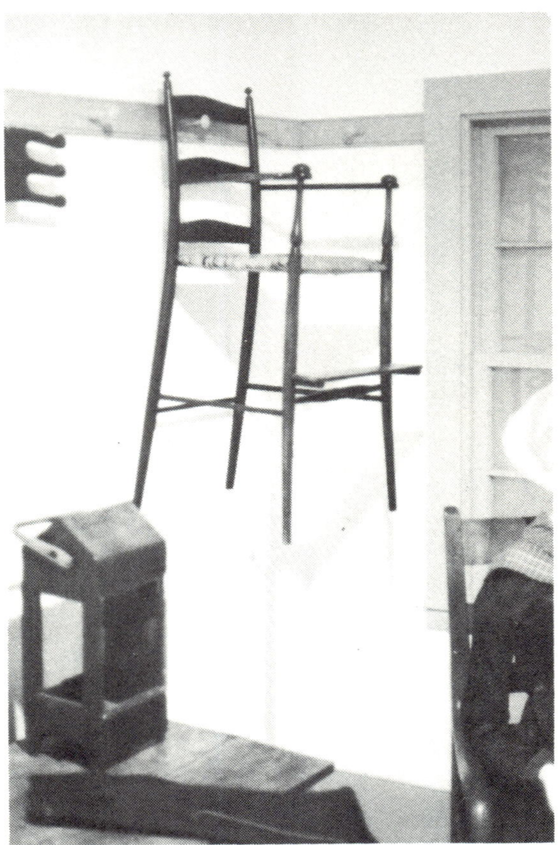

Mt. Lebanon high chair relecting the fineness of Shaker craftsmanship in the chair industry. (Western Reserve Historical Society Museum, Cleveland).

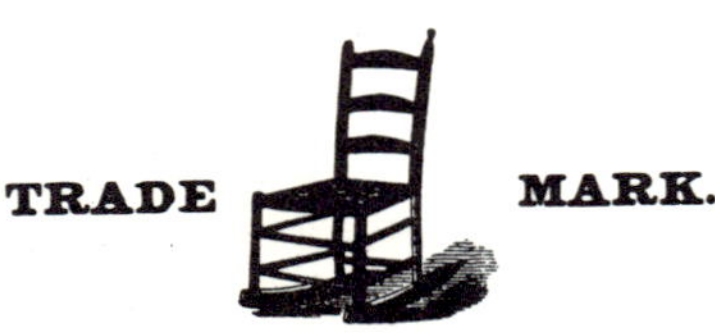

The above Trade-Mark will be attached to every genuine Shaker Chair, and none others are of our make, notwithstanding any claims to the contrary.

NOTICE.

All persons are hereby cautioned not to use or counterfeit our Trade-Mark.

A copy of the Shaker trade mark used on chairs manufactured at Mt. Lebanon, New York. A likeness of this as well as the size number is often found on the legs or slats of Shaker chairs.

Chairs

Whenever antique people think of Shaker they think of oval boxes and chairs. These two items seem to be the most desired of Shaker artifacts, perhaps because they are the easiest to definitely identify and are the most abundant of Shaker items. Chairs are significant also because they are the only pieces of furniture that were mass produced for sale to the world. All other Shaker furniture was made either for themselves or to meet a special custom order.

The topic of Shaker chairs is a difficult subject to consider because 1) it is a vast area to cover, and 2) there is surprisingly little information available. The first of these reasons can be seen by examing the catalogues of the Mt. Lebanon chair factory. Therein are pictured 42 different styles - all rockers. Add to these the same number made as straight chairs and other known chairs (such as the bentwood and spindle backs)

produced at Mt. Lebanon and better than an hundred variations can be quickly tabulated. Add even more by considering those manufactured at Hancock, Enfield (Connecticut and New Hampshire) as well as the other communities and it is apparent that there is an huge amount of material to be covered. The second reason why the consideration of chairs is difficult is the lack of information. Here again, considering the catalogued, mass produced chairs of the South Family at Mt. Lebanon, there are many questions that have not, to my knowledge, been answered. When did the arms change in style from a smooth curve to having an elbow? How can chairs be dated by the design of their finials? When did the use of screws instead of pegs to hold on the rockers begin? And beyond Mt. Lebanon, there is even less information. Union Village, Ohio, for ex-

ample, produced hundreds of chairs but a description of a "typical" Union Village chair has yet to be written.

Almost from the beginning, the Shakers made chairs to be sold. The November, 1889, issue of the Shaker publication, **The Manifesto**, places the date at 1776 in New Lebanon, New York, although this is ten years prior to the founding of that community. Dr. Edward Andrews, in **The Community Industries of the Shakers**, cites an early manuscript as the first reliable evidence: "In the daybook of Joseph Bennet Jr. on October 21, 1789, it is recorded in this book that three chairs were sold to one Elizah Slosson for 11 shillings." From that date on, there are numerous references to the making and selling of chairs.

The "mass producing" of chairs as a major business at New Lebanon developed about the mid 1800's. Earlier Shaker chairs had been equipped with the unique device that we now call a tilter. A small wooden ball was held in a hollowed out socket in the base of the rear legs and held in place by a leather thong fastened through the side of the leg. This device permitted the chair to lean backwards while staying flat on the floor. In 1852, George O. Donnell took out a patent on a metal variation of the tilter, undoubtably with the idea towards production. I have seen these in pewter and in brass with the latter one having the patent date stamped into it.

About the same time, Robert Wagan became trustee over the chair industry and used his skills to develop the industry into a prospering business. Under his leadership, a new factory was built (1872), catalogues were printed (beginning in 1874), and a gold stamp was used to guarantee the authenticity of the Shaker chair against imitations. (It is interesting to note that the Sufi, a contemporary commune, now owns the chair factory and is seeking to renew the manufacture of chairs there.)

While chair manufacturing continued at Mt. Lebanon until the 1930's, it had reached its peak in the last quarter of the 19th century when the Shakers proclaimed the high quality of their product:

"There continues a constant demand for the famous Shaker chairs, sofas, footrests, and numerous other articles...We are quite positive that the South Family at Mount Lebanon is the champion chair maker of the world. The work is of the very best and it is known that

They're useful -- ornamental Two grand principals combined.
You may search the whole world over,
Nor better chairs you'll find.
Then their sofas and their footrests
Are the best the world can give;
Do not try to find their equal,
For you cannot while you live."

(**The Manifesto**, July, 1895)

The chairs produced at the Mt. Lebanon factory came in eight sizes and were numbered accordingly. "0" was the smallest size with its seat measuring 12 x 10 inches. The "7" was the largest chair produced and had a seat of 22 x 18½ inches. Variations in the back included slats or cushion and included a rail across the top upon

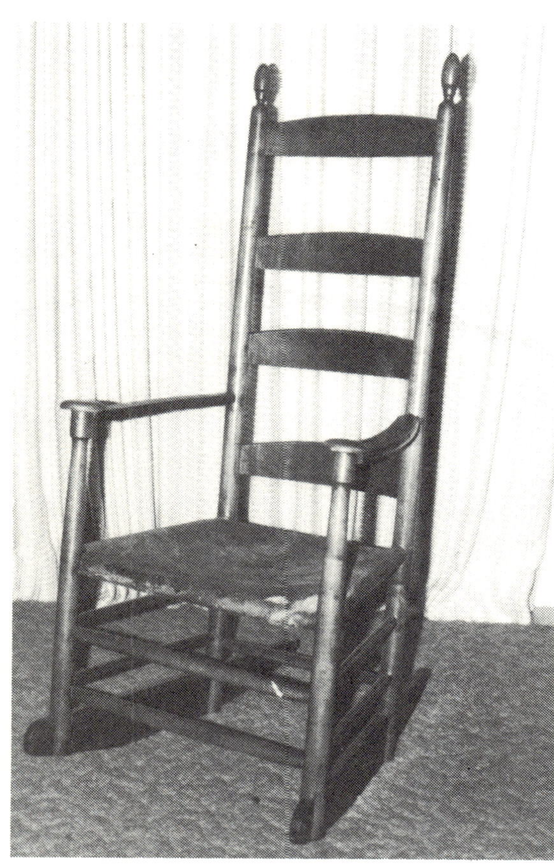

Very early (latter 18th century or early 19th) rocker from Hancock, Massachusetts. Private collection.

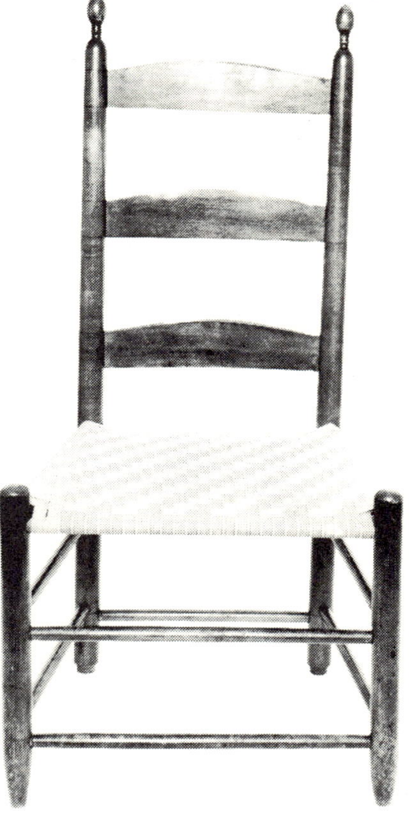

The delicate shape of the finial and taper of the back post attest to this chair's early date. The chamfered upper edge of the ladders is supporting evidence as well as the taper on all the rungs. Note the tilting buttons on the rear legs. Photograph and caption by John Kassay.

which to tie a cushion. The typical
Shaker seat was one of woven
tapes although braid and plush
seats could be ordered in fourteen
different colors, including pea-
cock blue.

A large mail order business in
chairs was established as well a
wholesale business and regular
trade routes throughout the
Northeast were developed. Shaker chairs were handled by furniture dealers in many cities including New York, Boston, Philadelphia, Chicago and Milwaukee.
The selling of the chairs through
these last two outlets would account for the occasional
"finding" of Shaker chairs at
country auctions in the Mid-west.
An attempt was even made to sell
the chairs in England as had been
done with the herbal products.

New Lebanon (called Mt. Lebanon after the establishment of a
post office at the Shaker community in 1861) had the major chair
producing business but all communities appeared to have made
chairs to sell. References to Richard McNemar of Union Village
note him as having produced
2,829 chairs up until May, 1821,
and he, as well as others, made
many more after that date. I often
wonder what ever happened to all
those Ohio Shaker chairs.

Next month's article will consider some general guides to the
desirability and purchasing of
Shaker chairs.

— February, 1977

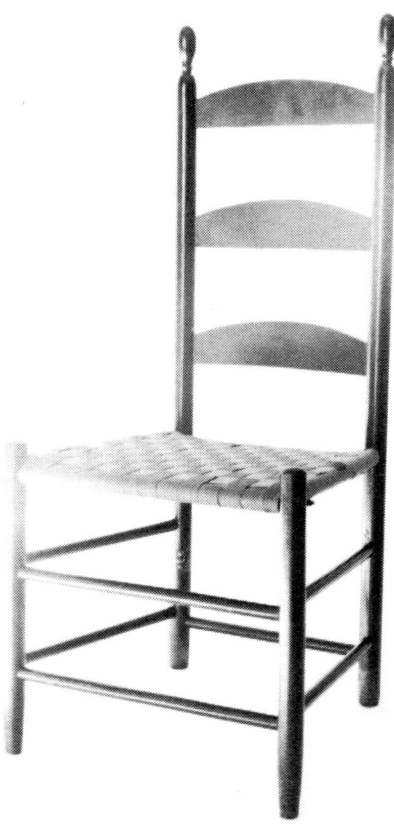

**Purchased from the chair factory at Mt. Lebanon,
the poorly shaped finial, lack of well defined taper
on the back post, general feeling of heaviness
throughout and the absence of taper on the rungs
makes the piece less desirable. Note the decal on the
inside of the rear leg. Photograph and caption by
John Kassay.**

Ohio Chairs

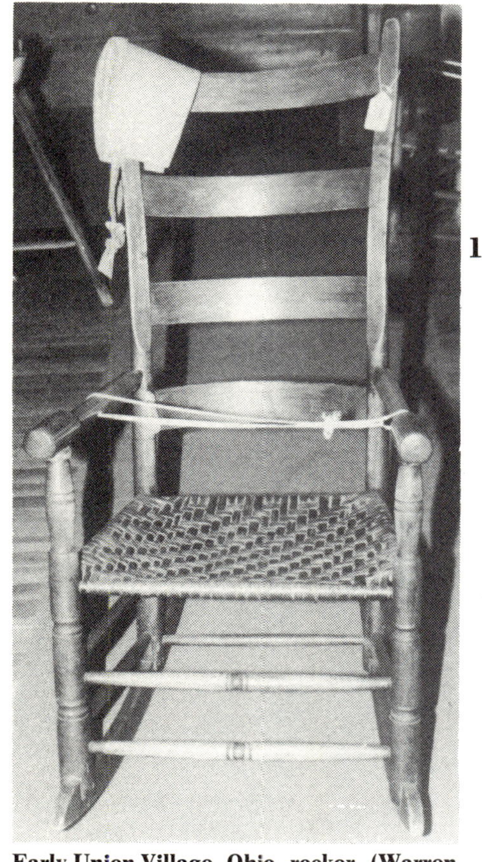

Early Union Village, Ohio, rocker. (Warren County Historical Society)

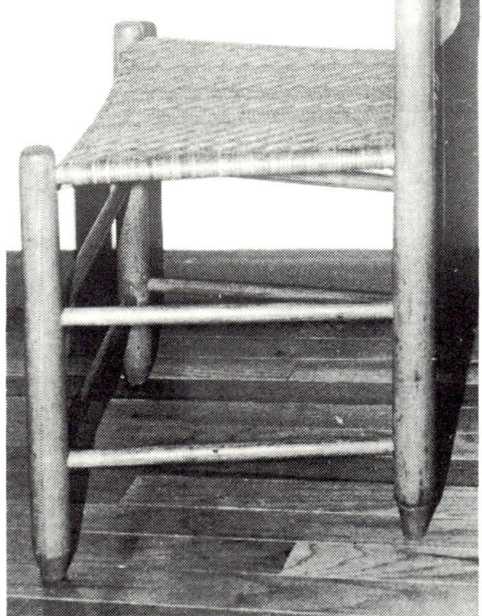

The nicely formed slats and shaped finials reflect the influence of Eastern design standards although the heavy uprights, the taper at the feet, and cantalope color indicate its Union Village origin. The top of front post is stamped #5. (Collection of Mr. and Mrs. Jack Rhodus)

In contrast to their Eastern counterparts for which a specific community origin can often be given, Ohio chairs are seldom properly acknowledged as Shaker. Many chairs are mistakenly called "Shaker" while the real thing is usually overlooked.

The chairs manufactured at the South Family in Mt. Lebanon, New York, followed certain patterns of style that were common in most of the New England communities for at least a century. The fineness of the slats, mushroom and curvature on the arms, rug cutter or bentwood rockers, simplicity of the uprights, and variations of the finials at the tops of the rear posts, all provide the collector who has even a little knowledge with insights into the Shaker heritage of a chair. Chair manufacturing in the East was largely standardized and reached its peak with the vast production at Mt. Lebanon in the 1870's and 1880's. There were, and still are, large quantities of Eastern Shaker chairs for purchase, examination and the determination of stylistic qualities. None of this is true with Ohio chairs. There are few well-documented Ohio Shaker chairs and few solid concepts of style can be learned from a study of these chairs.

Time is probably the major obstacle in studying Ohio (Kentucky and Indiana) Shaker furniture. Furniture is constantly being purchased today in the East from people who had received it from the Shakers when they left Alfred, Maine (1931), or Mt. Lebanon (1947), or Hancock, Mass. (1960). In fact, two of the Shaker communities (Canterbury, New Hampshire, and Sabbathday Lake, Maine) are still in existence. In contrast to this, the Shakers left Ohio more than sixty-five years ago and there are very few people around today who acquired furnishings directly from the Ohio Shakers.

Adding to the difficulties in finding and recognizing Ohio Shaker furniture is the brevity of the

One of the greatest problems confronting Shaker collectors is determining whether or not a piece of furniture is of Shaker origin. While this topic was considered in depth in the first article on Shaker to appear in the *Ohio Antique Review* (November, 1975), the subject of Ohio chairs points out the difficulty in recognition of Shaker.

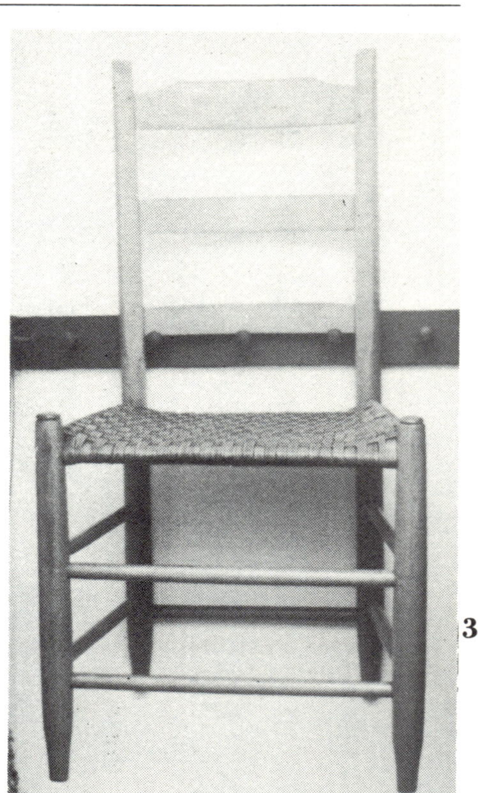

A donut turning appears on the top of the front legs of some Ohio Shaker chairs.

4.

From Watervliet, Ohio, this chair has a donut or biscuit turning on the top of the front legs. It also combines a notched slat with two straight ones. Another chair of this style in a private collection has D.R. (dining room) painted on the bottom. (Kettering-Moraine Museum)

3.

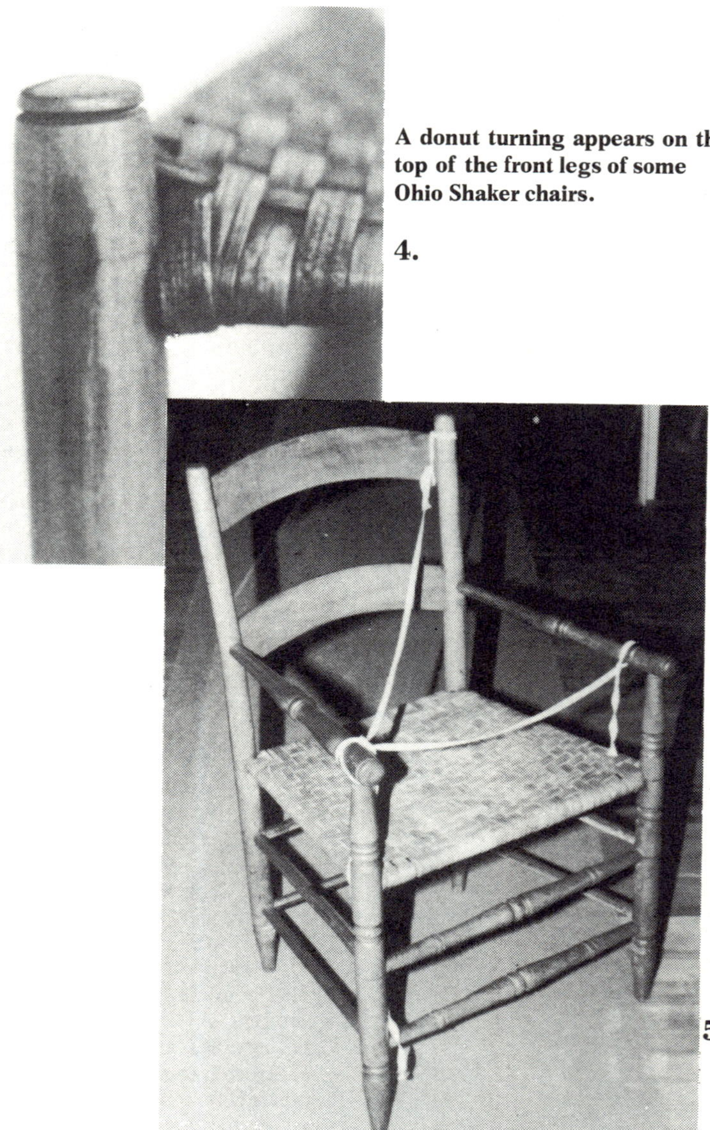

5.

Boldly turned arms, uprights and stretchers set Ohio Shaker chairs apart from their Eastern counterparts. The back on this chair does not reflect a high quality of craftsmanship. (Warren County Historical Society)

period of their initial organization. The first convert to Shakerism was made in Ohio in 1805. Within fifteen years, Union Village reached its peak of 600 members and then declined by almost half in the next fifteen years. This rapid growth and decline would suggest that the Shakers depended upon the furnishings brought by new converts and did not have the need or opportunity to standardize designs. This meant that much of the Ohio Shaker furniture reflected the styles and customs of the surrounding area rather than the classic Shaker lines that had developed in the East. This can be seen in the heavy, strongly turned, uprights of some examples shown in the accompanying photographs.

Early Ohio Shaker chairs had bold ring turnings on the uprights, front rungs, and, in some cases, on the arms. With the exception of an occasional small cap, mushroom hand holds do not appear on Ohio Shaker chairs. Instead, the arm is either turned or a variation of the cyma curve. The front upright often has a swell (Photograph 1) between the seat and the arm and in this respect is similar to the chairs of the Eastern communities. Where there are no arms, the posts often terminate above the seat with a delicate donut (Photographs 3, 4).

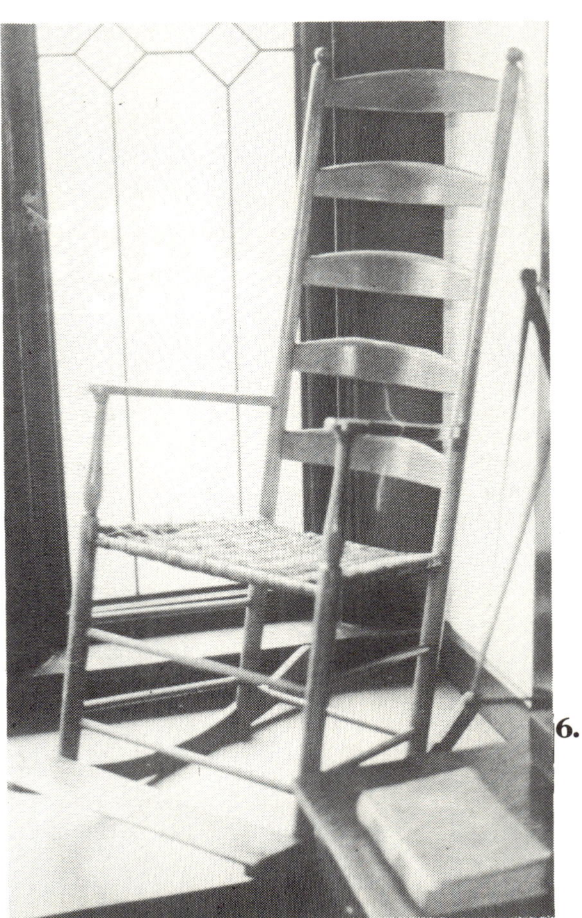

6.

Even the back stretcher has turnings on this early Union Village chair. (Warren County Historical Society)

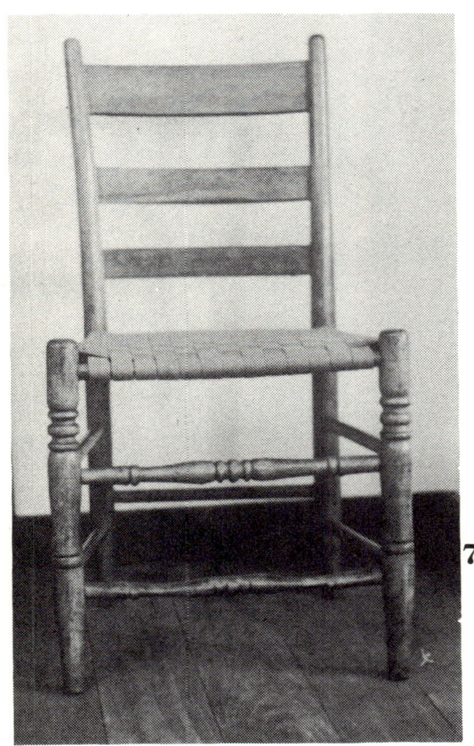

7.

Bold turnings and graduated slats such as seen on this Watervliet, Ohio, chair are not in keeping with most Shaker collectors' concepts or desires. (Kettering-Moraine Museum)

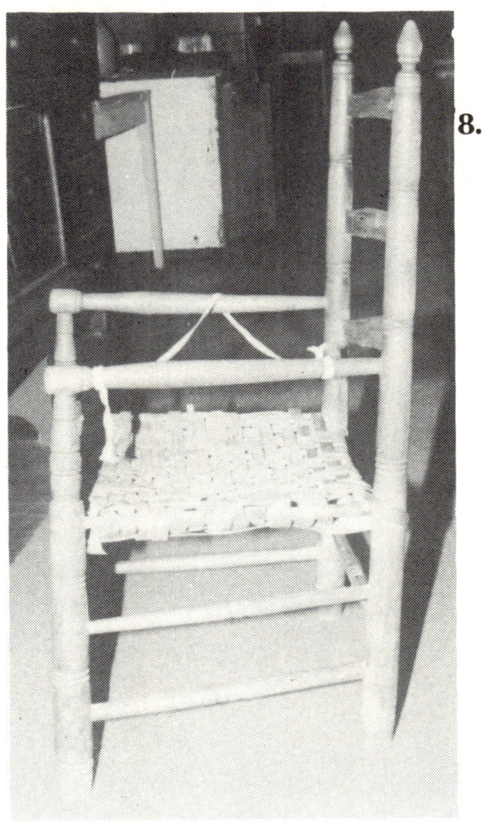

8.

These posts often meet the floor with an elongated heart shape which is also found on many Kentucky chairs (Photograph 5).

The rear posts terminate with a variety of forms: a flattened surface called "mule ears" (Photograph 1) finial in the shape of a ball or egg (Photograph 6); or simply cut off. The lack of any finial or special treatment to the top of the rear uprights is typical of Ohio Shaker chairs but unheard of (except on dining chairs) in the East.

The slats on Ohio chairs can vary from extremely thin, nicely bowed, (Photograph 2) to very heavy, straight examples (Photograph 7). The rise in the arch at the top of the slat also varies greatly. The most noticeable characteristic of the slats on the Ohio Shaker chairs is the notched corners (Photograph 9). Usually all slats are notched but, sometimes, only the top one is. The wide slats of thin pieces of wood, slight bow, notched corners, and fitted into uprights terminating in a mule's ear are the marks of an Ohio Shaker chair. Examine this example of a dining chair and the other chairs shown and then you will have an idea as to the difficulty in recognizing Ohio Shaker furniture.

— December, 1978

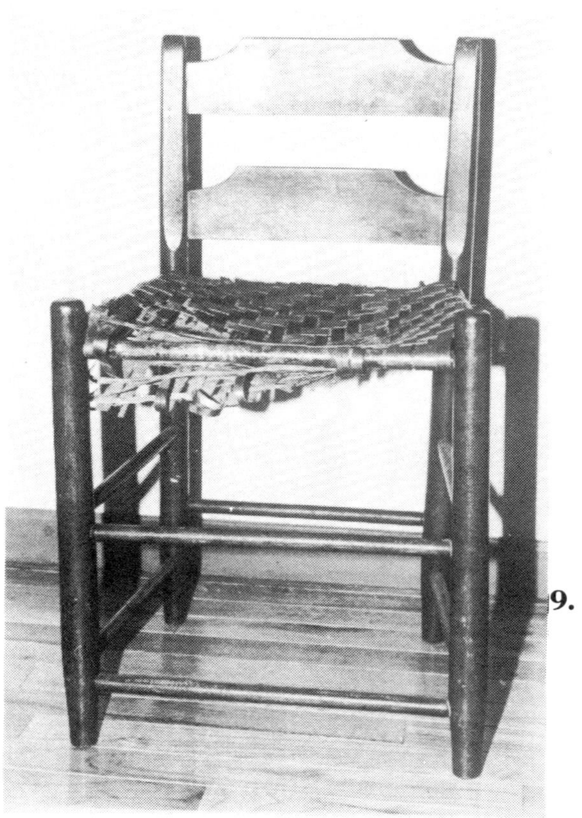

9.

Union Village dining chair in red stain has the typical notched slats. (Collection of Mr. and Mrs. Jack Rhodus)

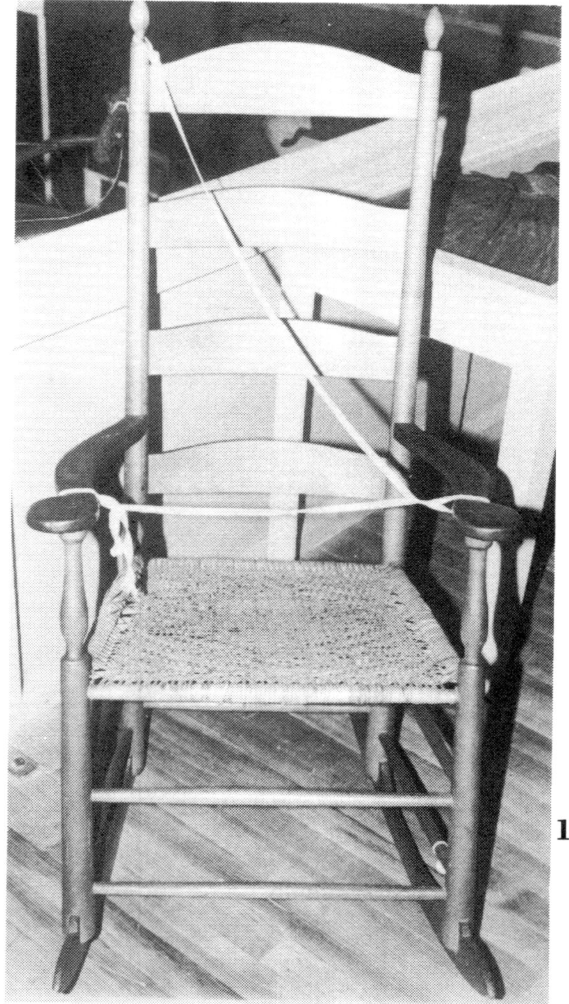

10.

The urn turning on the uprights between the seat and arms, cyma-curve arms and finely shaped slats give this Union Village chair a graceful style comparable to most Eastern chairs. (Warren County Historical Society)

Candlestands

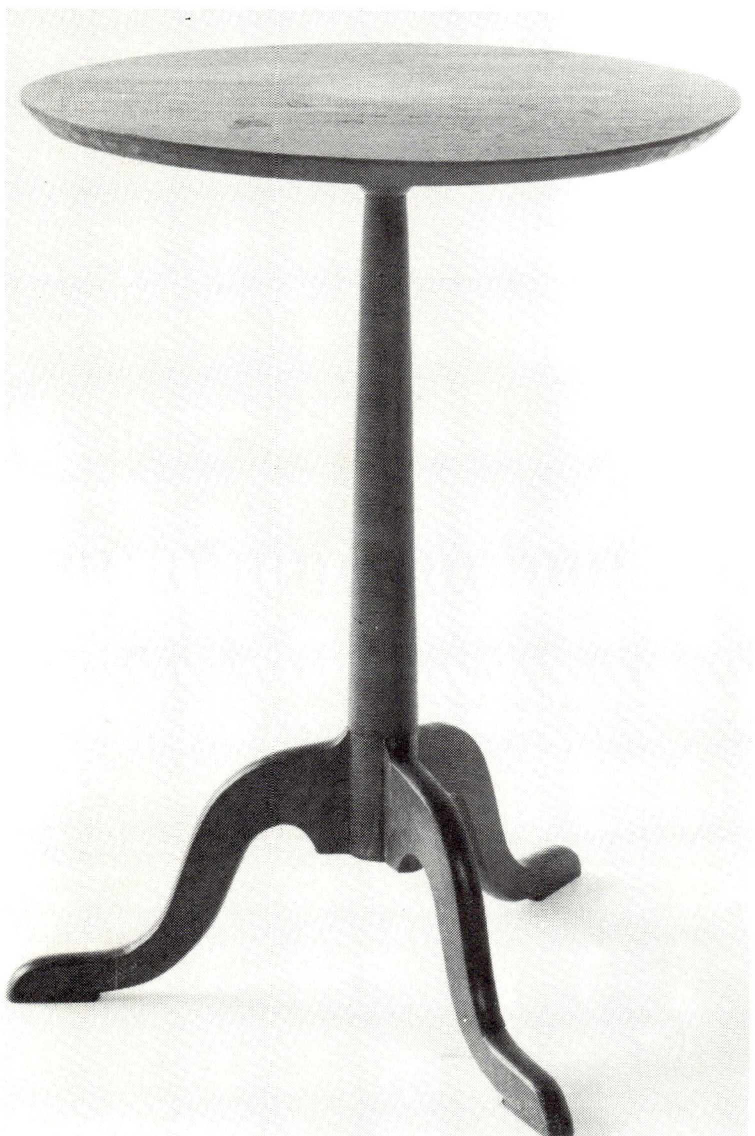

The round stand here illustrated has a less interestingly shaped edge **1.** than that pictured in Photo #3. It is more of a bend. The rod shaped pedestal is, in form, more severe and would take less time to produce than that of #3. The curved edge of the Queen Anne leg make it delightful - almost incompatable with the rest of the table. The working time saved on the pedestal was used here, except, I feel, the edges were shaped by machine. If that is true, the piece could be later than the 1850 attribution. Wood working machines made their appearance in America around 1840. The top is 19" in diameter and the heighth is 26". The wood is cherry. - Photograph and commentary by John Kassay; The Shaker Museum, Old Chatham, New York.

In studying Shaker candlestands, the results can often be more confusion than conclusion. While there are two classic styles that are definitely Shaker, there are many varieties besides these two that make it very difficult to attribute Shaker craftsmanship.

The two styles that are classically Shaker are the spider leg and a variation of the snake foot, both with a shaft that tapers only gradually from where the top sits to where the legs join. The spider leg is a convex arch with no embellishment from floor to upright. In its best form, the arch continues until it meets the upright at almost a right angle (Photo #2). This style leg was altered on many candlestands so that the top of the legs would curve upward to mesh with the lines of the shaft (Photo #3).

The second classic style is that of the snake foot (Photo #1) which is similar to the Queen Anne style legs of a half century earlier. The primary distinction between the two is that the Shaker foot has a continuous upward movement from the floor to the upright while the Queen Anne has a downward dip towards the floor at the point where the foot becomes a leg. A second distinction is that the Shaker snake foot usually does not have a well defined padded foot.

On either of the two classical style legs, the most identifiable and desirable shaft on a Shaker candlestand is the rod-like support that offers no fancy turnings and varies less than an inch in diameter from top to bottom (Photo #1). Often, the shaft becomes more bulbous where the legs are joined to it (Photo #3). Some of the uprights on the early stands are very crude in this bulbous portion and look like caveman clubs while those on the later stands are as elaborately turned as any non-Shaker stand. This variety of pedestals, matched with the classical snake foot, can be found on Shaker pedestal desks and sewing stands as well as candle stands.

More variety is found in candlestands in the legs and tops. Both the spider and snake foot vary greatly in quality from the very fine to the crude. Then there are stands with peg legs, some being doweled into the shaft directly and others being joined into a round block that in turn holds the shaft. There is one at the Golden Lamb Inn, Lebanon, Ohio, that has for its legs "bent sticks" that make up half the distance between the floor and the top.

Most Shaker candlestands have round tops although oval, square and rectangular tops are also found. Any of these have been made with or without rimmed edges. Tilt-top tables were reputed to have been made only in Maine and Massachusetts. Some stands were made with a thumb

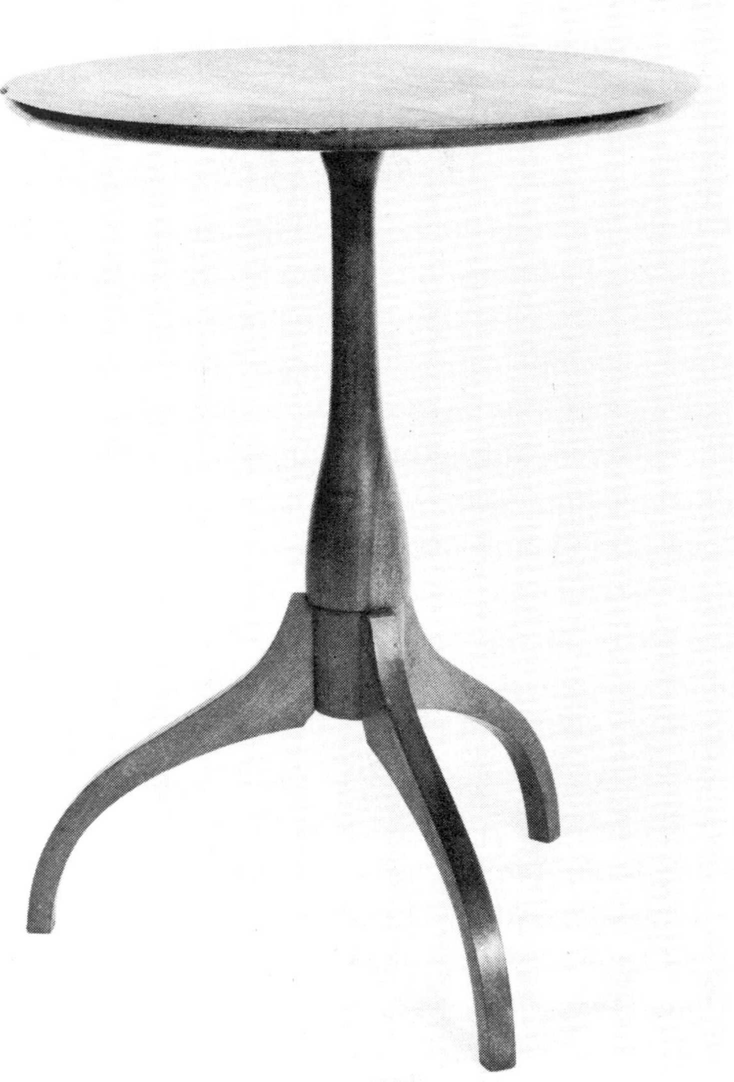

3. **This stand was probably made in the first half of the 19th century and is a good example of a one of a kind, made for their own use, stand. The shaped edge of the top is curved nicely. Also, the shape of the pedestal is curved interestingly. The umbrella or spider foot leg is nice but could be more pleasing if the leg were tapered more towards the floor line. - Photograph and comments by John Kassay; Museum of Fine Arts, Boston.**

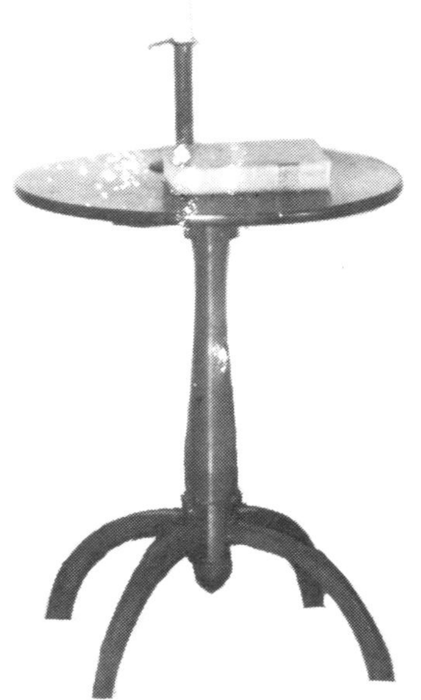

This round stand shows the 2. spider legs but is unique in having four instead of the usual three legs. Note the rod-like or club-like pedestal on this stand. It is a transition between those on the stands in Photos #1 and #3. Also note the added turning at the base of the shaft and the cleat top joining top and upright.
- Hancock Village, Mass.

screw where the pedestal and top meet so they could be lowered or heightened. Others had one drawer constructed between the upright and the top. Variety seems to be more the rule than the exception.

The construction of Shaker candlestands follows closely that of other stands of the period. The early stands had one piece tops while those made about the turn of the century and into the 20th century have two or three piece tops. These tops can be as much as an inch thick with a squared edge although the better made stands have tops that have been chamfered or beveled to make a fine crisp edge.

The legs, other than the peg legs, are dovetailed into the up-

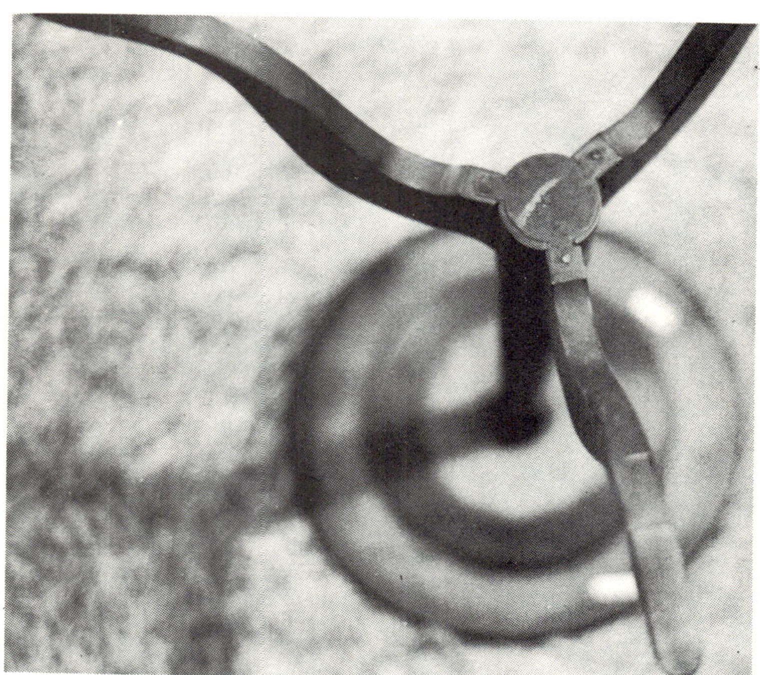

4. This photo shows the piece of tin that often covers the dovetail joints of the legs and shaft. In the background can be seen the round, chamfered donut base that is screwed into the top and holds the upright.

right. Often a piece of tin covers the dovetailing. On the underside of the top is either a cleat or a donut shaped base that is screwed into the top for the purpose of receiving the upright support. The pedestal then fastens into this base of the top either by being threaded or by friction and glue.

If it seems that, as you read this, very little definite has been said, then you have come to an understanding of Shaker candlestands. Beyond a few classically Shaker characteristics looms uncertainty. A person only needs to walk through the still functioning Sabbathday Lake community to become aware of this. In each room, there is a candlestand that is different than the one in the previous room and will be different than the one in the next room...even some that have had the base and top married over the years. Line them up side by side and study them. Seek out the common elements. And soon a conclusion will be reached: there is a lot of variety among Shaker candlestands!

— April, 1977

Desks - tall

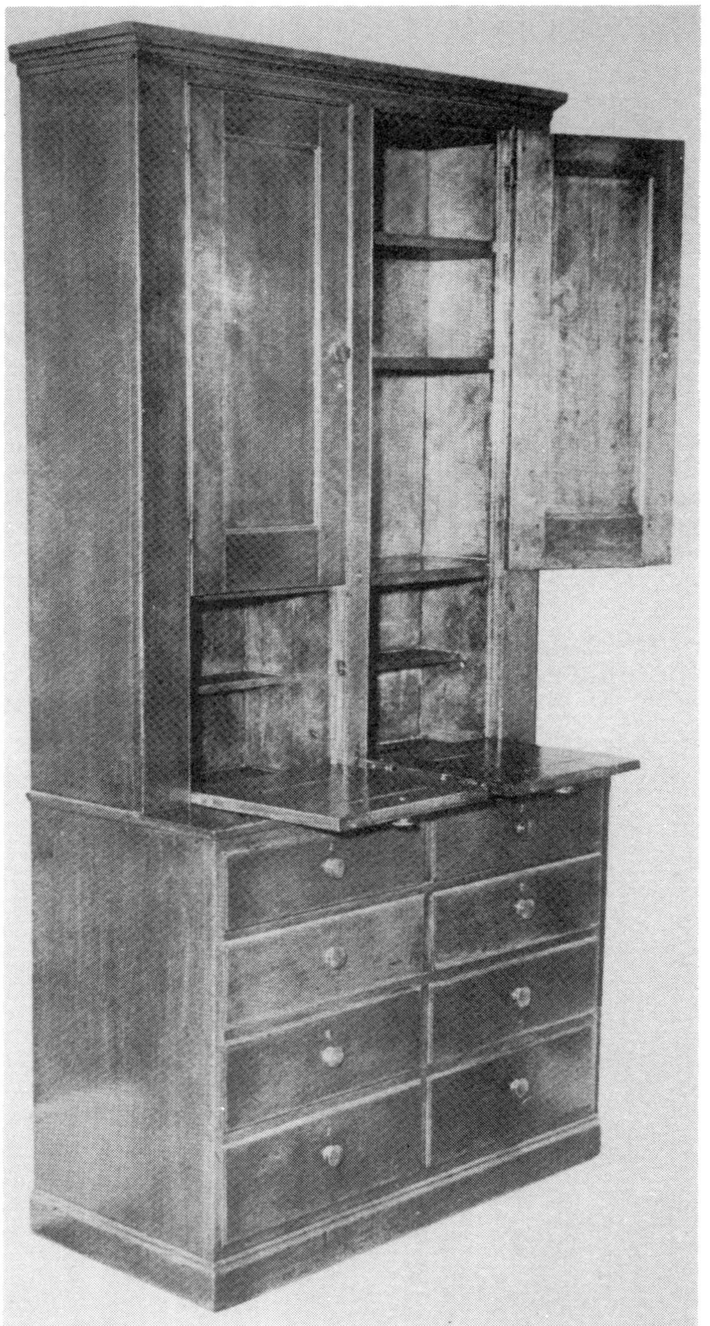

Figure 1

Private Collection

In the category of Shaker desks, there are four subdivisions. The first is what I call Tall Desks or Secretaries. These have cupboard or book space above the writing service. The second is built-ins. These were often in workshops and have a drop front for a writing surface which is surrounded by drawer space. The third division is, for lack of a better title, small desks. These would include a slant front with drawer space below as well as the desk on frame. These would be any stationary desk without a cupboard top. The final division is **table-top or portable** desks. These usually have a slanted writing surface and a drawer that pulls out the side.

Tall desks or secretaries **are a** good place to begin an examination of Shaker furniture. Many of the characteristics of tall desks are reflective of some of the generalities of almost all Shaker furniture. Let us look at the three desks in the photographs and see some of these characteristics.

Before we do that, though, a side comment might be made about these three desks. All three are in Ohio and have been purchased within the last couple of years. These ought to serve as encouragement for new collectors for they are evidence that good quality Shaker furniture is still available and does come on the market with some regularity.

The first generalization that can be derived from these desks is that the Shakers made furniture for themselves. Therefore, **any Shaker desk is not just** Shaker made but also Shaker used. With the exception of the Mt. Lebanon chairs, and some custom orders, the Shakers did not make furniture for the public outside their communities. Upon occasion, they would make a cupboard or some other piece at the request of a neighbor. I have seen a bow-front chest of drawers that was made at Canterbury, New Hampshire, on a special order. But generally speaking, major pieces of Shaker furniture were made for themselves and to be used within the community.

This leads to the second idea which is that each Shaker piece is an individual creation. While there are certain guidelines and styles, it seems that each major

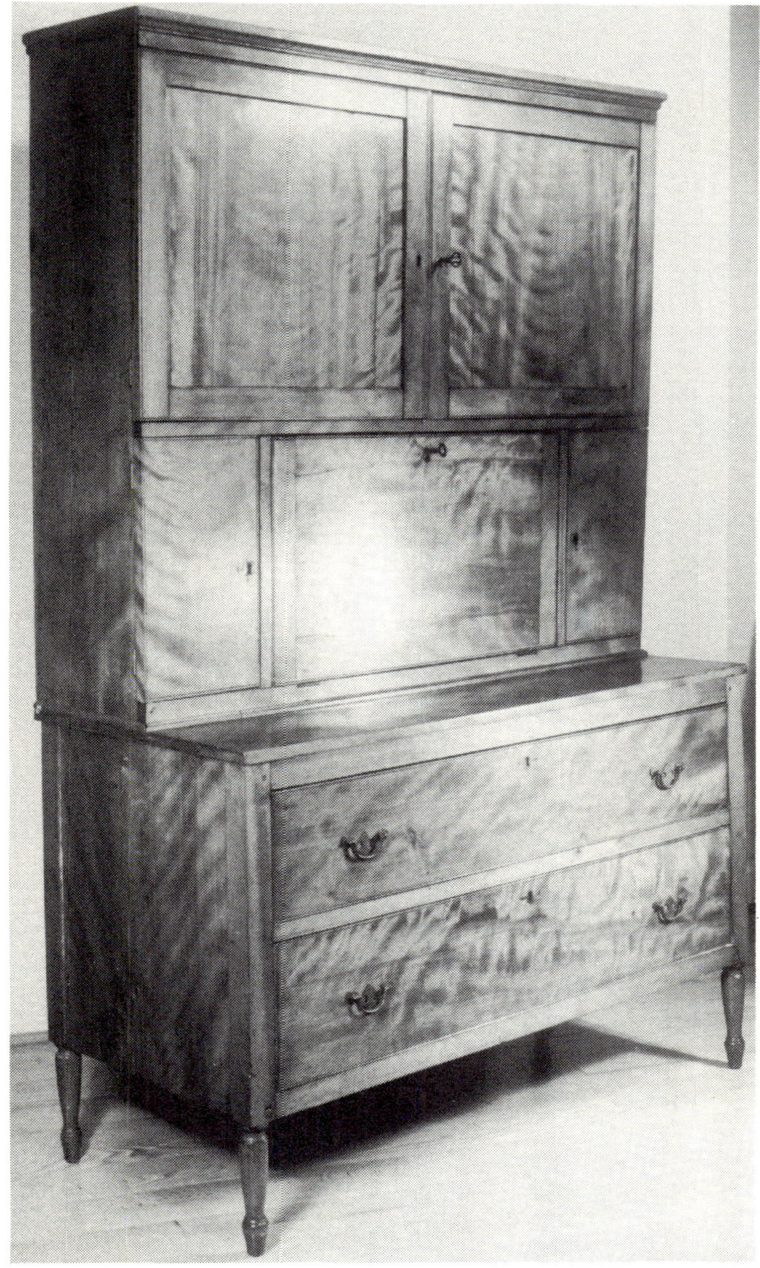

piece of Shaker furniture was made for a particular purpose and a particular place and therefore is distinctively different from any other piece made for a similar use. This can be easily seen in the three desks pictured. In addition to these, I have seen a dozen secretary type desks and no two are alike. The desk in Photo No. 1 is similar to the double trustees desk from Pleasant Hill, Kentucky, and to a bookcase desk at the Mt. Lebanon school but is still quite different from those. The desk in Photo No. 2 has an identical base to one pictured in ANTIQUES AT AUCTION but that one has a slant front and is three pieces. This desk is also similar in proportion to one in the New Hampshire Historical Society. The desk in Photo No. 3 is unlike any other. Each and every desk has its own individuality that makes it distinctive.

Pictured here are three excellent pieces of Shaker furniture. They were used for similar purpose and, yet, they are strikingly dissimilar in style and structure. The desk in Photo No. 1 is one piece construction while that in Photo No. 2 is two pieces and No. 3 is three pieces. Most major pieces of Shaker furniture are individual creations of the craftsman.

A third generalization of Shaker furniture is its superb use of space. In these desks, this is apparent in the storage space and in the writing surfaces. All three desks have large and numerous drawers and ample room for keeping journals, ledgers, or other books. The drop front writing surface makes for compactness when not in use. The slide-out writing surface in the elegant desk in Photo No. 3 is a common occurrence on Shaker pieces, especially sewing desks. Perhaps no other furniture makers have made as much use of slide-out shelves as have the Shakers. Shaker furniture has plenty of useful space and surface.

One last generalization can be seen in the desk in Photo No. 2. Before the influence of Victorian styles after the 1880's, the Shakers made little use of decoration or ornamentation. Often, the only decoration used in their furniture was the natural color and grain of the wood. This desk is curly or flaming birch. There are chairs to match as well as others in curly or bird's-eye maple. Sometimes contrasting walnut and maple were used to give an extra touch. The Shakers often permitted the beauty of the wood to speak for itself.

— April, 1976

Desks - small

As mentioned last month, Shaker desks find their design largely in the purpose for which they were to serve. In order to understand this, it might be helpful to relate the structure of government within the Shaker world. The top level was that of the Ministry. The Ministry might have charge of two or more Societies. For example, the Ministry in the West resided at Union Village, outside Lebanon, Ohio, and was in charge of all the Societies in Ohio, Kentucky and Indiana. The Central Ministry which governed all of the Shaker world because it was the first community to be structurally organized resided at Mt. Lebanon, New York, until its demise in 1947.

There were 20 Societies in the World of Shaker that existed for more than ten years. Each Society was divided into families of 50 - 100 members. Union Village had six families and Pleasant Hill, Kentucky, had eight while Watervliet, Ohio, and West Union, Indiana, had only two apiece. Elders or Eldresses had the same responsibilities as the Ministry but limited to the family in which they resided.

While the Ministry and Elders were in charge of the total leadership of the Shakers, the management of temporal concerns was delegated to the Trustees, and Deacons. The Trustees managed real estate, property and business contacts with the outside world on behalf of the Society. The Deacons and Deaconesses gave oversight to the temporal work of the Family. At each level of government, there were two Brethren and two Sisters.

From this division of responsibilities, it can be seen why desks

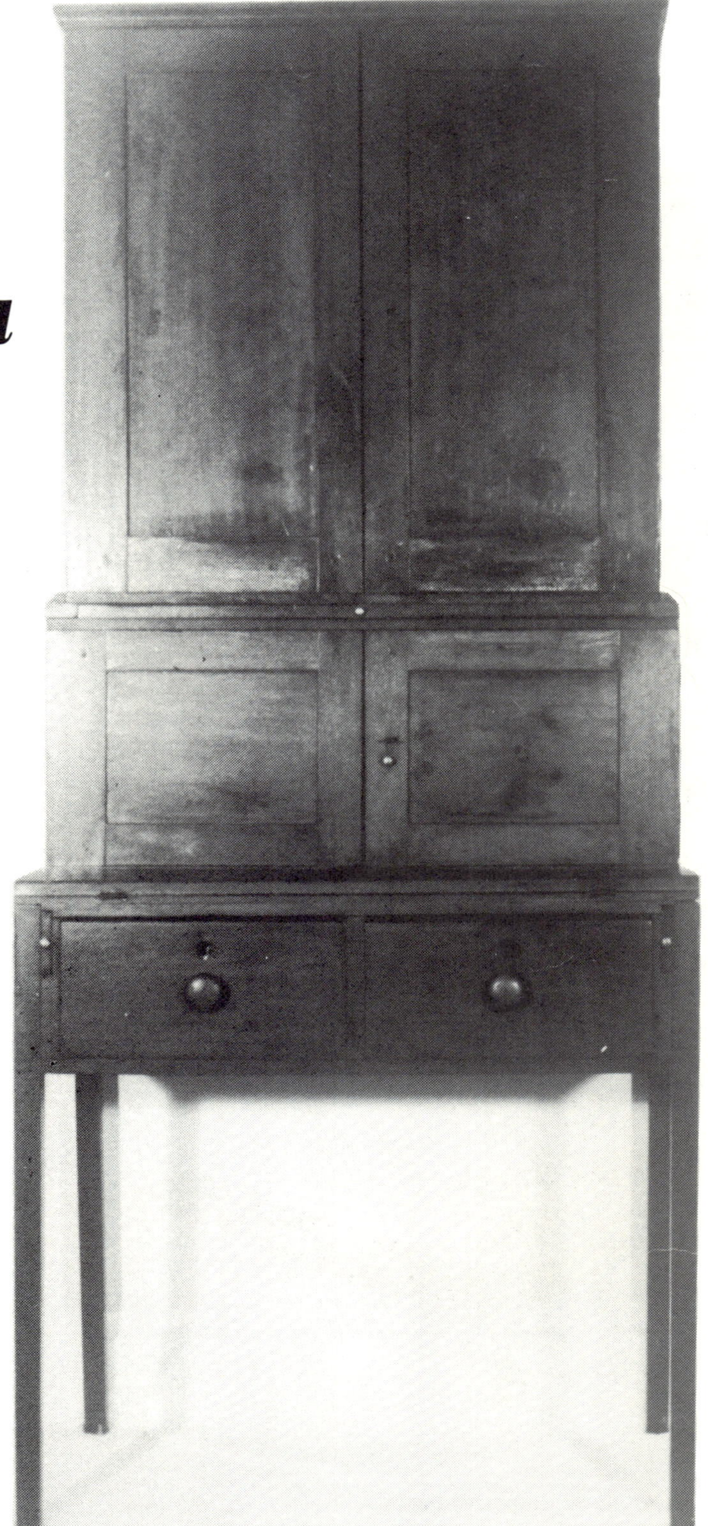

Figure 3   **Private Collection**

intended for use in the Ministry and for Trustees had to provide more book shelves and drawer space than did those to be used by the Deacons. It is probable that all small Shaker desks were intended to be used by the Deacons or Deaconesses or those of lesser stature in the community but not the general members. By lesser stature it is meant the persons in charge of certain departments and shops such as the weavers, basketmakers, herbalists, etc. Detailed records were to be kept of production and business contacts. Desks were needed for work purpose.

With the exception of children in school, the general membership had little or no reason to have access to a desk. Since the Elders and Deacons assumed the responsibilities of most transactions that might need to be made, the general membership's primary need for a desk would be correspondences to friends and relatives. Such communications were not encouraged. In *Shakerism Unmasked* (1828), William J. Haskett suggested the reason for this:

'It is contrary to order to receive or write a letter without the Elders' perusal of it. When a member receives a letter for himself, he is obliged to carry it to the Elders first, and in their presence to open it. He is forbid opening a letter, unless in their presence. If he be a suspicious character, the Elders read the letter; if not, he is permitted to. When a member would correspond with a friend or relative, he must ask permission of the Elders of the family in which be resides, and by whom he is closely questioned as to his business in correspondence; and if congenial to their views, he is permitted to. His letter must be submitted to the perusal of the Elders, and sealed in their presence. By this means any disaffection on the part of the member and the intention of his friends is exposed.

Shaker desks - tall and small - were made for specific purposes and places. Each one was created by a craftsman who probably knew the exact spot where that piece was intended to sit for the next decade or century. Therefore, there is much variance in design depending on the place and function. The desk in photo No. 1 stands out as a superb piece of craftsmanship different than any other Shaker desk. It is cherry with delicately turned legs beginning at the frame in the typically Shaker pencil post. The pull out surface above the drawer is another typical Shaker characteristic in getting the most use from a limited space. While it is often suggested that Western Shaker furniture is more clumsy and less refined than that of the Eastern communities, this desk is as fine as any.

Photo No. 2. This is not a trestle desk for the case is set upon two individual pedestals. It was a poorly conceived design and was subject to the "wiggles." For this reason, the stretcher had to be added at a later date to stabilize it. The design of the pedestal and feet on this desk can be found on other Shaker desks, candlestands and sewing stands. The most common style of Shaker small desks is a similar, but smaller, case centered upon a single pedestal with tripod feet. Such desks were used in school at Enfield, Connecticut, and by the Deaconesses at Hancock, Massachusetts. The feet on these are

Figure # 1

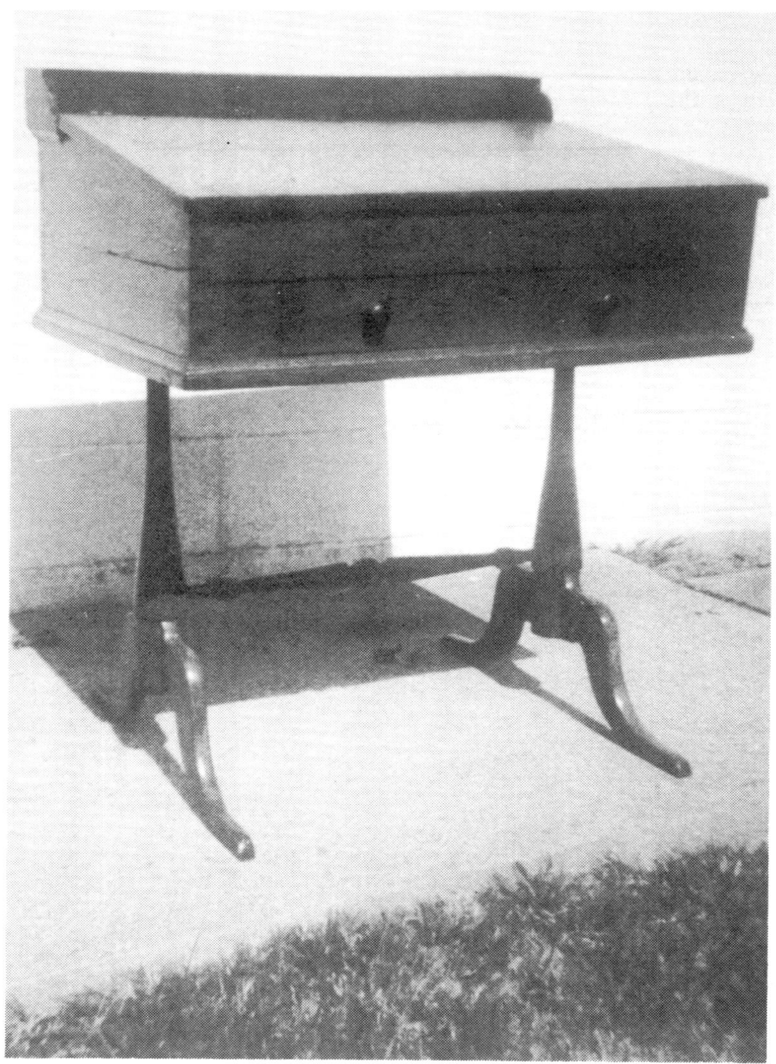

Figure # 2

similar to but not as finely executed as the snake feet on Period Furniture. The top of the leg moves continously downward and does not have an upward surge at the ankle as it begins the foot. This style of desk has unfortunately encouraged "marriages" of nice table desks with left-over bases from Chippendale candlestands.

The lap desk in Photo No. 3. does not lend itself to being combined with a base for it is too small. Edward Andrews in *Shaker Furniture* quotes the following from a 1834 Journal: "Rule for making writing boxes, 22 inches long, 15 inches wide and six deep. 1 drawer for paper. 1 for an inkstand. If any desire it they may be made slanting." Because of the uniformity and relative great number of these, it is believed that these were made for sale to the world rather than restricted to use within the community.

— May, 1976

Figure # 3

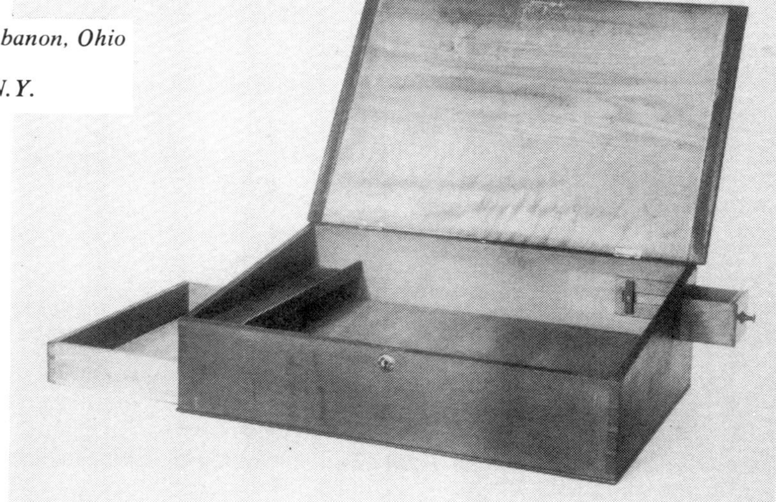

PHOTO CREDITS:
1. Warren County Historical Society, Lebanon, Ohio
2. Private collection
3. The Shaker Museum, Old Chatham, N.Y.
*   Photograph by John Kassay*

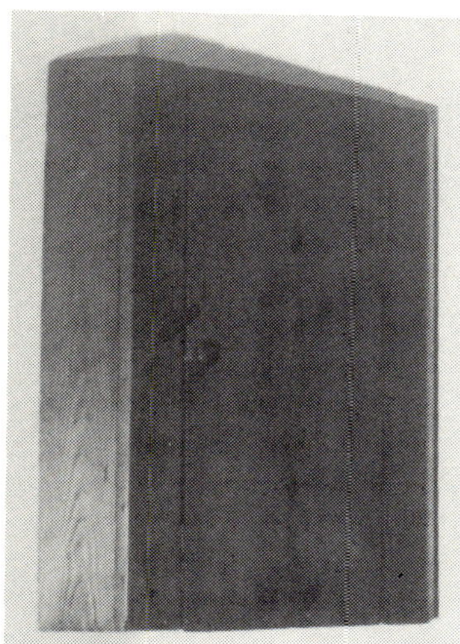

Less than two feet tall, this hanging corner cupboard is from Enfield, Connecticut, and retains its original red stain.

Corner Cupboards

One of the notable differences in furniture of the Eastern and the Western Shaker communities is the corner cupboard. Corner cupboards existed throughout the New England states from the early 18th century but Shaker examples in that section are very few. There are two in the kitchen of the Dwelling House of the Church Family at Hancock, Massachusetts, which are built-ins without doors.

Although a built-in corner cupboard in the former home of Dr. and Mrs. Edward Deming Andrews was erroneously labeled as Shaker in an early *Antiques* article, Mrs. Andrews has commented that she is unaware of examples other than those at Hancock. She has suggested that the Shakers had a dislike for corner furniture and desired to have all furniture to be aligned parallel with the walls. The lone exceptions in the East to this idea seem to be from Enfield, Conn., a community which had a tendency to be eccentric in its designs.

Of four examples from that community, all are hanging corner cupboards varying in size

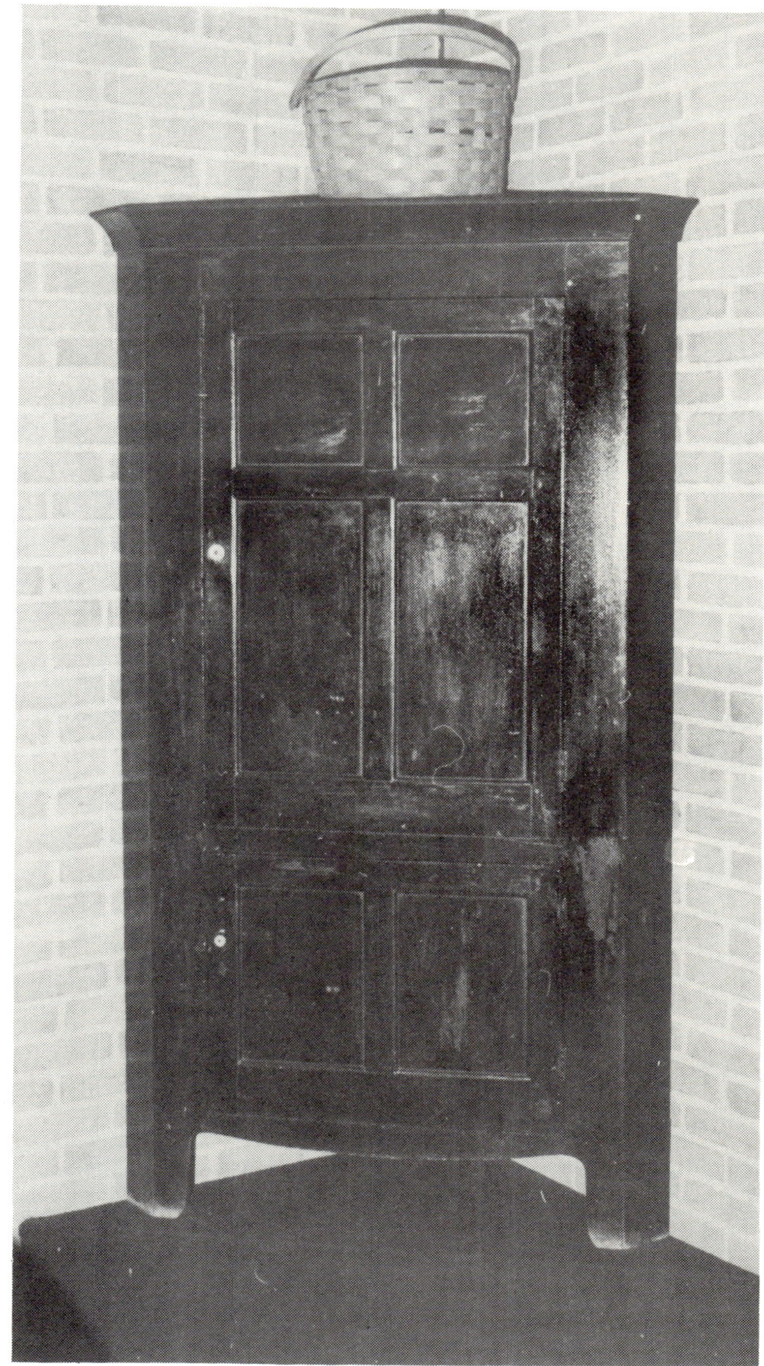

Perhaps the finest of Shaker corner cupboards, this one is only six feet tall. It has the cove molding and the typical Union Village scalloped base as well as the quarter round molding on the panelled doors. (The Otterbein Home, Lebanon, Ohio)

from 12 to 23½ inches in height. The most delightful of these has a glass panelled door and would fit nicely into any home. The pair of built-ins at Hancock and the four hanging ones from Enfield would appear to be a full representation of corner cupboards among the Eastern Shaker communities. John Kassay, who has done elaborate research in preparation of a book on measured drawings of Shaker furniture, has visited major Shaker collections throughout the United States and abroad and confirms this opinion. Free standing Shaker corner cupboards from Eastern communities are unknown.

In contrast to the East, there are numerous examples from Ohio and Kentucky. Pleasant Hill, Kentucky, has a couple of fine examples in the Center Family Dwelling House as well as a superb one resting on the chair rail in the dining room. By far the majority of Shaker corner cupboards seem to have originated in Union Village, Ohio. The Warren County Historical Society in Lebanon and the Otterbein Home, formerly Union Village, have numerous examples. One antique dealer has spoken of buying many for $25 each at the auctions of the former Union Village property in the 1950's.

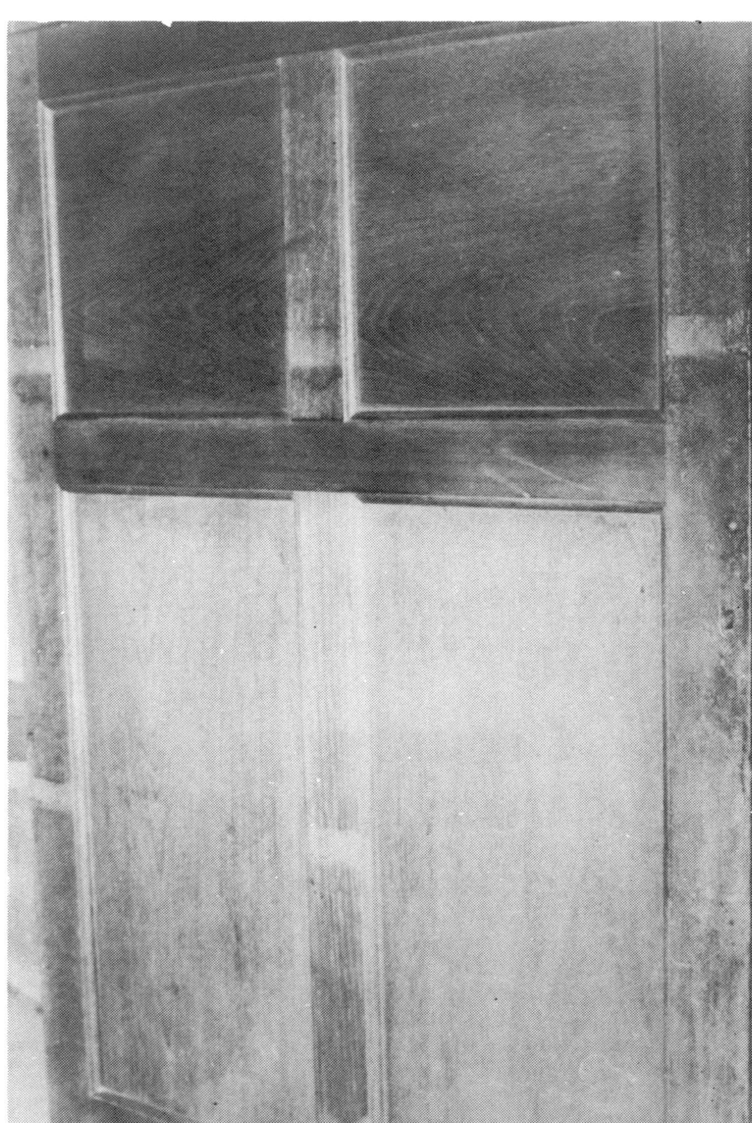

A close up photograph of the interior of the walnut corner cupboard at The Otterbein Home shows the pinning of the stiles and the Shaker quarter round molding around the panels. This quarter round is not an added strip but cut into the stiles, and is distinctive of Shaker cupboards. Note that the grain on the top panel is horizontal while that on the bottom panel in this door is vertical.

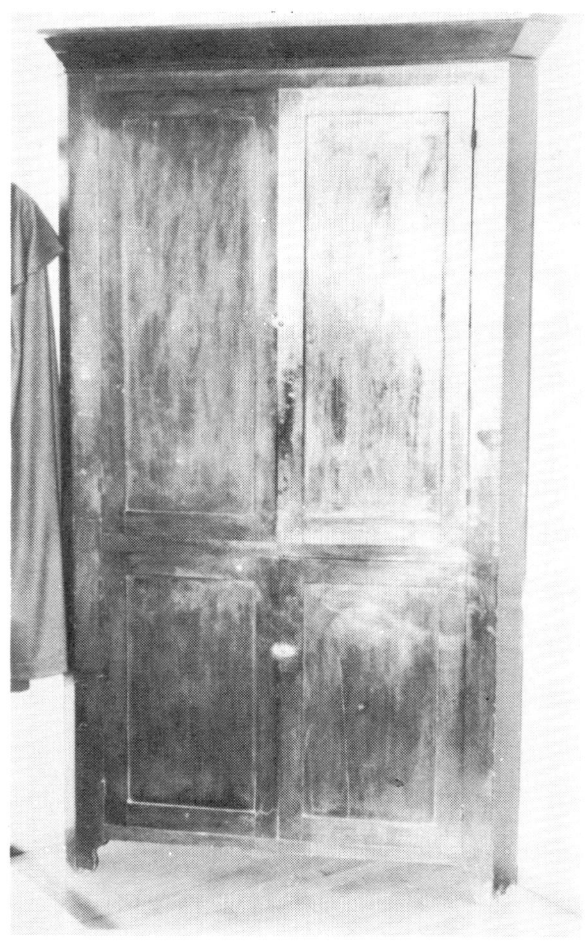

This Shaker corner cupboard from Union Village, Ohio, is indistinguishable from those made in the area by non-Shakers. (Warren County Historical Society, Lebanon, Ohio)

While most Shaker corner cupboards are indistinguishable from corner cupboards made in the world, some do possess those features that are typical of Shaker furniture. With the exception of the small hanging one from Enfield and the built-ins at Hancock, all Shaker corner cupboards have blind doors. Because of their adversity to vanity, the Shakers had little reason for glass doors behind which to display their china, although Mt. Lebanon, New York, did have ironstone bearing their name that would be worthy of "showing off."

The Western Shaker corner cupboards are constructed of walnut or cherry, the dominant woods of Ohio and Kentucky. Most are free standing and have panelled doors, usually made of two panels with the top one being approximately half the height of the lower. The grain in the wood of the top panel runs horizontal while that of the lower is vertical. This is a typical, although not exclusive, Shaker characteristic.

As has been stated, most Shaker corner cupboards can not be distinguished from others of rural Southwestern Ohio or central Kentucky. But there are two features that are worth pointing out because of their strong likeness to other Shaker furniture. The curved front skirt on Western chests of drawers and cupboards, particularly those from Union Village, is readily indentifiable to the trained eye. The quarter round molding around the panel in the door shows the strong awareness in the Western communities of the Eastern patterns. This quarter round molding is not a separate added strip but an integral part of the stiles, having been planed into those boards surrounding the panels. It is a typical mark of the Shaker furniture craftsmen.

Corner cupboards have been virtually overlooked in the literature on Shaker furniture. Perhaps this is because they are more characteristic and prominent in the West than in the East and, unfortunately, most of the attention given to the study of Shaker has focused on what is considered the classic styles that came out of the Eastern communities in the 1820-1850 period. An examination of corner cupboards points out the need for greater study and recognition of Western Shaker artifacts.

— May, 1978

NOTE: *There are two sets of "fancy" dinnerware known to have been used at Mt. Lebanon. China made by T. Furnival and Sons of Bombay was imported from England and used by the trustees. The other was ironstone with a green band and the Shaker name on it. It was first ordered from the Union Porcelain Works, Greenpoint, New York, in 1875. Since most of that was destroyed by a fire, the ironstone was reordered in the 1890's.*

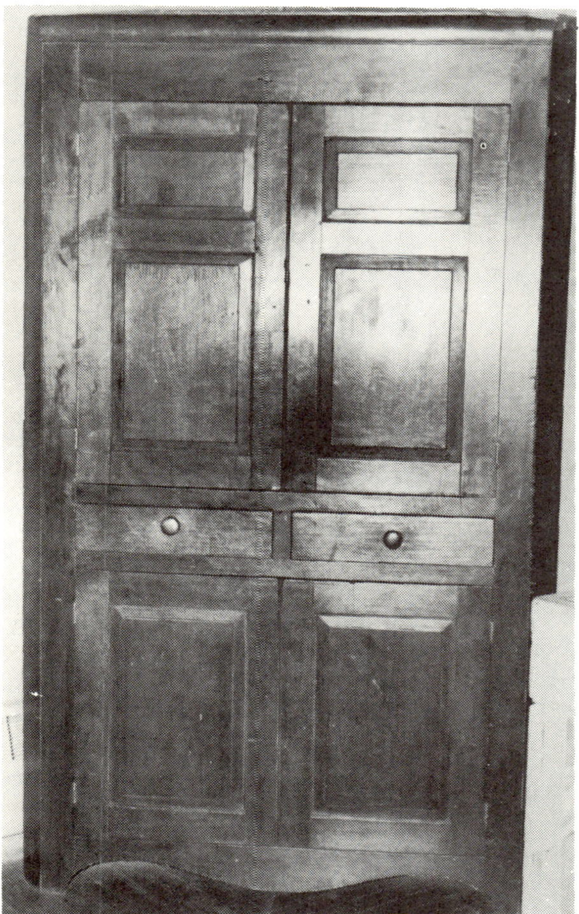

Also from Union Village is this raised panel corner cupboard with cove molding and a scalloped skirt.
(From the Jones Collection, Warren County Historical Society)

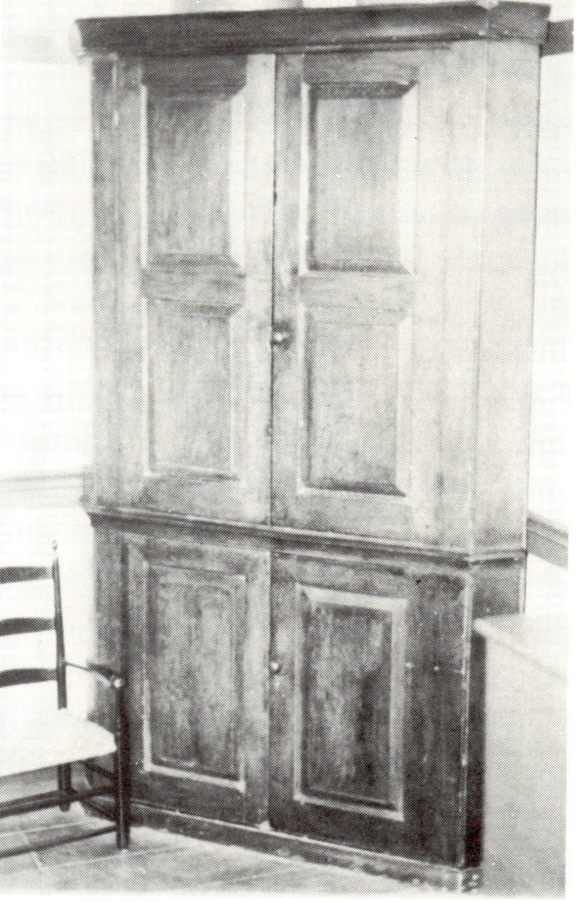

While the cove molding is similar to that found on Union Village pieces, the division of the top doors into two equal portions on this cupboard at Pleasant Hill is different from the arrangement on Ohio ones.

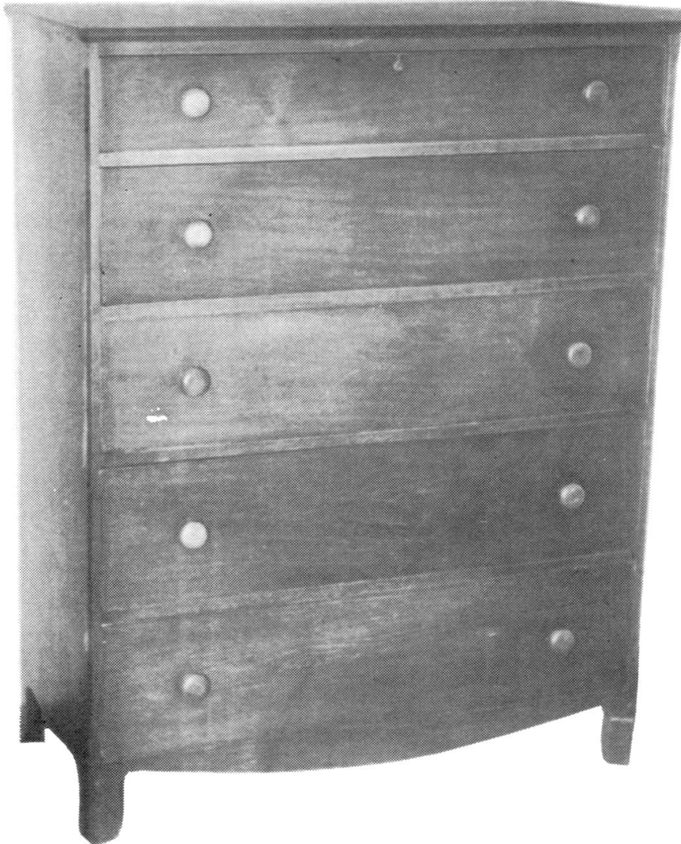

Union Village Chests of Drawers

It is often suggested that Western Shaker furniture is less identifiable as "Shaker" than its Eastern counterparts. While much of the furniture of the Kentucky communities incorporates the contemporary Sheraton and Southern styles, that from Union Village near Lebanon, Ohio, is easily recognizable to those familiar with the products of that community. Chairs (see O.A.R. July, 1977), tables (O.A.R. December, 1978) and chests of drawers have certain characteristics of design and construction that set them apart from the furniture of the world and of other Shaker communities.

One of the consistent design features of Union Village furniture is the use of the cyma or double curve. This is seen on the bracket feet and skirts of all chests of drawers except built-ins and a few with panelled sides. It is also seen on the skirts of cupboards. In some cases, an overlay of the curvature of the feet would be a match to that of the arms on early Union Village rocking chairs. The cyma curve base is in contrast to the straight skirt and half-moon cutout on many Eastern chests and the turned legs on Kentucky ones. The exceptions to this design are the few known examples of chests with panelled sides. In these cases, a single graceful curve moves from the bottom of the foot into the skirt. Union Village separated itself from other Shaker communities with its use of the curve.

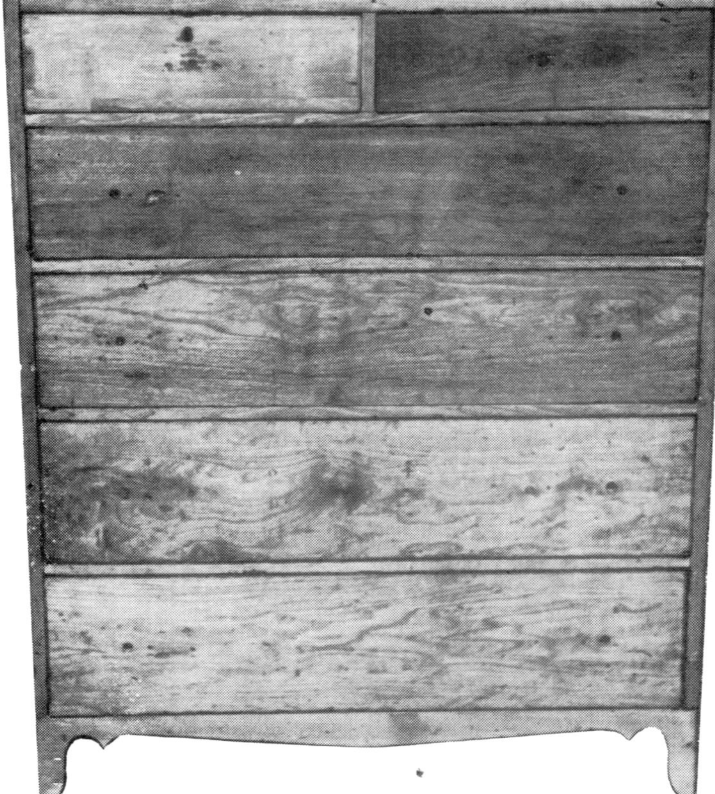

Separating this chest from others of Union Village is its use of both walnut and butternut as primary woods. The front is butternut while the sides are walnut.

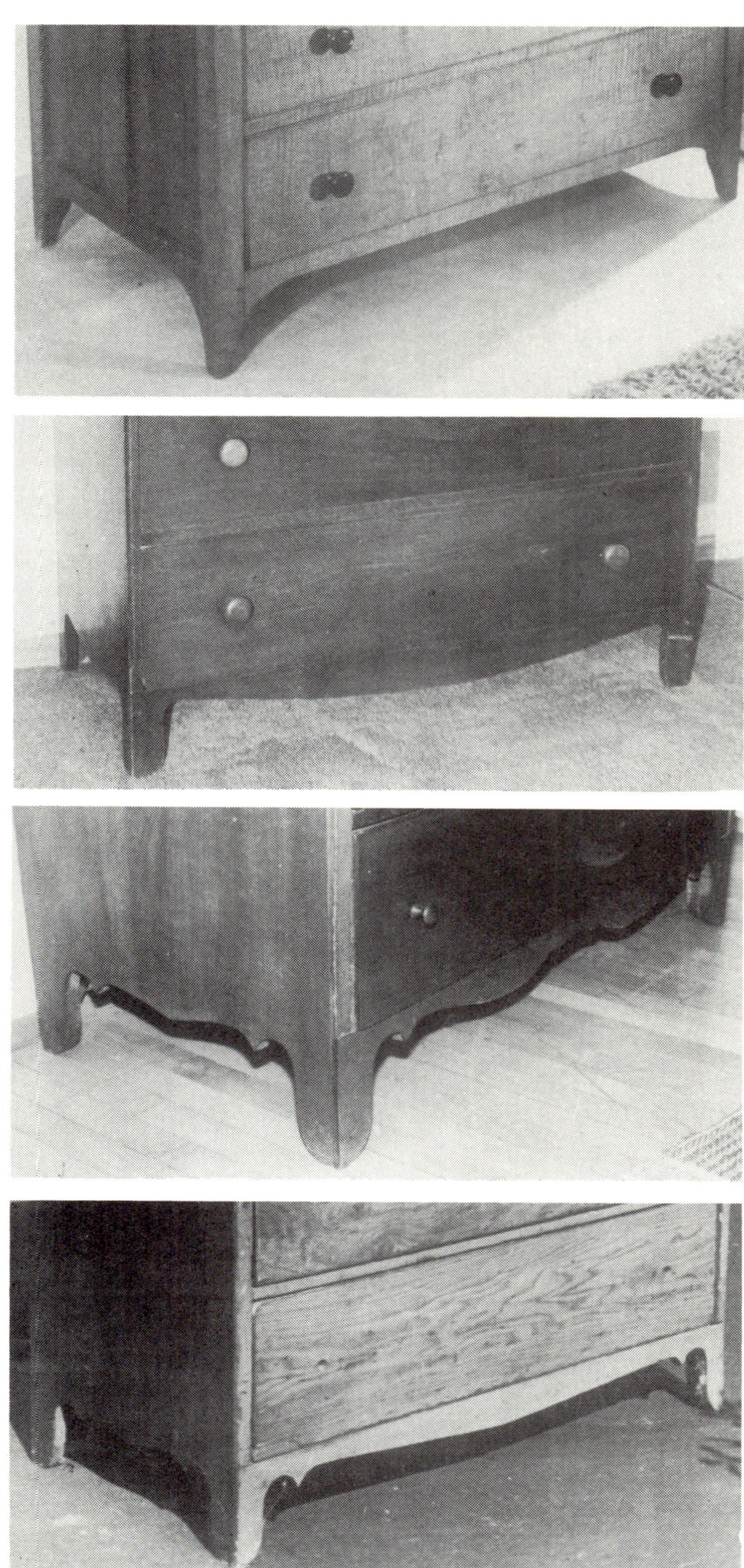

These photographs show the variations in the skirts of Union Village chests of drawers. The styles are easily identifiable and distinguish these chests from those of other Shaker communities.

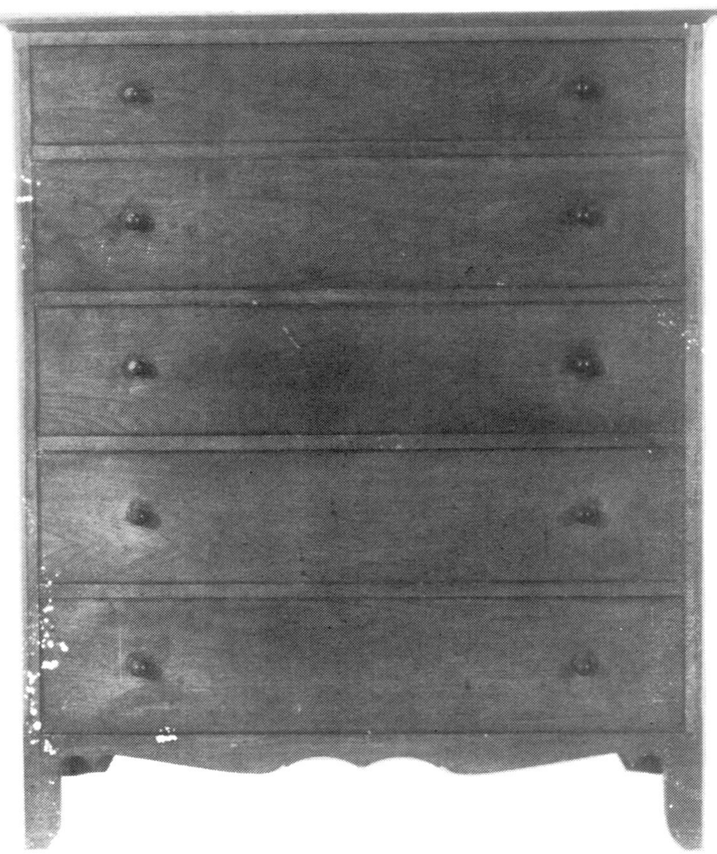

This superb five-drawer butternut Union Village chest was sold at Robert Skinner's auction in Bolton, Massachusetts, for $900 on August 4, 1976. The price was low for a piece of such quality because it and its value were unfamiliar to the Eastern market. Two mates to this chest, except for having two drawers at the top, one dated 1827, are in the Warren County Historical Society in Lebanon, Ohio.
(Photograph courtesy of Robert Skinner, Inc.)

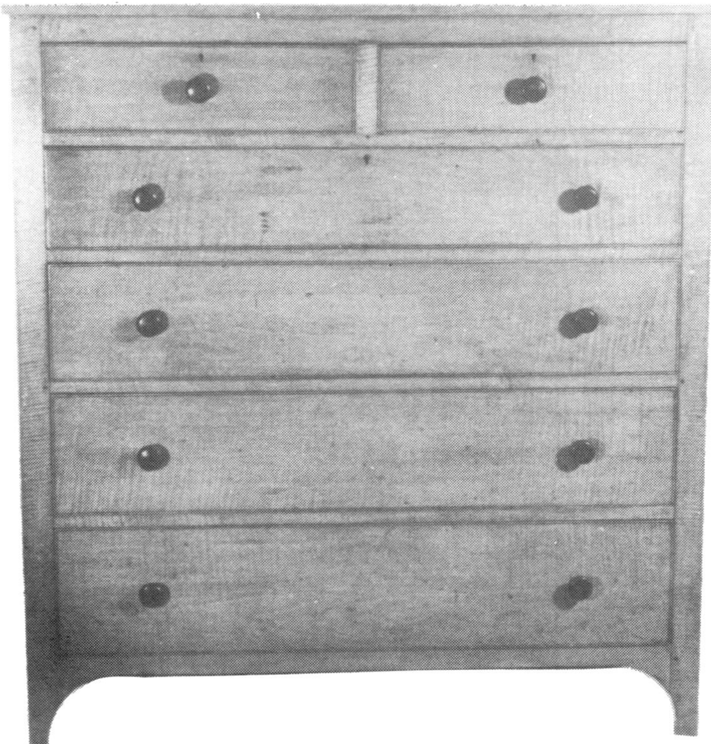

This curly maple chest has panelled sides and lacks the typical cyma curve skirt.

Another consistent design characteristic of Union Village chests is beading around the drawer fronts. To the best of my knowledge, this is present on all built-ins and free-standing chests except for one double chest. In addition, the frames of chests often have chamfered corners. The knobs on these range from large mushrooms with flat heads to small pegs.

Shaker furniture made in the East will differ from that of the West in the wood used for construction. Pine, common to most Eastern furniture, is only used occasionally as secondary wood in Western Shaker articles. The most common woods for Union Village chests are walnut and butternut with curly maple also having been used. The secondary woods are usually poplar, sometimes pine, and even some cherry.

There are two basic styles of Union Village free-standing chests which are distinguished by their sides: solid and panelled. The solid end chests have the stiles separating the drawers dovetailed into the sides and front strips applied to cover the dovetailing as well as to form the skirt. The chests with panelled sides have the corner posts continuing to the floor to form the legs. The panels are usually four, forming a cross of the stiles. This is different than the chests of North Union, Ohio, or Kentucky which have single panel sides. On all of the chests, the top is held to the

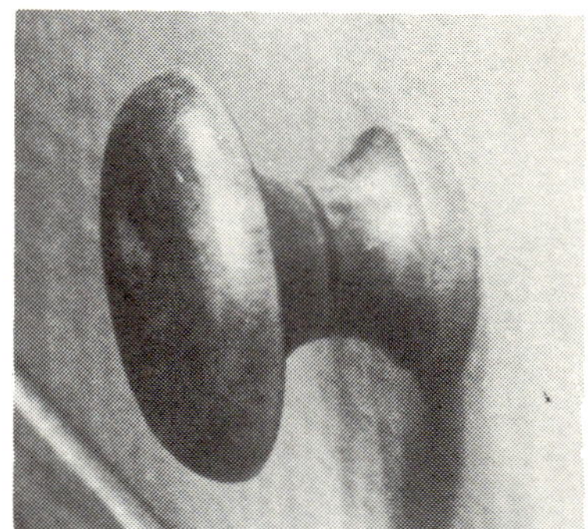
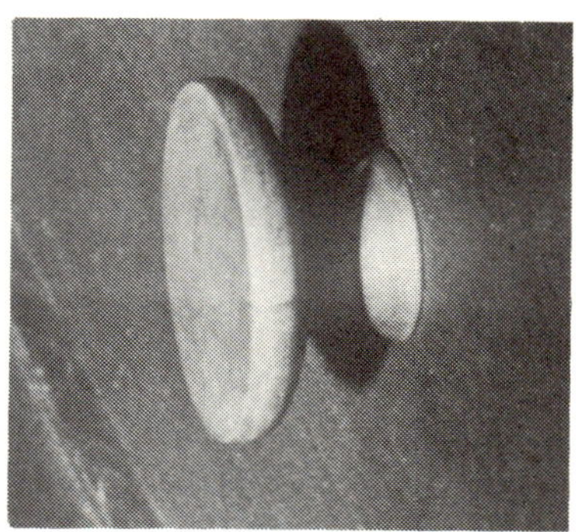
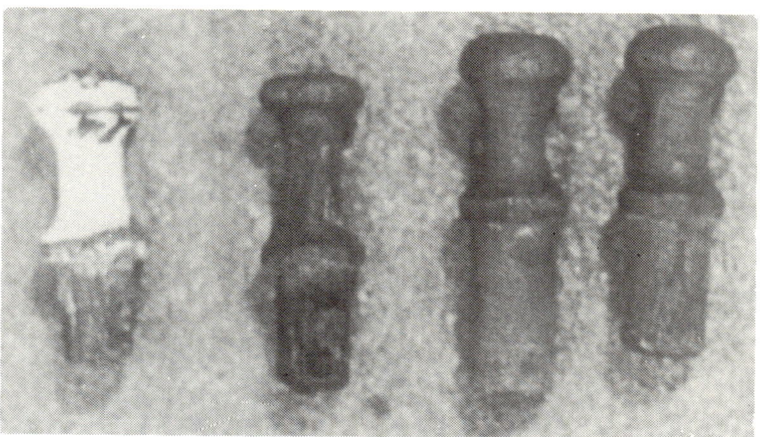

The knobs are from the curly maple chest shown, a double chest and a built-in. The flat head on the knobs of the double chest is not an alteration, but original.

frame by screws from beneath and is of two boards. A center bracing is under the joint of the two boards, runs the length of the top, and is dovetailed into the sides. This seems to be an unique construction feature to these as it is a form of construction not found on non-Shaker chests. The chests of drawers of Union Village are distinctive because of their design and their construction.

NOTE: *At least one Union Village chest has a single board top. But even with it, a center bracing is dovetailed directly into the sides. See photograph on page 10.*

— July, 1979

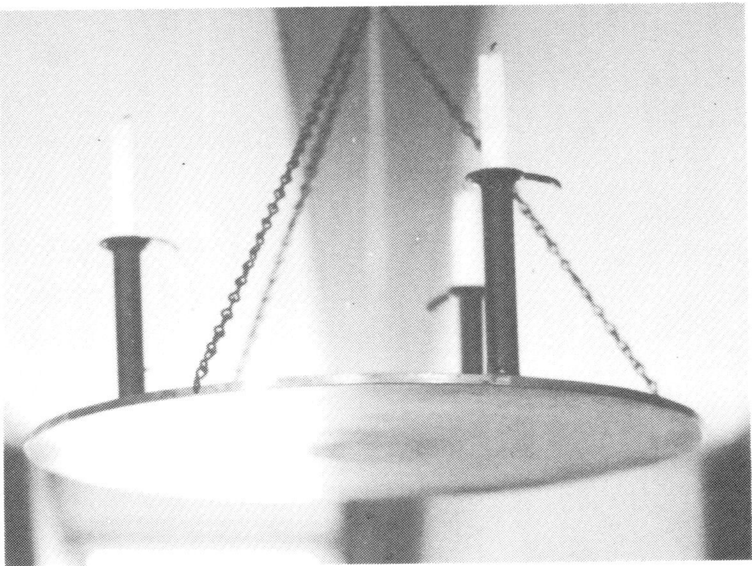

Lighting fixture at the Shirley, Massachusetts, Meeting House, now a restored structure at Hancock Village. This brass plate holding the candlesticks is described in a visitor's 1795 account. Attached by rope and pulleys to the side wall, it could be lowered and raised for the lighting and extinguishing of the candles. A larger fixture in the Mt. Lebanon, New York, Meeting House had a winch to aid in the lowering.

Meeting House Furnishings

2.

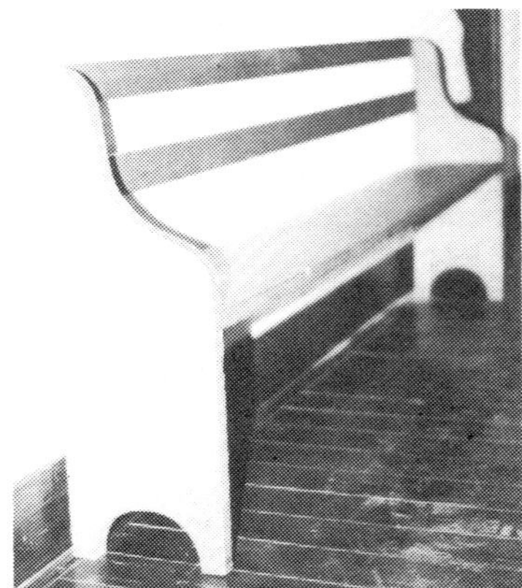

Typical slat back Meeting House bench. Hancock Village, Massachusetts.

So many times in the study of Shaker, we forget that the Shakers were, first of all, a religious sect and that their life style and furniture designs evolved from the religion. Their faith influenced the design of buildings, the simplicity of their furniture and their dedication to fine craftsmanship. The Shaker Meeting House reflects this fact. In keeping with the philosophy of separation of the sexes, two doors and internal symmetry are present. Simplicity directed that there be no ornamentation outside or inside. And, from the insulated walls of the 1792 Canterbury Meeting House to the massive columns under the 1824 Mt. Lebanon one, there are no better built structures of the period.

Mrs. Faith Andrews, author with her late husband of many books on Shaker, has stated that she feels the craftsmanship of the Shakers can never be reproduced because the faith of the Believers is gone. Her thought is borne out in the history of the Shakers themselves. Students of Shaker furniture consider the 1820-1850 period to be the prime time of Shaker craftsmanship. I believe it is not chance that this period was also the time of the greatest religious fervor of the sect. Membership can also be seen in correspondence to the vitality of the faith. John McKelvie Whitworth emphasizes this in his recent book *God's Blueprints.*

3.

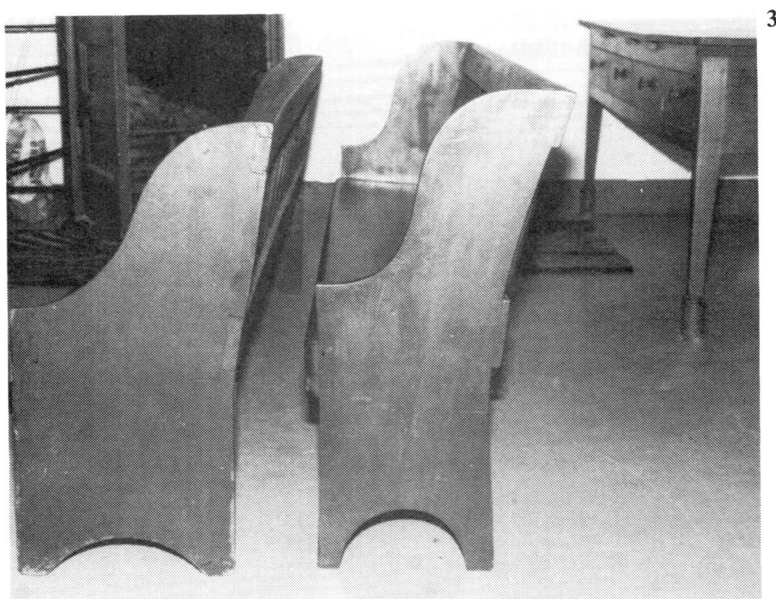

Two Meeting House benches from Union Village, Ohio. Note the similarity of the curvature on the arm and the arched base on these and the Eastern one in Photo #2. (Private Collection)

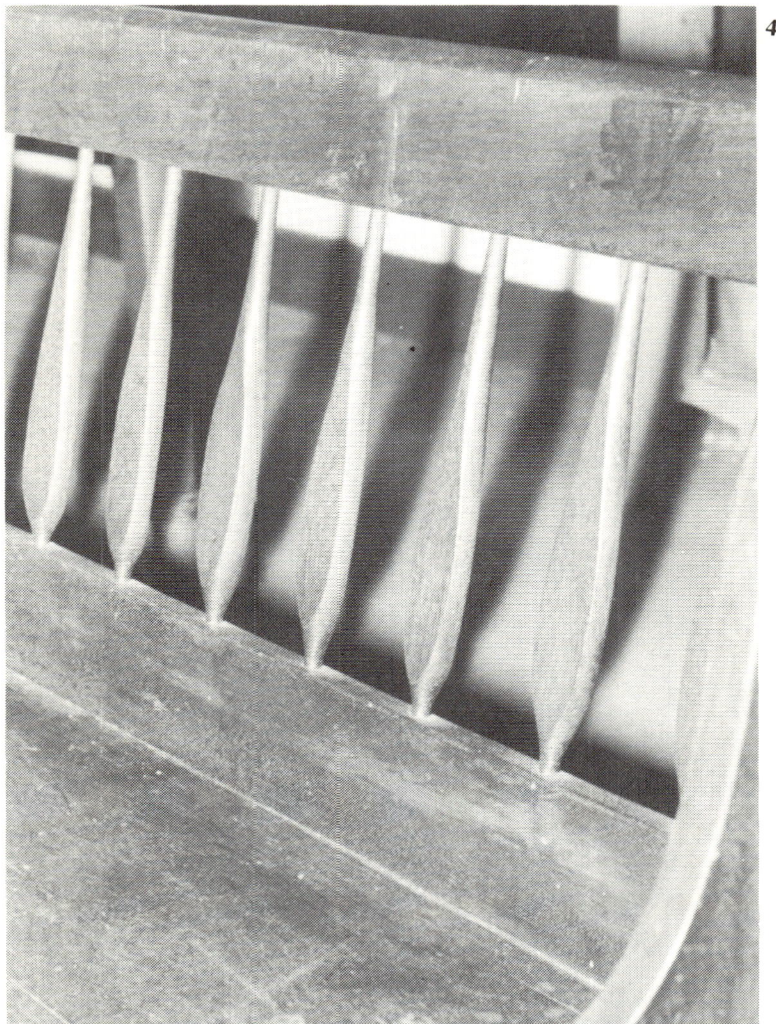

4.

Perhaps the most famous Shaker saying is Mother Ann's "Put your hands to work and your hearts to God." There is a direct relationship between the products of the Shaker hands and how closely their hearts were atuned to God. Not only do we see the best craftsmanships and designs during the time of religious revival but we see the poorest when faith waned. In 1893, the Meeting House at Hancock, Massachusetts, stopped being used. Two years later the Trustees' Office building was "Victorianized." With the decline of the faith, separation from the world and the keeping of simplicity gave way to keeping up with the times. Maybe the same relationship between faith and work can offer insight into the sometime lack of purity and recognition of Western Shaker. J.P. MacLean in his 1903 article on the *"Watervleit Shaker Community"* offers the following:

"On August 1, 1868, the Mount Lebanon ministry, in company with that at Union Village, arrived at Watervleit. The former was astounded that the meetinghouse had not been used for services since 1865, and that no public meetings had been held since 1834." Is it any wonder that so little Watervleit, Ohio, furniture has been recognized?

The tear-drop spindles on the back of the benches in Photo #3 appear to be unique in Shaker furniture.

6.

How does this bench strike you if you think of Shaker as simplicity at its best? The CHH stands for Church Family. The chair to the right is a chapel chair, numbered 3 and having a plywood seat. Darrow School, Mt. Lebanon, New York. Photo by Clark Rice.

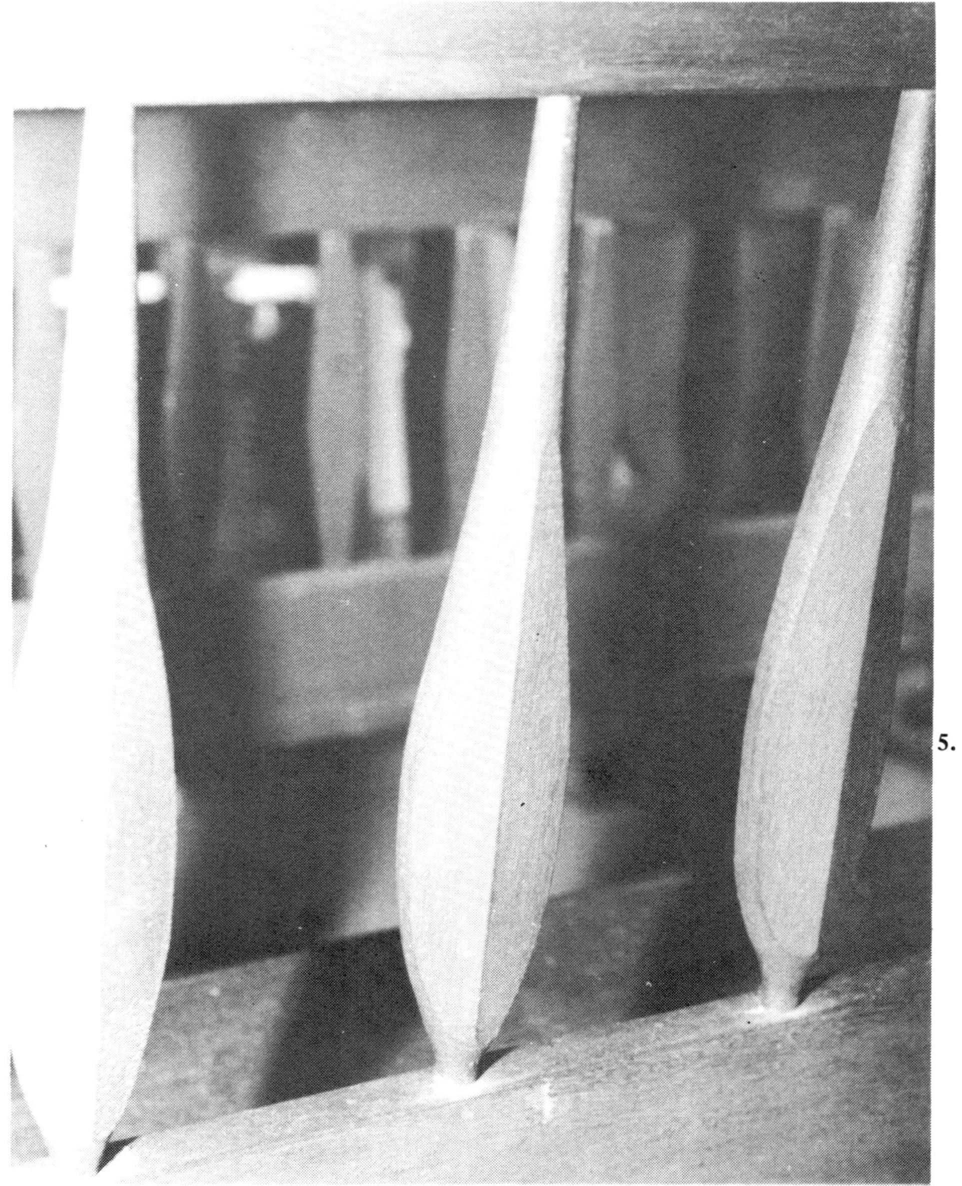

Rear view of tear-drop spindles of the benches in Photo #3.

The Shaker Meeting Houses were constructed and furnished to accomodate their style of worship. Their praise of God was expressed in exhortation, song and dance. There was no need for altars or stained glass. The construction was solid to withstand the rythmic marching and dancing. Pegboards were provided to hold the hats and coats of the dancers. And sometimes benches were built-in for the seating of spectators who were potential converts. The typical Shaker stoves stood at the ends to warm the buildings in the winter.

The only other furnishings were the lighting fixtures and moveable benches. The lighting fixtures were round disks (made of brass at Hancock) that held candlesticks. These disks were fixed with ropes and pulleys so that they could be lowered for the lighting of the candles and then pulled up out of the way of the dancers. The benches, too, were moveable. After listening to some words from the Elders and

5. Elderesses, the benches were moved back and then a square order shuffle, a circle dance or some other exercise of devotion was commenced. The benches from the Shaker Meeting Houses are eight or ten feet in length, usually with a back and ends having a sloping S curve at the arms and the typical Shaker semi-circular arch cut out of the base. There are two notable exceptions to this. Both are from Mt. Lebanon, Ohio. The first is the use of chairs, dating from August, 1887. These are numbered 3 on the top of the back slat and have punched plywood seats. They differ from regular #3 Mt. Lebanon chairs in the use of the plywood and the fact that the stiles holding the seat are square instead of the usually round. Robert Meader in his *Illustrated Guide to Shaker Furniture* says that the seats were made by the Gardner and Company of New York. This company also made benches to be used in railroad stations. It is fair to assume that they also made the second exception to Shaker Meeting House benches...the ones like that in Photo #6. This bench is a visible expression of the parallel decline in Shaker faith and work.

— September, 1977

Union Village Tables

In recent months there have been numerous Shaker tables to come on the market. These range from a small one drawer stand to one of 15 feet in length. One has turned legs. Another has square tapered legs. And yet another is a trestle table. Each of these is a unique piece of furniture. Add to these stretcher base-tables and those with various arrangements of drawers and the topic is indeed vast. Therefore, this month, let me take the suggestion of one reader, who thought I ought to say more about Western Shaker, and write about Union Village, Ohio, tables.

Few examples are available from Watervliet and North Union, Ohio. Whitewater, Ohio, appears to have favored tables with square tapered legs in the Hepplewhite style. But Union Village, being the oldest and largest of the Ohio communities and the Bishopric of the West, produced a variety of tables with the finest of craftsmanship.

The classic of Shaker tables is the trestle table. While many of the other communities seemed to have used a table with turned legs or square tapered legs for dining purposes, I have seen only trestle dining tables from Union Village. There are numerous four legged tables from Union Village but with a drawer or drop leaf and, therefore, intended for work purposes.

The Union Village trestle tables vary from those of other communities in four distinctive ways. First, walnut is the most often used wood. Secondly, the stretcher is down low. Eastern

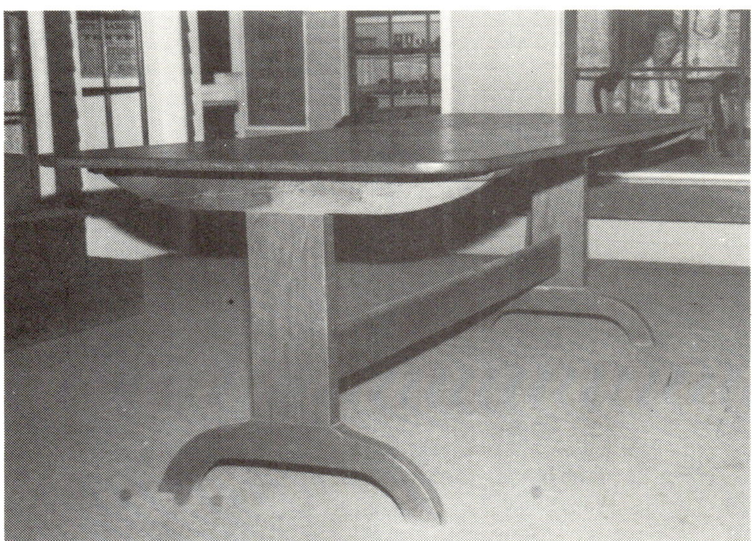

#2 - Union Village trestle table of walnut (Warren County Historical Society, Lebanon, Ohio.)

#1 - This Union Village trestle table of cherry, with a marble top added by the Shakers in the 1890's, is presently used in the private dining room of the Otterbein Home, United Methodist retirement center in Lebanon.

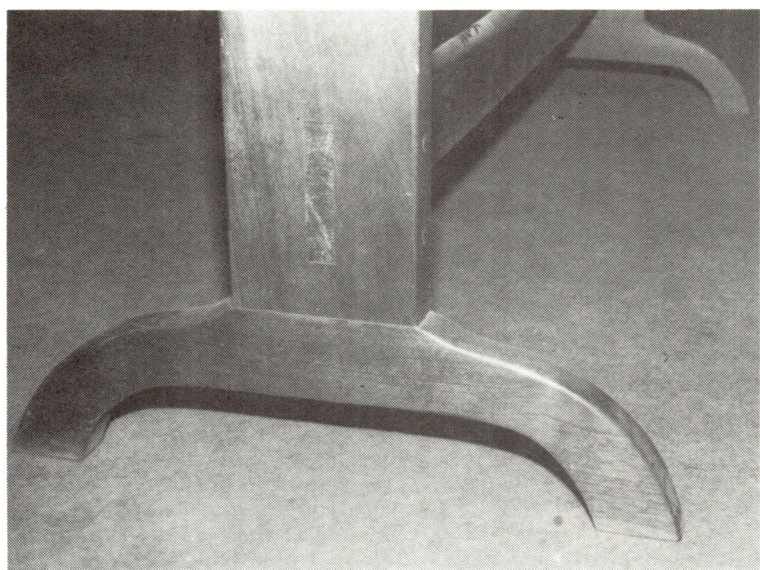

#3 - End view of walnut trestle table. Note the slight rise in the foot as it joins the upright.

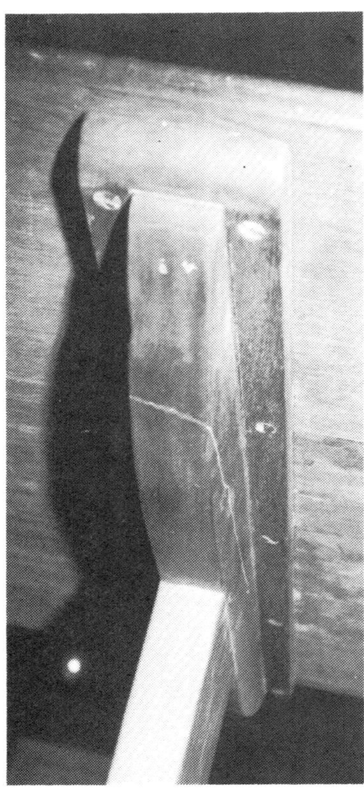

#4 - Underside of walnut trestle table. Note the method of using a batten to fasten the top to the base. All Union Village trestle tables are done in this manner.

and Kentucky tables have the stretcher within 6-8 inches of the top boards while those from Union Village are only about a foot from the floor. Thirdly, Union Village trestle tables differ from those of other communities in the treatment of the foot and the joining of the foot to the upright. There is a slight rise on the foot where it meets the upright support. (Photo #3). Trestle tables from other communities have the foot meeting the upright at a right angle. The fourth difference is the attachment of the top to the base. Eastern tables usually are fastened directly to the underside of the top. Kentucky tables have the top fastened to battens which are attached to the uprights. Union Village tables have a batten that is joined by screws to the top at the same time it is screwed into a cross support which terminates the upright. (Photo #4).

It can be seen from Photo #1 how sturdy is the construction of these tables. The upright is mortised into the cross support as well as into the one piece foot. Union Village trestle tables are probably more sturdily constructed than any other Shaker table. The one in this photo bears a

104'' x 40'' x 1¼'' marble top that was added by the Shakers in the 1890's. For 80 years these tables have withstood the 600-700 pound weight without a crack.

The trestle table in Photo #2 serves as a good example of how bewildering the study of Shaker can be. The top is made up of five walnut boards of random size with only one running the entire length. It is certainly not a proper treatment for a table top. Why would the Shakers make such a beautiful table and then lay a pieced top upon it? But the real bewilderment is stirred when it is considered that there is another Union Village table in California that is identical to this one…even to the same arrangement of the five board pieced top!

Among the smaller tables, those from Union Village are distinguished from those of other communities by their predominant use of walnut and by the treatment of the legs. Walnut was

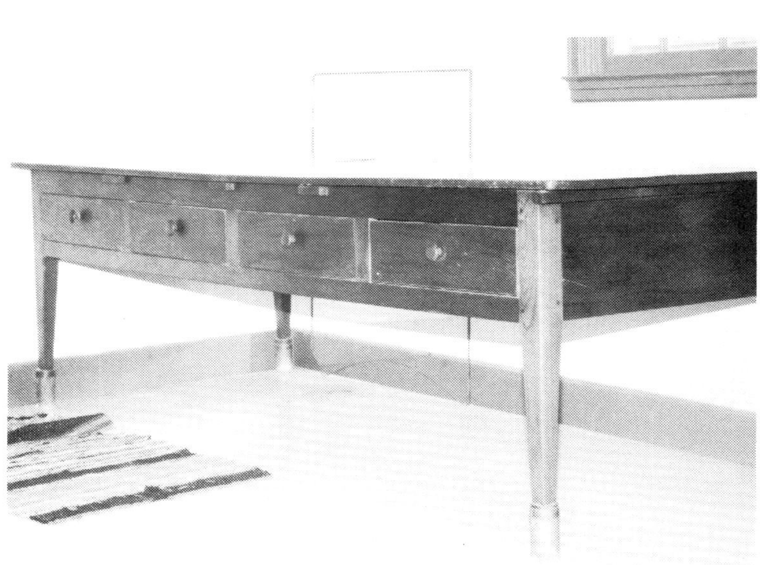

#5 - This Union Village work table at one time had rollers. The round sockets for the rollers are fastened to square tapered legs. Interest is added to this table by two squares that had been cut out of the top and put back in at a later time. Perhaps it was a convenient way to sweep excess material into the drawers? (Private Collection)

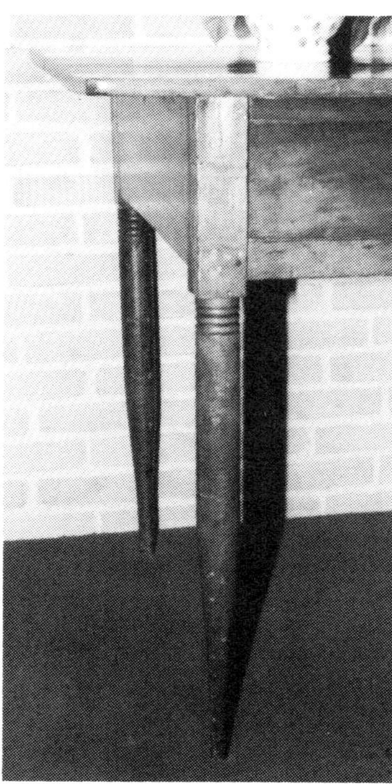

#6 - The gracefulness of this leg is enhanced by its added heighth. Used as a canning table, it is 34 inches tall. The turned leg reduces in diameter to less than an inch where it meets the floor. (The Otterbein Home, Lebanon, Ohio)

the favorite wood of most of the rural craftsman in Southwestern Ohio in the early 19th century. Most of the old homes between Dayton and Cincinnati used much walnut and the Shakers were no exceptions. Their buildings and their furniture were made with this wood.

Union Village small tables, and those of Pleasant Hill, Kentucky, exhibit a characteristic treatment of the legs in which they change from the square at the skirt of the table to a round leg. There is no slight taper or turnings, rather, the transition just below (¾ inch) the skirt is immediate and sharp. Then follows one of numerous variations. The most common seems to be a slight taper in the round leg all the way to the floor. Another will follow the same taper until about two thirds of the way to the floor where the taper becomes decidedly more pronounced. Yet another will go to within two inches of the floor before it is turned to a finer point. Following the same taper, some legs have what John Kassay calls a pencil post. About two inches from the floor, the leg becomes concave. This feature is also found on the legs of many Union Village chairs. The first two variations mentioned appear to be common to Kentucky stands as well as to those of Union Village while the last two are exclusively Ohio.

Another style that seems purely Union Village is one in which a square ornamentation is formed about halfway down the leg. While all of these tables of which the author is aware had a

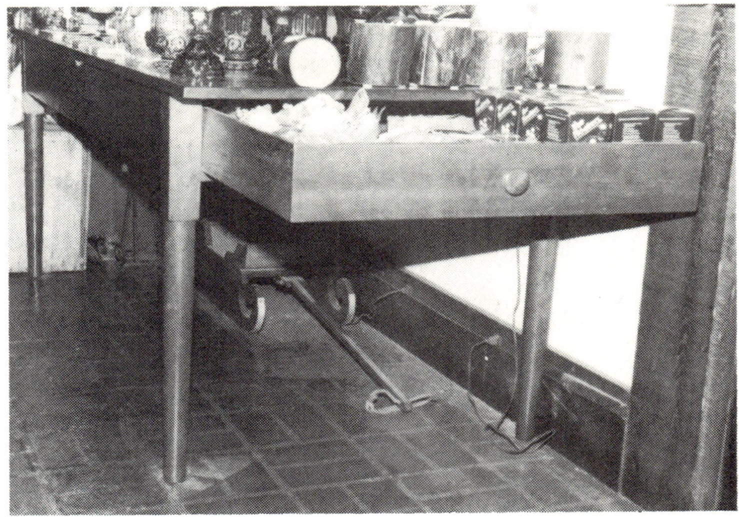

#7 - Cherry one drawer table. Note the sharp change from a square to the tapered round leg. (Golden Lamb Inn Gift Shop, Lebanon, Ohio)

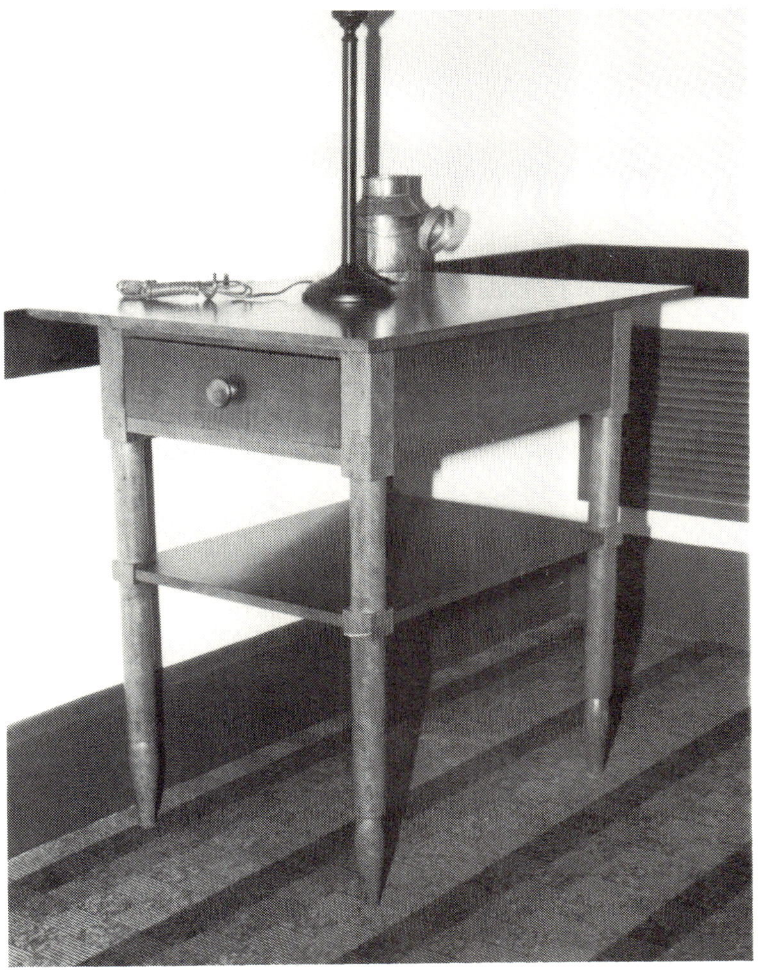

#8 - The shelf is probably a later addition. Of special interest is the square decoration on the leg and the turnings at the base of the foot. (Otterbein Home)

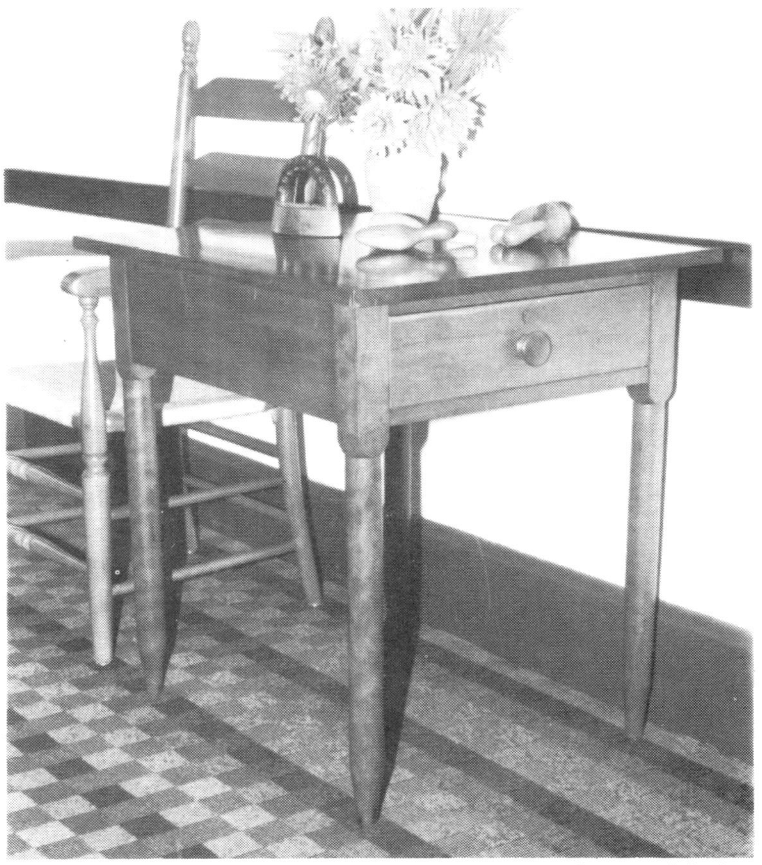
#9 - This cherry table illustrates the rapid decrease in the size of the leg as it nears the floor. (The Otterbein Home)

shelf, as does the one in the photograph, it is believed that the shelf is not original. These tables came out of the Otterbein Home, present owners of the former Union Village buildings, and had been used in the rooms of children or the elderly. The shelves were probably added during their use in these residents' rooms.

It can easily be seen the Union Village tables are among the finest of Shaker furniture. Legs mortised and pinned to the apron, screws to hold on the tops, and glue blocks to strengthen the joints were favorite methods of the Union Village craftsmen. Their tables stand out for their structure and design.

— July, 1977

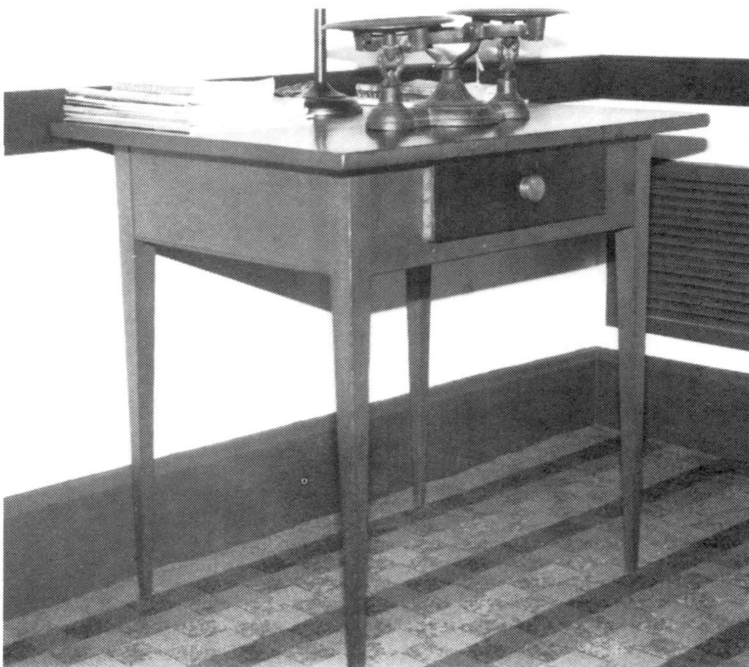
#11 - The Hepplewhite style leg tapers to a round at the floor. (The Otterbein Home)

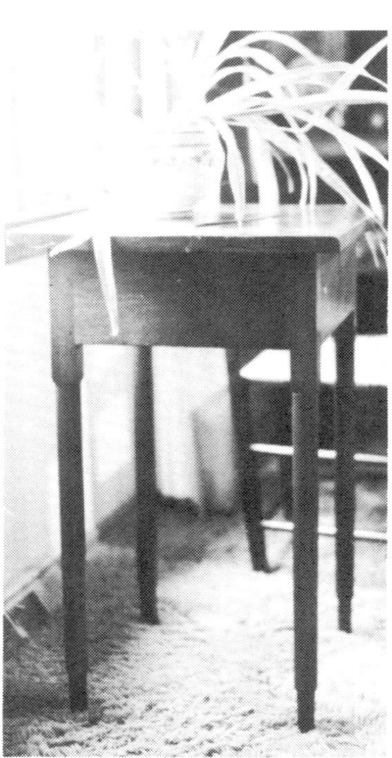
#10 - A typical Union Village walnut stand with pencil post legs. (Private Collection)

Folk Art

The exhibit opening May 2nd at the Hirschl-Adler Gallery in New York City is a rare opportunity for the Shaker and /or folk art enthusiast. Entitled ''The Gift of Inspiration, Art of the Shakers,'' the exhibition will feature sixty spirit drawings, maps and architectural sketches by and about the Shakers. It is the first major showing of Shaker drawings in New York since the Whitney Museum display in November of 1935. And it may be the last major showing of these little known pieces of folk art. The Hancock Shaker Village, as well as some of the other twenty contributors to the exhibition, have decided that these rare and priceless artifacts shall not be loaned in the future.

The Shaker Community (Hancock) outside Pittsfield, Massachusetts, is the beneficiary of the three week showing, the result of a Berkshire vacation by Norman Hirschl who visited Hancock and was impressed with the restored village and the products of the Shakers. While all of the drawings in the exhibit are on loan and not for sale, the Hirschl and Adler Gallery will be displaying American folk art from their collections that would have been contemporary with the Shakers. June Sprigg, Curator at Hancock, suggests that this will be the first showing of Shaker compared and contrasted with other folk art.

In this time of increasing awareness and discussion of folk art, it is proper that a major art gallery give attention to Shaker expression in drawing and painting. The first recognition of Shaker as a worthy subject of folk art was in a 1935 *Antiques* when editor Homer Eaton Keyes wrote the following: ''I shall have fulfilled my intention if I convince my readers that these works of art are worthy of study as independent phenomena, whose resemblance to other primitive creations is not due to any process of imitation but instead is the evidence of a kinship of the subconscious so deeply and univer-

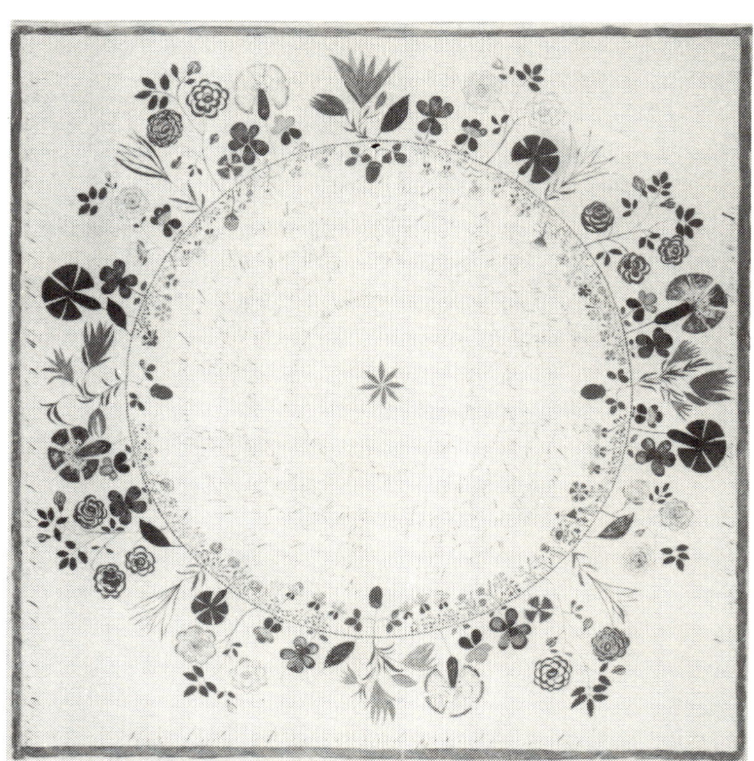

Floral Wreath. Hancock, 1853. The inside circle reads: ''Farewell in love from Father James Father Joseph Mother Lucy and Mother Dana. Written by an inspired Inst. Dec. 12, 1853.'' Ink and water color.

Photographs courtesy of Shaker Community, Inc.

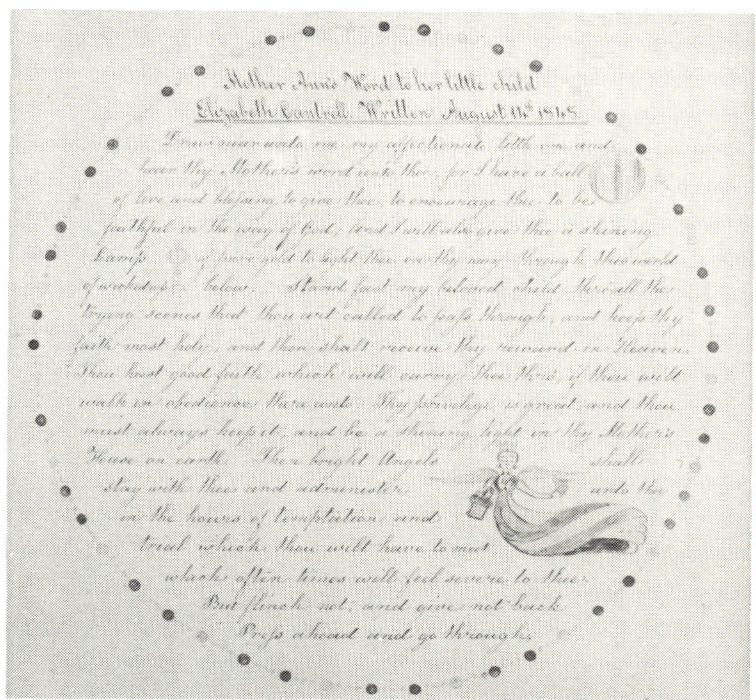

''Mother Ann's Word to her little child Elizabeth Cantrell. Written August 14th, 1848,'' New Lebanon, New York. Ink and water color.

sally implanted in humankind as to be almost unaffected either by differences of physical circumstances or by discrepancies of time."

Some years later, Jean Lipman and Alice Winchester gave a page to the subject in *The Flowering Of American Folk Art*. With the exception of these and Edward and Faith Andrews' book *Visions Of The Heavenly Sphere*, Shaker has been largely ignored by those interested in folk art. Kenneth Ames states in *Beyond Necessity: Art In The Folk Tradition* that "Perhaps because there is no widely shared single definition of folk, there is disagreement about whether or not the Shakers qualify as folk."

It is apparent to me, though, that whatever the definition of "folk art," Shaker needs to be given major consideration. Whether from the perspective of an anthropologist who is concerned about small, isolated, homogeneous societies or that of the sociologist who focuses on the material culture of a society, Shakers qualify as folk and the products of their minds and hands as folk art. One of the earliest commentaries, *American Folk Art*, catalogue for the 1932 exhibition at the Museum of Modern Art, offered the simple definition of folk art as "the work of peoples with little book learning in art techniques, and no academic training." Hoger Cahill concluded this discussion with "the folk artists tried to set down not so much what they saw as what they knew and what they felt." Certainly the Shakers meet these standards.

In the May, 1950, *Antiques* forum on folk art, Janet MacFarland and Louis Jones classify the subject into three divisions. The first of these is "those utilitarian objects which have an esthetic appeal for us deriving from their basic design. Those unadorned tools or utensils recommend themselves to us because the designer-artist combined perfectly the necessities of function with the grace of form." This definition is parallelled by the Shaker definition of beauty: "Beauty rests on utility. That which has in itself the highest use possesses the greatest beauty." The Shaker concept that beauty is a product of function suggests that most all Shaker products are to be considered as folk art.

Another classification of MacFarland-Jones includes "all types of folk art which are simply decorative and have no ulterior function." It is under this area that the exhibit opening in New York can be considered. The spirit drawings seem to be the expression of some internal forces within the artist. Although sometimes given as gifts from one individual to another, they were never circulated. MacFarland-Jones state that "Much folk art is created with a very limited and intimate audience in view, the members of the artist's family and his immediate circle. It is created out of the emotional needs of the artist and for his personal pleasure..." Such was

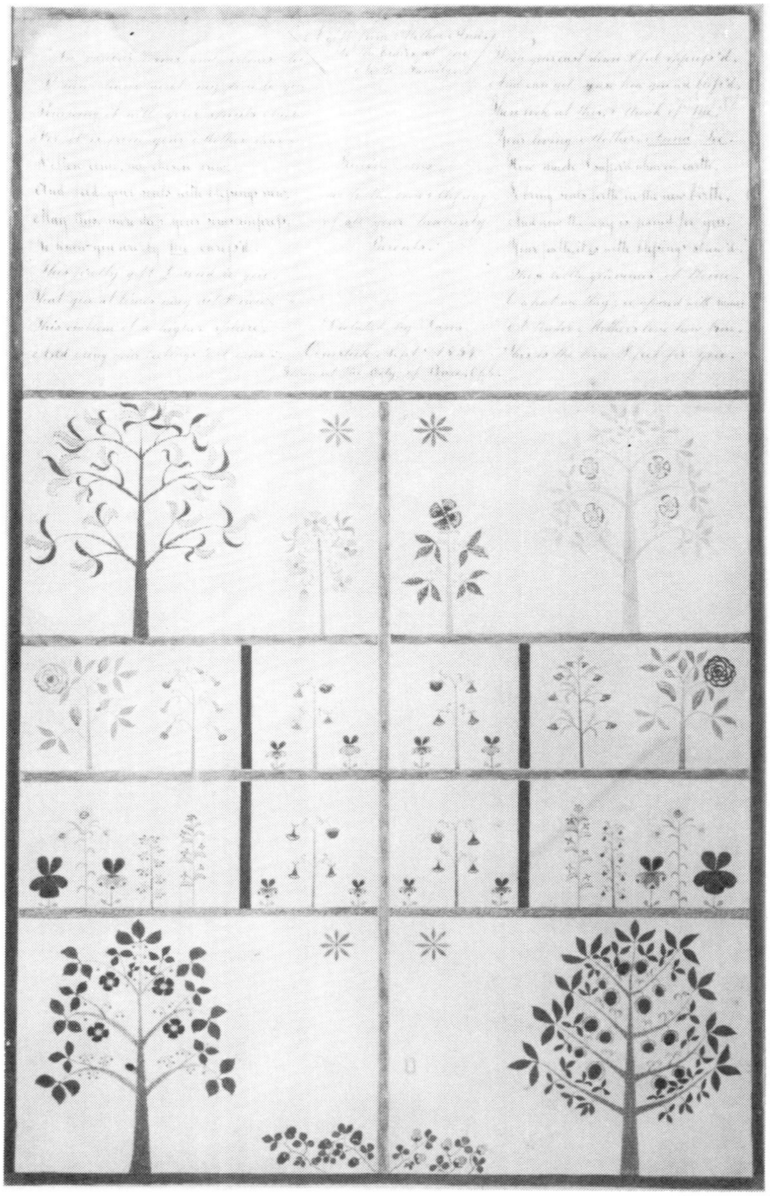

"A gift from Mother Ann to the Elders at the North Family." Hancock, 1854. Ink and water color.

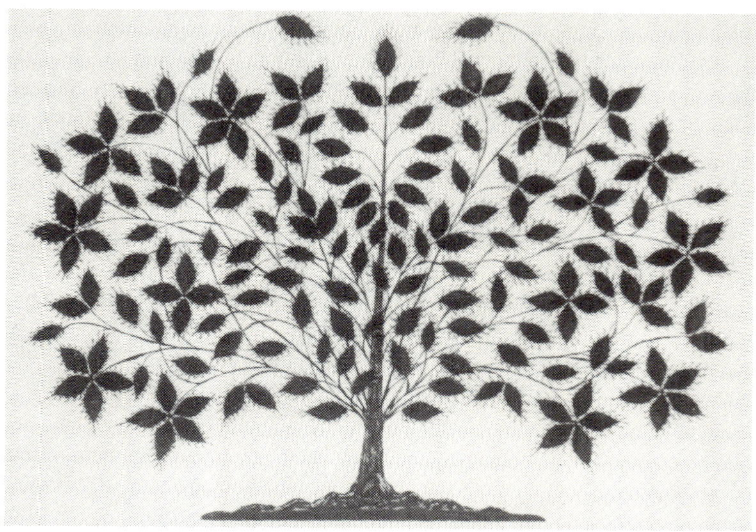

"The Tree of Light or Blazing Tree," Hancock, 1845. "Seen and received by Hannah Cohoon in the City of Peace Sabbath Oct. 9th 10th hour A.M. 1845, drawn and painted by the same hand," Ink and water color.

the case of the Shaker inspirational drawings.

The manifestation of the Spirit of God is a part of the history of the Shakers. It was a vision that brought Mother Ann Lee to the United States in 1774. It was a vision that caused the Shakers to send missionaries to Ohio and Kentucky in 1804. Other manifestations are to be found occasionally throughout the early years of the Shaker until 1837 when visions, songs, messages, dances and revivalistic rituals came in great numbers. It was during this time of great spiritual activity that the spirit drawings began to appear. But it is interesting to note that the more elaborate and colorful drawings were products of a time following the end of the revivalistic years. Andrews states that "the culmination of religious ecstasy was reached between 1842 and 1845." But the major inspirational drawings date after those years and as late as 1859. This would suggest that the drawings were not so much inspired by supernatural forces but by a rich

radition. They were the symbolic expression of previous religious experiences.

The drawings progress in elaborateness from simple geometric shapes (1834) to leaves (1845), hearts and fan cards (1847) to those of Hannah Cocoon (1854-56) who stated that she had been shown how to copy these works from an angel. Some of the interesting drawings are what Miss Sprigg calls "moon and machines drawings." Eight of these were produced between 1845 and 1847 and have a heart in the middle of the drawing. Various emblems such as wings, sun, moon, bird cages, clocks, birds and trees are common to all of them. Although these are not signed, the common symbols suggest that they might be the product of one hand.

It is apparent from Shaker writers of the time that the drawings were not known to the community at large. Shaker rules forbade hanging them or any other decorative objects. They were not used for the edification of the

Believers. They were usually unsigned and surrounded with an element of secrecy.

From the documentation available, all of the works were done by females. Neither the styles of the drawings nor the history of the artists seem to suggest any connection between the school girl art of the early 1800's and the Shaker inspirational drawings. They are products of the Shaker way that is imbued with spiritual manifestations. As Andrews said, "Although these manifestations are the work of individuals, they reflect the workings of a communal, or folk, mentality deeply tinted with mysticism." They are the products of unique individuals set in a distinctive culture. They are folk art at its best.

(A fully illustrated catalogue with essays by Nina Fletcher Little and June Sprigg is available for $5.00 from Shaker Community, Inc., P.O. Box 898, Pittsfield, Mass. 01201.)

— May, 1979

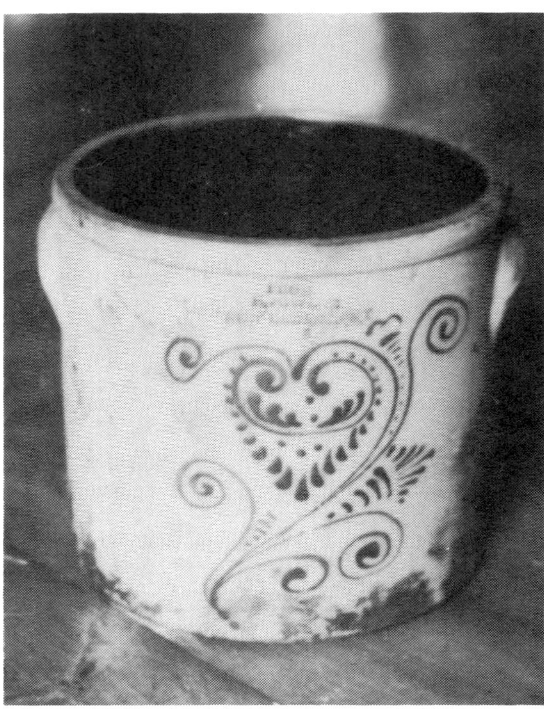

This well decorated stoneware crock was made for the Shakers but bears the marking "Fowler, New Lebanon, N.Y." Edward Fowler was a trustee in that community.

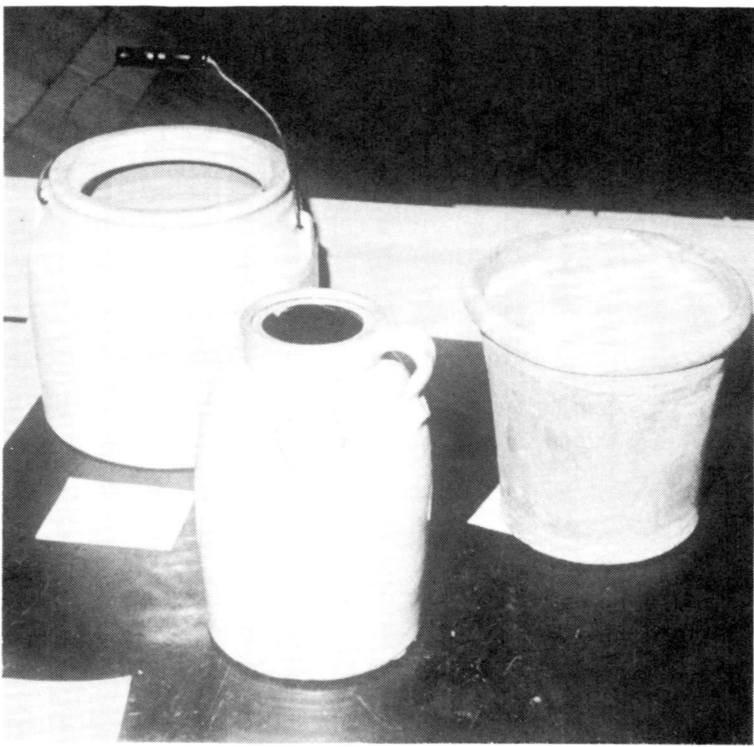

While these three pieces came from the Shakers at Union Village, it is likely that the two white clay products were purchased in the world. The crude flower pot might have been made at the brickyard of the West Family. (Warren County Historical Society)

Pottery

Pottery is one area of Shaker productivity for which little knowledge and documentation exists. While it is the general consensus that Shakers purchased jars and jugs from outside their communities, they did produce some clay articles of their own.

The Shakers made great use of the local raw materials in building their homes and shops. Thus, Pleasant Hill, Kentucky, and Enfield, New Hampshire, quarried limestone to use in the erection of their huge family dwellings. Canterbury, New Hampshire, and Harvard, Massachusetts, extensively employed the native timber surrounding those areas. Both Canterbury and Pleasant Hill, as well as Mt. Lebanon, New York, and the Ohio communities, took advantage of the clay on the land and made bricks to be used in the construction of their buildings. The second oldest Shaker structure west of the Hudson River. Rose Cottage in Union Village, Ohio, was made of brick in 1811 and still stands. The center House in the same community was finished on January 13, 1846, and used one million bricks in its construction. It also still stands and is currently used as a residence for elderly. A description of that building in an old journal relates that the "brick was burned on Shaker property and the timbers from their woods."

The same red clay and kilns that were used for the making of bricks could have been used in the production of other low temperature clay articles. It is known that drain tile was manufactured at Mt. Lebanon, Pleasant Hill and Union Village. Robert Meader, former Director of the Shaker Museum, has found shards of brick and drain tile at the site of the former brickyards at Mt. Lebanon. The tile that has been unearthed on the grounds of that former community measure about two feet long and four inches in diameter.

Two pieces of pottery from Union Village would indicate that products other than bricks and tiles were made by the Shakers in their brick plants. An unglazed redware flower pot in the museum of the Warren County Historical Society has an attribution to Union Village. The second piece is a finely formed redware jar with black manganese glaze measuring slightly more than sixteen inches in height. With an excellent provenance, it has the following inscribed on its base: "August the 17, 1827; Stephen." It seems probable that this is the work of Stephen Easton who is listed as "potter" in an 1834 account of the members of the West Brick Family. He was later to become the Deacon in the Second Family. That same listing includes three other men called potters: Elder Ely Houston, Elder John Gee, Jr. and James Morris.

The Alfred, Maine, community also appears to have had some potters in its membership. From information in the archives of the Shaker Museum, the names of Josiah and Stephen Emory, who joined and left the society three times, are given as potters. There is reference that a pottery was in operation there in 1805.

Other than these few examples, the only other pottery production of the Shakers seems to have been that of pipe making. In his book *The Community Industries Of The Shakers,* Edward D. Andrews relates "The bowls were made of both red and white clay. ...The first record appears in 1809, when 'some pipes' were sold for $1.62." He continues by saying

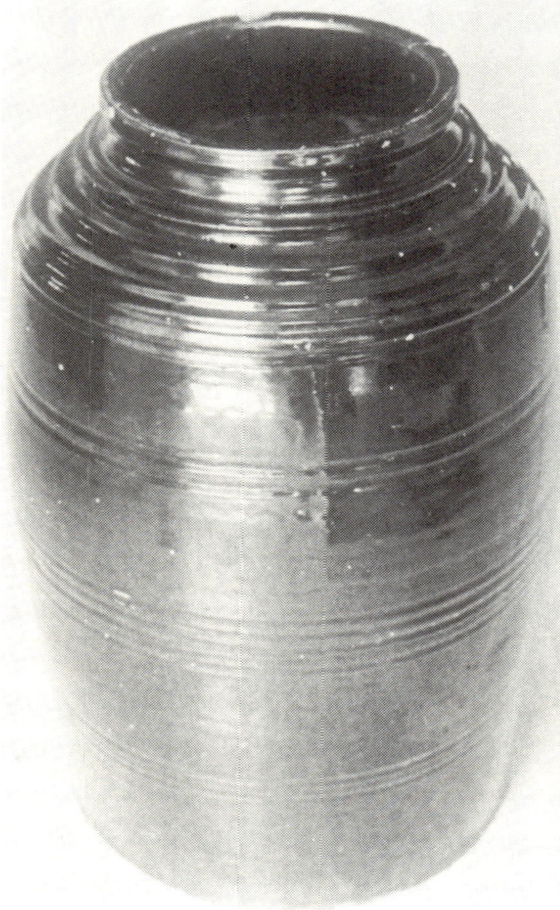

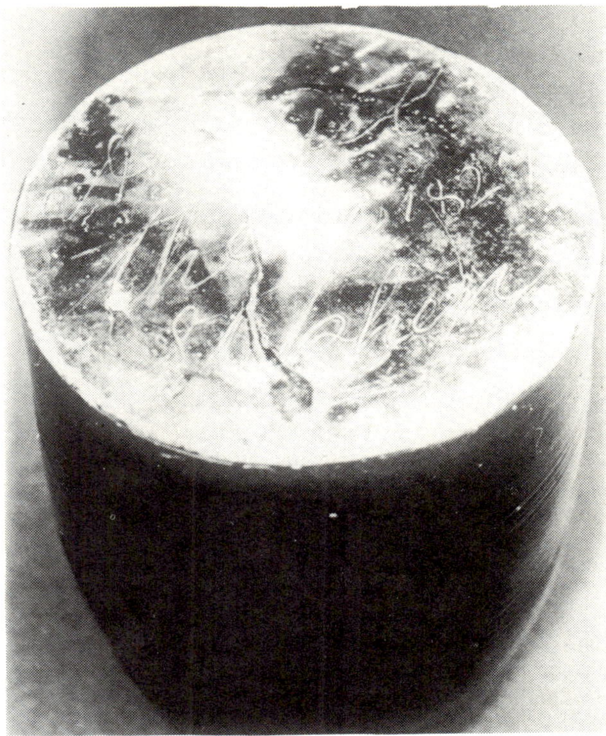

On the bottom of this redware jar is the inscription "August the 17, 1827; Stephen." Measuring 16⅛ inches tall and 9⅝ inches across the base, it is the only known piece of signed Shaker pottery. The "Stephen" was probably Stephen Easton, a potter in the West Brick Family at Union Village. (Owned by Mr. and Mrs. Nelson Melampy)

that the pipes were sold in 1835 for eight dollars a thousand and were being sold as late as 1853. They were also being produced and sold in the nearby communities of Hancock, Massachusetts, and Watervliet, New York.

In the West, at least two of the communities were in the pipe business. The *Index Of American Design* includes an illustration of pipes made at Pleasant Hill while an 1813 Shaker account book tells of sales from Union Village. Under a heading of "Received for sundry articles" is the following listing:

beans, flaxseed, small basket, tobacco, sawmill cotton, seeds, tacks, for lodging six travellors, garden seeds, pipes, cheese baskets, 25 bushels of lime, chair frames, for pasturing sheep, for 1,000 bricks, early seed potatoes, pine pail, cotton cloth, salt, one set of plow irons, for keeping two horses, chair, tacks and nails, boards, black pepper, rakes, for reaping, one quart of whiskey, towel linen, for mending a vice, ginger, cherry plank, for use and damage of a rifle gun lent, set of chairs, two ewes, ram, tea, bull calf."

Pipes and bricks were a part of the early industries of the Shakers. The production of pipes probably terminated shortly after the Civil War as smoking was looked upon in disfavor.

There are pieces of white clay pottery that are attributed to the Shakers. Since white clay was used in the making of the pipes, it is not unreasonable to conclude that some crockery might also have been made from this material. But most of the examples are of the late slip cast style and would have been manufactured at a much later date than the known references. By mid-1800, the Shakers were purchasing their glass and pottery from outside sources. An 1856 invoice contains an order from the Sandwich Glass Company of Massachusetts. Other notes refer to the purchase of stoneware from Fort Edward, New York, and the E. and L. P. Norton Company in Bennington, Vermont. Some of these pieces can be readily identified as having been made for the Shakers because the name of the trustee of the Church Family at New Lebanon is imprinted. "Fowler, New Lebanon, N.Y." is occasionally seen on a finely decorated piece of stoneware.

Although the Shakers are known to have produced bricks, tiles, pipes, and some crockery, it would be impossible to identify their pottery without an excellent provenance. The exception to this is the stoneware manufactured for the Shakers and bearing the name of the trustee.

— June, 1979

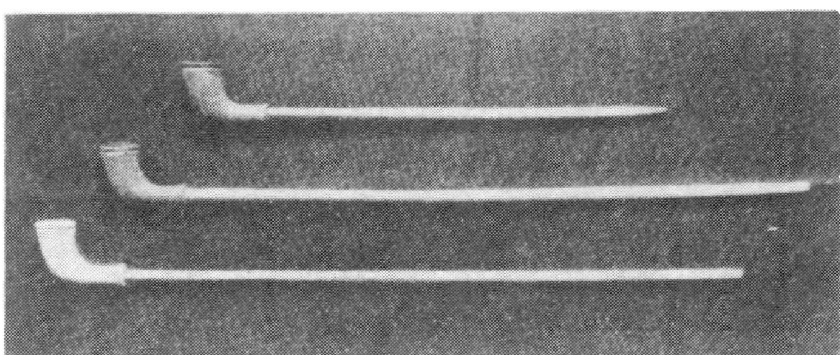

Red and white clay was used in the manufacturing of the bowls of pipes at New Lebanon. The stems were wood.

NOTE: *Brother Thomas Whitaker has been a scholar of the South Union Shakers since being on those grounds as a member of the Saint Mark's Priory for the last twenty-five years. Upon reading the above article, he sent the author a letter including information from the microfilm file at St. Mark's Priory. Dated October 7, 1836, addressed to "Beloved Ministry" and signed by "The Ministry of Union Village," one entry reads as follows: "In the great move last winter, it so hapened (sic) that all the Potters, were moved from the west Brick, to the north Lot, Brother Rufus knows where. Well in consequence of this change it became necessary to build 2 considerable sized buildings in order to accommodate the pottery business at the nort (sic) Lot, or second Family. One of these buildings were built with brick, the other frame. They also had to build a large kiln for burning their ware &c. This has all been done, & the Ware Making started, so we have been informed by letter, a few days since." Brother Thomas of the Benedictine Order adds "it appears to me that they must have had quite an operation if it was necessary to erect '2 considerable sized buildings.' Looks as though they put pottery on the market." He has found no evidence of potters at South Union although bricks were molded and burned at the site and "one of the main men in the brick making and attending the kiln was David Barnett, a former slave." The 1854 Wash House was constructed of 273,000 bricks and "records indicate that there were several hired masons on the job" and "that the brick work was completed in '8 weeks to a day'."*

Victorian

Last summer at a Victorian Society picnic in Cincinnati, an award was given for the picnic basket prepared in the best Victorian style. The judges saw fit to give a separate, special award to one person who had prepared some Shaker dishes and brought his picnic lunch in oval boxes. But the judges were mistaken in separating the Shakers from the Victorian period through which they had moved. Victorian Shaker is frowned upon and degraded by the purist. Yet, it is important when seen in the spectrum of Shaker history. It stands very visibly for the ability and desires of the sect to change with the times. From their earliest days, the Shakers were given to adaptation and adjustment in their furniture design, life-style, and theology. By 1872 when the Mt. Lebanon, New York, community had erected its new factory for producing the slat back chairs so collectible today, Elder Henry Blinn of Canterbury, New Hampshire, referred to the styles as "old fashioned chairs of one hundred years ago." Forty years later, the diary of a sister notes the automobile and telephone and speaks of the Shakers as being "very much like the inhabitants of the section of the country where they resided." Today, celibacy is the only tenet of the faith left unchanged.

While the Victorian period should be important to the history of the Shakers because of its representation of their attempts to 'keep up', the Victorian influence in Shaker architectural and furniture styles is looked upon with disdain by Shaker advocates. The "Horrors" of the era are epitomized in the former Trustees Office at Union Village, Ohio. This structure was originally built in 1810 but remodeled in 1892-95 with the inclusion of seven kinds of marble for the interior floors. From these floors has come its present title of "Marble Hall." The building has been eyed with great distaste by the students and teachers of Shaker. It has been considered to be a Western phenomenon, occurring in Ohio and Kentucky which were far removed from the seat of authority and regulation. Change was not limited to the West; it was happening in every corner of the Society. Mary Lynn Ray, now of the New Hampshire Historical Society, deserves recognition as having well expressed the transition that was taking place amidst the Shakers following their period of revival in the 1840's and becoming more intense after the Civil War. The following is from her "Introduction" to the catalogue *True Gospel Simplicity: Shaker Furniture In New Hampshire:*

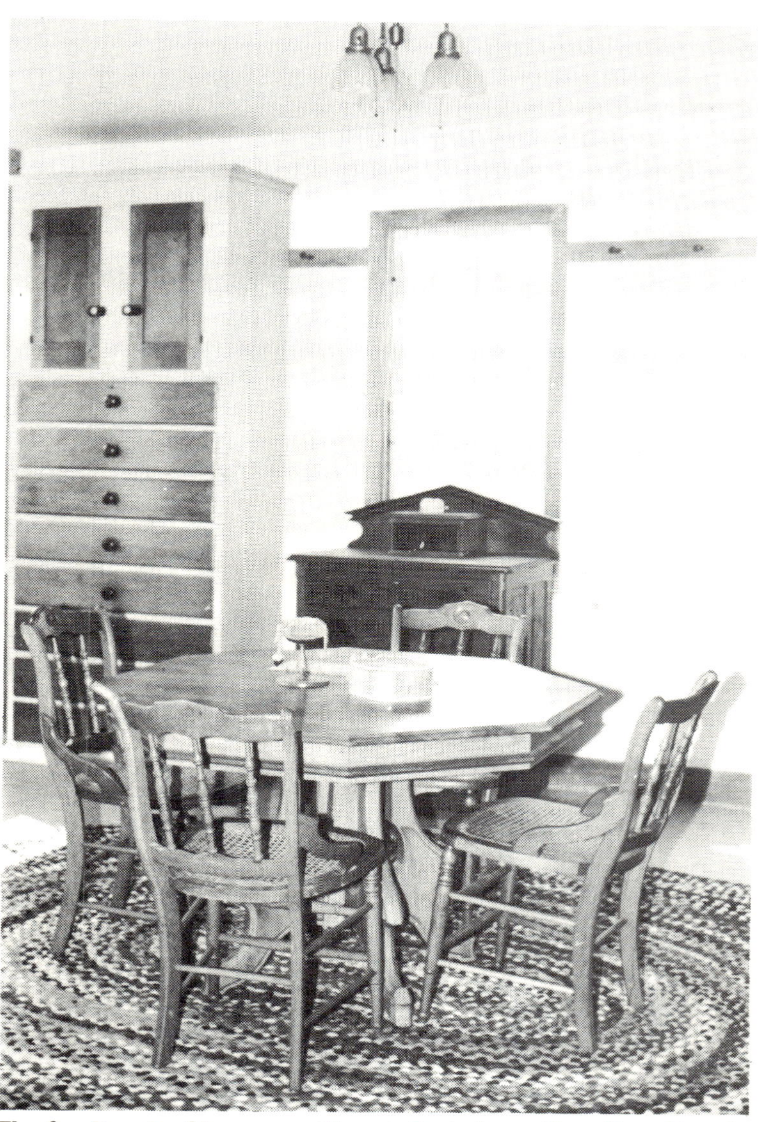

The furniture in this room setting at Canterbury, New Hamphire, is Shaker made. The chairs, attributed to Thomas Fisher, are fitted with tilters. Fisher was an Elder at Enfield, Connecticut, and is responsible for much Victorian style Shaker furnishings.

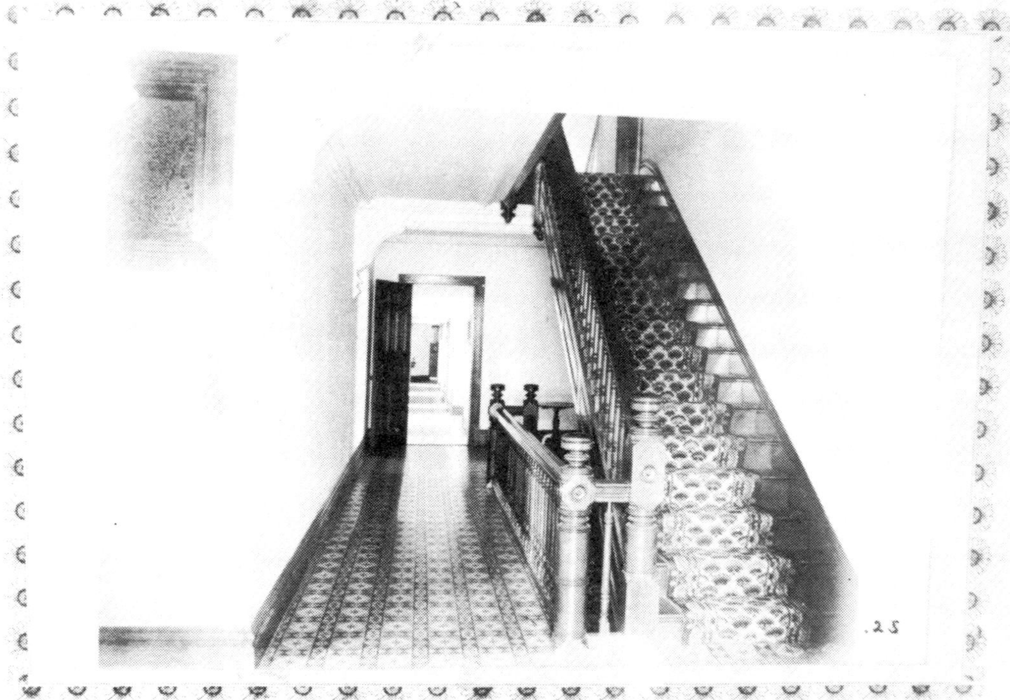

New England View Company.

These two photos point out that the desire to be contemporary occurred throughout the United Society. The old photo shows the second floor hall of the Trustees Office at Union Village, Ohio, while the other is its counterpart at Hancock, Massachusetts. The similarity in the use of turned bannister supports and floral patterns is striking.

". . .when the revival had passed, the Shakers were more and more exposed to fashion and change. Anxious to define themselves in modern terms, they adopted 'progressive' habits and, at Canterbury, discarded 'old-fashioned' relics of the earlier nineteenth century in a 'museum' room. . . .To discount Victorian Shaker furniture is to withold recognition from the climax of the Shaker experiment in New Hampshire. . . .after the Civil War, the

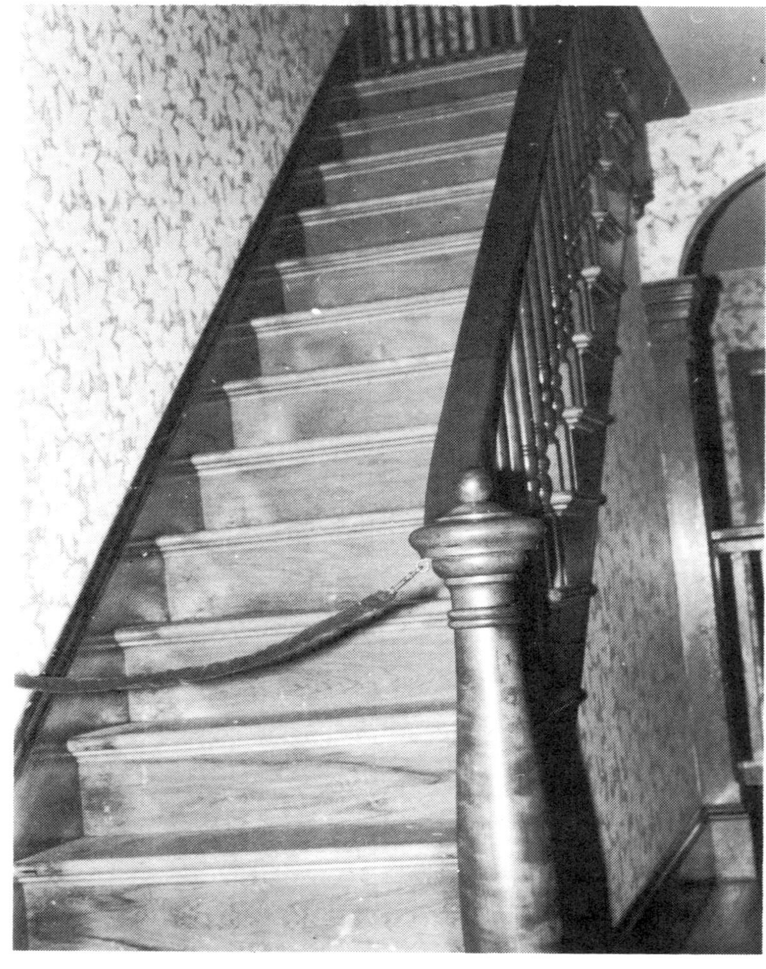

communities in New Hampshire were enjoying a renewal of vigor. The energy of the 1840's had resulted from an effort to withdraw from the world. . . .The vitality of the Victorian period was generated by an eagerness to acknowledge the contemporary world.''

Change was not happening in isolation in the extreme West, or East, of the United Society but permeated it. Elder John Slingerland was responsible for Marble Hall but he was a transplant from the central community of Mt. Lebanon and had started to gain an appreciation for the world's way while a member there. Ms. Ray, in an earlier article in *The Winterthur Portfolio* states: "A desk made for Eldress Augusta Stone 'after big fire at Lebanon, N.Y. 1875 by Elder Joseph Slingerland' is visually indistinguishable from writing desks used among the worldly.'' It is important to see that Slingerland had simply incorporated in Marble Hall many of the tastes to which he had become accustomed in New York. He had lived with elaborate turnings and marble for years before coming to Ohio. For example, marble topped trestle tables, for which Union Village is renowned, were first used at Mt. Lebanon in March, 1877.

The Trustee's Office itself points out the Society's wide acceptance of change and, yet, recognition of uniformity. A tour of the Trustees Office at Hancock, Massachusetts, (which the museum there has wisely decided to preserve in the Victorian manner) is little different than a stroll through its much maligned counterpart, Marble Hall. It is as though the same architect and construction crew had remodeled both. A study of Elmer Pearson's book *The Shaker Image* offers great insights into the desires of the Shakers to change with the times and to be contemporary. Such a study can also serve as

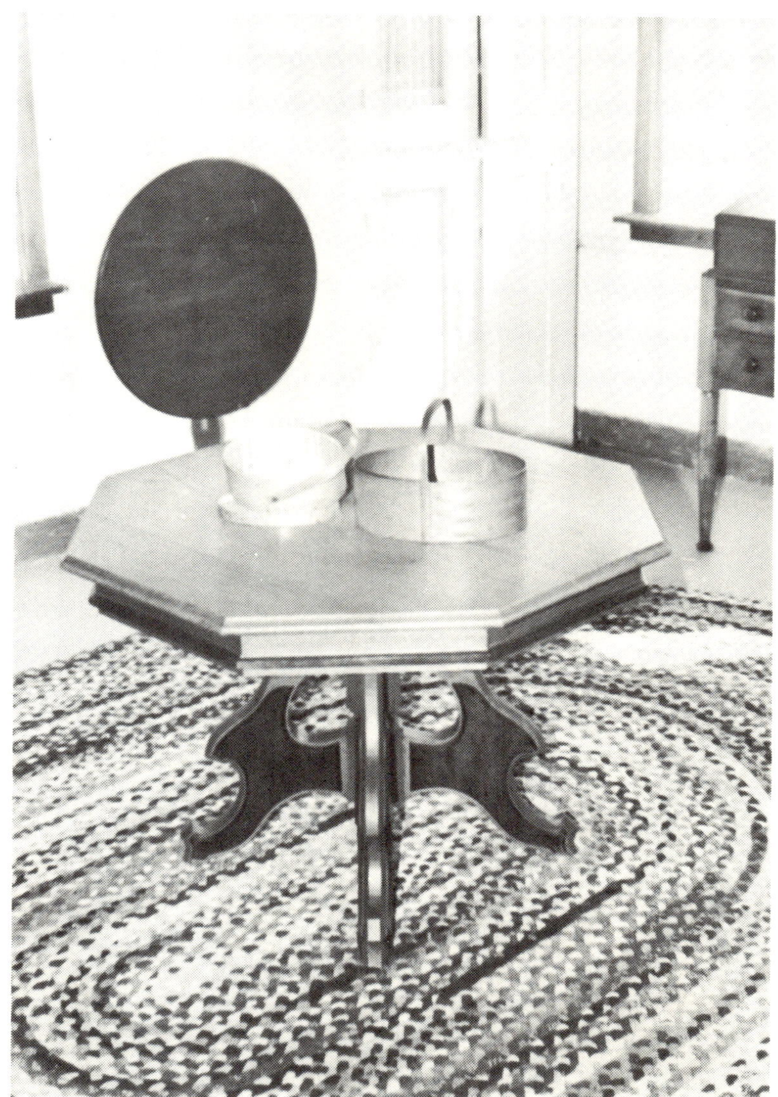

Another piece attributed to Fisher, this octogon top table is made of oak and trimmed with walnut.

recognition that change was taking place throughout the United Society of Believers.

Ms. Ray's statement about New Hampshire is applicable to the entire Shaker world: "Just as they rephrased their beliefs of a hundred years in the mode of modern grammar, the Shakers also restyled their traditional furniture forms to meet new needs.'' While the furniture of the latter century of the Shakers is more elaborate than that of the previous century, it is still simple in comparison to the styles of the time. The craftsmen of the time, far fewer in number than previously, felt the influence of the designs of their worldly contemporaries. But simplicity, quality, and usefulness were still concerns. Even though much of the furniture of the Victorian period was being purchased from the world, it was ordered to meet standards laid down by the Shaker elders. Victorian Shaker is important not only because of the continuing influence of earlier ways but because it symbolizes a period when the Shakers desired to prove to the world that their way was always timely.

— December, 1977

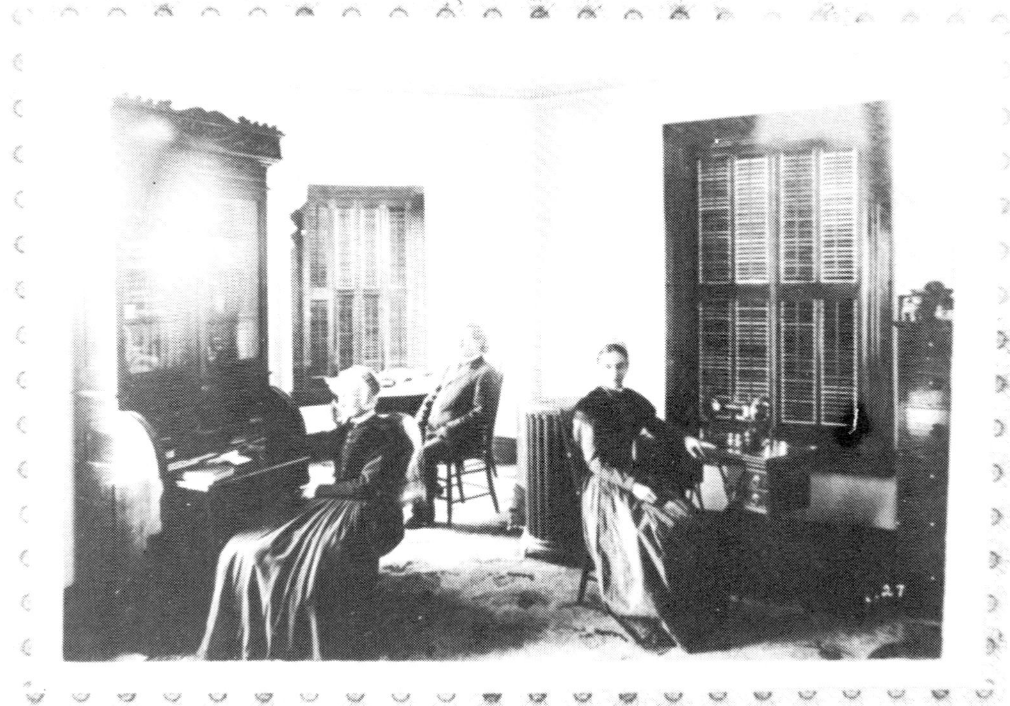

This photo of the remodeled Trustees Building (Marble Hall) at Union Village shows Elder John Slingerland in the background. Outside help was employed to do the remodeling. Furniture was also brought into the community from the outside as can be seen from the sewing machine. It is interesting to note the round radiators, invented at Mt. Lebanon, New York.

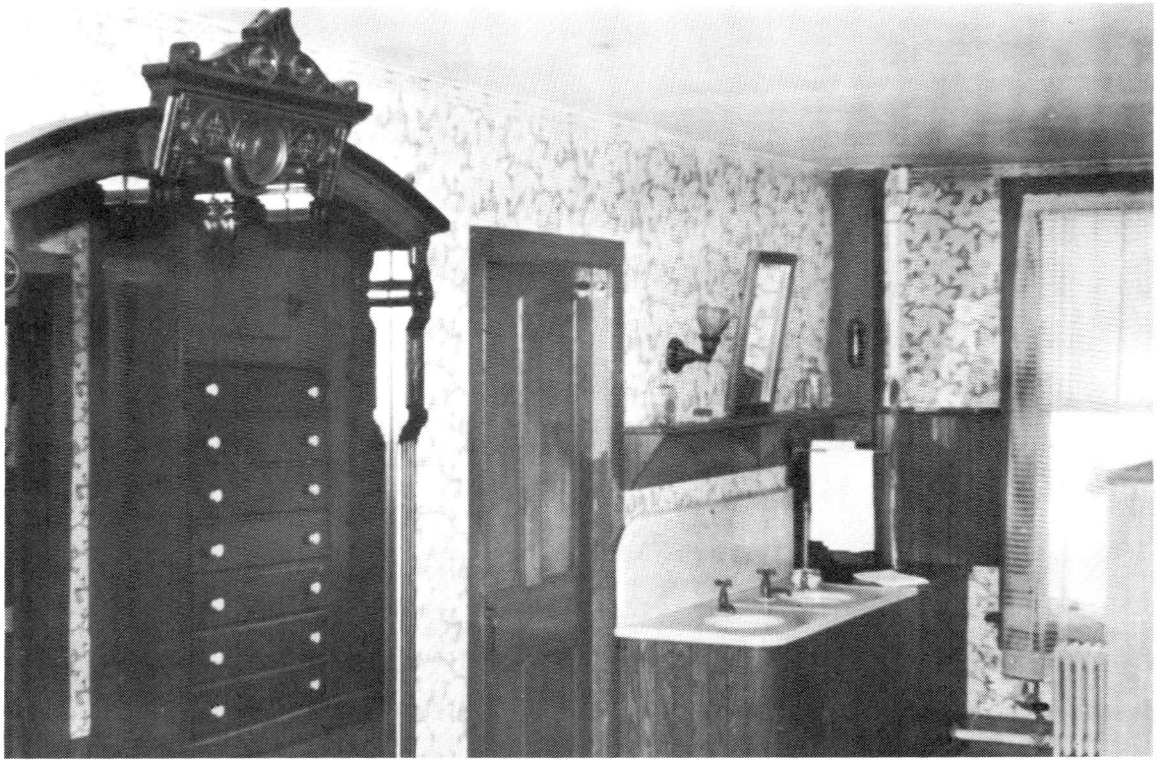

The hallway of the Trustees Office at Hancock, Massachusetts, shows much of the Victorian influence that had become a part of the Shakers around the beginning of the 20th century. Notice the marble sink, flowered wallpaper, porcelain knobs on the case of drawers reflected in the mirror, and the ornate mirror itself.

Influence on Danish

Long before I had any interest in antiques, I had an inclination towards furnishing any house of mine in Danish Modern with its clean, functional lines. With such an inclination, it was only natural that my taste in antiques be directed towards Shaker. Now, an exhibition from Denmark affirms the validity of my movement from modern to antique. Organized by the Danish Foreign Ministry for the USA '76 Committee in Denmark, *AN AMERICAN INSPIRATION: Danish Modern and Shaker Design* illustrates how knowledge of Shaker furniture influenced Danish designers.

In 1927, Kaare Klint, an architect and teacher, discovered a friend's Shaker rocking chair and had two of his students do measured drawings of it. In one of his books, Klint described this rocker as ''An American rocking-chair in the Colonial style...'' Shortly after discovering the first chair, one of Klint's collegues heard of another coming up at auction and sent a student to purchase it. How fascinating it is to think of purchasing a Shaker chair at an auction in Denmark! It was better than ten years, though, before these designers were to read Edward Deming Andrew's book on Shaker furniture, published in 1937, and discover the true manufacturers of their pattern chair.

Perhaps the closest relationship between Danish and Shaker chairs can be seen in a two-slat chair designed by Klint in 1943 (but not put into production) and the two-slat chairs of Mt. Lebanon. The lack of finials is the major difference. The shape of the upright supporting the arm and the use of a mushroom on the arm above the upright are very close. In fact, they are so close that I am glad Klint's chair was not produced en masse.

The Danish designers adapted some of the Shaker concepts in manufacturing as well as in design. The method of joining the arm support to the arm by means of a stud topped with a mushroom proved simple, efficient, and inexpensive. These were traits that were to be a part of a style called PORTEX. This style of furniture was conceived in 1945 to be produced and exported to countries devastated by the war

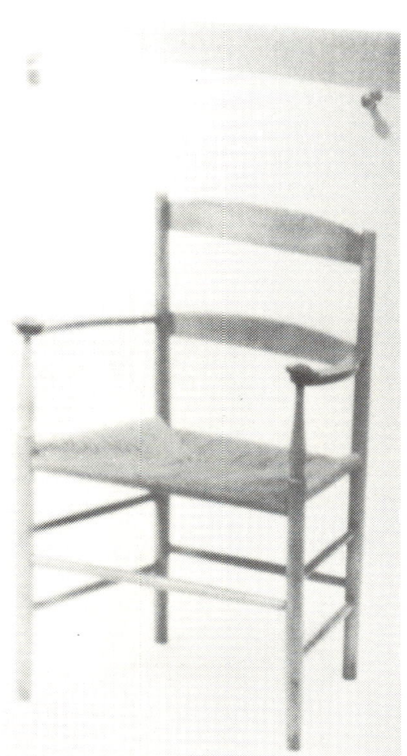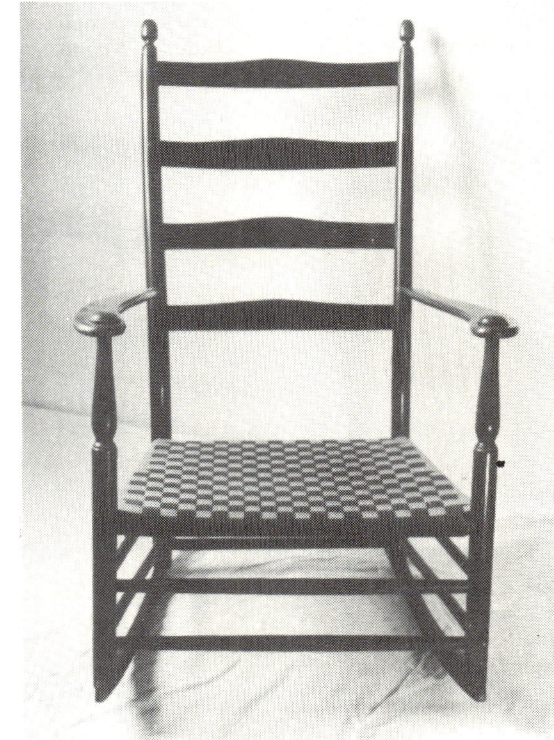

This chair (left) was designed by Kaare Klint in 1943. A striking similarity exists between this chair and many Shaker chairs. When this Hancock rocker (right) is compared to Klint's 1943 chair, the likeness in the slats, mushroom handholds and front uprights can readily be seen.

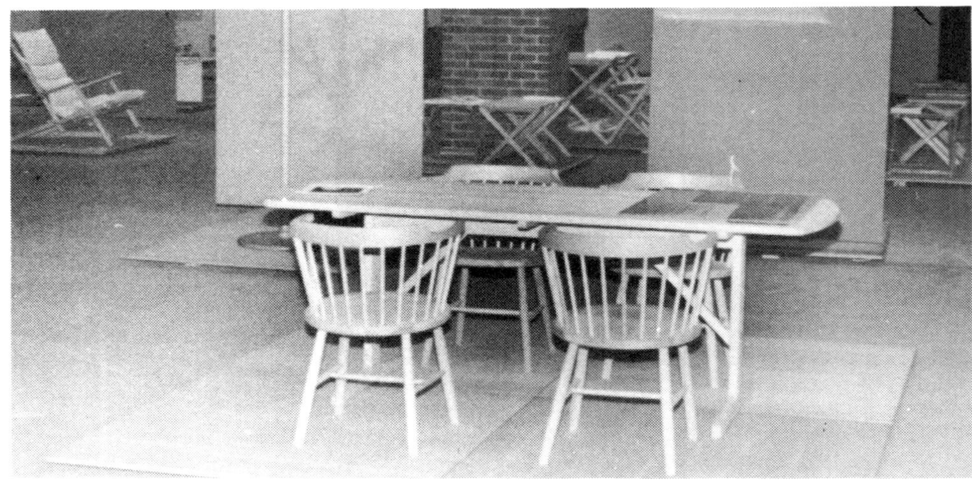

An overall view of the exhibition shows a Danish trestle table and spindle back chairs designed by Borge Mogensen in 1947 and still being produced. Compare the chairs to the Canterbury dining chair and Mt. Lebanon revolver in the photographs below.

and in need of inexpensive furnishings. It is interesting to note that one of the factors considered in the design of this style was ease of transport. Thus, the chairs were designed to stack exactly within a railroad box car. Besides the PORTEX furniture, other designs incorporated the idea of mass produced straight dowels for legs, stretchers and sometimes the back.

Chairs designed in 1947 by Borge Mogensen, a student of Klint's, reflect the spindle-back style of the Shaker revolvers or the Mt. Lebanon and Canterbury dining chairs. A tall spindle back rocker designed the same year by Hans J. Wegner is similar to the Shaker spindle-back rocking chairs. The rockers on the Wegner chair (which is still being produced) are almost identical to early Shaker carpet cutter type rockers. Mogensen also designed a trestle table to go with his chairs and it too reflects a knowledge of Shaker.

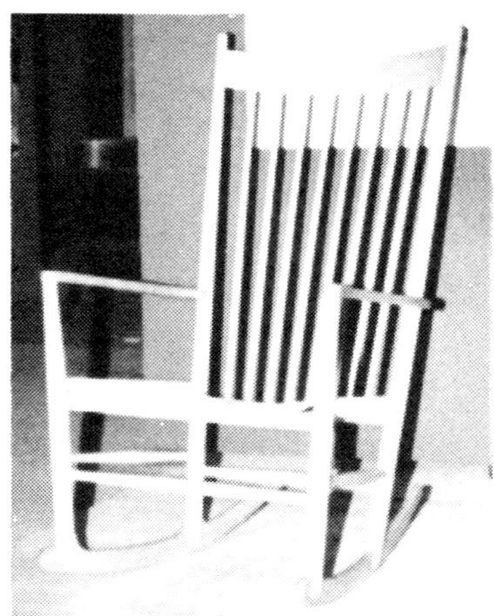

The rockers on this spindle back rocker by Hans J. Wegner are almost identical to those of Mt. Lebanon spindle back rockers.

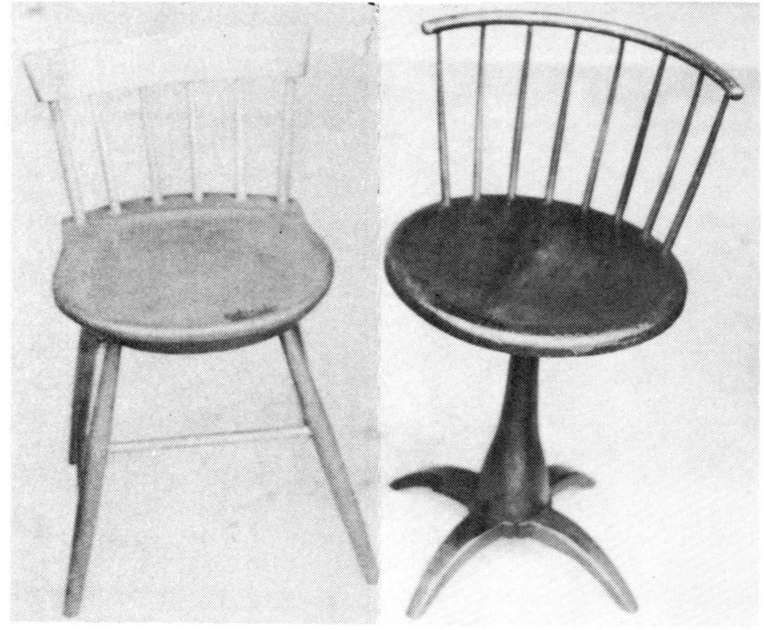

Canterbury dining chair and Mt. Lebanon revolver that probably served as the prototype for many Danish chair designs. Danish designers have produced an entire line of chairs utilizing straight turned pieces and plank seats.

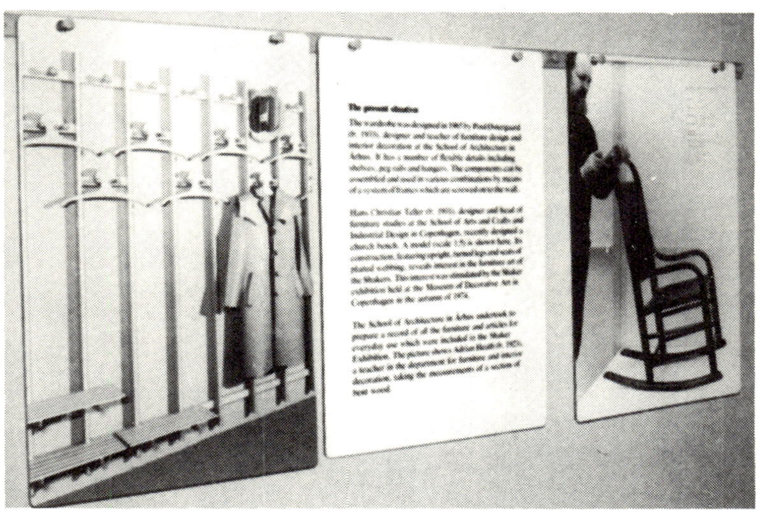

Present day Danish designers continue to incorporate the Shaker feeling into their furniture designs. Notice the use of pegboard and hangers in this built-in wardrobe. To the right, instructor Adrian Heath measures a Shaker bentwood rocker. He will have his students do the same.

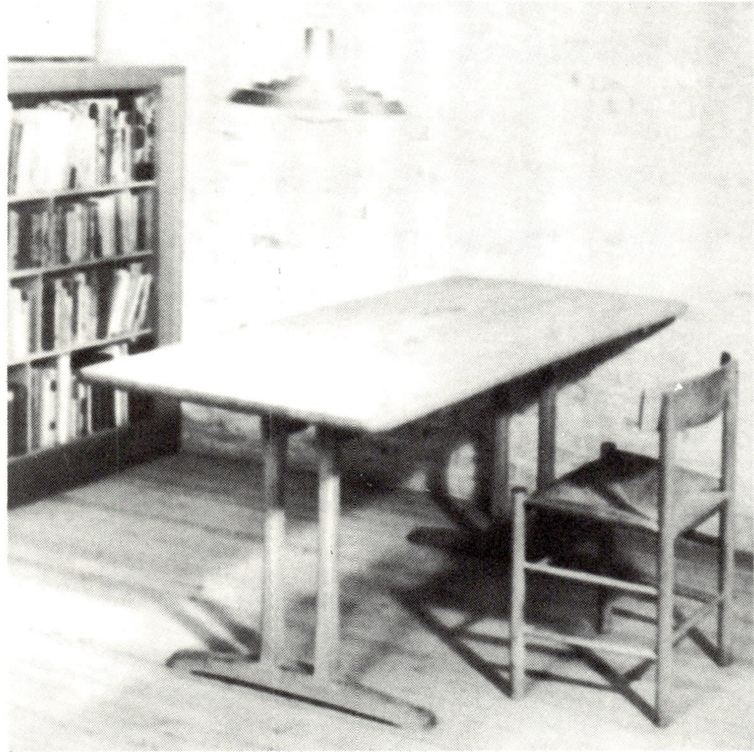

This placard illustrating a Danish variation of a Shaker trestle table and one slat dining chair served as the poster for the exhibition when it appeared in Boston.

Another Shaker feature that shows up often in Danish design is the peg. A recent design depicted in the exhibition is a wardrobe with the frame fastened to the wall and shelves, peg rail, and hangers adjusted as a person chooses. The peg is also seen under chairs. And one designer, Mogen Koch, created a line of yard furniture that could be folded and hung on pegs out of the way. The exhibition itself enhances the importance of the peg in Shaker and Danish design as the display material is suspended from pegs.

Along with the furniture and posters, the exhibition's creator, architect John Vedel-Rieper, documents the Shaker influence through illustrated materials that appeared in Danish architectural and design books. One of these, *Movelkunster,* (1955) by Ole Wanscler, speaks of the Shaker chair as "An example of a Shaker rocking-chair, clearly of Dutch origin, executed as late as 1850-1870. The slenderness of its construction is influenced by finical details, which in general could be sign of the artist-craftsman of both Europe and America of the period around 1850."

The contention is expressed in the exhibit that the Shaker influence is still being felt. An exhibition of Shaker furniture was held in 1974 in Copenhagen and later toured Europe. Inspired by

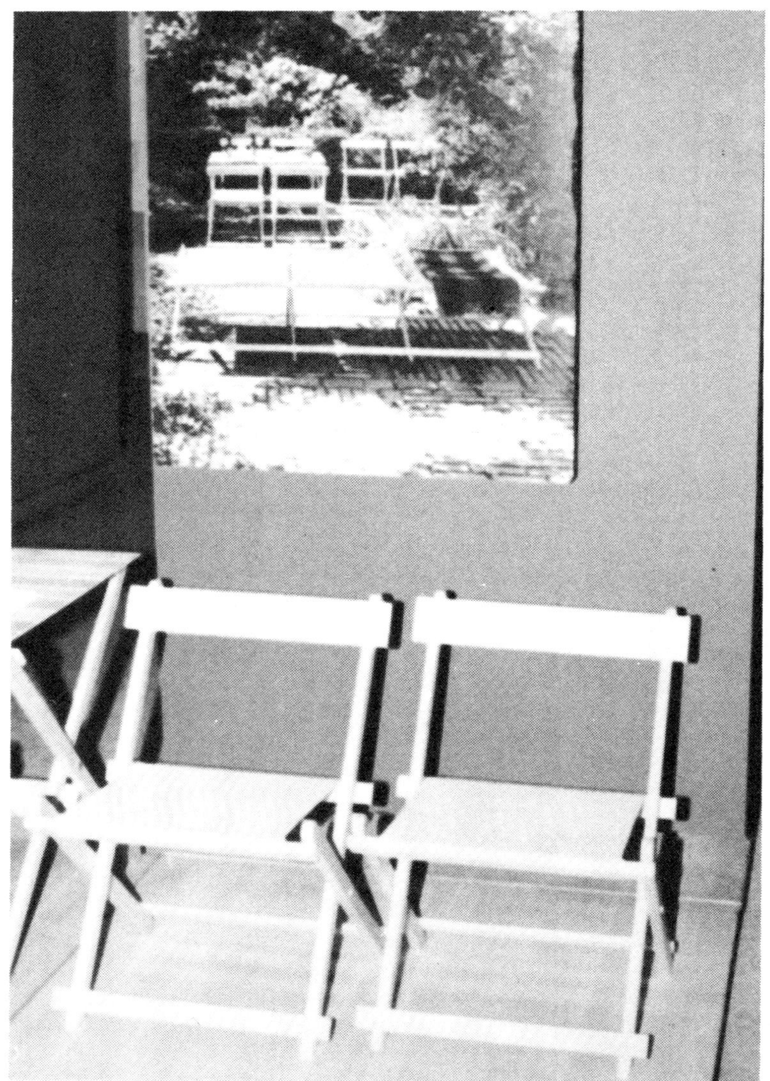

While the designer of this folding garden furniture does not attribute Shaker inspiration for his concepts, he produced this line to be hung from pegs. Incidently, folding chairs such as this were first illustrated in *Rural Homes* in 1853.

this exhibit, Hans Christian Teller designed a very simple and functional Church bench. Present teachers in the School of Architecture in Arhus are now having their students do as Kaare Klint's did 50 years ago—do measured drawings of a Shaker chair.

This exhibit is being circulated by the Smithsonian Institution Traveling Exhibition Service and is on display at the Midland Center for the Arts in Midland, Michigan, until November 13th. The Midland Art Council has added some original Shaker furnishings from a local collection to enable the viewer to see more clearly the similarities between Danish and Shaker.

— November, 1977

Collecting Shaker

One of the purposes of the *Ohio Antique Review* for which these articles were originally written is to report upon the marketplace of antiques...what is selling...for how much...and why? This third section of *The Shaker Way* includes such reports on Shaker as well as insights into collecting the artifacts of America's largest communal group.

It is in this section that the date when the material was first printed is particularly important. This date, printed at the end of the article, offers clues to the increase or stability of prices. It points out that time is a factor in the determination of values and prevents the potential customer from being misguided by the prices that appear here. But time is not the only influence on price; place; competition, authenticity, rarity, provenance and condition all contribute to what is paid for an item. For example, a built-in cupboard over drawers sold at the PB 84 auction in New York City in October, 1973, for $1,950 while a very similar one brought almost the same amount, $1,800, at Robert Skinner's auction in Massachusetts in July, 1979. And both of these far exceed the $510 that was paid privately for one about the same time as the Skinner sale. This is only to say that, in the final analysis, the fair price is determinded by what the potential customer/collector is willing to pay to possess a piece of history.

Over the last twenty years, Shaker artifacts have come a long way in gaining respect and appreciation among dealers and collectors of quality American antiques. Shaker is just beginning to be accepted in the same conversations with Queen Anne, Hepplewhite, Sheraton, etc. But the prices of Shaker furniture lag far behind those of the accepted classic styles and some of the better pieces are "good buys," because of their excellence in form and craftsmanship. Well designed, constructed and documented Shaker furnishings are worthy of a position in any collection of American antiques.

Why Collect ?

Why is Shaker such a talked about and collectible area of antiques? The answer is in its universality; it has a widespread interest to people in many and varied areas of life. Few areas of antique collecting are as encompassing as is Shaker. Whatever a person's depth of enthusiasm, personal economics, field of discipline or historical perspective, he can find a place in the world of Shaker.

Some people can spend a delightful afternoon at the restored village of Pleasant Hill in Kentucky or Hancock in Massachusetts and go away with a feeling of being familiar with the Shakers. But for those who desire to get to know the Shakers better, innumerable books, pamphlets, and manuscripts are available. In addition to the ready accessibility of information, Shaker collections in Dearborn, Michigan, Cleveland, Dayton, and Lebanon, Ohio, and in Pleasant Hill, Bowling Green, and Auburn, Kentucky, are also nearby for Midwesterners. For the advanced collector, person with advanced interests, visits to the communities of the East are possible.

Whether a person is content to simply eat a Shaker style meal once in a while or must visit every Shaker collection in the country, he can find satisfaction in the wealth of Shaker knowledge to be gained.

The same can be said for the collector. Shaker offers a wide range of challenge, price, and interest. For the beginner, many Shaker artifacts such as chairs,

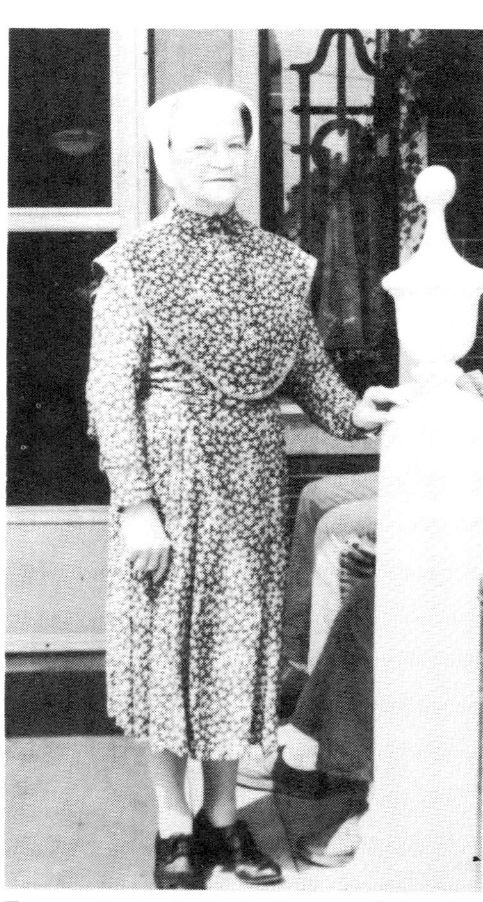

Eldress Gertrude Soule is one of the two Shaker sisters still living at Canterbury, New Hampshire.

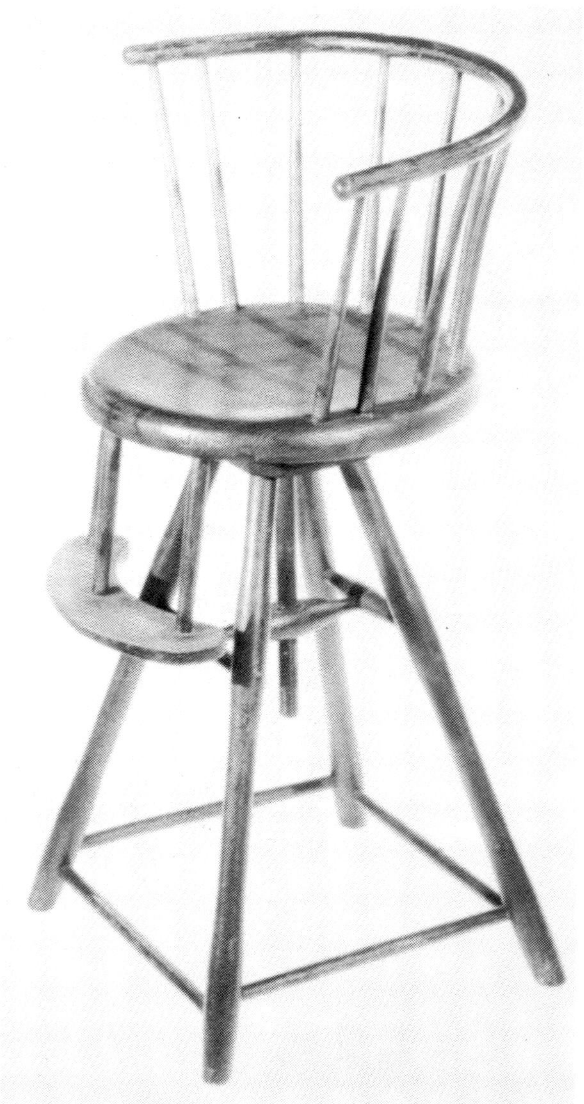

Designers, engineers and woodworkers are all interested in the lines and workmanship of a Shaker swivel high chair. (Courtesy of the Henry Ford Museum, Dearborn, Michigan)

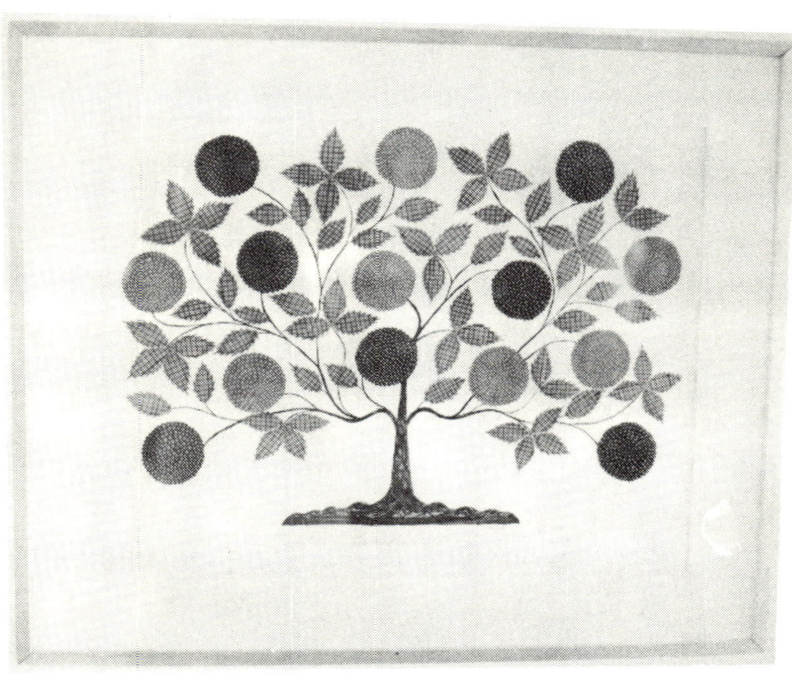

The Tree of Life with its vivid green and orange colors has become the standard logo associated with the Shakers. It was a vision seen and painted by Hannah Cohoon on July 3, 1854. Being an inspirational or spirit drawing, it represents the peak of Shaker collecting as well as the mystical element of the Shaker faith that is seldom understood but a challenge to theologians and psychologists.

almanacs, bottles, and treenware are labeled. Other artifacts such as poplarware and oval fingered boxes as well as many chairs and tables are very easily identified as Shaker. With the help of one or two good books and a visit to a Shaker collection, a person could begin to collect Shaker. But for the collector who wants a greater challenge, there is always the search for the uncommon...the signed piece of furniture, the Spirit drawing, the Union Village, Ohio, seed box, etc. A newcomer to Shaker will find easily recognizable Shaker items available for under $20 while the advanced collector might find it necessary to spend $20,000 for the table of his choice. And it is never too late to begin. In 1965, Charles Upton and his wife referred to their early days of collecting Shaker and recalled how people advised them in 1950 that they were too late to begin collecting Shaker. Today, the Uptons have a superb collection. A couple of good Shaker collections have been put together in Ohio and New York primarily within the last five years.

While Shaker offers a wide range of challenge and prices to collectors, it also touches the interests of many disciplines. The minister is attracted to the Shakers because of their unique theology. The sociologist discovers the Shakers as he studies Utopian societies. The pharmacist tries to distill rosewater according to the old Shaker recipe. Cookbooks offer the gourmet chef an opportunity to mix up a rich Shaker dessert. The architect approaches Shaker through the work of Micajah Burnett and his twin spiral staircases at Pleasant Hill. The professor of design is interested in the furniture of the Shakers with their form-following-function philosophy. The craftsman seeks to reproduce the finest of workmanship that is reflected in the products of the Shaker hands. The engineer is fascinated by the creativity of the Shakers in developing labor-saving machines. Periodicals on printing, pharmacy, decorating, woodworking, cooking, and design have all given attention to the Shakers and their work. Probably no other area of antique

collecting touches so many facets of life.

While Shaker offers a range of challenge in a range of prices in a range of disciplines, it also brings an almost timeless quality to antique collecting. With the exception of some of the huge built-ins, much of the Shaker furniture and crafts fit well...in space, practicability, and design...into modern homes. They are the product of a people who started in America in 1774 but who are still in existence today. Probably no other area of antique collecting presents so well the opportunity to search for the past and meet the present. Some of these people can still be met and the memories of these meetings cherished along with the other Shaker mementos. The Shaker collector can find joy in an 18th century piece of furniture or in a letter written just last week from Sister Mildred Barker, one of six Shaker sisters now residing at Sabbathday Lake, Maine. To the Shaker collector, the emery strawberries made by the Canterbury, New Hampshire, sisters last year are as desirable as the ones made 150 years ago. They are reminders of the people who have chosen a way of life and disciplined themselves in it. Touching the Shakers of today enhances the collecting of the artifacts of yesterday. In collecting Shaker, some people may be content to own an oval box or visit a museum but others may desire to not only collect, but meet a part of history.

— April, 1978

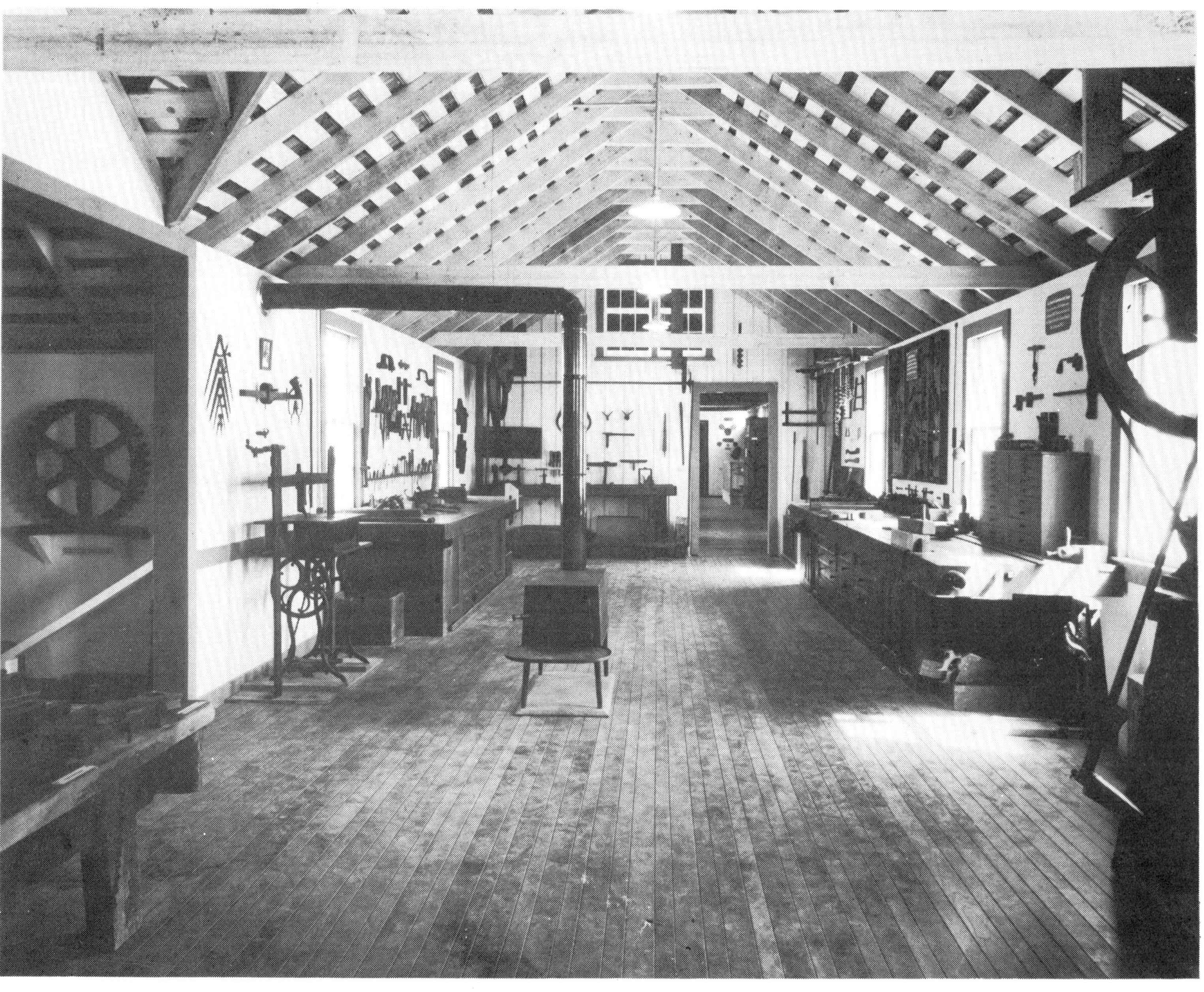

The carpentry shop at the Shaker Museum in Old Chatham, New York, offers a beginning or advanced collector many hours of enjoyment in the examination of the innovative use of machines in Shaker craftsmanship. (Photograph by Lees Studio, Chatham, New York, Courtesy of The Shaker Museum, Old Chatham, N.Y.)

How Do You Know It's Shaker?

Recently, a young man was describing to me a one-door cupboard that he said was "Shaker". I asked him in which community it was made or had belonged. When he could not answer this question, I pursued by asking the standard question: "How do you know it is Shaker?" His reply was also fairly standard . . . "Well, because it has simple lines!"

Sometimes the answers vary from "that's what the dealer I bought it from told me" to "it came out of up-state New York" or "it is so well made". In my ten years of following the Shaker trail, I have drawn some tentative conclusions. The subject is so complex, I feel there are no experts on Shaker furniture and artifacts. There may be an individual who knows well the items that were produced at the Mt. Lebanon, New York, community and another who is an authority on the Canterbury, New Hampshire, products and a lady who knows Union Village, Ohio, furniture. But it seems there is no one person who is completely knowledgeable in the vast field of Shaker artifacts.

When it comes to antique dealers, there is only one or possibly two whose expertise I greatly admire. As a matter of fact, opinions I favor most are those from non-professionals in the field . . . the long-time collector or scholar who is in it because of a deep appreciation for and a greater understanding of the Shakers' unique ways of work and worship.

How, then, can you know that an item is indeed Shaker made or used? In many cases, attribution may be impossible and, therefore, you will never know. With today's Shaker pieces commanding the high prices they do, you should not, and need not, settle for questionable pieces. The burden of proof should be on the seller to prove that an article is genuine Shaker rather than for the buyer to assume it is. Reputable dealers will not hesitate to supply the buyer with a signed and dated statement attesting to origin, probable date, and any other facts that affix unquestionable proof that an article is Shaker.

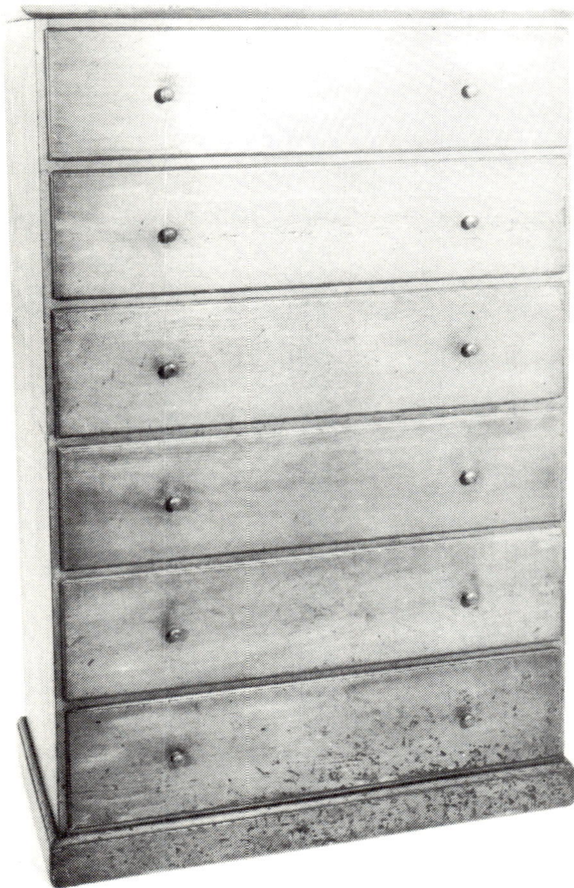

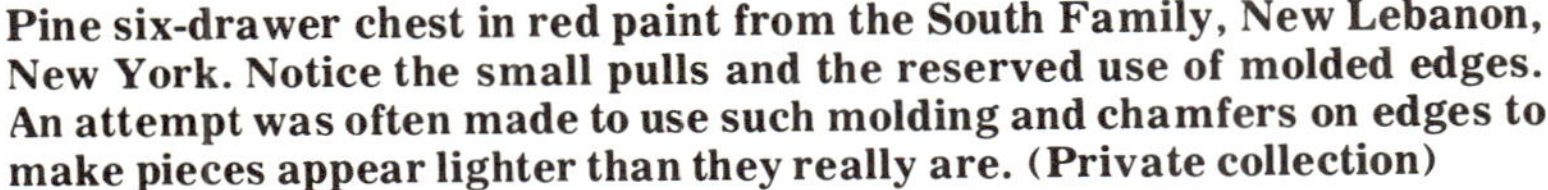

Pine six-drawer chest in red paint from the South Family, New Lebanon, New York. Notice the small pulls and the reserved use of molded edges. An attempt was often made to use such molding and chamfers on edges to make pieces appear lighter than they really are. (Private collection)

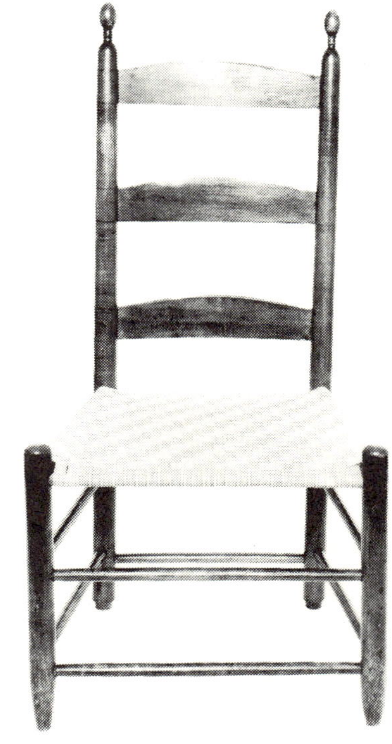

An "early" Shaker side chair with the distinctive finials and tilting buttons or "tilters" in the rear legs. (Private collection)

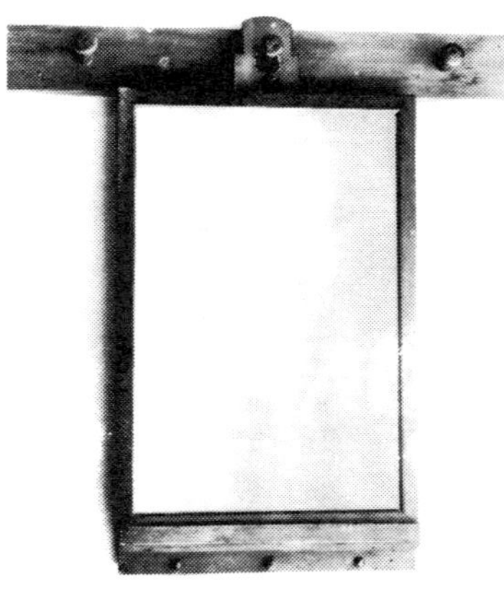

Looking glass is particularly distinguishable as Shaker because of the shaped upper end of the hanger. (Golden Lamb Inn, Lebanon, Ohio)

Many would suggest that Shaker articles possess a visual and physical feel. Simply put, it "speaks to them". The idea is that a person who has lived with Shaker and studied it for some time can "hear" the simple lines and construction saying "Shaker" to them. I recall the story about one "expert" in the field who visited an antique shop and chastised the owner for selling a stand as Shaker. The dealer knew the history of the stand and knew it to be right. So she simply put the stand away until another day when the acknowledged "expert" came. This time he raved about the stand as one of the finest examples of Shaker design and craftsmanship he had ever seen. In other words, there are many times when even trained eyes and feelings are wrong.

There are a number of factors that contribute to the problem of identification. Shaker craftsmanship was not always of the high quality which is associated with the items to be seen in books and museums. Most of the Shaker craftsmanship was adequate while some was excellent and some was poor. The period of Shaker production spans 150 years (1790-1940). During this time, the Shakers responded to changes in style, particularly those items made for sale to the world. Although the furniture of Ohio and Kentucky Shakers was more worldly and never reached the stylistic uniformity of the Eastern communities, Victorian and later designs influenced the construction in all of the communities. When you visit Marble Hall in Union Village outside of Lebanon, Ohio, with its French marble floors or the Trustees building at Hancock, Massachusetts, with its rooms papered in red Japanese patterned wallpaper or examine the ornately carved oak stands of Thomas Fisher of Enfield, Connecticut, you become very much aware that Shaker taste was not always simple and standard.

Let us return to the question, "How do you know it is truly Shaker?" I suggest that there are three exacting tests: I. Style; II. History; III. Mark. You can accumulate opinions (hopefully from knowledgeable people) that will lead you to believe a piece is Shaker. But being a skeptic, I like for a piece to have one or more of these three feature before I am willing to invest in an item as Shaker.

I. Style. There are many designs that are exclusively Shaker and readily recognized as such. The most notable of these are found in chairs. Distinctively shaped finials on the top of the posts and tilters on the bottom of the early (made for their own use) side chairs indicate Shaker-made. The form of the mass produced (made for sale to the world) Mt. Lebanon chairs are also readily identifiable. Other exclusive Shaker styles are oval boxes with Gothic fingers, trestle tables with arched feet, sewing desks with sliding shelf and multiple drawers, tables with rod like turned legs, table top desks with drawers, low back dining chairs with one or two slats or spindles, hanging shelves, and some small craft items. Even the untrained eye can determine that these are Shaker if the person has done a bit of reading in the books on Shaker furniture.

II. History. It is possible with most important pieces of Shaker furniture to be able to directly attribute them to a particular community. We are near enough in time to the demise of most of the communities that a tracing of the history of a piece of furniture is often obtainable. Whitewater in Ohio closed in 1907 but the property of the North Family had remained in the hands of the original purchasers until last year. Many of the communities were purchased by churches or states for institutional purposes and are still maintained by these groups. Articles have been sold to hired workers, nearby residents or through auctions and many are only one exchange of hands away

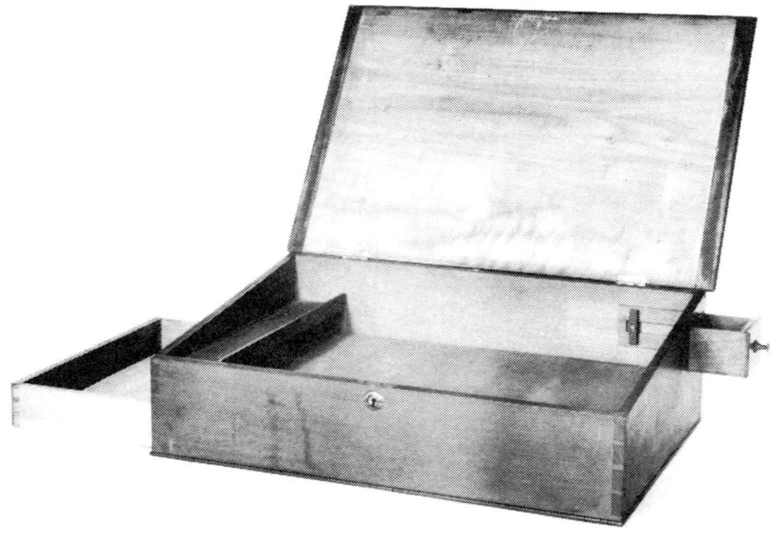

Mount Lebanon table or lap desk made of pine with maple bread board ends. (The Shaker Museum, Old Chatham, N. Y.)

from their original settings.

Darrow School at New Lebanon, New York, consisting of the North and Church Family buildings and furnishings was purchased in 1932 directly from the Shakers. The school held an auction in 1973 disposing of the contents of the North Family Dwelling. Hancock was not closed until 1960 and there were many pieces that people had purchased down through recent years directly from the Shakers before that community's end. In a week's stay at Mt. Lebanon this summer, I was amazed at the wealth of furnishings that are in private hands and which can be directly traced to their origin. Two of the Shaker communities are still functioning and have buildings furnished with a great deal of furniture and accessories. The Shakers are not out of the distant past but are relatively close in time. Their quality products live on . . . and so should the history of these items.

III. Mark. The easiest way to identify Shaker artifacts is by an identifying mark or sign. Seed boxes, sewing boxes, bottles, cloaks, and chairs often carry the Shaker name on labels. However, one should examine the label carefully for counterfeits are being made. Other Shaker articles carry the name of the Trustee under whose guidance the items were produced. Bottles from Mt. Lebanon bear the name David Meacham or just D.M. The name Babbitt appears with some Union Village medicines. Fowler or Fowlre is found on some stoneware used, but not made, by the Shakers. Additional identification can be found from the "world's" distributor of Shaker made items. Thus, A.J. White of New York is found on most almanacs and J.H. Sprague of Boston was a leading distributor of oval boxes.

The real highlight of Shaker identification, though, is not in labels but personal markings. Although it is said that Shakers did not personalize items, there is ample evidence to prove otherwise. Coat hangers with the names of the owners on them are numerous. Many small boxes and hat molds also carry the owner's name. And there is even furniture bearing the proud maker's signature. If you should find a name on a piece suspected to be Shaker, a check of some lists in THE SHAKER QUARTERLY published in Sabbathday Lake, Maine, or with the Western Reserve Historical Society, Cleveland, Ohio, could help in identification.

How do you know it is Shaker? You can tell by style, history, or mark. A red blanket chest that sold at a Whitewater, Ohio auction recently is a good illustration. The property had been in the same family since being purchased from the Shakers. The chest looked O.K. in construction and style but all blanket chests look pretty much alike. The history was O.K. since it came right out of a Shaker dwelling. But the final touch was added by the name on the back . . . "H.B. Bear". A quick check of the Whitewater history revealed that Henry B. Bear was Elder and Trustee there from 1846 until 1901. That blanket chest is Shaker for it has style, history, and mark.

(Acknowledgement is given to John Kassay, Professor, San Francisco State University, for his critical reading of this article and for providing the illustrations and their descriptions.)

— November, 1975

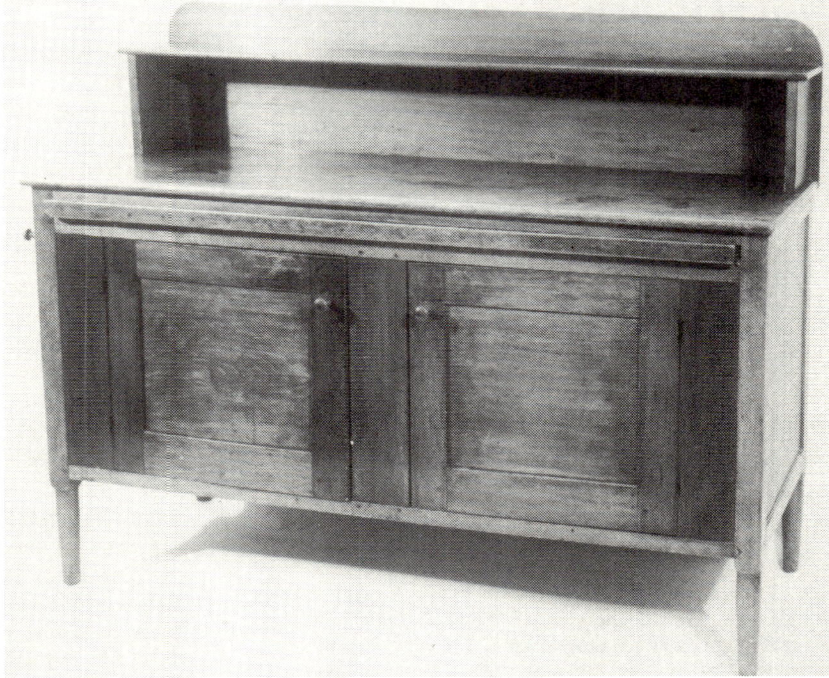

This sideboard is walnut, birch, and pine with traces of original red paint. It can be traced to its long use in the ministry dining room at Canterbury, New Hampshire. The legs and sliding shelf are typical Shaker styles. (Private collection)

One-of-a-kinds

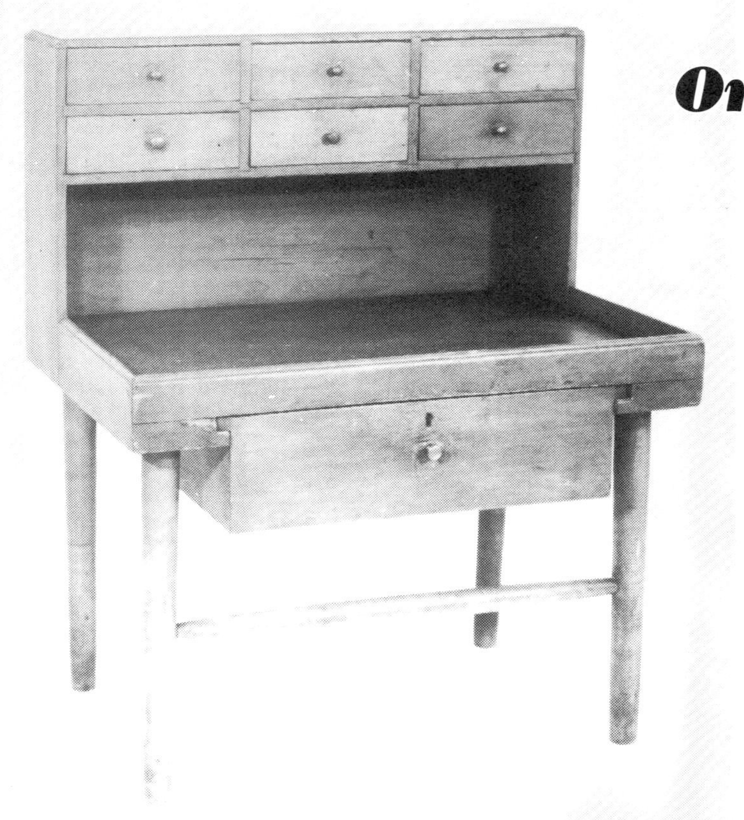

From Harvard, Mass., this pine, painted red, sewing table is unique. It dates from the first half of the 19th Century and is currently on exhibit at the Fruitlands Museum in Harvard. With small drawer pulls and plain turnings, it is a one of a kind piece. What would be its value? (Photograph by John Kassay)

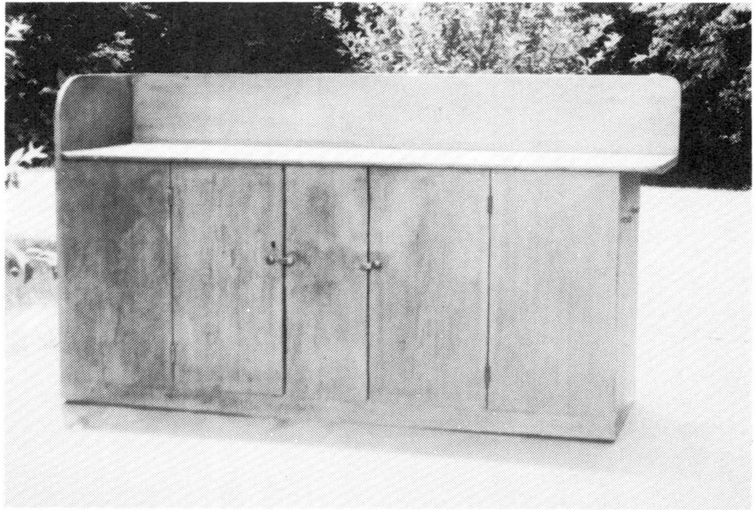

While there must have been numerous wash stands in the Shaker communities, this particular one exhibits the best of the craftsman's skills. The one board side on the left is champhered from the sink top to the upper edge so as to match the cant on the rear splash board. The two small pegs on the right end are threaded. The condition, construction and simplicity of lines sets this piece apart from others and make the determination of its value difficult for seller and buyer.

One of the great problems in distinguishing and determining the value of fine Shaker artifacts is the lack of comparative pieces. Like any products of a religious sect or an ethnic group (Pennsylvania Dutch, Zoar, Harmonites. Norwegian, etc.), those of the Shakers compose only a small part of the vast amount of furniture and accessories made in the 19th century. At their peak, the Shakers numbered about 5,500 of the United States' population of over 17 million. The small size of the Shaker order contributes to the lack of availability of comparative items.

Some items can be compared, though, because they were manufactured in volume for sale to the world. The Shakers were well aware of the market-place of the world and were not above merchandizing their wares. They designed and manufactured fancy goods for strictly commercial reasons even though the products were too ornate for their own use. They developed regular sales routes, printed catalogues, and promoted their products through heavy advertising and personal endorsements. Herbs, medicinal products, seeds, oval boxes and carriers, sewing kits, cloaks, ketchup, pickles, ink pens, stoves, bonnets, stools, chairs and much more were often made for the primary purpose of producing income. Since these were mass produced, style and quality were uniform and present values can be ascertained from studying the sales of similar items. Thus, red and black labeled Mt. Lebanon seed boxes are basically the same with only the price varying - from $25 ten years ago to around $200 today. Consideration of mass produced Shaker articles points out an interesting paradox.

Having been made by the thousands, often by use of machines, and for wordly consumption, these products of Shaker hands do not have great intrinsic worth. On the other hand, they are readily identifiable as Shaker (many times bearing the Shaker mark or label) and are greatly desired and sought by today's antique collectors.

With the exception of chairs, the opportunities for comparison between pieces of Shaker furniture are not great. Almost all of the established Shaker communities manufactured chairs for sale to the world. The Mt. Lebanon, N.Y., community even marked theirs, catalogued them by size, and wholesaled them to major furniture stores from Boston to Milwaukee. Other articles of furniture were occasionally made to order for a neighbor or friend. But the overwhelming majority of Shaker furniture was produced for use within the community. This means that the total production of candlestands would be limited by the total number of bedrooms in the communities. With regard to the furniture in sitting rooms, the "Millinnial Laws, or Gospel Statutes and Ordinances" states that "One rocking chair in a room is sufficient, except where the aged reside. One table, one or two stands, a lamp stand may be attached to the woodwork, if desired." The number of elders desks would be limited to two for each of the eighteen settlements. It is difficult to make accurate comparisons in Shaker furniture because the supply is relatively small...limited by the number of Shakers themselves who could have used the pieces.

The points of comparison become even fewer when we consider the variance in style from one community to another. There was a tendency for each community to reflect the environment in which it was located. The two Kentucky communities used plantation desks, a form common

to the area but unheard of in the Eastern Shaker settlements. The Ohio communities had large corner cupboards, again common to the area but not found in the Eastern families. Conversely, the multi-drawered sewing desks appear to be a style found only in the East.

Finally, one needs to remember that when a Shaker craftsman made a piece of furniture he usually made it for a specific place. Sometimes this did mean uniformity as on the occasion of furnishing a new building. As the structure neared completion, the cabinet makers would produce large numbers of stands, tables, beds, etc. More often, though, a craftsman made a piece of furniture in response to a particular request or need. A cupboard at Pleasant Hill, Ky., was made to fit between the two entrances to the dining room. Because of the opening of the doors, the sides of the cupboard are canted. That

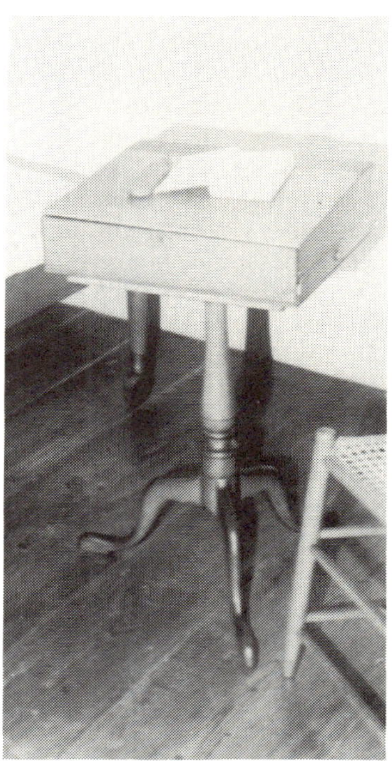

Tripod based pedestal desks are rare in Shaker furniture but the drawer in the side puts this one in a class by itself.

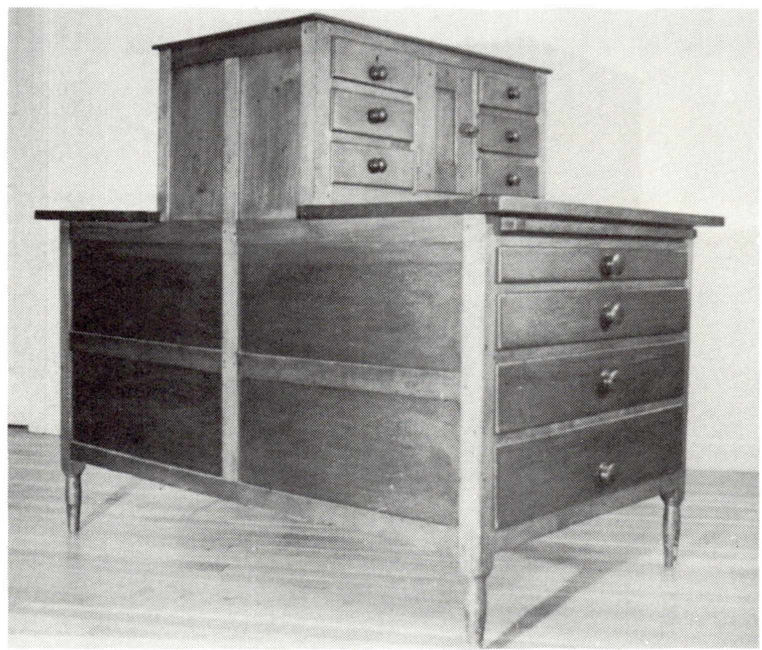

While there are a number of multi-drawered sewing desks, this one is in a class by itself. The Sabbathday Lake Shaker community in Maine has a matching pair of sewing desks but this double one from Harvard, Massachusetts, is one-of-a-kind. Since there are no comparative pieces, the value of this superb piece can not be adequately determined unless the collector were to put it up for auction. (Milt Sherman Collection)

cupboard was built for that particular spot and would fit no where else. The same idea applies to most Shaker furniture. This becomes especially visable in the late sewing desks where the backs are also finely finished because they were made to stand in a specific location protruding into the room and allowing all sides to be seen. The majority and best of Shaker furniture was made as an individual piece for a specific location and a particular purpose. This motivation of construction makes comparison all but impossible.

Quality and prices can be compared in the mass produced items. Even chairs, tables, stands, cases of drawers, and candlestands can find some points of comparison since many of them were made to fulfill similar functions within the Shaker communities. But how can a person evaluate a double sewing desk or a library ladder or an infirmary screen? These items are individual creations and have no specific point of reference to other pieces of Shaker furniture. The answer is a simple "whatever the market will bear!" That market often appears exceedingly high as the prices of tables, chairs, seed boxes, etc. are examined. But the unique, one-of-a-kind item still has not reached its peak. To the best of my knowledge, only one piece of Shaker furniture has sold for over $10,000. While that may be high for the average collector, it is behind the market for similar quality in non-Shaker American antiques.

— November, 1978

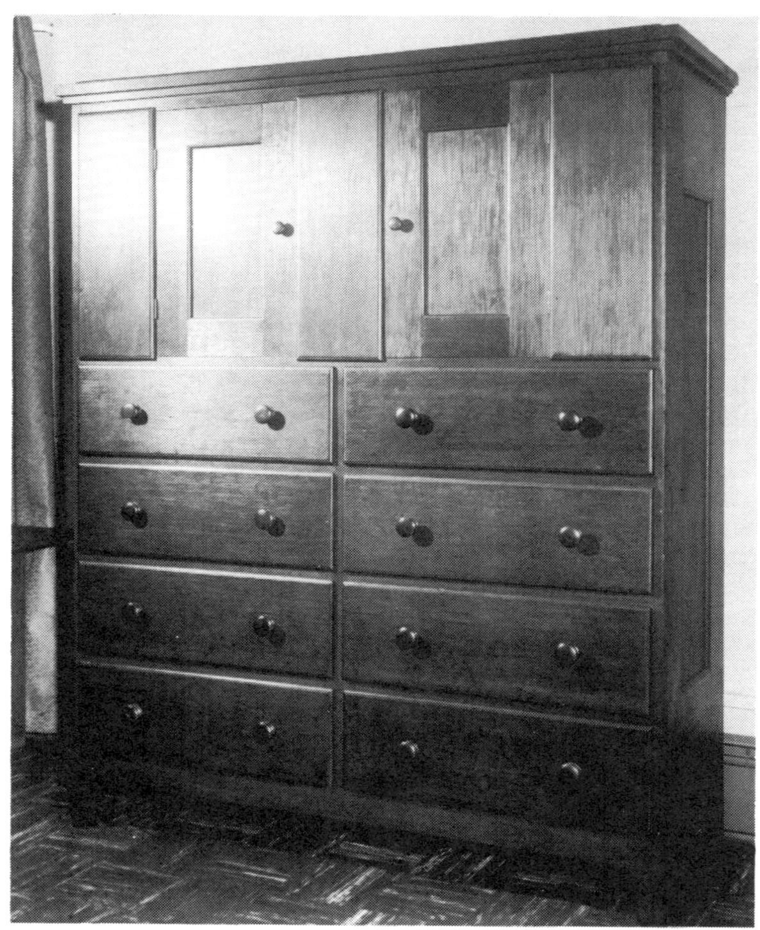

The raised panels on the front make this cupboard over case of drawers different from similar cupboards-over-drawers. If this were available on the antique market, there would be no comparative pieces to help in determining its worth.
(Photograph courtesy of Shaker Museum, Old Chatham, N.Y.)

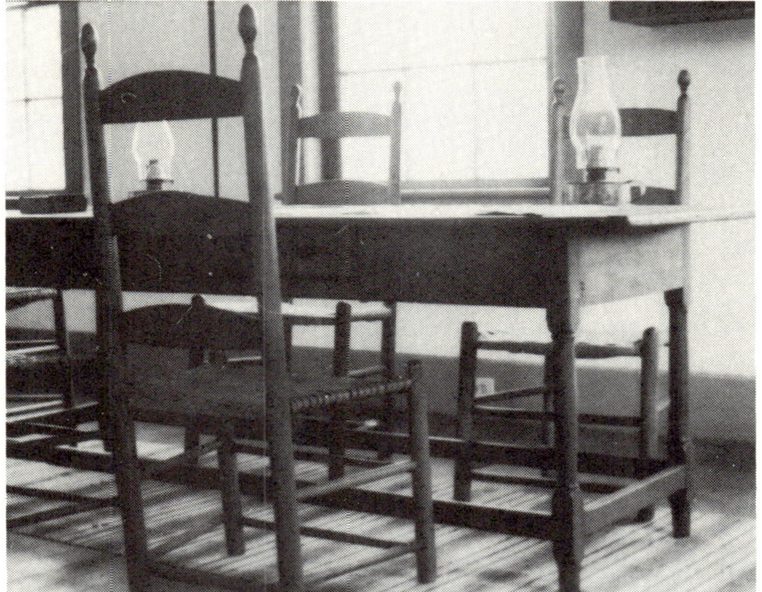

1. Large stretcher-based table (Hancock Village).

2. Cross stretcher-base work table (Hancock Village).

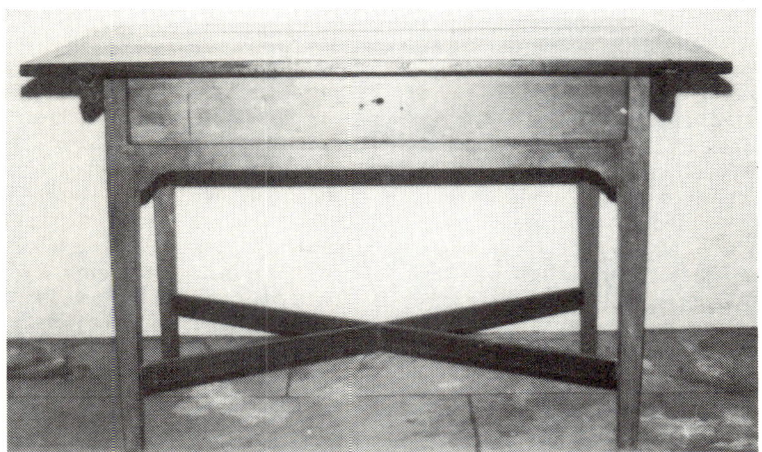

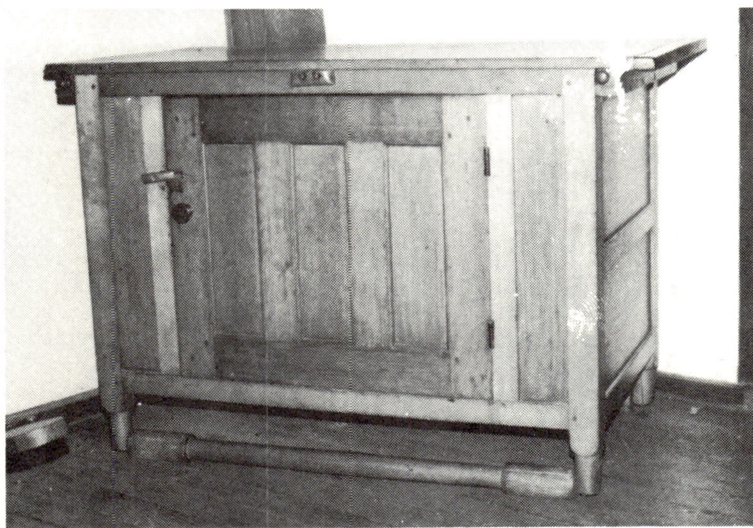

3. Unique cabinet-table with supports for additional leaves (Shaker Museum, Old Chatham, N.Y.).

Words of Caution

Like most antiques, Shaker artifacts have increased considerably in value in the past couple of years. The public sale of a few exceptional pieces at seemingly outlandish prices has a tendency to draw upward the price of any Shaker item regardless of the quality. This in turn has lead to an abuse of attributing items to be Shaker which may or may not be. Finely made country tables and stands with delicately tapered Hepplewhite style legs are the most common victims of such abuse in attribution. I think it is fair to say that square tapered legged tables can not be proved Shaker without knowing their histories.

Stretcher based tables (Photos #1 and #2) are another area for caution for, while they are rare in Shaker furniture, they can be true. The Shakers made stretcher based tables in many sizes, from about three to eight feet in length. Do not exclude a table from being Shaker simply because it has a stretcher base. But do exercise great caution for their numbers are very small.

On the other hand, hutch or chair tables can be excluded from the ranks of Shaker furniture. Many of us would be anxious to see a well-documented Shaker hutch table. Doug Hamel, of Concord, New Hampshire, worked with the Shakers in his younger days and is now one of the most knowledgeable and reliable antique dealers in Shaker. He says that neither he nor Bud Thompson, Director of the Canterbury Shakers museum, have ever seen a Shaker hutch table. Along with other museum directors, antique dealers, and collectors of Shaker, the same perspective is shared by Mrs. Faith Andrews, author with her late husband of SHAKER FURNITURE, RELIGION IN WOOD, THE PEOPLE CALLED SHAKERS, etc. In her better than 50 years of collecting, studying and writing about the Shakers and their furniture, she never came into contact with a Shaker hutch table. The form is inconsistent with Shaker methods.

Where added work area was needed in the Shaker kitchens and elsewhere, they would use the addition of leaves to tables. Numerous tables were made with a single drop leaf that could be raised when the table was pulled out from the wall. Leaves could often be added on the front by pulling out supports and laying a board across. The unique piece in photo #3 reflects both these characteristics. At one time, a leaf had been on the back. The small pullouts on the ends make it possible for a board to have been added to the front. Of special note on this piece are the unusual rollers.

Another table form that is inconsistent with Shaker design is

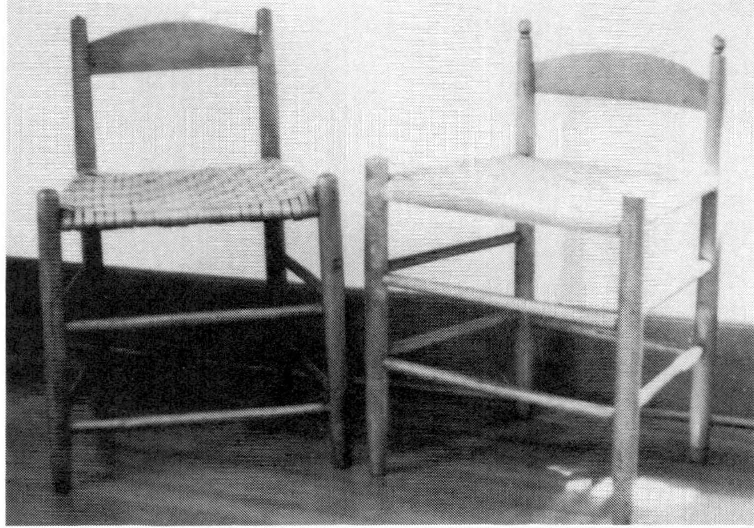

6. One slat Shaker dining chairs: left, Watervliet, N.Y.; right, probably Hancock, Mass., (Hancock Village).

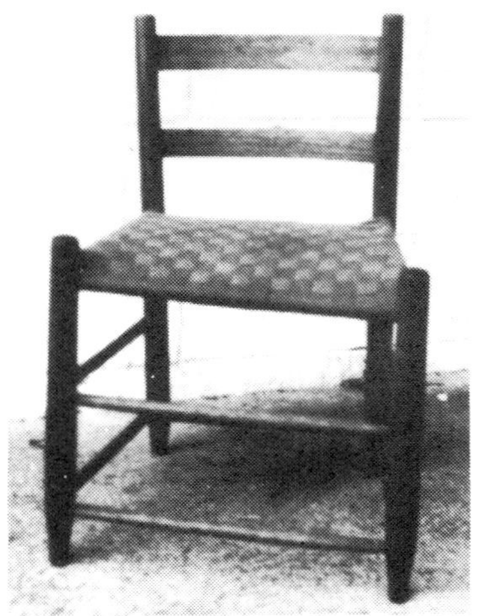

4. Tall slat back chair cut down top imitate Shaker dining chair (Private Collection).

5. True Shaker dining chairs: left, from Canterbury, N.H.; right, from Watervliet, N.Y. (Hancock Village).

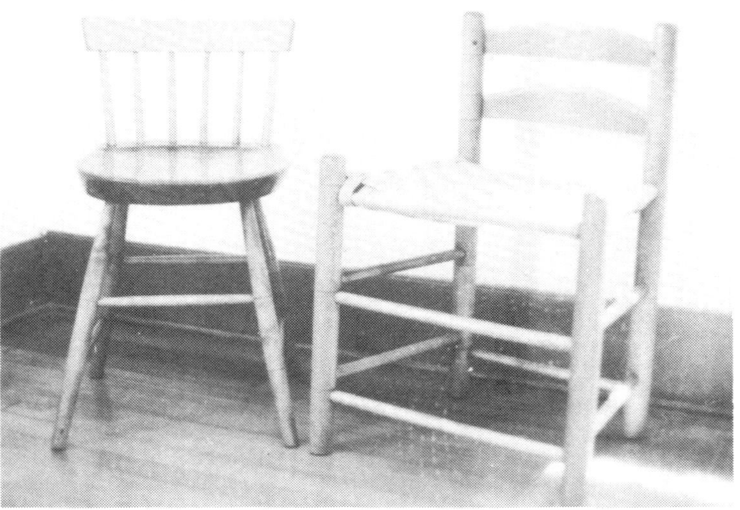

the large round table. There are many round stands and, in later years, round pedestal tables of 42 inches breadth. But for dining or general work purposes, it is an incongruous form. The Shaker brothers and sisters were separated at every point in living. Males and females would have to sit on opposite sides while dining. Therefore, tables would have to be rectangular in shape. In addition to this, round tables encourage conversation which was forbidden in the Shaker dining room. "The Millenial Laws" state "No talking, laughing or playing is allowed of when going to, coming from, or at the table." Mrs. Andrews says that she can not recall any round Shaker table larger than the Mt. Lebanon pedestal tables. Her response to the mention

of a round lazy susan table that was once sold at an Ohio auction as "Shaker" was "Ridiculous!"

Another area for caution is Shaker dining chairs. Dining chairs were made with short backs so that they could be pushed under the table at the end of the meal to make cleaning easier. Since talking and visiting at the meal were ruled out, there was no reason for higher backed, more comfortable chairs. It can be seen how very easy it is to take a country slat back chair and cut off the top slat or two in order to come up with the chair in photo #4. Sold as a Shaker dining chair, the saw marks are readily visible on the top of the posts. Photos #5 and #6 show Shaker dining chairs at the Hancock Shaker Village in Massachusetts. Of special note is the two slat chair from Watervliet, N.Y. in photo #5. It is earlier than the others and heavier. In fact, it is of heavier construction than the imitation of photo #4 and illustrates that lightness of lines and weight are not necessarily an indication of Shaker craftsmanship. Note also the curvature of the slats in the chairs in photos #5 and 6 as well as the finials at the top of the posts for these help to separate the true from the "made-to-be-Shaker" chairs. Also, the slats in true two slat dining chairs are set closer together than if the chair had at one time had three slats.

Be cautious! If you are going to pay Shaker prices, be sure of an item's authenticity.

— September, 1977

Chairs

Last month's article discussed Shaker chairs and their history. But what if you want to purchase a Shaker chair to add to your collection of antiques? Which would be the most desirable? How much would you have to pay? What are some of the factors to consider in buying Shaker chairs?

Perhaps the first consideration ought to be your purpose for the chair. Do you want a collector's item or just a Shaker piece to add to your other antiques? If it is the latter, then you will probably be interested in a # 6 or # 7 Mt. Lebanon rocker with the gold decal. (See last month's article for a copy of that decal). These reflect the style and fine craftsmanship of the Shakers (the largest chair weighs less than ten pounds) and at the same time are useful pieces of household furniture.

If you want more than just an example of Shaker, then you must consider other factors such as age, condition and style. Age is often difficult to determine since there was not much change in style over almost a century and a half. One sign of age, though, is the shape, or lack of it, on the rungs. The earlier the chair, the more taper there is to the rungs as they meet the legs. By 1890, the rungs had lost any taper. Another sign of age is the angle of the back. The earliest chairs had back posts that were straight up and down. During the first half of the 19th century, the posts became canted backwards until about 1860 when the uprights were bent at the seat to make a more comfortable chair. Other factors being equal, the older the chair, the more desirable it is.

More desirability also applies to original condition and finish, although I will not stick to that on the seats. There is not too much concern for the original seat since most of the taped kind have been previously replaced. And, too, it is important that a chair can be used. It loses its identity as a chair if it can not hold a person. The exception to this would be the beautifully colored plush seats.

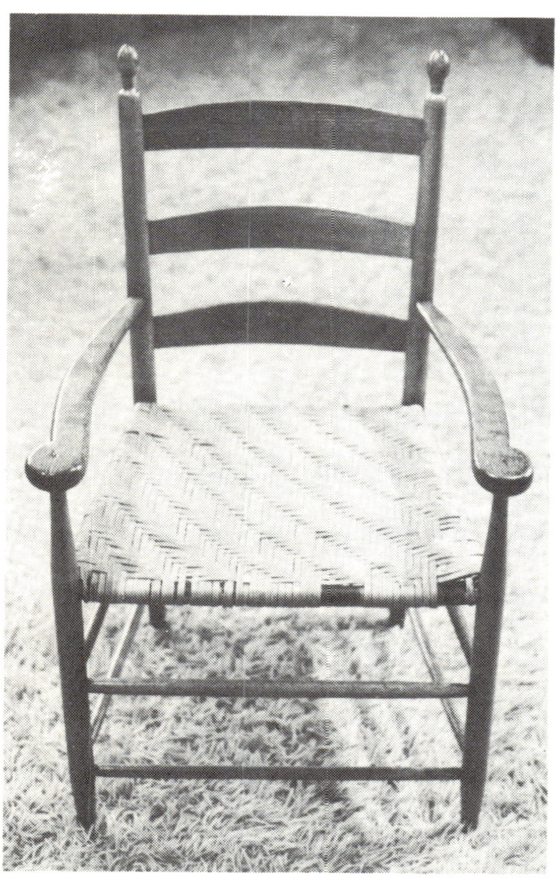

This is the only armchair with the patented brass tilters of which the author is aware. Plain tilter sidechairs sell for about $400. A sidechair with the brass tilter sold wholesale for $700 last summer. This chair probably could command $1,200.

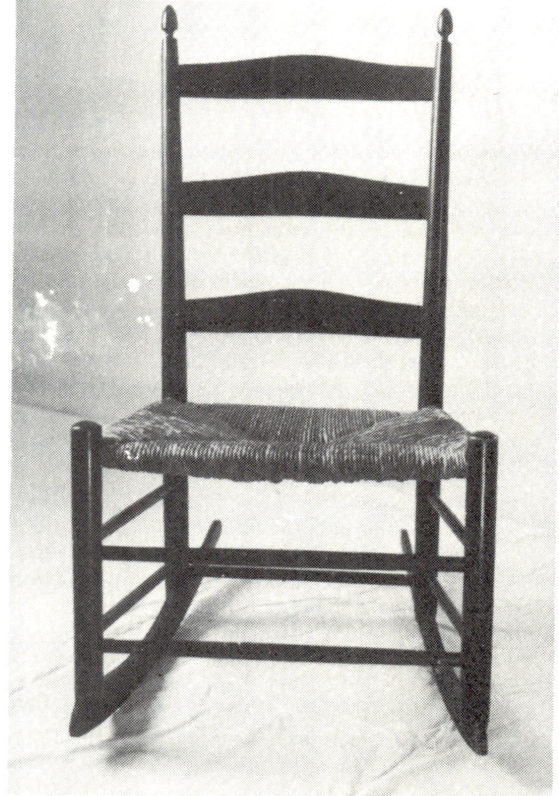

This #3 Mt. Lebanon rocker has the stamp of the Shaker factory on the back of the third slat. The gold decal is usually found there or on the inside of the rocker or the inside of one of the rear legs.

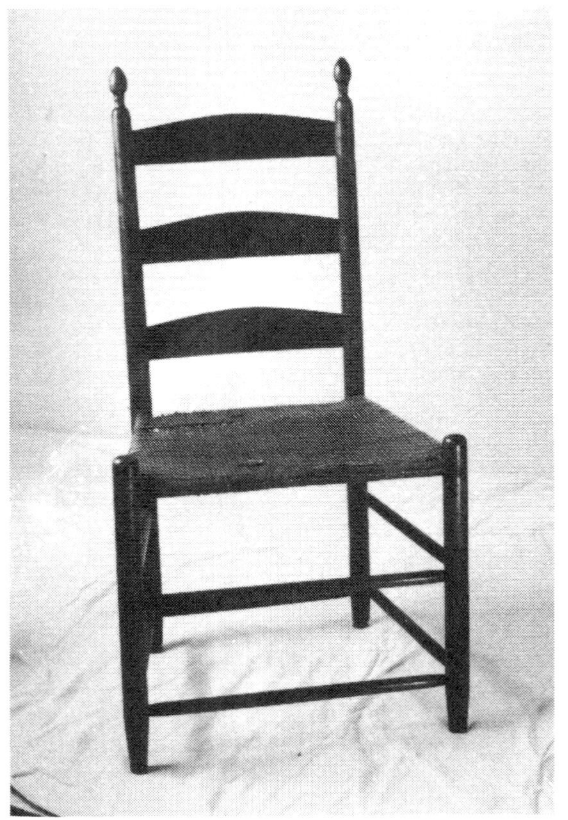

Whenever a number of desirable characteristics are met in one chair, the value of that chair is greatly enhanced. The cant of the back and the strong taper near the legs on the stretchers show this chair to have been made prior to 1850. Age, coupled with the delicate lines and the wooden tilters make this a chair of high quality. But this chair also shows the Shaker's love for beauty in wood in that it is constructed of curly birch. In addition, it is one of a matching pair. All this adds to its value. While ordinary wood tilter side chairs might sell for $400, an unordinary chair like this could bring $650 - $700.

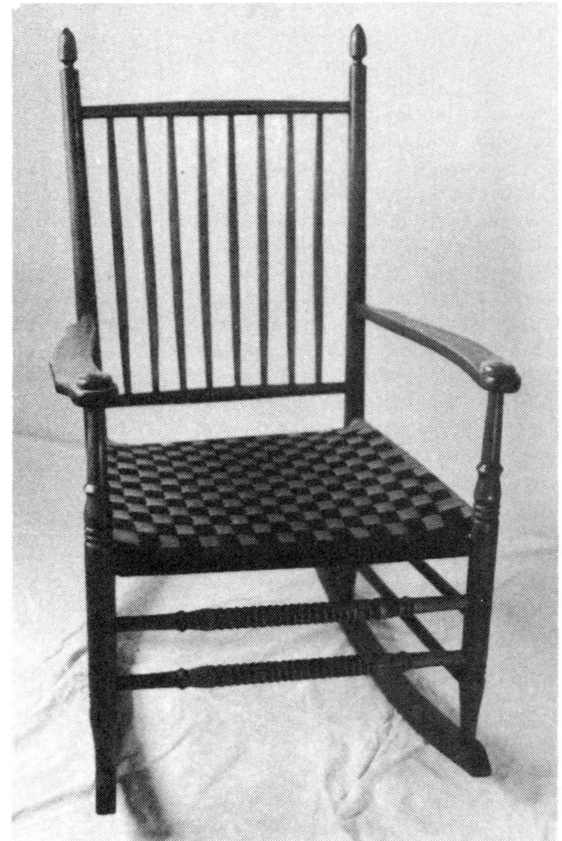

Because of the large finials and the fancy turnings on the arm supports and front stretcher, this spindle back rocker can probably be dated at about the turn of the century.

Their original condition would add value.

The finish and wood are important with Shaker chairs, as with other antiques. Many chairs had a red stain or orange paint (Union Village, Ohio) or yellow paint (Hancock, Massachusetts). These are desirable. Variations in woods also contribute to desirability with curly maple being a favorite of the Shaker craftsman and the collector. And any museum or collector would love to own the birds-eye maple chair now in a private New Hampshire collection.

After you have considered your purpose for the chair, possible age, and condition, then look at the various types or styles. The most desirable Shaker chairs are spindle back benches, sofas and revolving chairs. One unique chair is the swivel rocker in the Western Reserve Historical Society collection. These types are rare and are truly collector's items. Another very desirable style is the dining chair (see September, 1976, photograph). The Shakers did not talk during meals and, after eating, pushed the chairs under the tables to make for easier cleaning. Therefore, the dining chairs were made with short back, one or two slats, or spindles. While these chairs are a collector's delight (usually at a cost of about $525), their desirability goes back to a consideration of purpose. A low back dining chair is O.K. next to the telephone but not in the family room for T.V. watching.

One variation of Shaker chairs that is quite desirable and still obtainable is the tilter. The ball and socket arrangement on the rear legs made it possible to tilt backwards in the chair while keeping it firmly on the floor. The most desirable tilters are those with a brass cup and ball with the inscription ''Patented, 1852'' stamped into it. Pewter was also used although wood was the most common material. ($400 seems the going price on tilters with wood balls. Brass and pewter would probably command twice that amount.) Examine a tilter closely to see if the tilter has been replaced. It is interesting to note that the Shakers patented this style better than a hundred years ago and, now, most of the desks and chairs in our schools and universities are using it.

Going on down the line in order of desirability, other factors being equal, are the armed straight chair, side chair and rocker. I have only seen a couple of armed straight chairs ($400) for sale in the Mid-west in the last ten years. Side chairs, other than labeled ones, are generally considered to have been made for use in the community and are, therefore, more desirable ($250). Most rockers that are for sale are the Mt. Lebanon manufactured vari-

ety and are less desirable than chairs that were not factory made.

There are other variations in style such as the spindle back, rope twisted and bentwood. All of these were made after 1875. The spindle back ($150) is a variation of the Mt. Lebanon chair with pointed finials and mushroom knobs at the end of the arms. They vary from the more common styles by having windsor spindles in the back where there is usually a cushion, tape or slats. The rope twisted chair is similar except all uprights, and sometimes the front stretcher, are made to look like rope. The bentwood ($275) is completely different from any other Shaker chair. One continuous piece of wood is used for the two back posts and the cushion rail across the back. The front uprights are bent to form the arms and meet the back posts. Robert Meader, in his book THE ILLUSTRATED GUIDE TO SHAKER FURNITURE, classi-

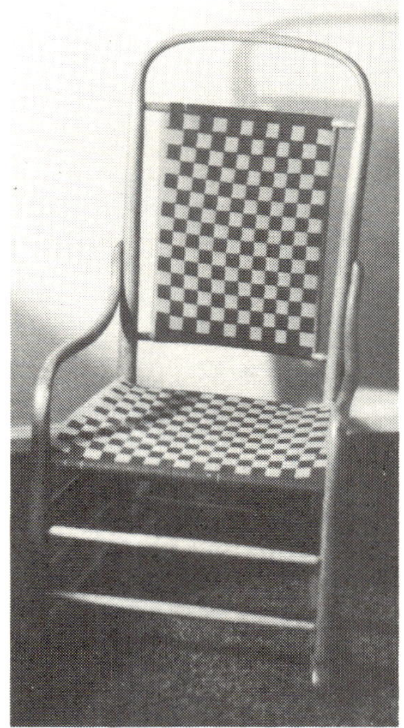

This bentwood rocker was made after 1875. While it does not reflect typical Shaker style, it is very desirable for its comfort.

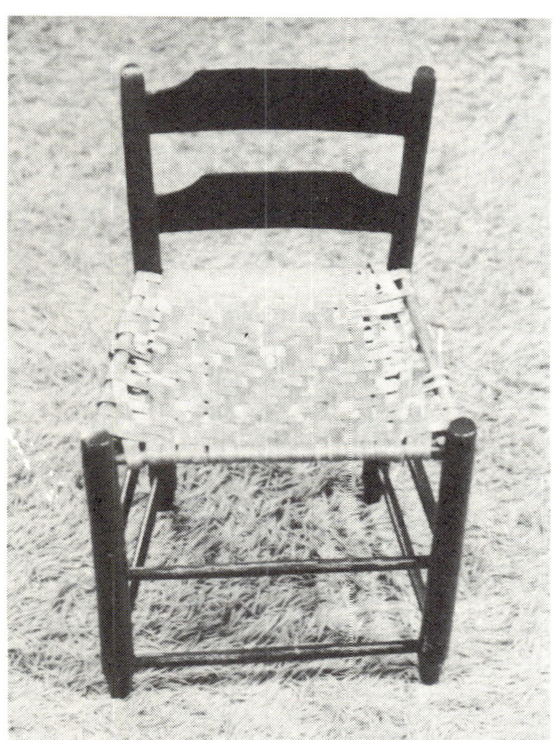

Union Village, Ohio, dining chair. Notice the notched slats and the taper at the bottom of the legs.

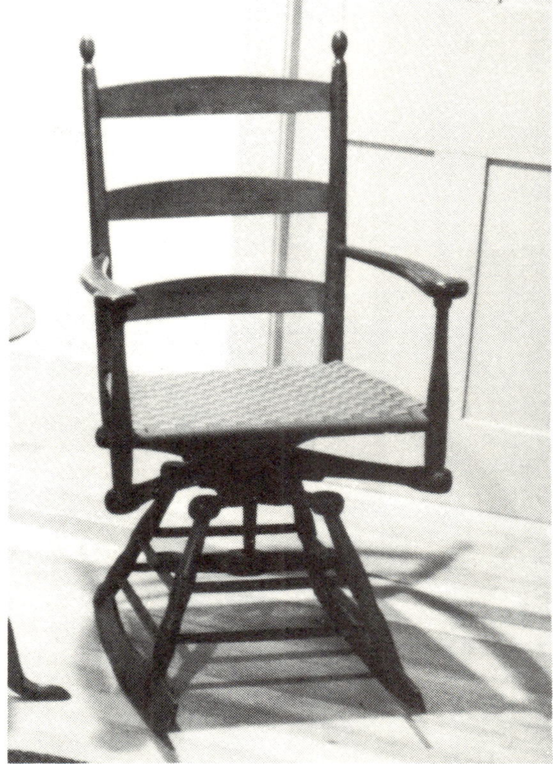

Very unique swivel rocker! Who can set a price on a one of a kind chair like this? (Western Reserve Historical Society, Cleveland)

[123]

fied these three styles among the "decadent." He uses this classification as much for the period in which they were made as for the design. It was the declining years of the Shakers and the last gasp of the chair making industry. The Shakers tried to keep up with the times and the Victorian styles. The chairs of this period shall stand as a symbol of a noble way of life trying to adjust to changing times.

In the consideration of Shaker chairs, though, these stand just about at the bottom. But herein is where personal tastes enter. I think the rope twisted chairs are ugly, uncomfortable and undesirable and would not want one at $50. Someone else sees the same chair as unique, rare, beautiful and very collectable and thinks $300 is a more realistic price. On the other hand, I like the bentwood rockers. While they do not truly reflect Shaker styles, they have very pleasing lines and, for me, are as comfortable as any

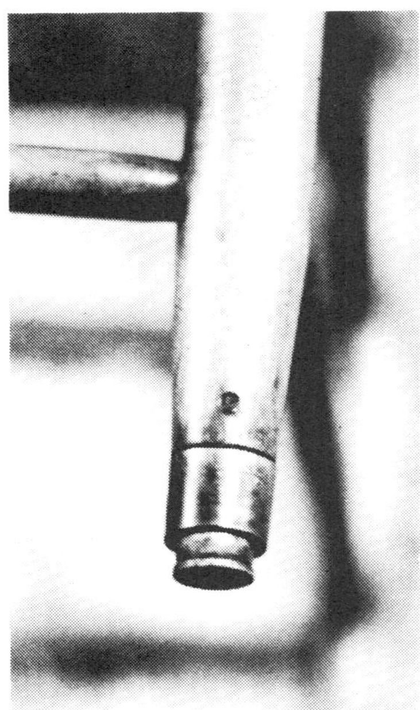

The brass tilter has "Patented 1852" stamped into the socket of the chair in Photo 1. The original brass ball has been replaced with wood one. The chair is so rare that this replacement does not detract from the value of the chair. Note the leather thong which holds the ball to the leg.

chair there is. It all depends on your taste!

Another consideration in desirability of chairs is whether or not a chair was a mass produced one or one made for use within the Shaker community itself. The latter would be the more desirable and would include dining chairs; chairs that had numbers stamped on the top of the front posts ($325) to indicate in which room the chair belonged; and most straight chairs. The mass produced chairs are more popular if they have the Mt. Lebanon label (1875-1930) although a collector will recognize that a non-labeled chair is usually earlier. I think people often make a mistake in insisting on the label, especially now that the labels are being reproduced. Chairs without labels often use wood pegs to hold on the rockers rather than the later use of screws and often have finer lines. The finest Mt. Lebanon chairs I have seen have not been labeled. But their style is indisputable and they did have the number on the back of the slat.

This number impressed on the slat will be 0 to 7 with the 7 being the largest size chair. The desirability of these chairs is related to how near to either end of this 0 to 7 scale the number is. The middle numbers, 3 and 4, are the most common and sell for around $200 without arms. 0 and 1 indicate children's chairs and are very collectable ($375) while the largest chairs, 6 and 7, prove to be very useful and are of about equal price.

There are other factors in desirability and price such as place of origin. Most Maine Shaker chairs tend to be less delicate than their upstate New York counterparts. A well documented chair from Groveland, New York, would be very desirable since there are, to my knowledge, none now. The combination of many of these factors also is important. An armed chair is nice. An armed chair with tilters is nicer. And an armed chair with the patented brass tilters is nicest.

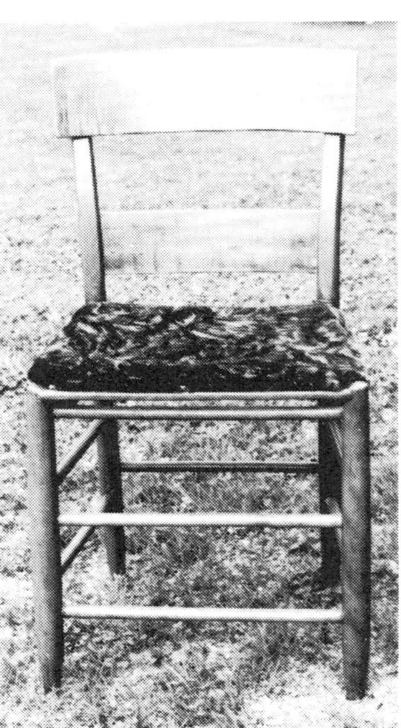

One of a set of chairs custom made by the Mt. Lebanon Shakers about 1890. The wood is tiger maple and the seat is a Kelly green crushed velvet. Note the lack of taper on the stretchers that is characteristic of the later chairs. This is unquestionably a Shaker chair but is it desirable? Some would consider it worthless because it is contrary to Shaker style while others might consider it a treasure because it is rare and demonstrates the Shakers' attempt to change with the times.

Desirability and pricing are awkward to consider since personal use, tastes, and finances are important. If I did not have any Shaker chairs, and had a choice, I would consider a rocker in some form. Although not as old or as classic as a tilter with the patent on it, it would be sturdier and more serviceable. The tilter becomes a decorative art object but a rocker can be used while reading the evening paper and without much worry about the children breaking it.

— **March, 1977**

NOTE: *As of August, 1979, $75-$175 should be added to values mentioned.*

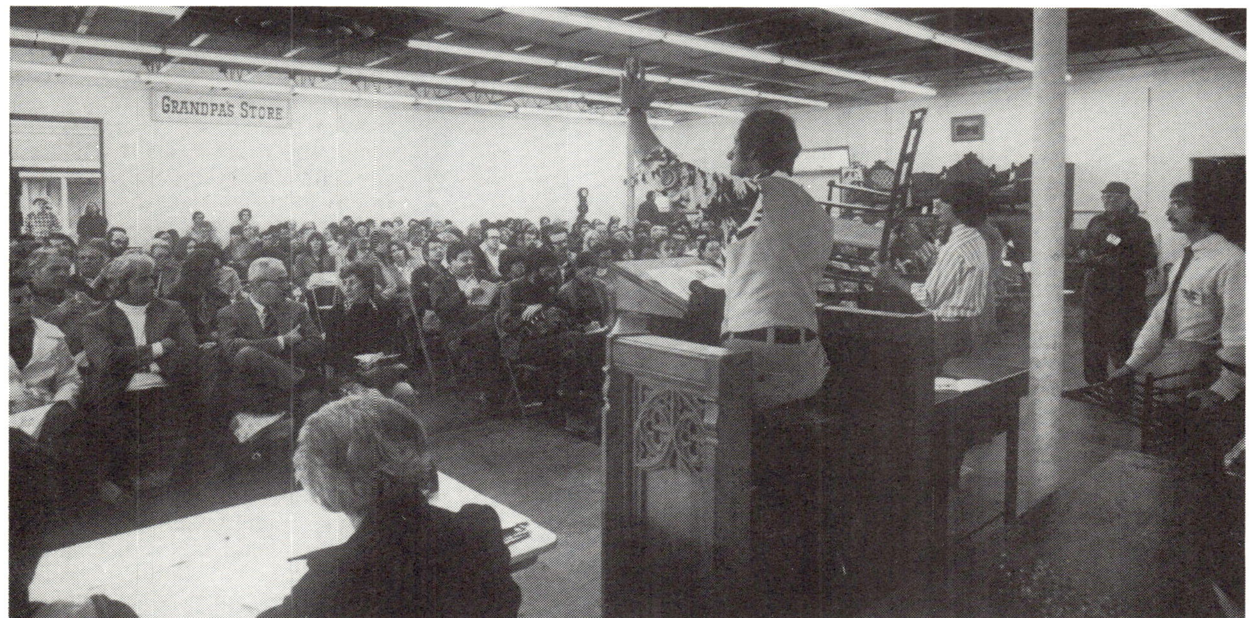

Lou Caropresso kept the auction moving at a steady pace as he sold almost 300 items in less than six hours without taking a break. The rocker being sold is the No. 6 with label, original seat, and cushion rail ($275) while the next item to come up was a footrest to be attached to the front stretcher of a chair ($70).

(Photograph by Warren Fowler, THE BERKSHIRE EAGLE)

Lenox, Massachusetts, Auction

The Shaker auction at the Caropreso Galleries on October 26 left many people wondering whether something has happened to the prices of Shaker artifacts. Lou Caropreso had been building for this sale for better than four months and was surprised that the gross fell quite short of the anticipated goal.

A factor which might have affected the sale was the admission by catalog only and the late arrival of the catalog from the printer (only four days prior to the sale). Also, the catalog lacked definitive descriptions and the distinction between Shaker and non-Shaker items. In spite of these shortcomings, most of the New England Shaker dealers

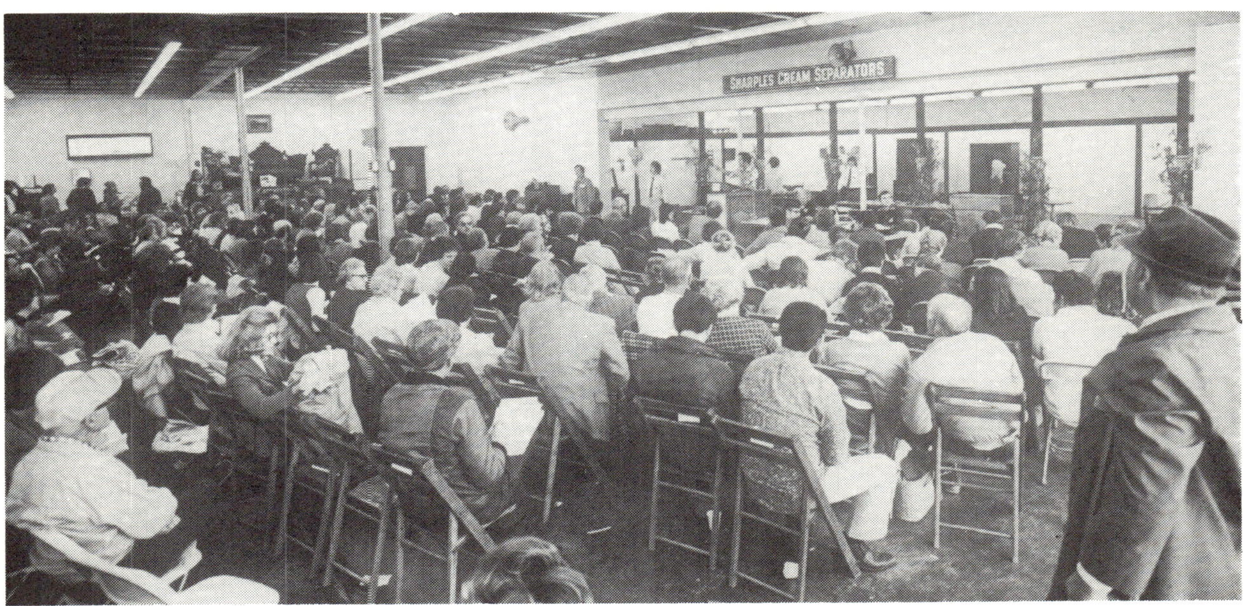

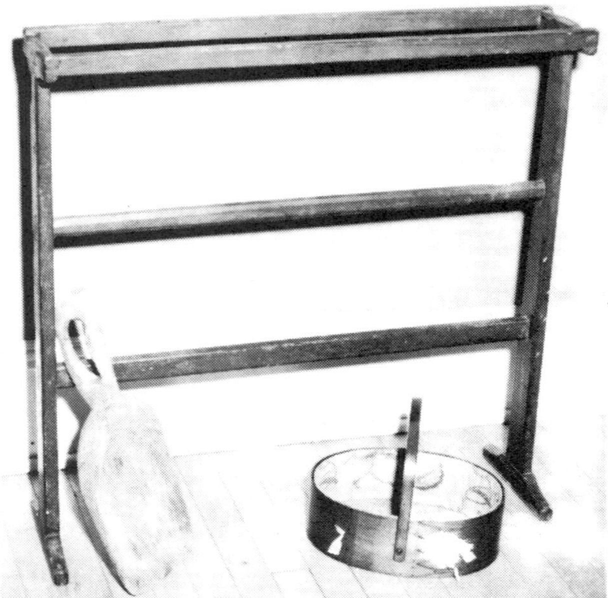

Shaker shoe foot towel rack ($120); Shaker scoop, well worn, ($155); Oval fingered sewing carrier with lining in poor condition and no sewing implements. ($95).

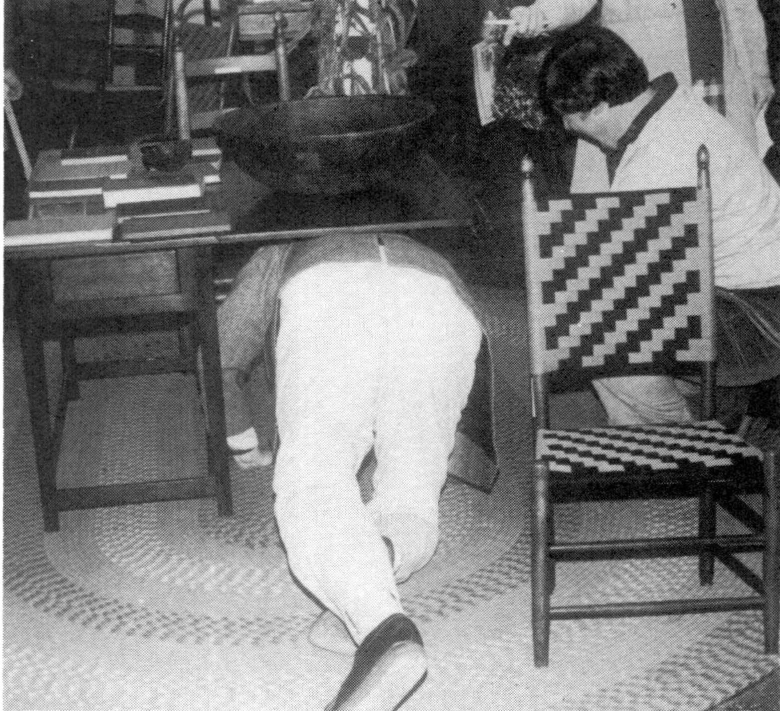

You can usually tell the collectors from the decorators by how they examine a piece. This fellow is giving the once-over to a rare cherry one drop leaf stretcher base table which brought $650. The large burl bowl brought $300 and the late Shaker side chair with tilters sold for $260.

(Photograph by Warren Fowler, THE BERKSHIRE EAGLE)

were present as well as many collectors, some from as far away as California.

While there were a couple of choice pieces and several good ones, the overall quality of the merchandise was only average. Many items were questionable as to their Shaker origins. Of the five candlestands in the sale, only one was classically and unquestionably Shaker. It brought $850 while $500 was the best paid for any of the others, that one being tiger maple with snake feet. I had the definite impression that there were more items being called Shaker after the auction than there had been prior to it.

But even the items that were unquestionably Shaker did not command the prices that were expected. The Shaker cloak brought $100, about half the going price. Bentwood rockers sold for $140 without a seat to $210 with one, about $80 under recent prices. All of the chairs manufactured for commercial purposes followed the same trend with the exception of a No. O child's rocker with arms that brought $450. A No. 6 rocker with arms, cushion rail, label and original seat brought $275 early in the day. That proved to be the top money for adult chairs as labeled No. 3's without arms sold for $140-180, a No. 7 with arms, finials and slat back sold for $250 and another No. 7 with arms and taped seat and back sold for only $200. The last was half what a similar chair brought at another Shaker auction five miles up the road one year ago. Among all the chairs, there was only one early one, a side chair with caned seat ($190).

Tables included a nice two-drawer sewing table ($500); a rare cherry one drop leaf stretcher base table ($650); drop leaf table from Enfield, Conn., with traces of red finish and the slides beautifully boxed in on the underside ($375); and another drop leaf with square tapered legs ($500).

Besides the tables, some of the other better pieces included a cherry washstand with cut out top for bowl and signed D. Merrick ($400); small eight-drawer spice box of butternut with dovetailed case ($350); one-door tall cupboard from Watervliet, New York ($775); drop front desk with three drawers beneath that had originally been a built-in ($380); and an excellent small Mt. Lebanon garment cutting table with folding legs and one drawer suspended under one end ($375).

Two choice pieces were the round sewing table with tripod base and a slant front desk. With a repaired leg and top, the sewing table sold for $1,300, well under expectations. The walnut desk, reputed to be from Watervliet, Ohio, brought the same price. What made this item exceptional were the Bible and picture of Elder Issachars Bates. Elder Bates was one of the three Shakers who journeyed to Kentucky and Ohio in 1805 and started the Western communities. Some prospective buyers had been scared from the sale by the rumor that a large reserve had been placed on this desk. They missed a real bargain AND TO OUR KNOWLEDGE THERE WERE NO RESERVES IN THIS SALE!

The best price of the sale came on the Trustees' Desk. With the exception of some replaced molding, drawer slides and knobs, it was in excellent condition. One knowledgeable person suggested that it was actually a bookcase desk used in the school. Others

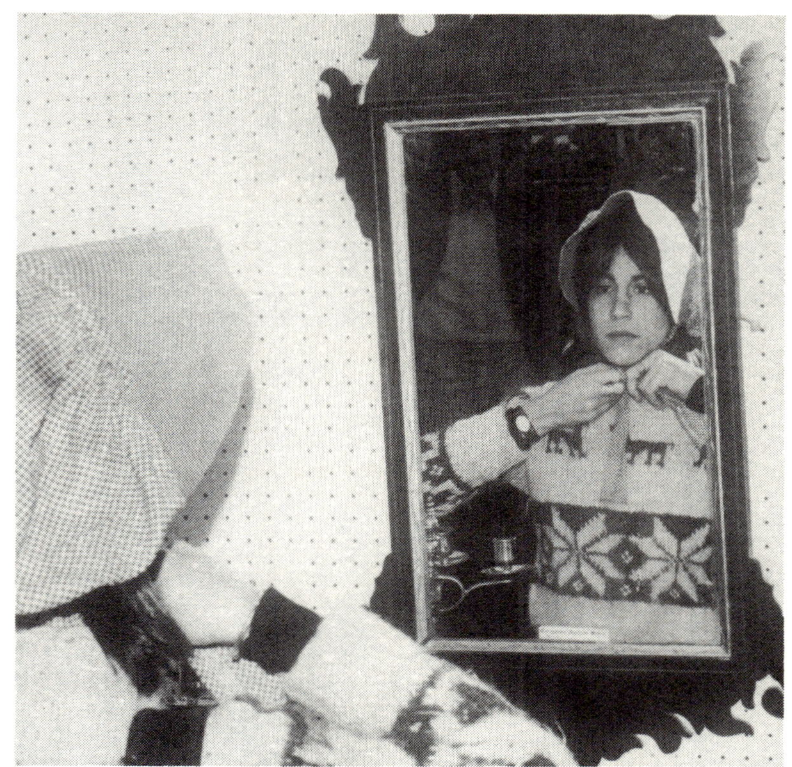

This young lady modeled the red and white checked Shaker bonnet ($5) in a Chippendale mirror that had some restoration ($150).

(Photograph by Warren Fowler, THE BERKSHIRE EAGLE)

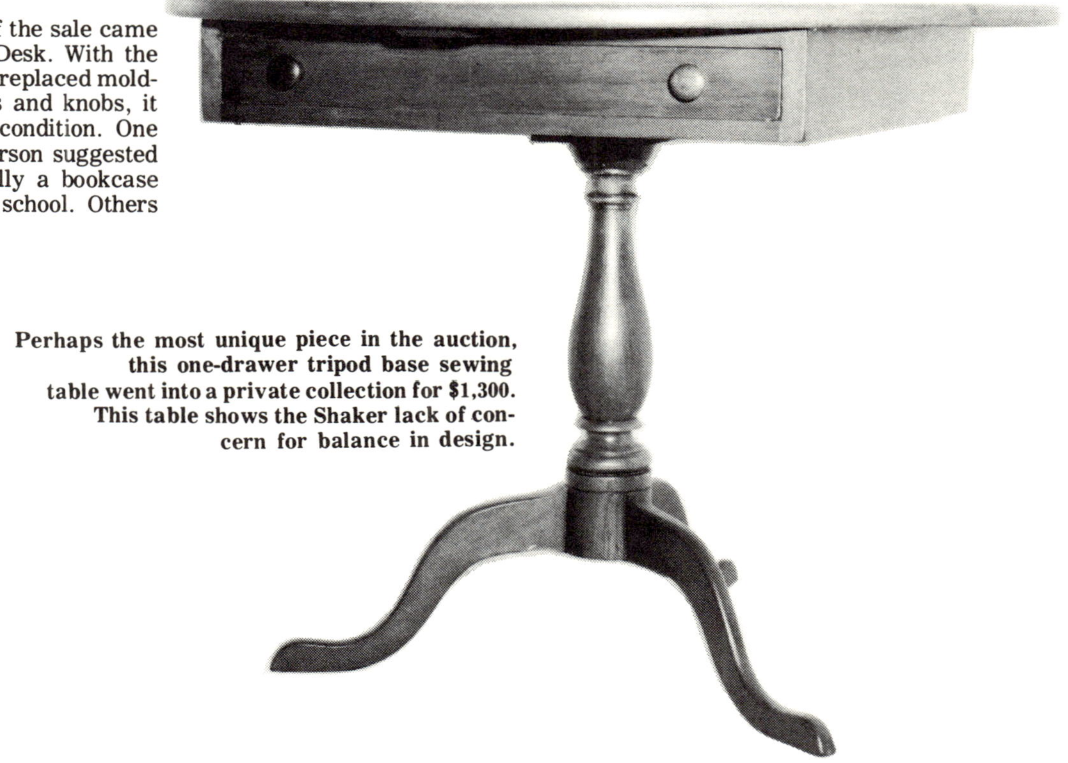

Perhaps the most unique piece in the auction, this one-drawer tripod base sewing table went into a private collection for $1,300. This table shows the Shaker lack of concern for balance in design.

thought that the medicinal odor in it marked it as having been used for pharmaceutical purposes in the infirmary. In any case, it reflects classic Shaker lines and illustrates the utilitarian purposes of Shaker furniture. Although pre-sale estimates had this piece bringing five to twelve thousand, $3,500 brought it to a private collector in Ohio.

Smaller items seemed to depend upon the particular desires of collectors. An old doll dressed in Shaker costume was sold to a lady for $120 while a man paid $165 for a pair of Shaker skis from Tyringham for his son's room. He didn't buy the next item though . . . a pair of crutches ($30). Another man bought an iron chimney cleanout door ($40) and intended to box it in as a cupboard to hang in his study. A darling folding stool about eight inches long went for $95 while a large, 16½'' height, taped stool with label brought $220. Shaker labels averaged about five dollars each (12 for $60; 13 for $55; 20 for $85) and pegboard commanded top value as pieces with two pegs, from Tyringham, went for $40-50 and one ten peg length brought $130.

Although the auction was billed as a Shaker one, there were many other early American items in the sale. Some of these proved to be good buys such as a 24 tube candlemold ($45), a 36 tube candlemold ($75), Nantucket basket signed A.D. Williams, 1923 ($210), another Nantucket basket with slight damage ($80), a pig weathervane ($350), and a nicely restored four-drawer inlaid Hepplewhite chest with drop panel ($400).

While the quality of the merchandise did not quite live up to expectations, it was a good sale for buyers, enough so to build anticipation for the next one Lou intends to have in February.

— December, 1975

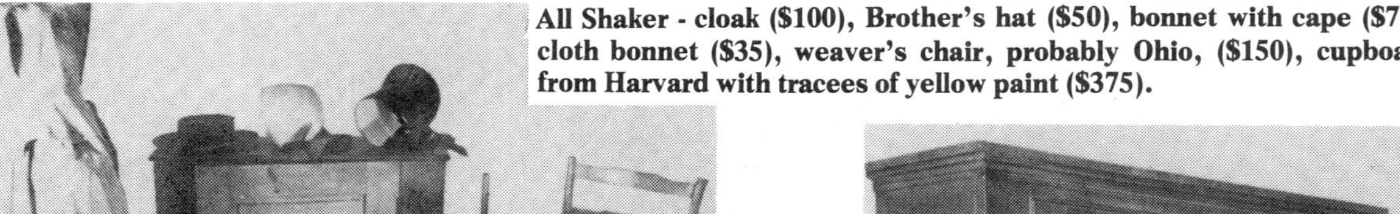

All Shaker - cloak ($100), Brother's hat ($50), bonnet with cape ($75), cloth bonnet ($35), weaver's chair, probably Ohio, ($150), cupboard from Harvard with tracees of yellow paint ($375).

Shaker two-drawer sewing table ($500).

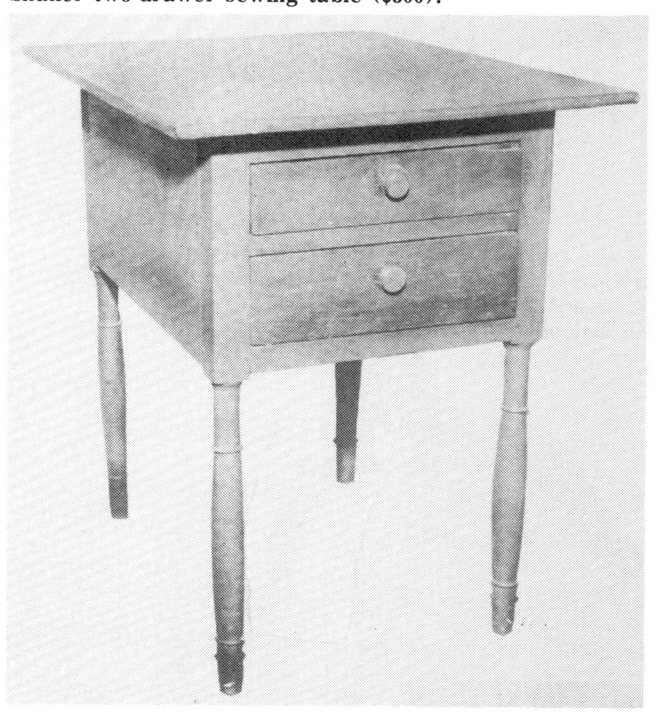

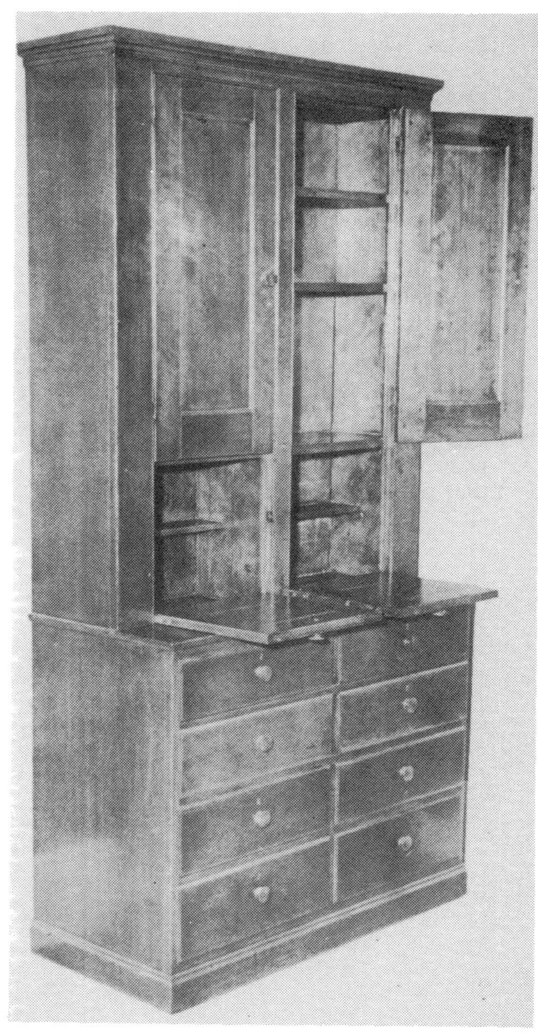

The top money of the sale ($3,500) was paid for this pine Shaker double desk, standing seven feet tall.

[128]

Auctions in Ohio

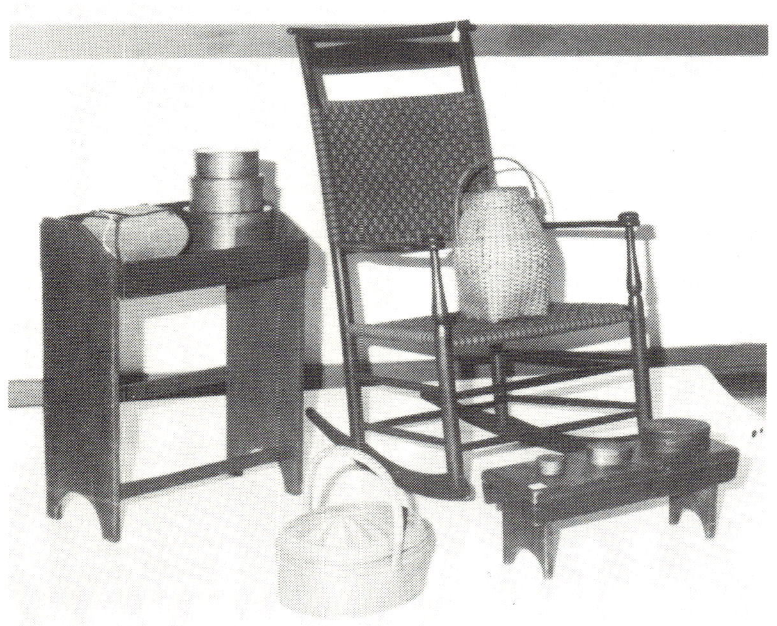

Someone got a good buy on this # 7 Mt. Lebanon Shaker rocker ($250). The Shaker milk house dry sink from Enfield, New Hampshire, went for $275 and the Hancock stool for $75. Oval Harvard style boxes with one finger went for $25 to $50 each.

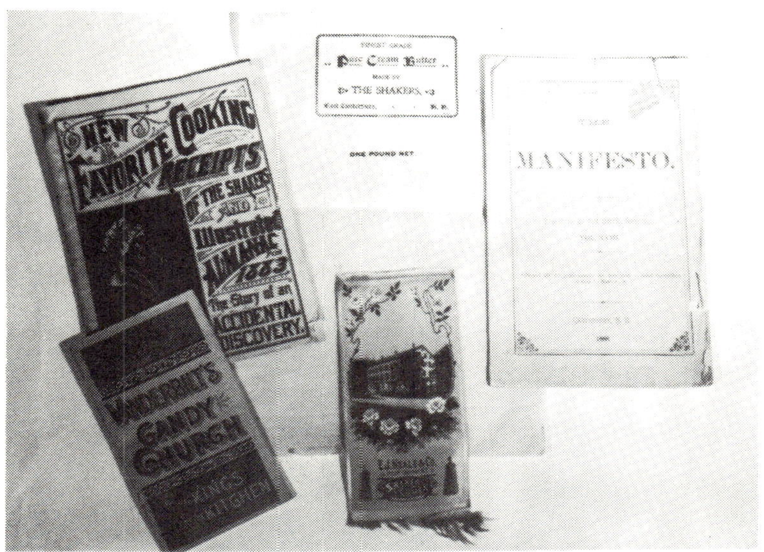

Some of the more interesting Shaker items in the sale were the small artifacts bearing the Shaker name. The unused "Pure Cream Butter" label went for $15. Other items were "Shaker Cloak" silk book mark - $15; a copy of "The Manifesto", - $15; and two almanacs - $12.50. All of these seemed good buys for such nice examples of Shaker memorabilia.

Not since the Bicentennial Shaker Auction at the Western Reserve Historical Society in 1974 has there been so much Shaker to go on the auction block in the Midwest as there was on two consecutive week-ends in April. On April 9th, Mike Clum conducted a sale 20 miles south of Columbus, Ohio, that included better than 50 lots of Shaker. The next week-end, Garth's, 20 miles north of Columbus, had a sale with 30 Shaker lots. The two sales complemented each other as the Kieffer-Stolzenbach sale offered a general line of Shaker artifacts including many small articles while the second sale consisted mostly of furniture.

The Kieffer-Stolzenbach sale in Lancaster, Ohio

Jack Kieffer closed out his shop in Maryland and discovered that Oriental and Continental antiques do not sell especially well at an Ohio auction, while Nancy Stolzenbach, thinning out her Shaker collection, was pleased with the number of collectors who were anxious to buy Shaker. Together, the two put on a catalogued sale that was satisfying to seller and buyer alike. This was the first time that Clum had held a sale with an ordered numbered catalogue although Garth's had done it for years. I believe we will see more of them in the future.

From the standpoint of Jack and Nancy, the catalogue was one of the great benefits of the sale. The catalogues sold for $3.00 each and enough were sold to cover the cost of printing. A great deal of time and effort went into the production of the catalogue but the sellers thought it was well worth the effort. The publishing of the catalogue elicited many inquiries and put the Kieffer-Stolzenbach names on the lips and in the minds of many antique dealers and collectors. It would be our hope that they would follow through with a price list for those who had purchased the catalogue.

In addition to the Shaker items, country things found a ready market among the more than 200 bidders. An early sawbuck table brought $230 while a two door, two drawer cupboard with a high arched splashboard and original red paint commanded $190. Other items and prices included the following: 8 hole tin candle mold - $37.50; double bar towel rack with shoe feet - $65; New England 6 board blanket chest with boot-jack ends - $90; half-round tapered leg table with triangular apron - $85; pine candle box, 11'' long, with green paint - $40. With the exception of a set of chairs, the best price of the sale was for a two-piece decorated wall cupboard with red-brown graining over yellow. It sold for $1,025, only one hundred dollars more than it had brought at Garth's about two years ago.

The center of the sale in attention and prices was the Shaker. These items sold well, and, almost exclusively, to collectors. The bargains of the day were the chairs. An armless rocker, probably a # 5 although the catalogue said a # 7, sold for only $135. An excellent # 7 armed rocker with taped back and seat and a cushion rail went for only $250 (a slat backed # 7 without arms and cushion rail sold at Garth's the next week for $230). The # 5 armed straight chair sold for $300. While these chairs did not have the desirable Mt. Lebanon decal, they probably pre-dated the use of the decals and were excellent examples of Mt. Lebanon Shaker chairs at very reasonable prices.

The accompanying photographs illustrate some of the other items and prices. We in the Midwest will be seeing more catalogued sales ... and hopefully more Shaker in those sales.

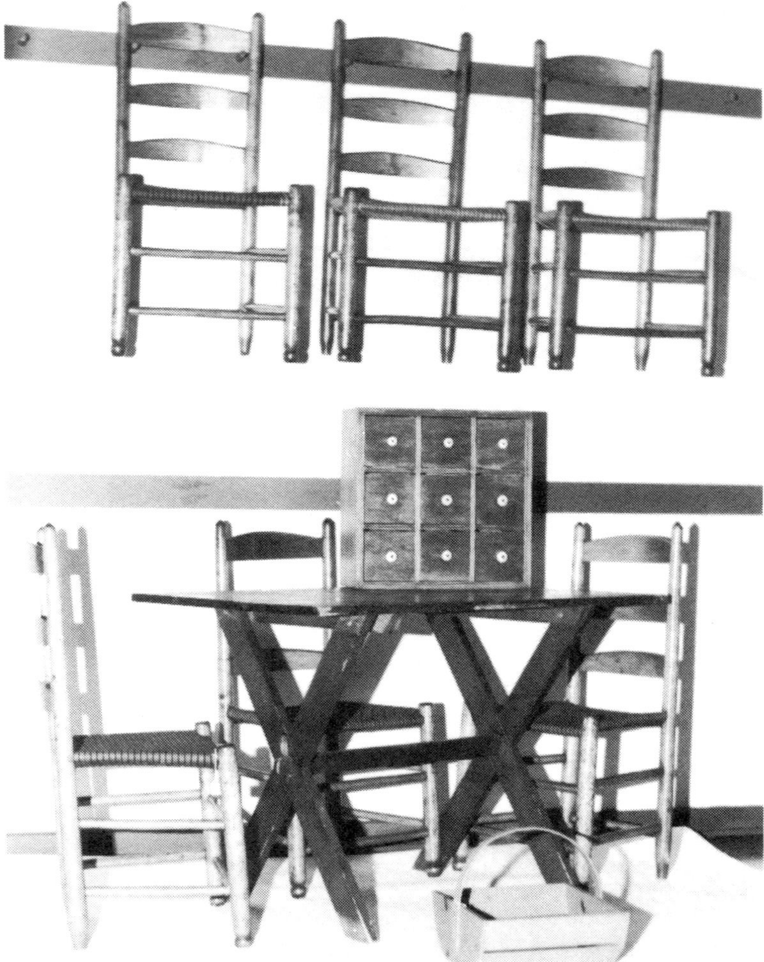

The highest bid of the sale went for the set of 6 Watervliet Shaker chairs - $180 each. The apothecary chest is from Canterbury, New Hampshire, Shakers and sold for $280. The case was dovetailed. The Shaker carrier on the floor brought $180 and the table $625. It was collapsible and was reputed to have been used by the Shakers as a traveling display table.

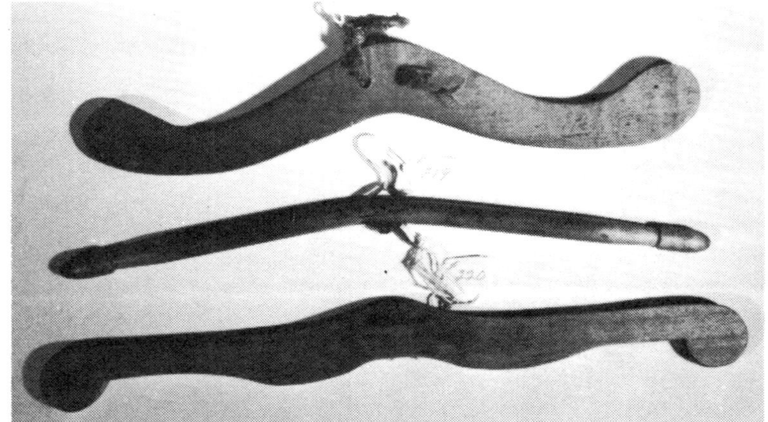

Shaker coat hangers: top - South Union, Kentucky, - $30. The other two are signed H. Wilson who was from the Enfield, Connecticut, community. - $35 and $25 respectively. The center one is a good conversation piece for those psychologists who insist on phallic symbolism in Shaker craftsmanship.

Included in the Putman Sale of April 15-16 (reviewed last month in O.A.R.) were a number of Shaker items from a prominent Shaker dealer in Connecticut who had recently closed her business there and moved South. She had had poor results with an Eastern auction house a year and a half ago (see December, 1975, O.A.R.) and decided to try the Mid-West. Unfortunately, not many Shaker collectors attended the sale and the better quality pieces did not command the money they should have.

Chairs are a good example of the low prices. Most of them were from the Shaker communities themselves rather than the mass produced Mt Lebanon variety and, therefore, more scarce. A Hancock, Massachusetts, side chair with repair to one finial had been purchased previously from Faith Andrews who, along with her late husband, has been writing about Shaker furniture for 50 years. That alone should have made it worth far more than the $160 it brought. An Enfield, New Hampshire, side chair with some repairs sold for $230 and an excellent Mt. Lebanon one brought only $235. Maybe part of the failure to bring top dollar could be attributed to the neglect of the catalogue to point out that these were rare and desirable tilting chairs. Both of these were far better than the Mt. Lebanon armless rocker that sold for $230. A # 0 child's chair, the smallest chair manufactured by the Shakers had the decal on the back of one slat and went for a strong $380.

All three case pieces in the sale were unique and interesting. The tin cupboard was only 69'' tall with one door and two drawers below that. It had originally been built into a right hand corner and had had some rebuilding to make it free-standing. With its quarter-round molding around the door panels, even the added top and base did not detract too much from this delightful piece ($475). The label cupboard had also been a built-in but had had no alterations. It retained a 1½'' face molding and could be conve-

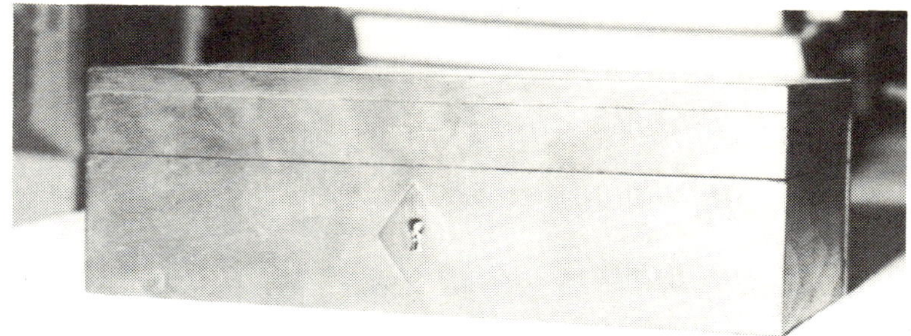

This small box (3'' x 5'' x 9'') was not listed as Shaker in the catalogue but was sold as such. On the lid was the notation "Sister A. Brooks, T. Fisher, '99." Sister Abigail Brooks died in 1901 and is buried in the Shaker cemetery at Enfield, Connecticut. Thomas Fisher was a Trustee at that community when he made this box. It sold for $45.

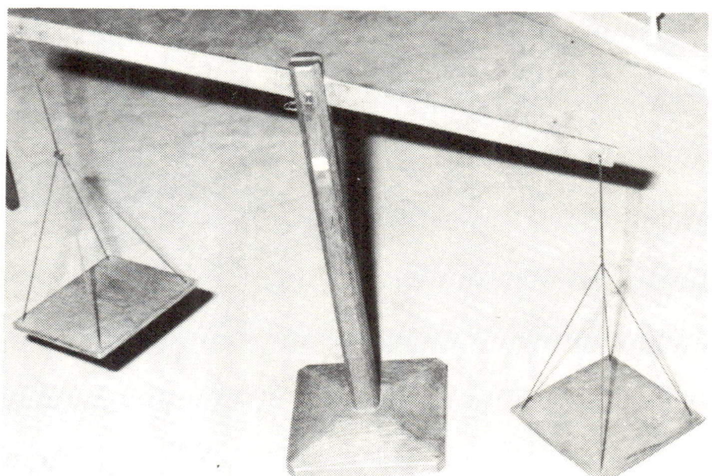

Beautifully constructed butter scales - $100.

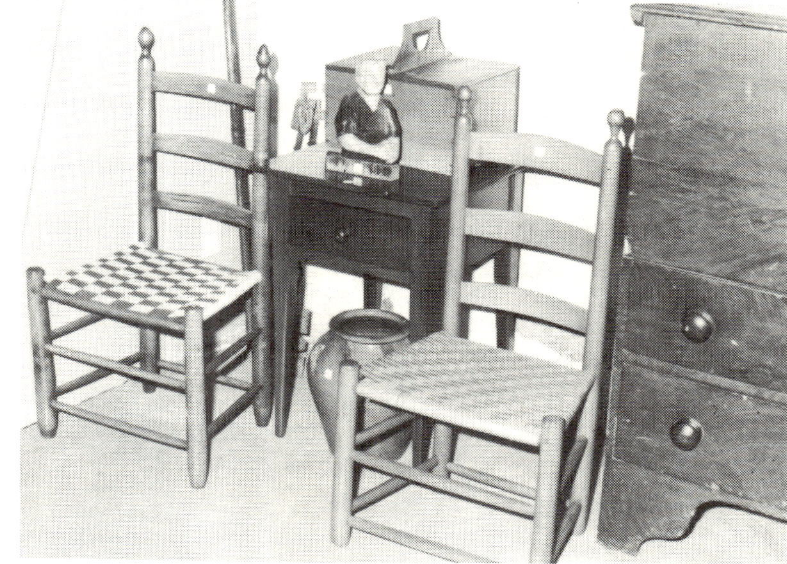

These two Shaker chairs sold for $55 and $160 respectively. The more expensive one on the right had been a part of the Faith Andrews collection (Like the other community chairs, these sold very reasonably!) The cherry one drawer table in the middle is reputed to be from the Canterbury, New Hampshire, Shaker community and brought $200.

niently recessed into a wall, original except some of the 144 pigeon holes had been removed. It featured a 45° molding around the door panels and three pegs in each corner to hold the mortised joints ($225). The third case piece was a 79'' tall pine cupboard of questionable Shaker origin. The catalogue said it was from Groveland or Maine. There is nothing from Groveland, New York, to which it could be compared. And one person at the sale suggested it was definitely Maine but not Shaker. Although the case was dovetailed, the piece lacked re-flections of a good craftsman. The drawers were nailed; the door panels were not chamfered; the mortised joints were held with a single pin; and the petition separating the two sides of the cupboard extended only two thirds of the way back. It was a nicely proportioned cupboard but lacked those qualities of craftsmanship characteristic of Shaker hands.

Some other Shaker items worth noting included two pieces of pegboard. One was 45'' long and had four pegs ($25). The other was 9 feet long and had 9 three inch pegs ($105). The first was an exceptionally good buy. An excellent wooden butter scale sold for $100 and a standing yarn swift went for $95. Both of these had finely chamfered bases. The most delicate Shaker piece in the sale was a towel bar made of a tapered cherry rod mortised into a pine block that hinged onto a wall. Two small pewter knobs were on the top of the bar to hold towels in place. It was unusual and delightful enough to be well worth the $195 it brought.

For the Shaker enthusiast in the Mid-West, it was an interesting April.

— June, 1977

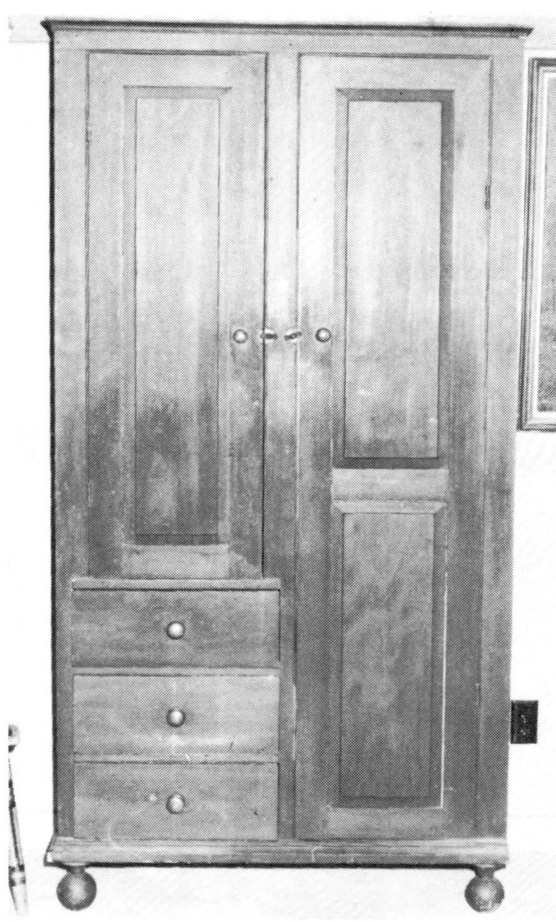

This painted cupboard troubled the author as well as many other people. If the ball feet are original and the piece is Shaker, the feet would be unique. The author is unaware of other examples of Shaker furniture with ball feet. (Although some pieces are known with bun or turnip feet.) $1500.

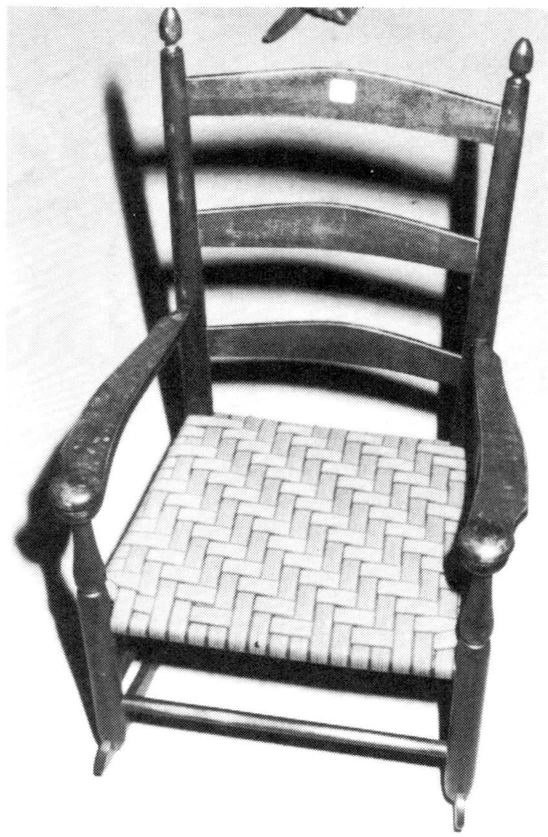

Child's # 0 rocker sold for $380. It had the Mt. Lebanon decal on the back of one slat which would date it after 1876 but the rockers were put on with the earlier method of wooden pins rather than screws.

[132]

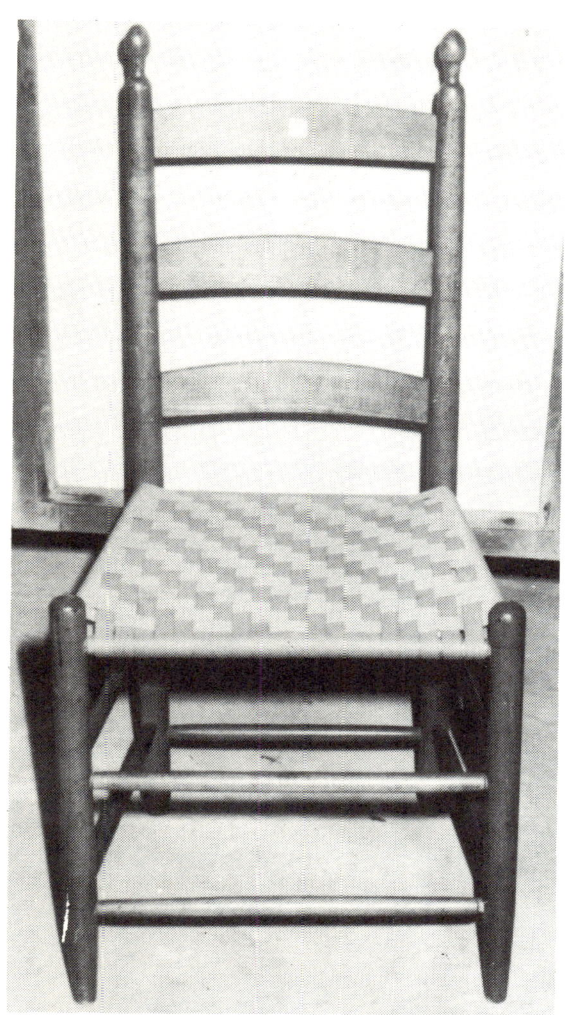

Mt. Lebanon, New York, side chair was unusually tall. Although not catalogued as such, it was a "tilter" and went to a collector for $230 - an excellent buy!

Too often Hepplewhite tables take on a Shaker identity but this pine one lost its. From the Enfield, Connecticut, Shaker community, this table sold for $260 without any Shaker attribution. A pencil marking inside the drawer had the name "Whito__." Might that be Henry Whiton, a Shaker who died in 1893?

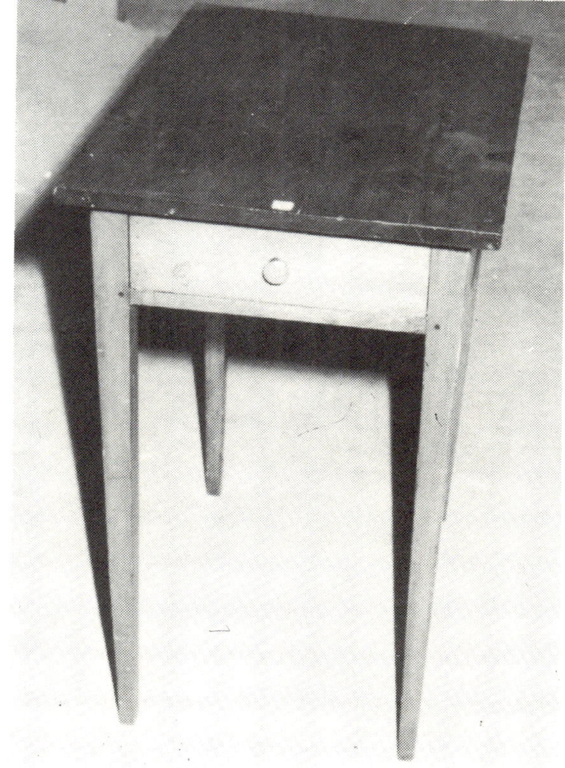

A Look At Prices

The sale on June 17th of a sewing desk and a few other Shaker items at Garth's Auction Barn in Delaware, Ohio, offers an opportunity to do some comparisons of prices on Shaker. Considered to be a unique Shaker form, the sewing desk, used occasionally as a writing desk in later years, is the ultimate desire of almost every Shaker collector. Although some variation of case pieces with drawers was developed as a sewing cabinet at an early date, it appears that the typical sewing desk with recessed drawers on top did not come into being until about midway in the 19th century. The earliest dateable one that I have seen was made by Lorenzo Brooks of Enfield, Conn., in the 1860's. Other desks can be attributed to William Briggs (1851-1899) and Henry Blinn (1824-1905) of the Canterbury community and Henry Green (1844-1931) of Alfred, Maine.

Most sewing desks contained two tiers of three drawers each in the base although some utilized only three larger drawers. A few examples are known which had one tier of drawers in the front and another entering from the side. This would permit two people to be using the desk at the same time. In almost all cases, a pull out work surface is built into the base. The recessed top is usually constructed in two forms: 1) two tiers of three drawers separated by a small cupboard and having no space between the top and base; 2) four or six drawers with a space between them and the base.

The desk which sold at Garth's was of the latter style and is almost identical to one which sold at the auction of the Shaker Society of Sabbathday Lake, Maine, on June 20, 1972. The prices were almost identical also — $3,250 in 1972 and $3,200 in 1978. Even considering that the desk sold in 1972 was attributed to Elder Henry Green and was being sold directly from the Shaker community, the price was seen as being high for its day. Another sewing desk with a cupboard included in the top section brought $3,500 in that same sale. The top price paid previously for a sewing desk had been $2,500 at the Jordan auction in September, 1968. It was 32'' long and contained drawers in front and side. Since 1972, a superb example was sold privately for $5,000; another was offered at the New York East Side Show last year for $6,800; and yet another has been on the market for an amount over $20,000. All of these would indicate that a bargain was obtained at Garth's last month.

This would be true of the Canterbury dining chair as well. One was offered at the Lebanon, Ohio, show in September of 1976 for $550 and sold to a collector. A set of six (four matching) sold at Skinners auction in Massachusetts in August, 1976, for $3,500. The one at Garth's in June brought only $360. The retail price of dining chairs has tended to remain steady at $400-$500 over the past three or four years while the mass produced, stamped, and labeled Mt. Lebanon, N.Y., chairs have showed a constant increase in value. At the Frank Reinhold auction in Maine in June, 1973, a #7 (the largest chair manufactured by the Shakers) slat back rocker with tape seat sold for $250. The same type brought $410 at Garth's in April of this year. While these are only two examples, they are representative of what has happened with

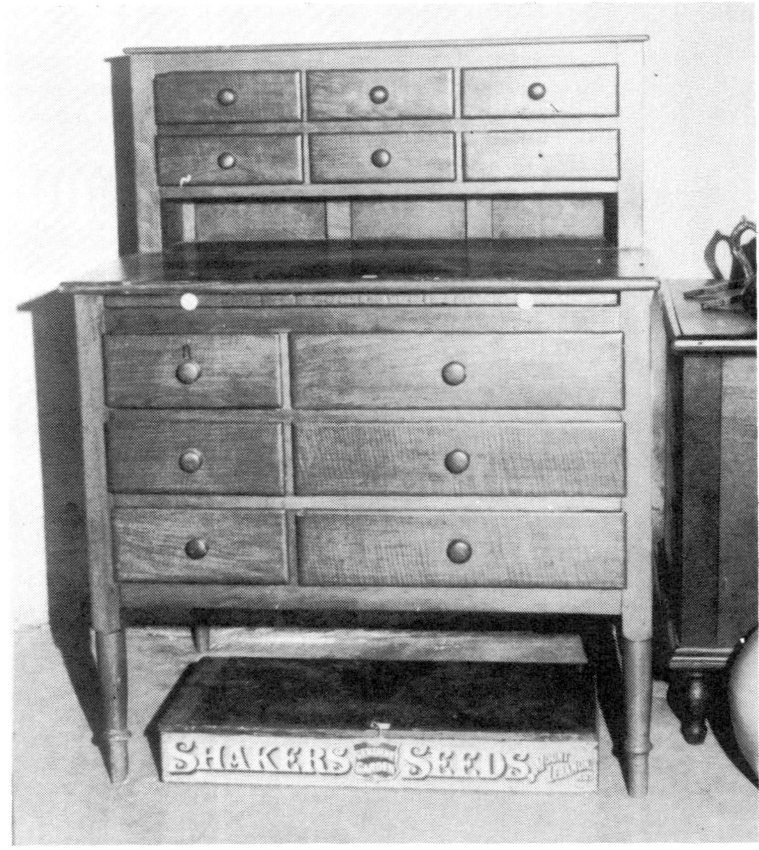

This sewing desk sold at Garth's last month was almost identical to one sold at Sabbathday Lake, Maine, in 1972 in form and price...$3,200 to $3,250.

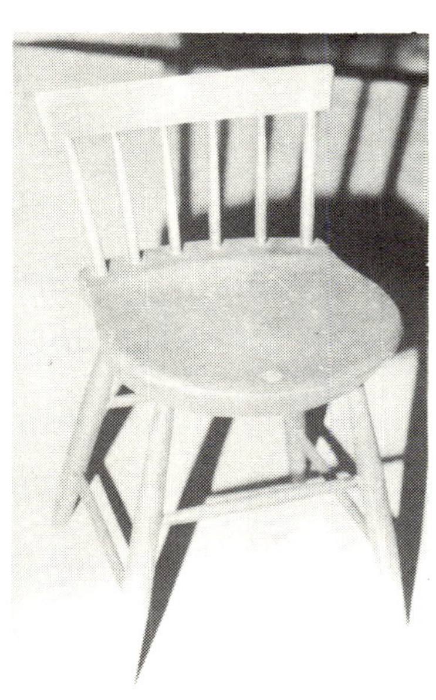

The Midwest market for dining and tilter chairs lags behind the East. This Canterbury dining chair brought only $360 at Garth's.

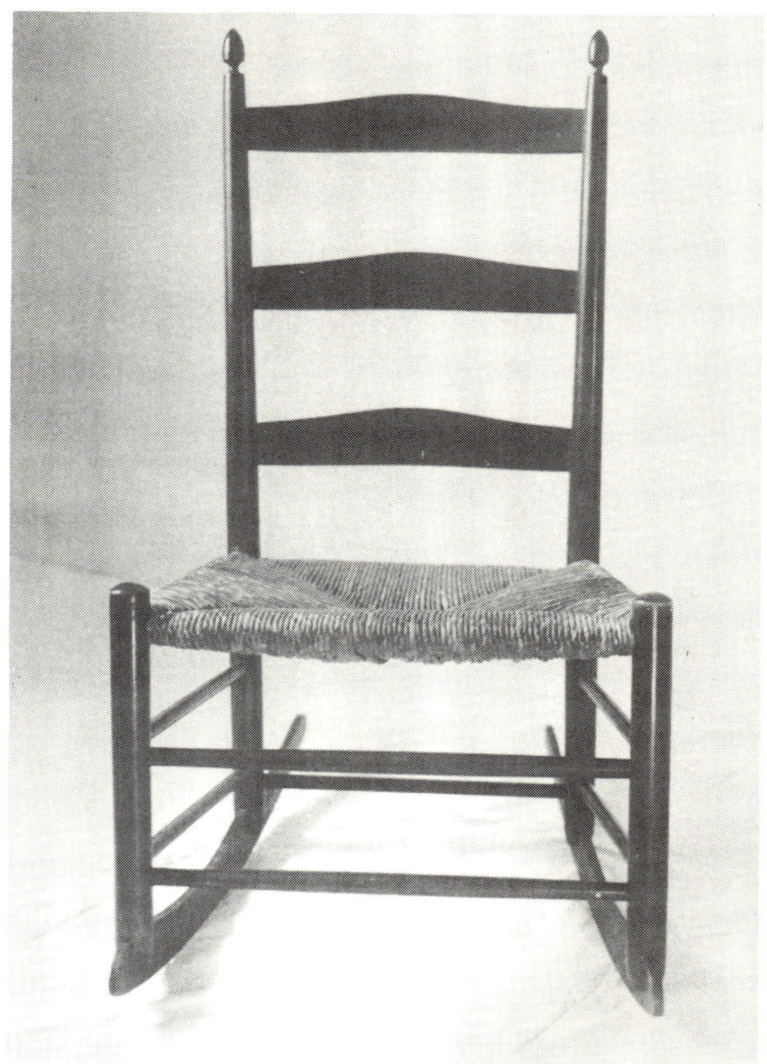

Prices on Mt. Lebanon, New York, mass produced, numbered for size, and labeled chairs has maintained a steady upward movement. For example, the average price on a #3 chair such as this has almost doubled in the last four years.

the prices of numbered production chairs. It can be seen also in the #3 armless rocker as ones of that size sold as follows: Reinhold (June, 1973) - $150; Caropressos Auction in Massachusetts (Oct., 1975) - $160 and $180; Garth's (April, 1978) - $250. The Mt. Lebanon production chairs have grown in price more rapidly than the older and, from a collector's viewpoint, more desirable community used chairs such as the dining chairs and early tilters. It is interesting to note that the exception to constantly increasing prices for the production chairs is the child's chairs with #0 chairs bringing $375 at Reinhold's; $450 at Caropresso's and $380 at Garth's in April of 1977.

Seed boxes offer another example of how people seem to be willing to compete for the more ordinary, and yet identifiable, Shaker items. A Mt. Lebanon seed box with the old red finish and the red and black label brought $177.50 at Garth's in the same sale as the sewing desk, even though the top was separated from the box and some questioned its belonging to that particular box. This style seed box, which dates after 1875, has shown a steady increase in price. In 1969, they could be readily purchased for $35 each. At the Sabbathday Lake auction in 1972, one sold for $62.50. In 1974 at the Shaker Bicentennial Auction of the Western Reserve Historical Society in Cleveland, one without a cover brought $115. I have seen them at shows recently for $200.

Small items such as labels and publications have also grown in price with some of these selling

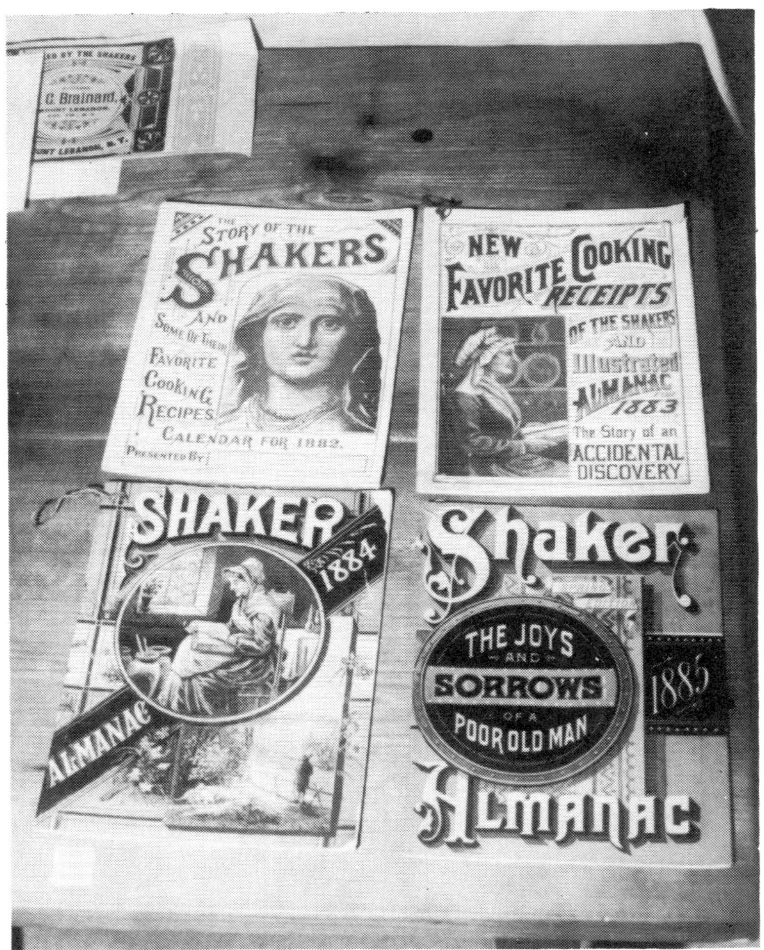

Prices on almanacs and other small Shaker paper items seem inflated to the author.

for $1.00 each a few years ago and about $20 now. Part of this increase might simply be that more people can afford labels than sewing desks. Almanacs sold for $22.50 and $25 at the Bicentennial Auction; two for $12.50 at the Kieffer-Stolzenbach Auction in Lancaster, Ohio, in April, 1977; and $37.50 and $47.50 at Garth's last month. These can still be purchased for $10-$25 at flea markets, shows, and old book stores.

It has to be remembered that all these prices involve many factors such as condition of an item; variations in form; how badly the two people present and bidding want a particular item; and the place and publicity of a sale. Many of the items in the Sabbathday Lake auction brought extraordinary prices because of their lack of distinguishing factors except for the identity that comes from being bought directly from the Shakers. It has now been six years since that auction and the Shaker market has been mixed since then. Some items such as candlestands ($750 in 1972 to $2,500 in 1977), trestle tables ($2,750 in 1972 to $5,500 in 1977), and superb case pieces have greatly increased in price. The same has been true with marked and labeled Shaker artifacts. But there is still plenty of room for ''good buys'' in stoves, tilter chairs, swifts, and perhaps even a sewing desk!

— **July, 1978**

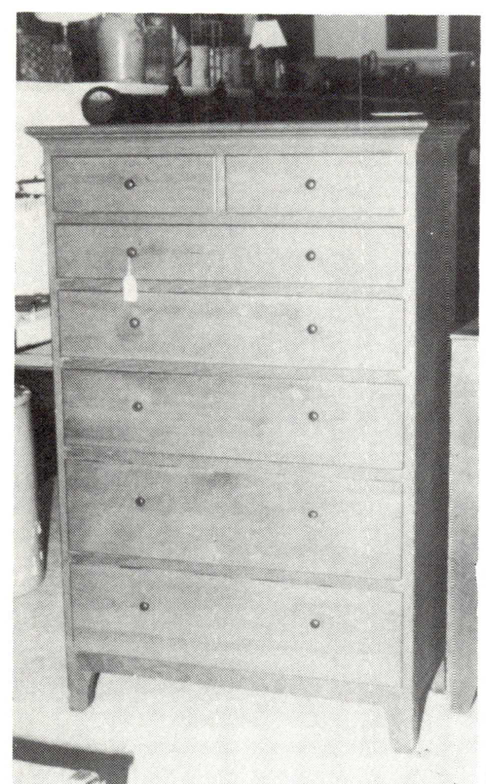

The Midwest has not for many years had the opportunity to buy as fine a lot of Shaker items as it had on July 4th at the John Banks auction in Ypsilanti, Michigan. And it did not respond to the opportunity; every major piece in the sale went East with its new owners.

The auction encompassed two days as the Banks were selling all their antiques to change their furnishings to modern, more in keeping with their new home. While the auction lasted two days, the more than 100 Shaker articles came up for bids on the second day. Except for sales at the time of the dispersal of some of the Ohio and Kentucky communities, I believe this was the largest amount of Shaker ever to be sold West of the Alleghenies.

Schmidt's auction room looked like a "who's who" of the Shaker dealer-collector world. The catalogue offered just enough information to wet the appetite of would-be buyers..."rare Shaker revolving office chair with eight spindles...Shaker printer's desk...Shaker Granny rocker..." etc. But upon close examination, most of the collection, early American as well as Shaker, had problems. I felt that only two of the Shaker pieces could be considered all original and in desirable pristine condition. Evidently there was some concurrence with this feeling by others, since these two pieces brought the top money of the sale (for Shaker). The finest item was a 10′ 7″ trestle table with a two board maple top (Photo #1). It sold for $7,750 to a dealer who expected to resell it immediately. A seven drawer chest in original red with superb blocked feet went to another Eastern dealer for $4,750 (Photo #2).

#2.

Major Midwest Auction

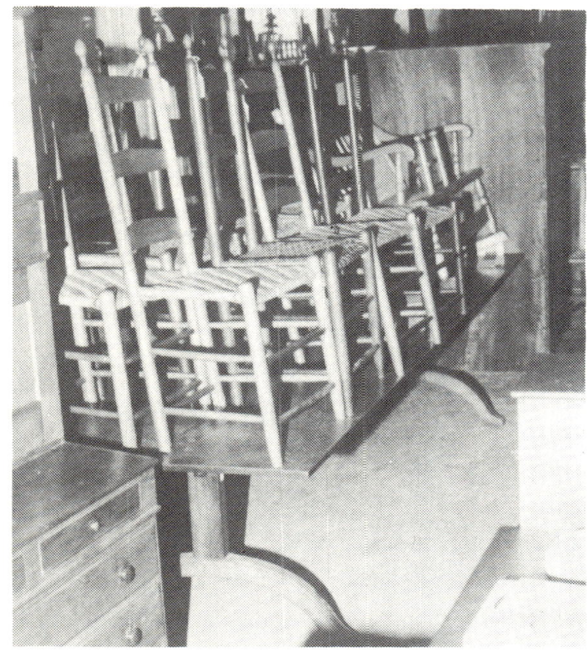

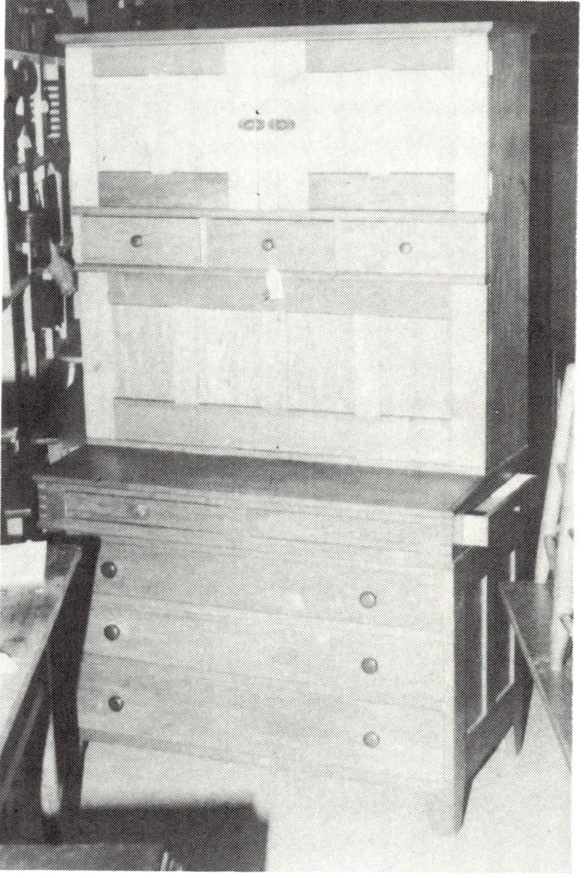

#1. Prices on these chairs ranged from $250 to $480 for a tilter. The table brought $7,750.

#3. Having been purchased for $2,500 in 1968, it sold for $4,500 in 1978. Note the drawer in the end and the fake drawer in front.

Four of the major articles in the auction had been sold in Sept., 1968 at the sale of the George E. Jordan collection in Concord, New Hampshire. The prices commanded in this sale for the four items were double those paid ten years ago.

The top price of the four was the butternut secretary (Photo #3), which sold for $4,500 in this sale as opposed to the $2,500 paid at the Jordan sale. While it is a beautiful piece and was purchased by an Eastern collector, it is of late origin and lacking many of the features of hand-craftsmanship that a person likes to see in Shaker items. The drawer on the end is unique. Bringing more than three times what it sold for ten years earlier...$3,750 in 1978 and $1,200 in 1968, a five foot tall cabinet with cupboard top and ten drawers had a small strip added to the back. Some retouching of the red paint did not detract from

its desirability (Photo #4). Some people thought that the use of the photo of this piece on the cover of the 1968 Jordan sale was a major factor in its price at the Banks auction. Also from the Jordan sale, a Hancock, Massachusetts, stove with tin warming oven (Photo #5) sold for $800 ($395 in 1968) and a pine yarn cupboard from Canterbury, New Hampshire (Photo #6) brought $925 ($285 in 1968).

A glance at a list of prices for the smaller items would indicate that they sold quite reasonably, but this can be very misleading since they lacked the fine points of quality that would make them most desirable to collectors. Most of the oval boxes were of the Harvard style with only one finger on top and one on the bottom. A nest of four of these brought a surprisingly high $325. An almanac of 1885 sold for $30, less than a similar one brought at Garth's

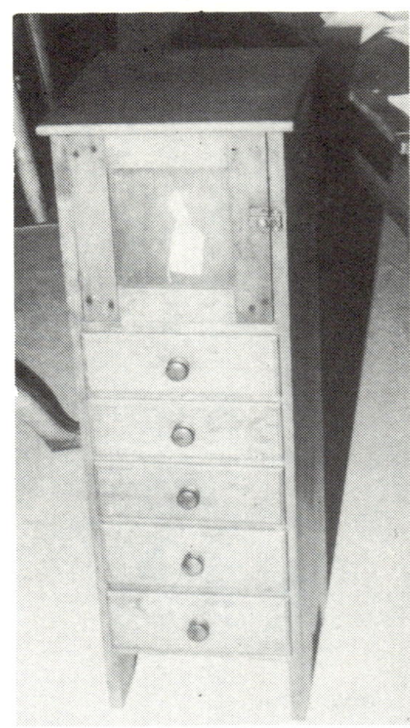

#6. Only 38½" tall and 12½" wide, this yarn cupboard sold for $295 in 1968 and $925 in this auction.

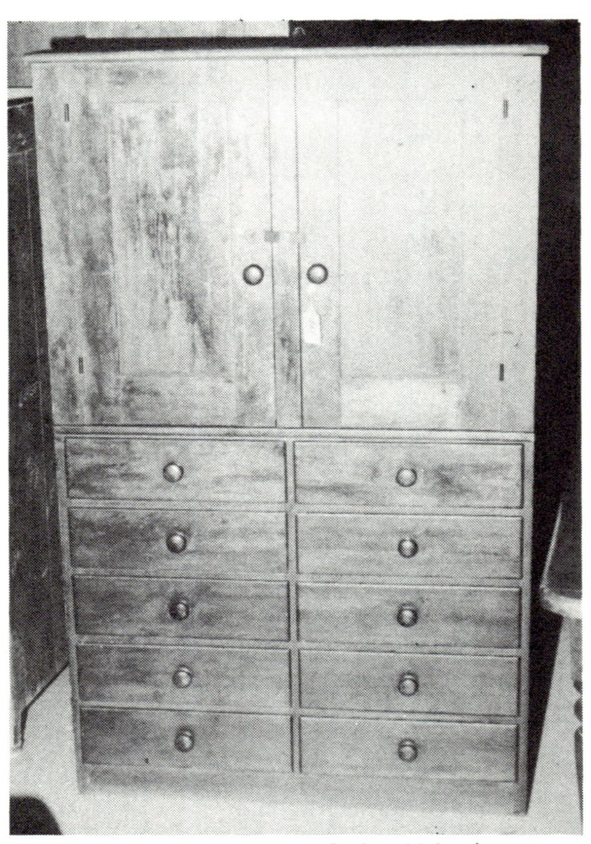

#4. $3,750 bought this piece which sold for $1,200 ten years ago.

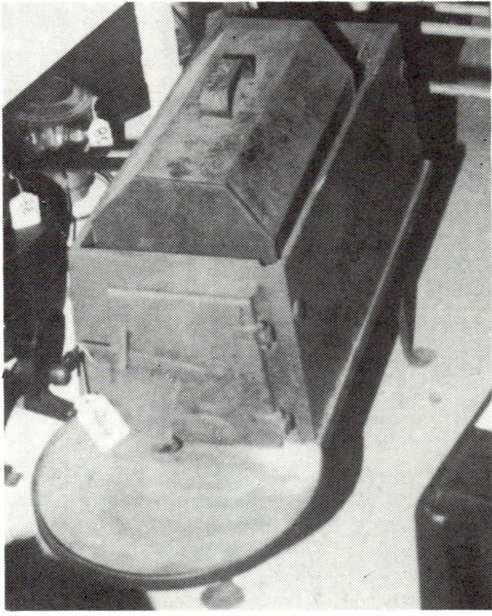

#5. The $800 paid for this excellent three legged stove was double its price of the Jordan sale.

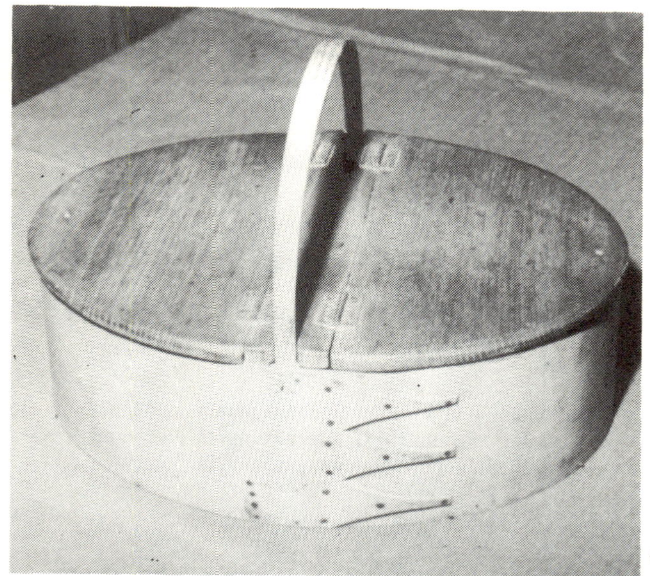

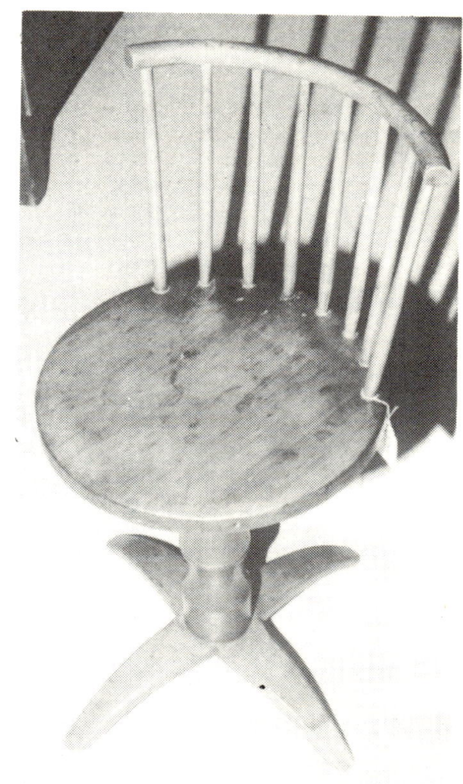

#7.

#8.

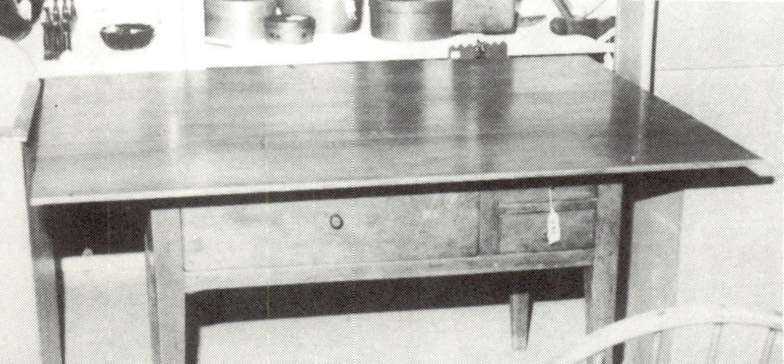

#9. **The arrangement of the three drawers made this table especially interesting. The top (made up of six boards) is probably a replacement ($1,600).**

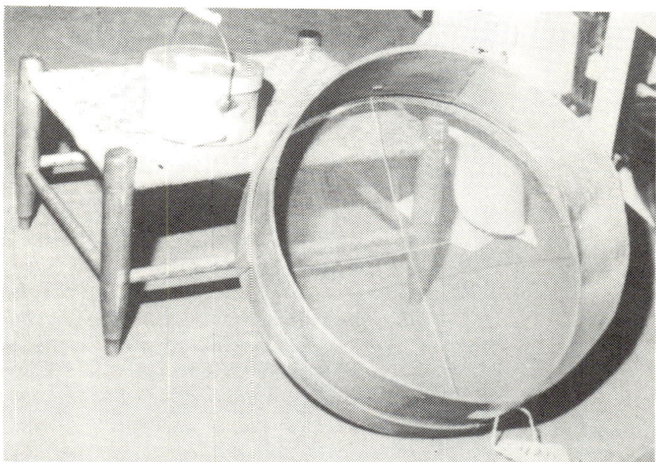

#10. **The sieve brought $50 and the stool $155.**

last month (see July ''The Shaker Way'') but the condition was not as good. An oval carrier with double hinged top (Photo #7) reminded me of the one that sold in the Mary Thornton sale at Garth's in January, 1976. But that one, which sold for $450, had four fingers and was originally made with the double hinged top. The one in this sale had only three fingers, and although the top appeared to be a later addition it is exactly like one in the museum at Canterbury, N.H. ($275).

The finest of the chairs were seven slat backs from Watervliet and Mt. Lebanon, N.Y. (Photo #1). These were chairs made for community use and ranged in price from $250 to $480 for one with tilters. The highest price paid for a chair was $650 for a revolver (Photo #8). The first impression is that such a price is a real bargain. On close examination though, the seat had been split and repaired, one leg had been pieced out, the donut was missing between the seat and the shaft, and the form was heavy and stiff.

The results of this auction offer a few interesting insights. First, the prices paid for items out of the Jordan auction suggest a constant upward market for quality Shaker furnishings. Second, none of the buyers—dealers or collectors—of major articles was active in the Shaker market at the time of the Jordan sale 10 years ago. This suggests that the market is not only constantly moving upward but is a constantly changing one with new faces, new collectors, and new money. Third, the Midwest collectors and dealers are not yet ready to be a serious part of the Shaker market.

— **August, 1978**

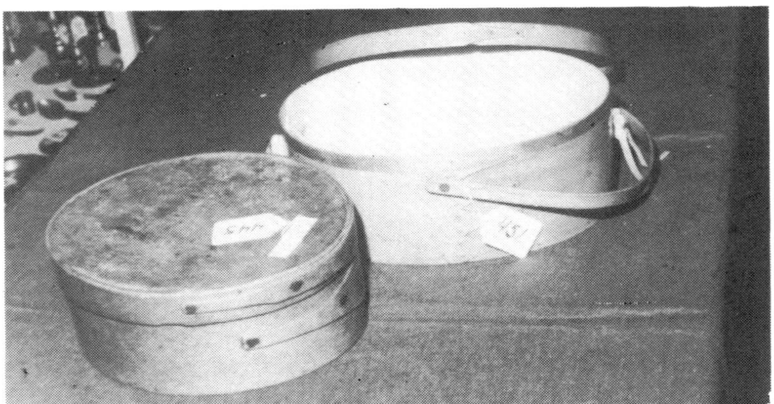

#11. The early box with the unusual placement of fingers on the end was worth its $90 winning bid. The sewing box showed wear and contained thimble, pincushions, beeswax, etc. ($500).

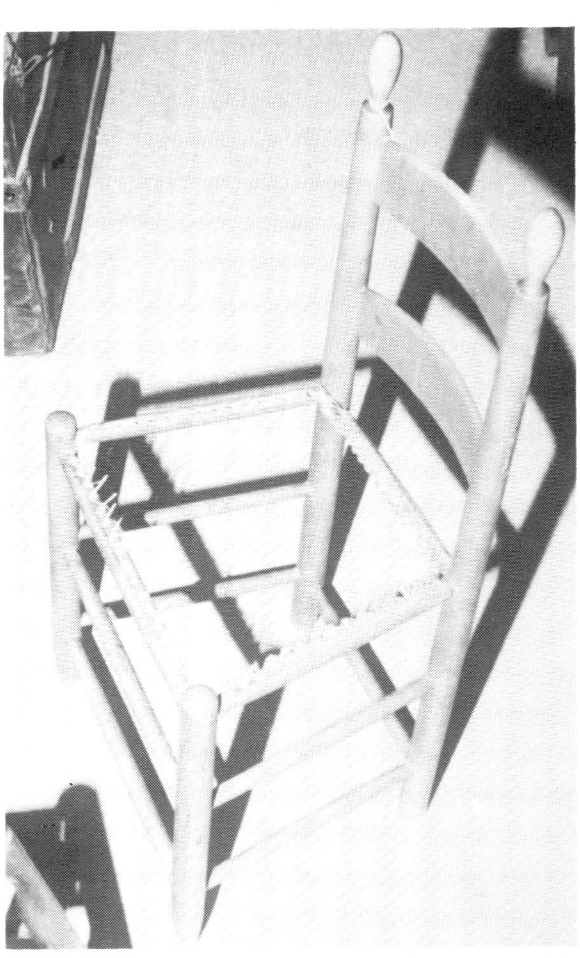

#12. With mellow yellow paint and without a seat, this child's chair from Harvard, Massachusetts, went to an Ohio collector for $425.

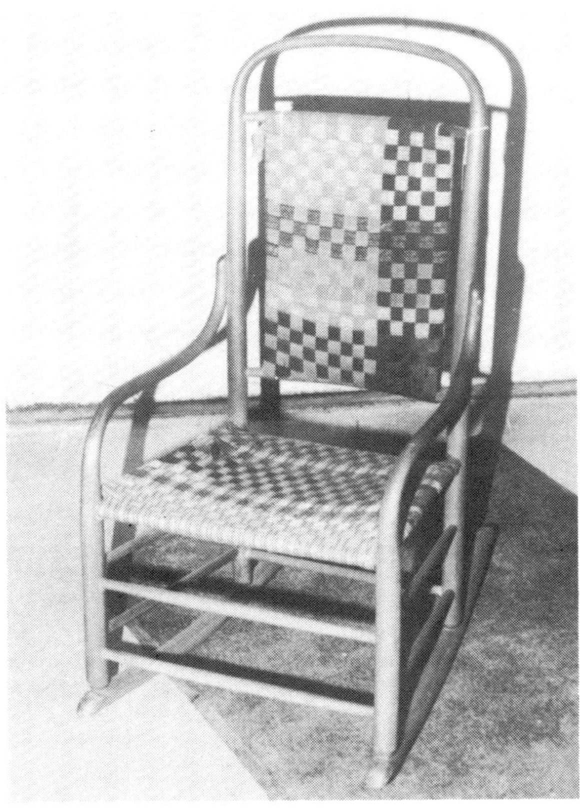

#13. Bentwood rockers sold for $225 and $400. The conglomeration of different colored tapes used in the seat and back of this one formed a pleasing pattern.

NOTE: *The seven drawer chest (photograph #2) was offered at the East Side House Winter Antiques Show in New York City the following January for $8,500 and sold. The desk (photograph #3) had been thought to have been altered by Mr. Jordan. This does not appear to be true because it is identical to the illustration of it in* THE TREASURY OF AMERICAN DESIGN, *volume II, page 739, except for five wooden knobs that replaced white ones. In some cases, the porcelain knobs had simply been painted brown. The yarn cupboard (photograph #6) changed hands since the auction and was pictured a year later in* McCALL'S *(July, 1979).*

The title of this month's column comes from a brief note from New York collector Milt Sherman. In earlier conversations, we had discussed his purchase of a Shaker drawing and some of his choice finds from local homes and auctions. The weekend of March 10th, he gained a few more pieces from an auction in Cohoes, New York, and commented: "More Shaker has been available during this past year than I have seen in the years I have been collecting."

After hearing reports of the offerings and prices in New York City during January, an Ohio collector said: "I'm glad I have what I do. It looks like I'm not going to be able to afford Shaker anymore." To that statement, I replied: "That's what you said five years ago and look at what you have obtained since!" In a more recent conversation, he spoke about some of the superb articles he hoped to add to his collection in the very near future. Shaker is increasing in popularity and it is increasing in price but it is certainly available.

Rita Reif of *The New York Times* entitled her January 21st column "Soaring Demand for Shaker Design." She began with the insight that "Not since the celebration of the Shakers' Bicentennial in America in 1974 has there been so much activity in the innovative and superbly crafted designs that this celibate religious community produced..." She then cited the exhibitions and sales taking place in New York City and the show at the Albany Institute of History and Art.

On March 30 and 31, Yale Divinity School will sponsor a symposium on "Visible Theology: Emblems of Shaker Life, Art, Work and Worship." To the best of my knowledge, this is the first time that a theological school has used Shaker as the focal point of a seminar. In May (3-31), the Hirschl and Alder Galleries in New York will present fifty-six spirit drawings in a benefit exhibit for Hancock Shaker Village. During the summer months, Elmira College of New York State will hold its fifth annual Shaker Seminar. This year it will be at Pleasant Hill and South Union,

Kentucky, on July 9-13. The University of Maine in Portland will probably again this summer sponsor its two week course at the Sabbathday Lake Shaker community. For the Fall, the Museum of American Folk Art has scheduled "The Shaker in New York State" as the subject of their exhibit (September 13 - November 21). Add to these events the tremendous growth in attendance at Hancock Shaker Village, Massachusetts, The Shaker Museum in Chatham, New York, and Pleasant Hill as well as the needed expansion of the Warren County Historical Society in Lebanon,

Ohio, and it can easily be seen that Shaker continues to rapidly increase in interest and popularity.

The growth in popularity is paralleled by the upward thrust in prices. A trestle dining table sold at a Michigan auction for $7,750 in July (see August, 1978, *O.A.R.*). Rita Reif informs us that Israel Sack, Inc. of New York City has a 13-foot long table for sale at $18,000. Small drop leaf tables have been selling for $2,400 to $4,000. The sewing desk and revolving chair exhibited by Ed Clerk at the East Side Settlement Show (see last month's *O.A.R.*)

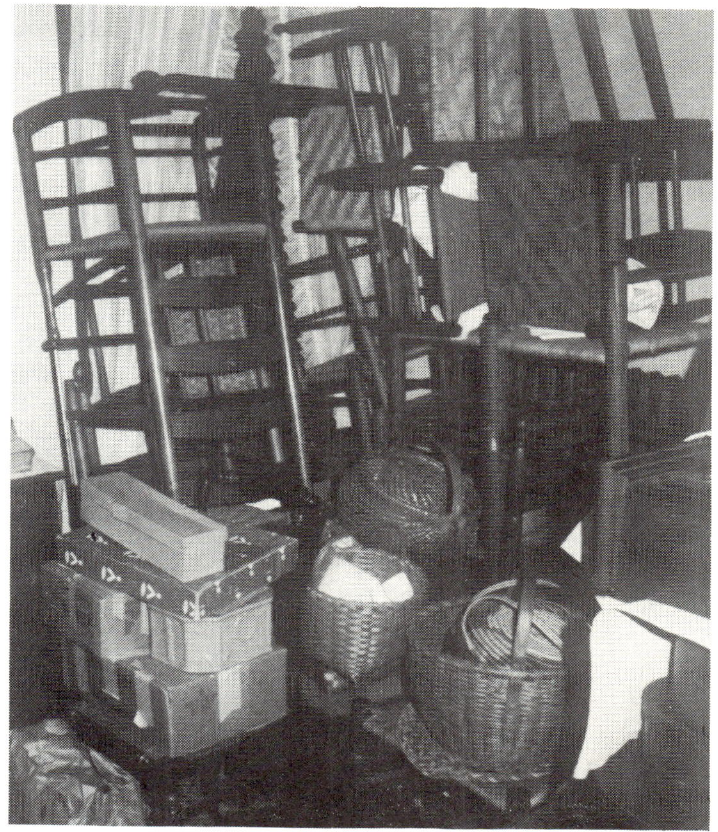

Auctioneer Warner found one room of the King house stacked with Shaker.

was offered for $12,000 for the two pieces. It sold, as did a $8,500 case of drawers. About the same time, the American Folk Heritage Gallery placed on exhibit, and sold, a small Shaker goat cart that had carried a tag for $2,250. $550 was paid for a #6 rocker at Christie's auction house in January and an early rocker was priced at $1,675 by a New York dealer. Then came an auction this month in which two rockers were sold… not just offered…for $2,450 and $1,600 each. Such prices are disheartening to the person of average income who would like to own some Shaker. It is discouraging for many to examine a lovely trestle table and realize that they would probably never be in a financial position to own one. But what is true of Shaker is an axiom of the antique world: quality always commands top dollar. As Ed Clerk says: "Important items of any furniture style have commanded the price from collectors who could afford it." The best pieces in any area of antiques go to the collector who has the means to pay for it.

It is the opinion of numerous collectors and dealers that the seemingly high prices have brought more pieces of Shaker into the marketplace. Richard Rasso, a New York dealer who specializes in Shaker, commented that "It is not really more difficult to find Shaker today than five years ago. It is available but we are buying it from collectors who have a good idea of the market value." He coupled the statement with the remark that "it is harder for dealers to buy small items at auction now." The difficulty for a dealer buying Shaker at auction was seen in the King sale.

Under the gavel of auctioneer John Blaine Warner, the private collection of Rose and Harold King was brought up for sale on March 10th and 11th. On this, the first week-end of four to sell the more than 5,000 objects, the Shaker was offered. The Kings had lived in Niskayuna, New York, the town of the first Shaker settlement, Watervliet. Much of their acquisitions had been obtained more than thirty years ago and contained some very early Shaker artifacts. The five slat rocking chair which sold for $2,450 (refinished and with a new seat) is an example as well as the four slat rocker with tiger maple arms and a foot rest ($1,600).

Oval fingered boxes brought $100 to $500 for one with a handle while baskets averaged $130-$150 with one selling to a dealer for $250. Chairs with tilters brought around $500, even though they lacked the desirable old finish. The manufactured Mt. Lebanon rockers sold for $425 (a #6 and a #7) and a surprising $600 for a #0. A one drawer stand was signed "Channcy Miller, 1838," had a beaded top and sold to a collector for $2,750. The purchaser was offered a $1,000 profit before he left the premises by a young couple who had not brought enough money with them. With an oval wooden piggin bringing $200 and a broom rack selling for $240, it appears that Shaker prices are indeed strong at a well publicized auction.

While Shaker is often priced beyond the reach of a large segment of the growing number of people interested in it, it is available. It should be pointed out that the recognizable high prices are for the "Tiffanys" and "blockfronts" of the Shaker world. The collector of limited means should

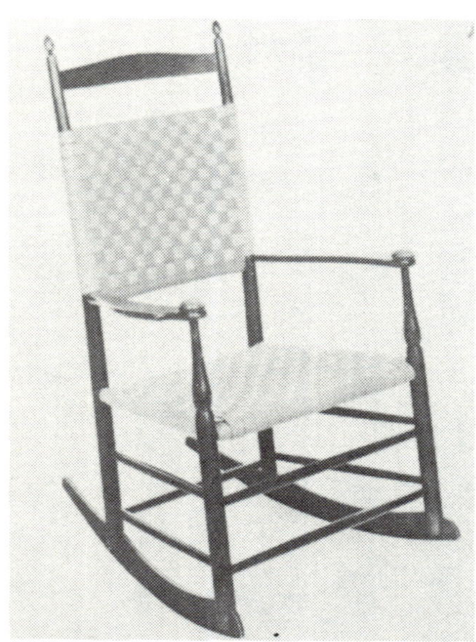

No. 6 Mt. Lebanon rocker brought $550 at Christie's.

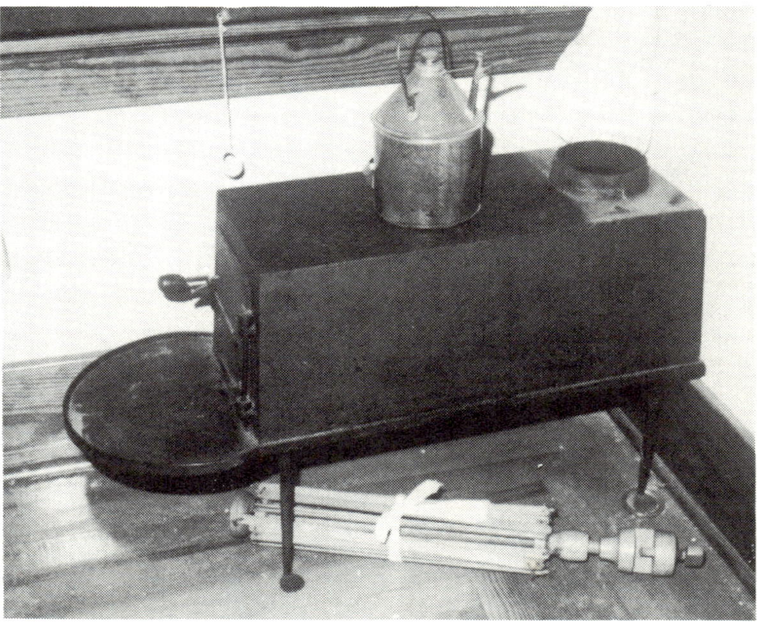

Three penny foot stoves sold for $650, $650 and $975. The Hancock swift brought $110 while the tin coal oil lamp filler can received a top bid of $70. (King auction)

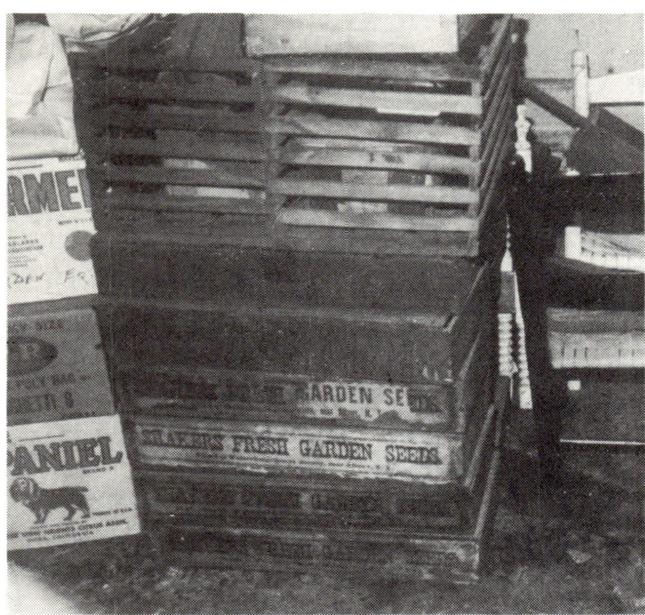

Seed boxes from Watervliet sold for $100 and $110. (King auction)

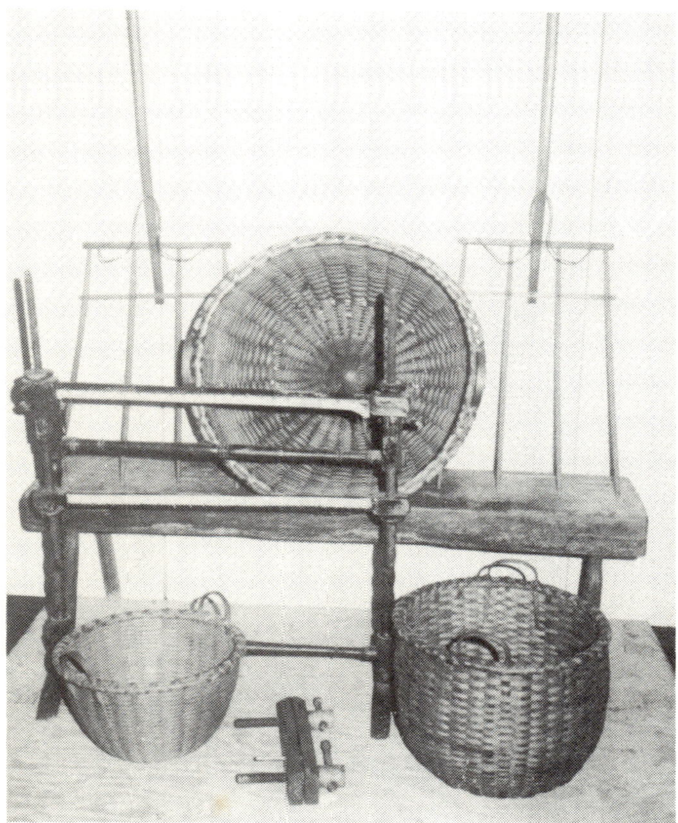

The baskets in the King auction were in excellent condition, average $130 - $150 with one large gathering basket bringing $250.

be neither blinded by nor discouraged by these prices. Mediocre quality and/or priced Shaker may appear to be a "good buy" in comparison to the "blockfronts" but, in reality, are too much for the quality. As an unnamed New York collector says, "there is much more marginal Shaker today" and "poor Shaker often brings too much." On the other hand, there is middle-priced Shaker that reflects the fine craftsmanship of the sect and is well worth the money.

I have found great encouragement in the experience of that well-known upstate New York collector who was advised in 1950 not to collect Shaker. She and her husband were told "it was too big, too cumbersome and too plain. You can't find it any more. It is all in private collections or museums." It was two years before these words of warning were put aside and one of the nation's finest Shaker collections was started. Even in 1952, it was a "matter of finding it...detective work." The same is true today.

While an early rocker may bring $2,450, a rope twist example (certainly of far less desirability) sells for $70 at the same location two months earlier. One Shaker foot stool brings $300 at the King auction but another sells for $27.50 at Garth's. While a Mt. Lebanon production rocker brings $550 at a New York City auction gallery, another from the same factory exchanged hands for $33 at the Fairhaven, Ohio, Antiques Festival last June. Straight chairs may carry a price tag of $300 in New England shops but have been bought recently for $85 in an out-of-the-way shop in Indiana. Shaker is still available today...and not always at top dollar.

— April, 1979